GRAPHIC INDIGENEITY

GRAPHIC INDIGENEITY
Comics in the Americas and Australasia

Edited by Frederick Luis Aldama

University Press of Mississippi / Jackson

The University Press of Mississippi is the scholarly publishing agency of
the Mississippi Institutions of Higher Learning: Alcorn State University,
Delta State University, Jackson State University, Mississippi State University,
Mississippi University for Women, Mississippi Valley State University,
University of Mississippi, and University of Southern Mississippi.

www.upress.state.ms.us

The University Press of Mississippi is a member
of the Association of University Presses.

Copyright © 2020 by University Press of Mississippi
All rights reserved

First printing 2020
∞

Library of Congress Cataloging-in-Publication Data

Names: Aldama, Frederick Luis, 1969- editor.
Title: Graphic indigeneity: comics in the Americas and Australasia /
    edited by Frederick Luis Aldama.
Description: Jackson: University Press of Mississippi, 2020. | Includes
    bibliographical references and index.
Identifiers: LCCN 2020001512 (print) | LCCN 2020001513 (ebook) | ISBN
    9781496828019 (hardback) | ISBN 9781496828026 (trade paperback) | ISBN
    9781496828033 (epub) | ISBN 9781496828040 (epub) | ISBN 9781496828057
    (pdf) | ISBN 9781496828002 (pdf)
Subjects: LCSH: Comic books, strips, etc.—History and criticism. |
    Indigenous peoples in literature. | BISAC: LITERARY CRITICISM / Comics &
    Graphic Novels | LCGFT: Essays. | Literary criticism.
Classification: LCC PN6714 .G7388 2020 (print) | LCC PN6714 (ebook) | DDC
    741.5/9—dc23
LC record available at https://lccn.loc.gov/2020001512
LC ebook record available at https://lccn.loc.gov/2020001513

British Library Cataloging-in-Publication Data available

Contents

ix   Nourishing Minds and Bodies with Indigenous Comics: A Foreword
Lee Francis IV

xi   Graphic Indigeneity: Terra America and Terra Australasia
Frederick Luis Aldama

Part I: Mainstreamed Indigeneities

5   "We the North": Interrogating Indigenous Appropriation as Canadian Identity in Mainstream American Comics
Brenna Clarke Gray

27   Jack Jackson, Native Representation, and Underground Comix
Chad A. Barbour

53   "Goin' Native!": Depictions of the First Peoples from "Down Under"
Jack Ford and Philip Cass

75   Representations of Indigenous Australians in Marvel Comics
Dennin Ellis

100   The Wisdom of the Phantom: The Secret Life of Australia's Indigenous Superhero
Kevin Patrick

Part II: Decolonial Imaginaries *Terra South*

127   Outsmarting the Lords of Death: An Amerindian Cognitive Script in Comics
Arij Ouweneel

144 Memory in Pieces: Chola Power's Origin Story and the Quest for Memory in Peru
Javier García Liendo

168 Visualizing an Alternate Mesoamerican Archive: Daniel Parada's Comic Series *Zotz* in Historical Perspective
Jessica Rutherford

181 Critical Impulses in Daniel Parada's *Zotz*: A Case Study in Indigenous Comics
Jorge Santos

197 The Battle for Recollection: Maya *Historietas* as Art for Remembering War
Brian Montes

210 *Turey El Taíno* and *La Borinqueña*: Puerto Rican Nationalist and Ethnic Resistance in Puerto Rican Comics Dealing with Taíno Cultural Heritage
Enrique García

Part III: Decolonial Imaginaries *Terra North*

237 Securing Stones in the Sky: Word-Drawn Recreations of Oral Trickster Tales
Jordan Clapper

254 Super Indians and the Indigenous Comics Renaissance
James J. Donahue

273 Seeing Histories, Building Futurities: Multimodal Decolonization and Conciliation in Indigenous Comics from Canada
Mike Borkent

299 Deep Time and Vast Place: Visualizing Land/Water Relations across Time and Space in *Moonshot: The Indigenous Comics Collection*
Jeremy M. Carnes

316 Deer Woman Re-Generations: Re-Activating First Beings and Re-Arming Sisterhoods of Survivance in *Deer Woman: An Anthology*
Joshua T. Anderson

340 Indigeneity, Intermediality, and the Haunted Present of *Will I See?*
Candida Rifkind and Jessica Fontaine

361 Afterlives: A Coda
Susan Bernardin

365 List of Contributors

371 Index

Nourishing Minds and Bodies with Indigenous Comics: A Foreword

Lee Francis IV

My dad used to tell the story of when I was a boy of four or five how I would welcome guests and family members, any new visitor to our house, with a bright "hello!" And a, "may I get you some coffee?" My father would smile at the memory of how folks were always taken aback at this display by such a little guy, a tiny barista.

That welcoming spirit was something my father was proud to have imbued in me at such a young age. It was something welded into his DNA, something that connected us to his home in Laguna Pueblo. Everyone was welcome there and, during feasts and family gatherings, the house would sing with the energy of people talking, laughing, eating.

This welcome is an invitation to join us in a feast for the mind. Just as food and prayer nourish our body and spirit, so too must we nourish our minds. We must take the time to engage and allow complex, dynamic thoughts and ideas to root, expand and grow, and fill our thoughts with color and energy. It is the energy of home, of people telling stories, of creative tension and release, of conversation and creation. It is an invitation to join us in a celebration of learning and understanding.

What this collection also offers is a reframing of Western discourse in order to bring the work of Native and Indigenous comic and pop culture artists to the center of the conversation in the way that continues to illuminate and reinforce LeAnne Howe's concept of Tribalography; the positioning of works by Indigenous creators as central to the discourse and valid on their own merits for critical scholarship and intellectual dialogue. This repositioning is crucial in fostering a more robust and deliberate literary exploration of Indigenous works while also encouraging more work to be created and explored.

Further, by utilizing pop culture and comics as a way of exploring Indigeneity and Indigenous identities of the Americas and Australasia, the scholars in this collection have created a deliberate access point for all readers to engage with the material and concepts in a way that seems familiar. This familiarity allows for deeper and more satisfying understandings of the ideas and frameworks. It also creates a space for more expansive reflections around various cultural touchpoints, such as comics, and the ways in which identity is formed, cultivated, reinforced, debated, and reconciled.

So welcome! Enter this incredible book as you would a home place. It is warm and engaging. It is thoughtful and thought provoking. It is nourishing and rewarding.

Graphic Indigeneity: Terra America and Terra Australasia

Frederick Luis Aldama

> *I learned to read with a Superman comic book. Simple enough, I suppose. I cannot recall which particular Superman comic book I read, nor can I remember which villain he fought in that issue. I cannot remember the plot, nor the means by which I obtained the comic book. What I can remember is this: I was 3 years old, a Spokane Indian boy living with his family on the Spokane Indian Reservation in eastern Washington state.*
> —SHERMAN ALEXIE, *Los Angeles Times*, April 19, 1998

For as much as Alexie is today *persona non grata*, he speaks a truth here. That many of us raised in the ethnoracial and socioeconomic margins found our way to our ABCs along with a reprieve from poverty in and through our encounters with comics. It also speaks to how, in spite of the history of mainstream comic books focusing on creating superheroes that *don't* look like us or come from our communities, we have long cocreated them on our own.

Times are changing. While there continue to be egregious misrepresentations of people of color in mainstream comics, there are some who are getting it right. And, we're seeing, too, how creators of color are not sitting around waiting for a sea change. They are clearing important spaces of self-representation—and from everywhere around the world.

This brings me to the pulse that beats at the center of *Graphic Indigeneity*: to throw scholarly light on how mainstream comics have clumsily (mostly) distilled and reconstructed Indigenous identities and experiences of *terra America* and *Australasia*; and to spotlight how Indigenous comic book creators are themselves clearing new visual-verbal narrative spaces for articulating more complex histories, cultures, experiences, and identities. To this end I bring together scholarship that explores both the (mis)representation of Indigenous subjects and experiences as well as scholarship that analyzes and brings to the fore the extraordinary work of Indigenous comic book creators. As Lee Francis IV so beautifully and forcefully identifies above, the volume seeks to center-stage Indigenous creators and their work as important, powerful transformative forces within the shaping of the visual-verbal narrative arts writ large.

Of course, the scholarship that makes up this volume doesn't exist in a vacuum. Important scholarly inroads have been made on Indigenous comics, image-text, and mixed-media creations generally by scholars such as Chad A. Barbour, Susan Bernardin, Jorge L. Catalá Carrasco, Sarah Henzi, Sheri Huhndorf, Elizabeth LaPensée, Claudia Matos Pereira, Nickie D. Phillips, Dean Rader, Deanna Reder, Candida Rifkind, Michael Sheyahshe, Niigaanwewidam James Sinclair, Lindsay Claire Smith, Miriam Brown Spiers, and Staci Strobl, among others. *Graphic Indigeneity* seeks to build on and solidify these important incursions that shed light on the ways in which indigeneity is *geometrized* in the comic book narrative arts of *terra America* and *Australasia*. By this I mean the way comic book creators (mainstream and Indigenous) use the shaping devices of comics (layout, balloon placement, ink lines, perspective, character posture and facial expression, among others) to distill Indigenous subjectivities and experiences (past, present, and future) then reconstruct this in word-drawn narratives. Artful drawing and word craft skills along with a responsibility to subject matter leads to the geometrizing of narratives that adds kinetic energy to the word-drawn narrative; that directs our eyes, our minds, and our hearts in the filling in of motion and emotion; that breathes life into Indigenous identities and experiences. When not done well, it can and does lead to the reproducing of denigrative stereotypes: sidekick buffoons, thieves, threatening hordes, hypersexualized seducer, frozen-in-time mystics, noble savages, alcoholics, and preternatural race-betrayers, and criminals. When not done well, they destructively delimit what has happened, what is happening, and what might happen in the future for Indigenous subjects.

The volume's wide-armed embrace of comics by and about indigeneities of *terra* America and Australasia is ambitious. It is also a first step to understand deeply how the histories of colonial and imperial domination across the globe connect the violent wounds that continue to haunt the existence of Indigenous peoples across hemispheres and continents. We feel very present yesteryear's coloniality of power as it swept across the Americas and Australasia—the globe. We see today the scars of this in our communities that continue to suffer external and internal forms of racism, sexism, and classism.

Wounds connect us, but so, too, do resistance movements create a global web that connects Indigenous and first nation peoples across the planet. Resistance to histories (past and present) of expropriation, oppression, exploitation, and genocide also connects Indigenous communities. I think readily of the resistance movements of the Indigenous Māori and Aboriginal and Torres Strait Islander, who share deep decolonial re-occupations and revolts with those in the Northern Americas: the Māori resistance movement against the Treaty of Waitangi in Aotearoa, New Zealand, shares a like impulse with the Indigenous resistance movement of Columbus Day and, as well, with resistance movements to the US annexation of the Hawaiian Islands, the occupation of Alcatraz, the Trail of Broken Treaties, the occupation of the BIA in Washington, DC, the revolution at Wounded Knee, South Dakota, and many others. (See Paul Chaat Smith and Robert Allen Warrior's *Like a Hurricane: The Indian Movement from Alcatraz to Wounded Knee*.)

From these violent wounds we have survived. We are mestizos. We are Mexipinos. We are Asiatic and Indigenous admixtures. We are Canadian métis. We are Taíno, African, Latinx métissage. And from these wondrous new spaces we have been able (against the odds) to create dynamic, syncretistic cultural phenomena, comics included. As Rudy P. Guevara sums up the colonial and capitalist global practices in the trans-Pacific, they have created "a long historical web of interconnectedness that underpins the mestizaje that began in the sixteenth century" (*Becoming Mexipino* 327). From the trans-Pacific to and from the Canadian arctic to the Southern Cone, nations that make up Americas north and south can, as Earl E. Fitz states, "claim a Native American history and cultural heritage, and in many, if not all, of these modern nation-states this heritage lives on, becoming finally, the common denominator of our multiple American identities" (15). In *Comparative Indigeneities of the Américas* Arturo Aldama and his coeditors identify how a "shared history of colonization, genocide, displacement and Eurocentric racism and sexism" (1) connects Indigenous peoples globally, and thus necessitates a hemispheric approach to the study of cultural phenomena by and about Indigenous subjects. It's from our shared open wounds (Gloria Anzaldúa's *heridas abiertas*) that Rachel Adams asks that we consider how "transnational cultural networks" (5) from New York to Quebec to Mexico City interconnect Indigenous spaces, creating a vital Indigenous transnational imaginary.

This volume likewise seeks to articulate a transnational framework. In this regard, it seeks to build on scholarship of those like Rachel Adams just mentioned along with Shari Huhndorf, James H. Cox, Daniel Heath Justice, and Chadwick Allen. And, like these scholars the scholars that make up this volume are respectful of the situated histories and politics that have shaped different Indigenous subjectivities and experiences. In *Continental Divides* Rachel Adams sums this up nicely when she writes how a transnational framework "does not seek to ignore borders or to bypass the nation altogether, but to situate these terms within a broader global fabric" (18). For Adams, the identifying of these transnational cultural networks are not just reactions "to the fractious power of the nation-state" (35). They are the "resumption of alliances and networks of filiation that were severed by the conquest and its aftermath" (35). In *Mapping the Americas* Shari Huhndorf's analysis of post-1980s Native art and literature puts front and center how national and Indigenous nationalist political structures along with global capitalist structures of power have shaped in contradictory ways the Native cultural phenomena such as fiction, performance, photography, and film. Likewise, in their introduction to *The Oxford Handbook of Indigenous American Literature Online,* editors James H. Cox and Daniel Heath Justice discuss the transnational move in Indigenous literary criticism as one that seeks to identify and build on "coalitions among Indigenous and allied scholars across institutional, tribal national, and settler-colonial borders" (1). We see this transnational scholarship in action in Cox's *The Red Land to the South.* Cox analyzes early and mid-twentieth-century Native American (northern) authors such as Todd Downing, Lynn Riggs, and D'Arcy McNickle and how Mexico's precolonial indigeneity became inspiration for these authors to once affirm local, tribal national spaces and to create a revolutionary "indigenous American transnational" imaginary (19).

In putting coalition building and networks of coalition Indigenous imaginaries front and center, these scholars destabilize the concept of "transnational" that has historically privileged the colonizer and settler-invaders. As such, the concept of transnational has been deployed as a tool of, in the words of Chadwick Allen, "scholarly deracination of the Indigenous" and the "engulfment of the Indigenous within and beneath systems of meaning-making dominated by the desires, obsessions, and contingencies of non-Indigenous settlers, their non-Indigenous nation-states, their non-Indigenous institutions, their non-Indigenous critical methodologies and discourses" ("A Transnational Native American Studies? Why Not Studies That Are Trans-Indigenous?"). In a like spirit, Danika Medak-Saltzman warns of the scholarly deployments of Indigeneity in ethnic studies. This can erase important specificities of historical, political, and cultural contexts. If we do not become conscious of such moves in our scholarship, we simply perpetuate the colonial and imperial logics of power) that continue to haunt critical ethnic studies fields (paraphrase 29).

It's this kind of critical self-conscious about one's position as a scholar of Indigenous cultural phenomenon that at the heart of scholars like Cox, Huhndorf, and Allen among others. For instance, Alice Te Punga Somerville declares that while she is doing comparative work on Indigenous texts from a number of contexts, she does so as a Māori scholar inhabiting Māori lands—a situatedness that, she identifies, "both guides and underpins my comparisons" (25). And we see in Chadwick Allen's book, *Trans-Indigenous: Methodologies for Global Native Literary Studies,* a careful and critical articulation of a trans-Indigenous approach to Indigenous cultural phenomena by those of the US America, Canadian First Nations, Indigenous Hawai'i, New Zealand Māori, and Aboriginal Australia. For Allen, cultural creators and intellectuals who "self-identify as Indigenous and/or who are claimed by Indigenous communities" are situated within specifics of time and places of "survivance" as well as across trans-Indigenous layers of "diversity and complexity," made up of "seeming paradoxes of simultaneity, contradiction, coexistence" (xxxii).

In addition to Native authors of literature mentioned above, the transnational model has also been used in approaching cultural phenomenon such as art and film as specific instantiations of Indigeneity *and* as cross-coalitional. Such an approach can lead to the articulation of "create a cross-genre discourse of resistance," as Dean Rader states in *Engaged Resistance* (2). Such an approach allows Chris Teuton to articulate and analyze the transcultural connections that inform Mesoamerican writing, Navajo sand painting, and Iroquois wampum belts.

* * *

Cultural phenomena by and about Indigenous identities, histories, and experiences circulate far and wide. However, not all such phenomena are made equal. Not all such phenomena serve to enrich an understanding of the complexity of Indigenous subjectivities. This is the case with films, animations, TV shows—and comic books. In an interview with Elizabeth LaPensée, Michael Sheyahshe decries, "Whether it's the whooping, attacking horde of Indians in the early 'cowboy' movies, the notion of Native American as a crack-shot and/or expert tracker in comics, or the continued (mis)representation in video games (some mentioned above), pop culture media serves to mirror the emotional consensus of how mainstream America sees us." In *Indian Stereotypes in TV Science Fiction*, Sierra S. Adare critically dismantles a whole range of these destructive stereotypes in sci-fi shows where we see constantly reproduction of "Indian" stereotypes (7). Other scholars have turned their sights to mainstream comic books and comic strips to critically sleuth out and dismantle the "Indian" stereotypes. For instance, in Michelle Bauldic's analysis of the Canadian comic strip, "Ookpik" (1964–1966), that was meant to be a symbol to unite the Canadian nation, she reveals how Oopik becomes a stand-in for First Nations peoples portrayed as idiots disconnected from land, history, and culture. For Bauldic, Ookpik represents an "imaginary space that is the frontier, empty, white, blank and belongs to Canada; and the ideological North that is an empty page used to project Canadianness against the urban Canada" (143). In *Native Americans in Comic Books*, Michael A. Sheyahshe carefully retraces mainstream superhero comic book archaeologies built out of the pernicious stereotyping of Indigenous peoples. He also identifies the tradition in comics of the "Mohican syndrome" whereby white saviors play "Indian" (Plastic Man, Captain Marvel, Superman, Batman, and the Phantom) to fight for justice and restore the white American way of life (10). In *From Daniel Boone to Captain America,* Chad A. Barbour analyzes how white heroes and superheroes slum it in "Indianness" with little connection to the "genuine history, ongoing traditions, and particular peoples" (5–6). In these scholarly archival reconstructions of mainstream comics we see the construction of white fantasies of heroic manliness with a global reach, and always at the expense and erasure of complex Indigenous identities and experiences. Conversely, in mainstream comics from the Americas to Australasia, scholarship here and elsewhere identifies how Indigenous superheroes are tethered tight to community; they never have the global reach of a Superman, for instance. (See Chadwick Allen's "Tonto on Vacation, or How to Be an Indian Lawyer" and also Nickie D. Phillips and Staci Strobl's *Comic Book Crime*.)

It's worth mentioning that not all non-Indigenous-created comics get it wrong. There's the complex rendering of the *mestiza*, Maya Lopez as Echo (cocreated with Joe Quesada) along with today's revamped Red Wolf. For instance, with S'Kallam Indigenous consultant Jeffrey Veregge brought on to help shape *Red Wolf: Man Out of Time*, the comic book narrative resists locating Cheyenne indigeneity in a frozen past by teleporting him from the nineteenth century into a twenty-first-century world filled with racism; notably, the comic includes a history of mistreatment of Indigenous peoples. We journey with Red Wolf as he grapples with his outsiderness and his deep connection to community. In DC's published *Quarantine Zone* (2016) Cherokee writer Daniel H. Wilson (along with artist Fernando Pasarin) recreates a future where Indigenous issues percolate under the surface: spreading the virus identified as "Malnoro" leads to rounding up those infected in a so-called Quarantine Zone—an extrapolation of the way Indigenous peoples have become prisoners to the impoverished conditions of reservations. And in New Zealand we see a certain degree of willful reconstruction of Māori culture in Jim Davidson's *Moa*. Davidson states how he wanted "to produce books that teach children about the land they inhabit, the history they all share, and the mythologies that surround them" (*From Earth's End* 116). For instance, in issue 3 of *Moa* (2013) he willfully introduces into the story the Māori concept of the life principle, or Mauri of a Forest as concentrated in objects like stones.

While I will leave the lion's share of analyses of the different ways that comics offer "cross-genre discourses of resistance" (Dean Rader) to the scholars in this volume, I would like to mention some Indigenous comics creations as well as Indigenous created spaces for connecting with readers and audiences. For many such creators, the word-drawn narrative spaces of comics offer important ways of dynamically geometrizing Indigenous identities and experiences otherwise erased or pejoratively reconstructed in the mainstream. And, just as importantly we see in these comics creations the materialization of imaginations shaped by non-mainstreamed cultures, histories, and mythologies.

Indigenous comics cross all genres, topics, and drawn-word forms. There are those that spring from and make vitally new myths such as those collected in *Moonshot Vols. 1-2*, Matt Dembicki's anthology, *Trickster*, and Michael Nicoll

Yahgulanaas's *Red* (2009). There are those that follow the superheroic mode such as Andrea Grant's *Minx: Dream War*, Jon Proudstar and Ryan Huna Smith's *Tribal Force*, Arigon Starr's *Super Indian*, Jen Murvin Edwards and Tom Lyle's *Chickasaw*. In Steven Keewatin Sanderson's *Darkness Calls*, for instance, we meet the bullied high schooler, Kyle; to escape his brutal everyday existence, he turns to making comics—until, that is, his encounter with his grandfather, a storyteller who conjures epic battles between Wesakecak and Wintiko; the stories have a transformative effect, empowering Kyle in his everyday life. And Sanderson's *Journey of the Healer* follows Rosa's superheroic journey and transformation into a warrior as she travels across dark swamps and battles monsters; she saves her grandmother and her community: "That's how our people survived. Because a girl found courage to leave her home so she could come back and heal it." Such Indigenous-created comics, as Darren Préfontaine writes in the introduction to *Stories of Our People: A Métis Graphic Novel Anthology* (2008), are a vital way "to show respect for the storytellers and stories themselves" (Préfontaine v).

There are those comics that follow an alternative, testimonial mode like David Alexander Robertson and Scott B. Henderson's *Sugar Falls: A Residential School Story* and David Alexander Robertson's *The Life of Helen Betty Osborne*. And, there are those that take an historical approach such as Gord Hill's *The 500 Years of Resistance Comic Book*. For instance, in "A Necessary Antidote" Sarah Henzi analyzes *The Life of Helen Betty Osborne*, *Kiss Me Deadly*, and Hill's *The 500 Years of Resistance Comic Book*, as narratives that use the visual and the textual to enable "an exploration of different means to reconnect the elements of the past with those of the present and the future" (29). Moreover, for Henzi they are necessary "interventions" that wake readers to the legacy of the violent colonialism that has led to the "tragedies of abused children in residential schools, teen suicide, and missing and murdered women" (29).

We're seeing the rise of important Indigenous-grown spaces for connecting with Indigenous audiences. I think of the yearly Indigenous Comic Con in Albuquerque, INC: The Indigenous Narratives Collective, Native Realities Press, and HAN (Healthy Aboriginal Network)—a publisher that seeks to promote "health, literacy & wellness through the production of visual resources for youth" (https://thehealthyaboriginal.net/). The Internet has also become an important platform for individual creators to reach audiences. I think of Arigon Starr's Rezum Studios (http://superindiancomics.com/), which features not only her *Super Indian* comic book, but also her webcomics, art, and podcasts.

These Indigenous creations and the many that are analyzed in this volume not only resist histories and reconstructions of Indigenous identities and experiences warped by the mainstream. For Susan Bernardin, Indigenous comic books "proliferate the imaginative possibilities—present and future—of twenty-first-century Indigenous Wests" ("Indigenous Wests" 6). They clear new spaces for the articulation of possible, affirmative futurities.

* * *

The scholarship that takes the baton from the scholars mentioned above and others not mentioned, build on and extend the work on comics by and about Indigenous peoples and experiences in the Americas and Australasia. To this end, I divide the volume into three major sections.

"Part I: Mainstreamed Indigeneities" includes scholarship that traces the histories of non-Indigenous comic book creations. Brenna Clarke Gray's chapter, "'We the North,'" opens this section. Here Gray traces a Canadian comics genealogy grown from the appropriation of indigeneity: identities and practices. As such, Canadian comics have metabolized indigeneity as a way to package and market Canadian-ness in ways that ultimately sweep to the side the histories of the civil rights struggles of Indigenous people. I follow with Chad A. Barbour's chapter, "Jack Jackson, Native Representation, and Underground Comix." Going against expectation, Barbour explores and analyzes how US Anglo underground comix creator Jack Jackson willfully distills and reconstructs Indigenous identities and experiences in a complex and progressive way. Barbour locates Jackson's work within the contexts of resistance movements such as Alcatraz and Wounded Knee to show how he interrogates "the parameters of historical recollection and nationalistic mythology in the United States." This section then moves from the Americas north to Australasia (specifically Australia and New Zealand) to look at their histories of representing Indigenous peoples and experiences. Historians Jack Ford and Philip Cass's "'Goin' Native!'" provides an overview of the history of *absenting* and misrepresenting Indigenous peoples of Australasia. And while they point out that the Australian and New Zealand comics markets were much smaller than those of the US, there was still a tradition of white male comic book storytellers creating both racist stereotypes *and* also complex Māori and Aboriginal characters and stories. As they state, "the worst excesses of Indigenous imagery have been largely avoided in both countries." I follow with Dennin Ellis's chapter, "Representations of Indigenous Australians in Marvel Comics." Ellis focuses on the distillation and reconstruction of Aboriginal characters in the Outback Era of the *Uncanny X-Men* series. By focusing his scholarly lens on characters like Gateway, Talisman, and the Reavers he analyzes how Marvel missed an opportunity to wake readers to the "real-world evils" of colonization and imperialism in committing acts of genocide against Indigenous Australians. I end this section with Kevin Patrick's chapter, "The Wisdom of the Phantom." In a move to tease out how Indigenous readers and audiences are not passive consumers of non-Indigenous mainstream comic book superheroes, Patrick takes us on a journey of the Phantom's active transformation by Indigenous communities throughout Australasia, Papua New Guinea inclusive. Patrick carefully unpacks how this superhero, who represents the evils of colonialism, can be reconstructed for Aboriginal audiences and by creators in ways that serve their own needs and aspirations.

"Part II: Decolonial Imaginaries *Terra South*" brings together chapters that focus on the complex ways that comic book creations in the hemispheric Americas south graphically texture indigeneities. I open with Arij Ouweneel's chapter, "Outsmarting the Lords of Death." Ouweneel uses insights from the cognitive sciences to consider how a series of comic book creators from across the Americas reschematize Euro-Christian national myths that leave out Indigenous histories, cultures, practices, and peoples. In his analysis of how creators like Rhode Montijo, Francisco Miro Quesada Cantuarias, Carlos Castellanos Casanova, Martín Espinoza Díaz, and Ricardo Walter Rodríguez, among others use an Amerindian cognitive schema in their comics to clear a space for affirming Indigenous cultural memory, Ouweneel posits that by "keeping the Amerindian cognitive schema's alive, comics like *Pablo's Inferno, Supercholo, La Chola Power, Turbochaski,* and *Supay* are key mediators of Amerindian memory." I follow with Javier García Liendo's analysis of La Chola Power—a daughter of the Incan sun god sent to fight crime and heal Peruvian society. In this chapter, "Memory in Pieces" García Liendo uses the concept of a "multidimensional" narrative of cultural and political memory to analyze how La Chola Power safeguards "the memory of a past that neoliberal society seems intent on burying forever." García Liendo analyzes how the comic book series at once reconstructs Peru's violent past and redeploys Indigenous epistemologies and linguistic codes (untranslated Quechua) to critique current contexts of exploitation and oppression in and through urbanization and mass migrations of Indigenous peoples.

The two chapters that follow were written in concert with one another, focusing on teasing out the rich complexities of Daniel Parada's comic book series, *Zotz*. Jessica Rutherford's "Visualizing an Alternate Mesoamerican Archive" identifies Parada's use of Mesoamerican myth and history as a way to occupy a space of *nepantla* (in-between-ness) that offers readers an Indigenous-anchored historical archive. She analyzes, for instance, how Parada's reconstruction of a Chiapanec legend of resistance to Euro-Spanish invaders wakes readers to the violence of colonization and conquest. In "Critical Impulses in Daniel Parada's *Zotz*" Jorge Santos builds dialogues with Rutherford's chapters to demonstrate how *Zotz* functions as an important, Indigenous-based knowledge repository. In the chapter that follows, Brian Montes focuses on the importance of the visual and verbal modes of narrating Indigenous histories. In "The Battle for Recollection" Montes analyzes the ten-page comic book, *Manuel Antonio Ay: El Primer Mártir de la Guerra de Castas*, revealing how the comic powerfully narrativizes Maya resistance as a stand-in for the sovereignty of Indigenous peoples across history and the Americas. Enrique García's chapter, "*Turey El*

Taíno and *La Borinqueña*," takes us into the Hispanophone archipelago where comics like *Turey El Taíno* and *La Borinqueña* place at their centers Indigenous Taíno and African ancestral histories and cultures erased by legacies of Spanish colonial caste systems and histories.

With "Part III: Decolonial Imaginaries *Terra North*" I bring together scholarship that focuses on comics that complexly *geometrize* and texture indigeneities in the hemispheric Americas north. I open with Jordan Clapper's "Securing Stones in the Sky," which analyzes how the visual strategies of comic book storytelling intensify the oral storytelling traditions recreated in vignettes collected in *Trickster: Native American Tales, A Graphic Collection*. Here Clapper radically retheorizes the narrator function as an extension of the oral function in Indigenous cultures and storytelling traditions. I follow with James J. Donahue's chapter, "Super Indians and the Indigenous Comics Renaissance." Here Donahue analyzes how Captain Paiute and Super Indian at once work within and complicate mainstream superhero conventions. As Indigenous-created superheroes they wake readers to the issues and problems that face tribal communities today. Their battles are with the legacies of the violence of the coloniality of power, the real monsters and super-villains that haunt and plague Indigenous peoples across the Americas north. In "Seeing Histories, Building Futurities" Mike Borkent analyzes how alternative publishing venues are producing comics that "challenge representational assumptions [and] transform colonial representations of Indigeneity in Canada." In analyses of comics such as *7 Generations: A Plains Cree Saga* and *The Outside Circle*, Borkent demonstrates how Indigenous-created comics clear spaces for "decolonial healing" as well as "cultural reclamation." For Borkent these and other Indigenous comics "offer a complex space to strategically display Indigenous stories, which can only continue to add to the important work of Indigenous literatures." In Jeremy M. Carnes's "Deep Time and Vast Place" we see how the willful use of space layout and gutters in comics can awaken readers to how land and water inform a cosmic, trans-Indigenous knowledge system. Carnes demonstrates how Indigenous word-drawn narratives use time and space to push readers to "think beyond any one specific community and point out how these complex relations of human, nonhuman, and land/water constitute each other in complex relations of deep time and vast place in the cosmos." In the chapter "Deer Woman Re-Generations," Joshua T. Anderson analyzes how the *Deer Woman* comics anthology presents word-drawn narratives of the Indigenous first being, Deer Woman, that clears a space for *re-membering* "dismembered bodies and histories" and re-activating *traditional* "arts practices through resurgent, regenerative networks centering contemporary Indigenous women." In "Indigeneity, Intermediality, and the Haunted Present of *Will I See?*" Candida Rifkind and Jessica Fontaine examine how the multimodal narrative (comic, animated video, and vocal recording) of the tragic murders of Tina Fontaine and Faron Hall create an alternative history and aesthetics of resistance; that the violence against Indigenous youth necessitates the creating of such multimodal narratives to enact a "politicized practice of empathetic witness." Susan Bernardin's coda, "After Lives," brings the volume to a close, powerfully reminding us of the significance of Indigenous comic book creation and exhibition in its power to heal in a social tissue that's increasingly ripped apart.

While we need to keep our eyes wide open for those lazy and willfully racist distillations and reconstructions of Indigenous peoples and experiences in comics from around the world, as *Graphic Indigeneity: Comics in the Americas and Australasia* begins to demonstrate, there is much to be excited about. There is a growing array of comics by and about Indigenous peoples and experiences, histories and cultures that powerfully make new our perspective, thought, and feeling.

Works Cited

Adams, Rachel. *Continental Divides: Remapping the Cultures of North America*. Chicago: University of Chicago Press, 2009.

Adare, Sierra S. *Indian Stereotypes in TV Science Fiction: First Nation's Voices Speak Out*. Austin: University of Texas Press, 2005.

Allen, Chadwick. *Trans-Indigenous: Methodologies for Global Native Literary Studies*. Minneapolis: University of Minnesota Press, 2012.

———. "A Transnational Native American Studies? Why Not Studies That Are Trans-Indigenous?" *Journal of Transnational American Studies* 4, no. 1 (January 2012) https://escholarship.org/uc/item/82m5j3jf5.

———. "Tonto on Vacation, or How to Be an Indian Lawyer." *Canadian Review of American Studies* 39, no. 2 (2009): 139–61.

Barbour, Chad A. *From Daniel Boone to Captain America: Playing Indian in American Popular Culture*. Jackson: University Press of Mississippi, 2016.

Bauldic, Michelle. "Allan Beaton's 'Ookpik' Was Here." *Canadian Review of Comparative Literature / Revue Canadienne de Littérature Comparée* 43, no. 1 (March 2016): 137–47.

Bernardin, Susan. "Indigenous Wests: Literary and Visual Aesthetics." *Western American Literature* 49, no. 1 (Spring 2014): 1–8.

Cox, James H., and Daniel Heath Justice, eds. *The Oxford Handbook of Indigenous American Literature Online*. November 2014. https://www.oxfordhandbooks.com/view/10.1093/oxfordhb/9780199914036.001.0001/oxfordhb-9780199914036.

Fitz, Earl E. "Indigenous American Literature: The Inter-American Hemispheric Perspective." In *The Routledge Companion to Native American Literature*, edited by Deborah Madsen, 15–27. London: Routledge, 2016.

Guevarra, Rudy P. *Becoming Mexipino: Multiethnic Identities and Communities in San Diego*. New Brunswick, NJ: Rutgers University Press, 2012.

Henzi, Sarah. "'A Necessary Antidote': Graphic Novels, Comics, and Indigenous Writing." *Canadian Review of Comparative Literature / Revue Canadienne de Littérature Comparée* 43, no. 1 (March 2016): 23–38.

———. "Indigenous Uncanniness and Popular Culture." In *The Routledge Companion to Native American Literature*, edited by Deborah Madsen, 469–79. London: Routledge, 2016.

Huhndorf, Shari M. *Mapping the Americas: The Transnational Politics of Contemporary Native Culture*. Ithaca, NY: Cornell University Press, 2009.

LaPensée, Elizabeth. "Aboriginal Territories in Cyberspace: Interview with Michael Sheyahshe." April 6, 2009. Web. December 31, 2014. http://www.abtec.org/blog/?p=118.

Medak-Saltzman, Danika. "Empire's Haunted Logics: Comparative Colonialisms and the Challenges of Incorporating Indigeneity." *Journal of Critical Ethnic Studies*. Special Issue: "The Perils and Possibilities of Comparative Work" 1, no. 2 (2015): 11–32.

Miner, Dylan. *Creating Aztlán: Chicano Art, Indigenous Sovereignty, and Lowriding across Turtle Island*. Tucson: University of Arizona Press, 2014.

Pereira, Claudia Matos. "Indigenous People in Comics: The Ethnographic-Semiotic Look by the Brazilian Artist Sergio Macedo/Povos Indigenas." *Revista: Estúdio, Artistas sobre outras obras* 5, no. 9 (2014): 79–84.

Phillips, Nickie D., and Staci Strobl. *Comic Book Crime: Truth, Justice, and the American Way*. New York: New York University Press, 2013.

Préfontaine, Darren. "Project Introduction." In *Stories of Our People/Lii zistwayr di la naasyoon di Michif: A Metis Graphic Novel Anthology*, edited by Norman Fleury, Gilbert Pelletier, Jeanne Pelletier, Joe Welsh, Norma Welsh, Janice DePeel, and Carrie Saganace. Saskatoon: Gabriel Dumont Institute, 2008.

Rader, Dean. *Engaged Resistance: American Indian Art, Literature, and Film from Alcatraz to the NMAI*. Austin: University of Texas Press, 2011.

Reder, Deanna. "Sacred Stories in Comic Book Form: A Cree Reading of *Darkness Calls*." In *Troubling Tricksters: Revisioning Critical Conversations*, edited by Deanna Reder and Linda M. Morra, 177–91. Waterloo: Wilfrid Laurier University Press, 2010.

Sheyahshe, Michael. *Native Americans in Comic Books: A Critical Study*. Jefferson, NC: McFarland, 2008.

Spiers, Miriam Brown. "Creating a Haida Manga: The Formline of Social Responsibility in Red." *Studies in American Indian Literatures* 26, no. 3 (2014): 41–61.

Teuton, Christopher. *Deep Waters: The Textual Continuum in American Indian Literature*. Lincoln: University of Nebraska Press, 2010.

Further Reading: Comics

Carey, Mike, Leonard Kirk, and Pat Oliffe. *Sigil: Out of Time*. New York: Marvel, 2011.
Deforest, Dale. *Hero Twins #1*. Albuquerque, NM: Native Realities Press, 2017.
Downie, Gord, and Jeff Lemire. *Secret Path*. New York: Simon & Schuster, 2016.
Durack, Mary, and Elizabeth. *A Book of Picture Stories*. Perth: Imperial Printing, 1942.
Eaglespeaker, Jason. *NAPI—The Trixster: A Blackfoot Graphic Novel*. Amazon CreateSpace, 2016.
Edmondson, Nathan, and Dalibor Talajic. *Red Wolf: Man Out of Time*. New York: Marvel, 2016.
Egan, Vincent, and Madison Henry. *Sun Tamer Graphic Novel*. Auckland: Māui Studios, 2016.
Englehart, Steve, Marshall Rogers, and Tom Palmer. *Coyote: Volume 1*. Portland: Image Comics, 2005.
Gaiman, Neil, and Andy Kubert. *Marvel 1602*. New York: Marvel, 2010.
Gladue, Stephen, ed. *The Indigenous Comics Collection Volume 2*. Toronto: AH Comics, 2017.
Grant, Andrea, Rey Arzeno, and Mike Williams. *Minx TP*. Ardden Entertainment, 2012.
Grell, Mike. *Shaman's Tears*. San Diego: IDW Publishing, 2011.
Grosz, Chris. *Kimble Bent: Malcontent*. New York: Random House, 2011.
Hawke, Ethan, and Greg Ruth. *Indeh: A Story of the Apache Wars*. New York: Grand Central Publishing, 2016.

Hill, Gord. *The 500 Years of Resistance Comic Book*. Vancouver, Canada: Arsenal Pulp Press, 2010.
Jackson, Jack. *Jack Jackson's American History: Los Tejanos and Lost Cause*. Seattle: Fantagraphics, 2013.
Jones, Stephen Graham, and Aaron Lovett. *My Hero*. Erie, CO: Hex Publishers, 2017.
Kinnaird, Adrian. *From Earth's End: The Best of New Zealand Comics*. Auckland: Godwit Press, 2018.
LaPensée, Elizabeth, and Weshoyot Alvitre. *Deer Woman: An Anthology*. Albuquerque, NM: Native Realities Press, 2017.
Lewis, Sean, and Caitlin Yarsky. *Coyotes*. Portland, OR: Image Comics, 2017.
Manfredi, Gianfranco, José Ortiz, and Serbian Bane Kerac. *Magic Wind Vol. 1: Fort Ghost*. San Diego: Epicenter Comics, 2013.
McNeil, Carla Speed. *Finder Library: Volume 1*. Milwaukie, OR: Dark Horse Books, 2007.
Nicholson, Hope, ed. *Moonshot: The Indigenous Comics Collection Vol. 1*. Toronto: AH Comics, 2016.
Odjick, Jay, and Patrick Tenascon. *Kagagi: The Raven*. Burnaby, Canada: Arcana Studio, 2011.
Ostrander, John, and Lonard Manco. *Blaze of Glory: The Last Ride of the Western Heroes*. New York: Marvel, 2002.
Pauls, Cole. *Dakwäkäda Warriors*. Vancouver, Canada: Moniker Press, 2016.
Proudstar, Jon, Ron Joseph, and Weshoyot Alvitre. *Tribal Force #1*. Albuquerque, NM: Native Realities Press, 2016.
Robertson, David Alexander, and Scott B. Henderson. *Sugar Falls: A Residential School Story*. Winnipeg, Canada: HighWater Press, 2012.
Sanderson, Steven Keewatin. *Darkness Calls: An Invited Threat*. Healthy Aboriginal Network, 2008.
———. *Level Up*. Healthy Aboriginal Network, 2008.
———. *Just a Story*. Vancouver, Canada: Healthy Aboriginal Network, 2009.
———. *Lighting Up the Darkness*. Vancouver, Canada: Healthy Aboriginal Network, 2011.
———. *An Invited Threat*. Vancouver, Canada: Healthy Aboriginal Network, 2013.
Smith, Paul Chaat, and Robert Allen Warrior. *Like a Hurricane: The Indian Movement from Alcatraz to Wounded Knee*. New York: New Press, 1996.
Starr, Arigon, Roy Boney, Theo Tso, Kristina Bad Hand, Johnathan Nelson, and Renee Nejo, eds. *Code Talkers*. Albuquerque, NM: Native Realities Press, 2016.
Starr, Arigon. *Super Indian*. West Hollywood, CA: Wacky Productions Unlimited, 2012.
Starr, Arigon, Jeffrey Veregge, Weshoyot Alvitre, Jim Terry et al. *Indigenous Superhero Sketchbooks 1 and 2*. Albuquerque, NM: Native Realities Press, 2017.
Sullivan, Robert, and Chris Slane. *Maui: Legends of the Outcast*. Auckland: Godwit Press, 1997.
Taylor, Drew Hayden, and Mike Wyatt. *The Night Wanderer: A Graphic Novel*. Toronto, Canada: Annick Press, 2013.
Truman, Tim. *Scout, Vol. 1*. Runnemede, NJ: Dynamite Entertainment, 2006.
Wilson, Daniel H., and Fernando Pasarin. *Quarantine Zone*. Los Angeles: DC Comics, 2016.

GRAPHIC INDEGENEITY

PART I
MAINSTREAMED INDIGENEITIES

"We the North": Interrogating Indigenous Appropriation as Canadian Identity in Mainstream American Comics

Brenna Clarke Gray

Indigenous characters—as appropriated by primarily white mainstream comics artists—are often coded as markers of Canadian identity in mainstream American[1] comics in a larger echo of Canada's own corporate, institutional, and governmental practice. In many ways, American mainstream superhero comics (and the scholarship written about them) are merely repeating a cycle of convenient and ahistorical appropriation that has been central to the branding of Canada, especially to a global audience, for much of its history. For example, in their 2010 article "Aboriginality and the Arctic North in Canadian Nationalist Superhero Comics, 1940–2004," Jason Dittmer and Soren Larsen begin a valuable interrogation of the way Canadian identity is often imagined in appropriated Indigenous terms.[2] While their work on the Canadian Whites-era of Canadian comics (sometimes called the Golden Age, through the Second World War) and *Captain Canuck* represents a substantial contribution to the study of comics in this country, which has not often focused on necessary questions of race and representation, their easy framing of *Alpha Flight*, wholly owned by Marvel Comics, as a "Canadian" comic—primarily because its creator John Byrne was Scottish-Canadian—offers grounds for further work. This chapter considers the implications of scholarly assumptions about so-called Canadian nationalist superheroes created and marketed by major American corporations and, more importantly, examines the appropriation of representations of Indigenous bodies to those ends.

The Canadian Nationalist Superhero and Superheroes Who Just Happen to Be Canadian

The concept of the nationalist superhero is one of the ideas most often discussed with regard to mainstream Canadian comics scholarship, and for good

5

reason: until the 1970s, the most popular comics made in Canada seemed to be expressly nationalist. Ryan Edwardson, in his article "The Many Lives of Captain Canuck: Nationalism, Culture, and the Creation of a Canadian Comic Book Superhero," notes that

> Distinctively national comic books are vessels for transmitting national myths, symbols, ideologies, and values. They popularize and perpetuate key elements of the national identity and ingrain them into their readers—especially, given the primary readership, younger generations experiencing elements of that identity for the first time.

When the comics are superhero comics, then, the superhero becomes emblematic of the expectations and stereotypes of the nation; their goals as heroes and do-gooders are aligned with the goals of the nation-state. Jason Dittmer notes in "Captain Britain and the Narration of Nation" that Captain America, with his pursuit of "truth, justice, and the American Way," "can be understood as a foundation for the nationalist superhero genre" (71). Think about the way Captain America is named for his nation-state and draped in its colors, symbols, and flag, and you have a visual representation of nationalist superheroes.

As Bart Beaty outlines in his article "The Fighting Civil Servant: Making Sense of the Canadian Superhero," "the temptation to provide the Canadian superhero with a distinctly nationalist identity, generally at odds with American-themed superheroes, has been one of the dominant hallmarks of the Canadian superhero genre" (429). This is rooted in the origin of Canadian comics; the Canadian comic book industry only emerged as a direct result of WWII rationing, which prevented the sale of US paper goods in Canada. Canadian publishers took up this opportunity to fill the void left, with titles like *Nelvana of the North* and *Johnny Canuck*. To speak plainly, these comics were simply not very good, having been created by people with passion but very little training or history in the production of comics; when the war ended and comics were once again imported from the United States, very few Canadian readers remained loyal to their Canadian comics. By 1955, the industry had collapsed, and there were effectively no English-language comics produced from 1955 to 1970.

As you might imagine given the time period, these WWII comics, known widely as Canadian Whites because of the paper stock they were printed on, were expressly nationalist in tone and content. Some characters, like Nelvana of the Northern Lights, were tasked with protecting Canada at home. Others, like the desperately and unintentionally hilarious Johnny Canuck, exist to fight abroad. As Bart Beaty points out, though, in their inherent Canadianness these characters are barred from being too exciting; they could be "active in the war, but not so active as to accomplish much of significance" (430). They were, if there can ever be such a thing, middle-power superheroes. They were nationalist in that they signaled a direct connection to the interests of Canada as a nation-state and often represented that nation-state, whether at home or abroad.

From 1955 to 1970, as noted, there were no Canadian comics of note published and thus the market was dominated by the mainstream American comics produced by big publishing houses like Atlas/Marvel and DC; this glut of American culture aligned with a Canadian centennial anxiety about the dominance of American culture in all aspects of Canadian life. *Captain Canuck* emerged as a response to this anxiety, and creator Richard Comely was expressly interested in engaging in nationalist sentiment in his comic. Edwardson notes that *Captain Canuck* primarily provides "Canadian comic book fans with a sense of national identity in a cultural arena where New York overwhelms New Brunswick, and one rarely sees a maple leaf" (199), particularly in the 1970s, when no other Canadian comics existed outside of the underground presses in Montreal and Toronto. Comely's mission in creating *Captain Canuck* was expressly to fill what he saw as a cultural absence and establish an icon of identity. Comely also saw *Captain Canuck* as an opportunity to reinsert religion into a largely secular cultural space; while Captain Canuck didn't explicitly share Comely's own Mormon identity, he did pray before every mission and connected overtly his mission to protect Canada with his own godliness. (Later iterations of the character have dropped this religiosity.) It is worth noting that Captain Canuck was far more successful as an idea and as a trademark to be sold than he ever was as a comic book—his representation on a t-shirt has always had greater cultural cache than sales figures of comics featuring him might suggest—but new iterations of Captain Canuck recur every decade or so nonetheless.

As far as mainstream comics go, nationalist heroes were it for much of Canada's publishing history in mainstream comics. So it's natural that this area is a focal point for comics scholars interested in trends and expectations in Canadian comic books. But there is a trend in comics scholarship to assume that all superhero comics featuring Canadian characters are necessarily nationalist, and *Alpha Flight* is the series most commonly caught in this, as we see in Dittmer and Larsen's article. This comes, I believe, from a comment Bart Beaty makes in his article where he notes that, compared to the mandated nationalism of Captain Canuck, Marvel's Alpha Flight team is actually more broadly representative of Canada, including a linguistic and racial diversity rare in comics of that era (and today, unfortunately) and absent from the bland and blond superheroes of the nationalist comics movement in Canada. But Beaty specifically notes that Alpha Flight and other American-produced Canadian superheroes—characters like Wolverine and Deadpool in the Marvel Universe, for example—actually "undercut [. . .] Canadian nationalism" by relying "on some of the most obvious clichés about the nation" and the stories "prove [. . .] difficult to quantify as distinctly Canadian" (436–37). Further compounding this issue, Dittmer and Larsen also commit the error of reading too uncritically our nationalist comic

Captain Canuck. From *Captain Canuck #1* (1974): cover. Reprinted by Chapterhouse Archive, 2016.

historian John Bell,[3] who tends to foreground creator nationality over corporate context in outlining the history of Alpha Flight. While it's true that Alpha Flight creator John Byrne lived in Canada and was trained at least in part at the Alberta College of Art and Design, of his own nationality he writes:

> I've been a citizen of three different countries. I was born in England, so I got that one the easy way. When I was 14, my parents became Canadian citizens, and I floated in with them. Then, in 1988, after having lived in this country the prerequisite number of years, I became an American citizen. (In full. I do not hold dual citizenship. I do not hyphenate myself.)[4] (Byrne)

As much as there seems to be an inherently Canadian drive to claim all tangentially related cultural figures as our own, it is clear here that Byrne does not see himself as Canadian; his choice of the phrasing "floated in with them" to describe how he acquired his Canadian citizenship suggests a lack of agency in or commitment to that identity.

Alpha Flight is really only Canadian because it was convenient for them to be Canadian, and they emerged at a time when Marvel was trying to expand the geographic base of its subscribers and diversify (mildly!) its offerings. This was around the same time as the launch of, for example, Captain Britain in the UK. The team was introduced as a foil to the X-Men in 1979, and then quickly achieved their own series. *Alpha Flight* was a viable title as long as it was making money. The most successful comic to feature Canadians—the first issue earned creator John Byrne a record-breaking thirty thousand dollars in 1984—was not a nationalist comic; indeed, as Beaty points out, it "helped to marginalize Canadian concerns within the so-called Marvel universe" in a single title about characters who regularly lost to American superhero teams. (To understand just how expressly *Alpha Flight* was not intended to be a nationalist comic for advancing Canadian interests, one can read the lettercols or letters to the editor from the 1980s and 1990s, where Canadians who write in to complain about geographic or cultural inaccuracies are roundly mocked by the creative team.)

We the North: National Identity Via Indigenous Appropriation

The "We the North" phrase of my title comes from the marketing of Canada's only (current) NBA basketball team, the Toronto Raptors, and indicates in a relatively minor way that the appropriation of northern and Indigenous identities stands in for discussion of Canadian identity. As we have seen from recent pop culture stories such as the DSquared² clothing line D-Squaw, appropriation of Indigenous identity as a signifier of Canadianness, particularly for an international market, is an ongoing issue. DSquared² is a fashion label owned by Italian-Canadian twins Dean and Dan Caten that sells a high-end conception of stereotypical Canadian identity to European clients[5] (one season featured a showroom draped in furs and flannel) with Canadianness obviously heavily coded through Indigenous imagery. The DSquaw line, launched early in 2015, was described by the Catens as, "The enchantment of Canadian Indian tribes. The confident attitude of the British aristocracy. In a captivating play on contrasts: an ode to America's Native tribes meets the noble spirit of Old Europe" ("Canadian Fashion Label Dsquared2 under Fire for #Dsquaw Collection"). This combination, including deeply troubling items like a wedding dress, seem to celebrate colonization and evince a celebratory tone; the sense is that this relationship and the coming together of these "contrasts" results not in rape and genocide, but beauty and fashion.[6] Groups like ReMatriate, a collective of "female fashion designers, singers, models, architects, artists, and advocates," are working to reframe these kinds of appropriations in explicit colonial terms, noting that for settler populations to treat cultural practices they once outlawed now as part of the public domain is deeply offensive ("ReMatriate Wants to Take Back 'Visual Identity' of First Nations"). Further, to call these images, ideas, and artifacts somehow inherently "Canadian" after the Canadian nation-state used generations of cultural violence to attempt to eradicate them is truly grotesque. But for generations, Canada has sought to have it both ways: to quash Indigenous nations at home while projecting Indigenous iconography as representative of Canada abroad. Take, for example, the branding for the 2010 Olympics in Vancouver: the use of Haida and other Indigenous nations' imagery (including the central logo, the Inuksuk, which is a symbol and practice of the Inuit and shares no territoriality with the site of the Olympics) belied the mass displacement of, for example, homeless youth—who are disproportionately Indigenous—from Vancouver for the Games. And even earlier attempts to brand Canada globally, like the Centennial and Expo 67 use of Oopik, an Inuit handicraft,[7] suggests that this has long been a corporate/government strategy: look to the Arctic North specifically and Indigeneity more generally to represent "authentic" Canada for a global audience.

This desire to appropriate without thought to obligation or responsibility is nothing new. In his *Souvenir of Canada* project, Douglas Coupland, Canadian artist and writer, tells the story of being asked to create a piece of Indigenous-inspired work for one of his first design jobs in 1984. Tasked with creating flash cards—one of which was to display Indigenous art—for a stadium in Vancouver, he writes:

> I was told to mock one up quickly for a meeting, so I invented a fake thunderbird-motif flash sequence. The meeting went well, and a week later I was asked to prepare a flash card sequence using genuine First Nations imagery. So I began to do research and generate designs [. . .] with none of them looking quite *right* to the committee. [. . .] It was finally decided to go with the original fake thunderbird sequence because it looked the most "Indian-y." (Coupland 95)

This idea of the inauthentic being read as more real than the authentic by ignorant settlers is, Coupland contends, the end result of misunderstanding and mistrust stoked by the government. It also underscores the ways in which Indigenous iconography is appropriated for non-Indigenous use by Canadian corporations and communities. The practice is coming into increasing scrutiny now, but countless organizations over the years have chosen, as Coupland's employers here did, to create for themselves an Indigenous iconography without following community practices and protocols, and often without involving Indigenous people at all.

We must also be mindful of how Canada is often explicitly sold abroad as a nation without colonial history; because Canada has not had expansionist global aims, it is easy to sell or represent Canada as a kinder, gentler face than other English-language nation-states like the UK or the US. Indeed, Canada's former prime minister Stephen Harper, famously speaking to G20 leaders in 2009, asserted that all nations want to be like Canada because of our unblemished record with "no history of colonialism" ("Every G20 Nation Wants to Be Canada, Insists PM"). This is an obvious untruth, violently eliding the experiences of Indigenous people and the Canadian government's historical desire for complete erasure of them. This is a mythology that seems to comfortably cross party lines, with Justin Trudeau echoing similar comments (though reflexively complicating the notion by referring to Indigenous people) in 2015 (Fontaine). What this suggests is another version of Canada's quest for difference from the United States and a sense of how we want to be seen by the world, regardless of reality. In this, as in the comics we will discuss, Indigenous people are treated less as nations and communities with uniquely territorialized histories and experiences, and more as set pieces to use or forget as is convenient to particular expressions of the Canadian global brand.

This is a particular problem in Canadian nationalist comics, where the intersection of a desire to represent the characters as expressly connected to the land and the unbearable whiteness of mainstream comics culture more generally often draws creators to appropriate Indigenous people, especially the Inuit, as symbolic characterizations of the Canadian landscape. The North functions as something of an internal Orient in Canada, comparable in some ways to the use of the American South in American discourse. As Sherrill Grace has noted, the North is "a construction of southerners, paradoxically invoked to distinguish [Canadians] from those who are more southern" (55). Indeed, evocations of northernness are an easy way to separate urban Canadians from urban Americans, even though their day-to-day life is demonstrably similar, though it is worth reflecting that this is often done in terms of lack (like the scathing rebuttal to the American tourist that, no, we don't all live in igloos and it doesn't typically snow in July). But the North is also "an archetypically Indigenous and aboriginal place," as Dittmer and Larsen note, and "aboriginality and northernness are often conflated in dominant Canadian cultural productions" (56).

Nelvana of the Northern Lights is a salient example of this. This is one of the comics of Canadian Whites WWII era, popular primarily as an accident of rationing that kept American comics on the southern side of the 49th parallel. Nelvana is, apparently, the daughter of the Inuit god Koliak, who manifests himself as the Northern Lights, and a white woman, but she is depicted as exclusively white throughout the comics. (It is interesting that a recent re-release of the Canadian Whites has colored Nelvana with a deeper skin tone.) She maintains a bizarre relationship with the Inuit people around her who rely on her for protection but are also confused by her: she is treated as a goddess, and her protection and salvation is always mystical, otherworldly. She is Inuit in name only, and in the comics appears as a white savior to, ostensibly, her own people. But she is also hemmed in by the construct of the land: while the other major titles of the Canadian Whites era were involved in the war effort overseas, Nelvana's role is limited to within Canadian borders and primarily with the protection of the arctic. She is a nationalist superhero insomuch as she represents the land and its protection and that her powers—for example, to travel at the speed of the Northern Lights—connect her explicitly to the geography of the arctic. And the history of Nelvana's character is entirely appropriative: creator Adrian Dingle got the idea from Franz Johnston's retelling of the real-life story of an Inuit woman from Coppermine, NWT, named Nelvana. Dingle liked the stories about this traditional-living Inuit woman, but didn't like that Johnston's photos and paintings depicted her as "an old crone" and so Dingle gave her "long hair and mini skirts" and "tried to make her attractive" (57); of course, in so doing he also makes her features whiter and her presentation more typically southern. Dittmer and Larsen note that Nelvana "herself embodies and constitutes both the categories of a colonial, white south, a colonized, aboriginal Arctic North, and the Canada that purports to unite them" (60). As Will Smith has articulated, "The erasure of particular histories and Indigenous sovereignties, whilst attempting to visualise Native characters, carries the sense of performing Indigeneity whereby vital and meaningful knowledge is sundered from the remaining aesthetic" (Smith).

But Nelvana was created exclusively for a Canadian audience, and her problematic depiction exists within a cultural and historical context. It assumes a certain amount of domestic buy-in—that Canadians do primarily see themselves as part of an arctic nation—as well as Canada's own founding in white supremacy with the reframing of Nelvana's story in white-coded terms to be more palatable. But we might hope that Canadians in the twenty-first century have some capacity to read critically these assumptions. We need to consider another layer when this appropriation is designed not to sell Canada to Canadians, but to package Canada for an external audience that may not have even the chance at holding the knowledge and history to contextualize the representations, as we find when John Byrne borrowed from the Nelvana canon to create his character Snowbird, one of the members of Alpha Flight, which launched in 1979 as a foil for the X-Men. As noted, Alpha Flight is not a nationalist superhero primarily intended to tell Canadian stories, but a Marvel comics property for primary sale in the United States. That complicates Dittmer and Larsen's reading in significant ways.

Alpha Flight: Progressive in Its Day, But . . .

For a superhero team launched in the late 1970s (they would get their own title in 1984), Alpha Flight was in many ways impressive. Alpha Flight has members who are gay and straight, white and nonwhite, federalist and separatist, French and English, representative of every region of the country, and the team is almost half female, with one female character even coping with a significant mental illness. There is no other mainstream comic from its era that tried so overtly to balance representation long before representation was the subject of lengthy blog posts. But there are only so many points to be awarded for effort, and many of these representations are shallow and underdeveloped. On the issue of representation of Indigenous characters in particular, Byrne made a lot of problematic mistakes. Some Marvel Comics canon is probably necessary here for many readers. The genesis of Alpha Flight, in terms of comics lore, was the Canadian government's contribution to the American Weapon X program, a supersoldier program rooted in technology liberated from concentration camps in WWII. This program in Canada, run by Department H, produced mutants like Wolverine and Deadpool (healing factor seems to be the primary quality shared by Weapon X mutants in Canada). But Department H also oversaw all superheroes in Canada, including Alpha Flight. Alpha Flight is introduced in 1979 when they are sent by then-prime minister Pierre Trudeau[8] to capture Wolverine from the X-Men and return him to the Weapon X facility. In the history of Department H and Weapon X, we see small examples of this appropriation of Indigenous identity in the construction of characters like the Native. The Native was captured by the Weapon X program and code-named Feral, and she was used as a test subject until she escaped, hiding out in a cabin in the mountains of British Columbia where she becomes pregnant with Wolverine's child (the unborn child dies when the Native is murdered by Sabretooth). The Native's origin story is not disclosed and she is not explicitly depicted as Indigenous, though by the time we meet her, she is deeply marked by her time as a test subject and her ethnicity is difficult to ascertain. But her name certainly connects her to Indigeneity, and in her imprisonment and use as a test subject it's hard not to read deep echoes of colonial projects like residential schooling.[9] However, the most significant intersection of the Canadian nation and Indigenous representation comes with John Byrne's development of the superhero team Alpha Flight and the characters of Snowbird, Shaman, and Talisman.

In Alpha Flight, the character of Snowbird is a product of John Byrne being heavily influenced by the Canadian Whites: Snowbird is supposed to be the daughter of Nelvana, though she is perhaps more explicitly depicted as Indigenous (though still the blond-yellow of comic book goddesses for generations), and her power is that she can shape shift into any animal that exists in the Canadian territory. This territoriality is part of how Alpha Flight has, in Dittmer and Larsen's terms, "bound the landscape to the Canadian state" (61): if Snowbird leaves Canada, she is powerless. Her powers are literally bounded by the national borders of the Canadian state. This explicitly codes Indigeneity as Canadian while imposing a colonial border upon Snowbird and universalizing her Indigenous identity as being specifically and exclusively Canadian. In effect, this imposes the colonial structure of the border more explicitly upon Snowbird than any other members of Alpha Flight, who do frequently leave Canada, which considering her Inuit heritage—the Inuit have an established

Shaman. From *Alpha Flight* #6 (1984): 18.

presence in their territories that predates the construction of the Canada-US border by thousands of years—is deeply troubling. This always calls to mind for me the Thomas King story "Borders," about a Blackfoot mother's rejection of colonially imposed borders and boundaries that limit her movement.[10] Snowbird is quite literally restricted, and critically wrested of her powers, by these same forces.

Both Snowbird and her mentor Shaman are used as cyphers for an ill-defined pan-Indian spirituality that is also deeply anchored to the Canadian nation: when Shaman doubts his powers, he retreats to "the Canadian Barrens" and to his ancestral homeland known only as the "North Country." There is an attempt, here, to reflect Indigenous spirituality in a way that might be considered refreshing after the Christian dominance of Captain Canuck, and Shaman himself is an interesting character vis-à-vis the typical stereotypical depiction of Indigenous characters in comics. Shaman's real name is Michael Twoyoungmen, and in his life before becoming a powered superhero, he was a medical doctor: in fact, he is recognized as the best surgeon in Canada. However, as part of this identity, he fully rejects the mysticism of his grandfather, and fails to heed his lessons until he loses his wife and realizes there is more than medical science. When he acquiesces to the spiritual demands of his grandfather (and, by extension, his elders and his people), he discovers his powers; these powers are connected to an appropriative notion of Indigenous spirituality, with Shaman able to summon objects from a medicine bag and beseech the spirits to assist Alpha Flight. (Likewise, his daughter, Talisman,[11] has the power to act as a channel for the will of the spirits.) Thus Shaman is a complicated figure of appropriation and representation: it is rare to see an Indigenous character connected to science and medicine, but it is troubling that these two halves of his self cannot coexist.

In addition to this spirituality, Shaman is connected to the land; for example, another power he wields is the ability to run at hyperspeed without disturbing the animals or plants on his path. But that doesn't mean his Indigeneity is recognized as connected to a specific place. Shaman's nation is defined as Tsuu T'ina, but that nation is not tied to a concrete geographic location in the

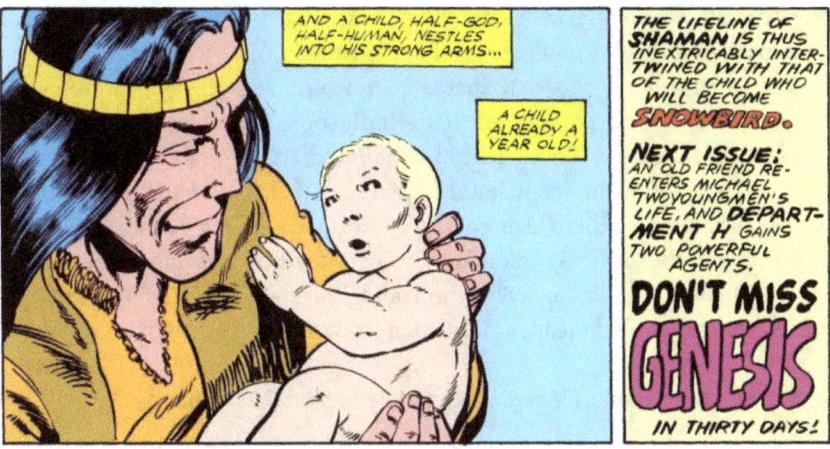

Shaman and Snowbird. From *Alpha Flight* #7 (1984): 23.

comic; it is, instead, somewhat generically rural Canadian. Likewise, Talisman's powers include things like the ability to conjure "spirit animals" or control the weather, so her powers connect to the land but again in generic ways. For each of these Indigenous characters, "land" is a generic concept that generally refers to the territory that is now Canada rather than reflecting a specific nation or community. It is an appropriation of Indigenous communities and their relationship to both territoriality and colonial governance to represent Shaman, Talisman, and Snowbird in these contexts, and we need to be mindful of the fact that although Alpha Flight's diversity is laudable for its historical context, it is part of a larger history of white comics artists depicting Indigenous characters for their own thematic ends; indeed, in all of Alpha Flight's renditions, right up to the current day where Alpha Flight is in a backing role to Captain Marvel's space defense project, these characters have never been written or drawn by an Indigenous creator. In the case of Alpha Flight, this use of appropriation is also about defining Canada in terms that are distinct from the United States. The foregrounding of Indigenous characters suggests a different kind of relationship to the land, nation, and north than is exhibited by, say, the X-Men, the superhero team Alpha Flight is most commonly either fighting with or against. The X-Men maintain a clear independence given that they are not expressly nationalist superheroes and are not even always aligned with the American nation-state, and their territoriality is often ambiguously defined largely because as mutants they are often seen as undesireables in America. Even a superhero team like the Avengers, with their explicit connection to the US government in story lines like Civil War, or a character like Captain America or USAgent, does not use Indigeneity to make some larger claim for nationalism. This appropriative relationship to Indigenous culture as a form of nation-inscribing branding is certainly a strategy used by the Canadian government, seemingly with enough success that it is a recognized way of framing Canadianness on the page of a mainstream American comic book.

It is worth noting, too, that Shaman, Snowbird, and Talisman were by far the most visible and popular explicitly Indigenous characters in the Marvel Universe in the 1980s. While their presentation certainly diversified superhero team offerings of the moment, it did so for thematic utility more than anything else. As part of a superhero team specifically located within a Canadian geopolitics, and with the explicitly colonial framing of their powers and physical bodies, the effect is that Shaman, Snowbird, and Talisman are a significant part of coding the Alpha Flight team as Canadian, and therefore other-than American.

Justice League Canada, I Mean, United: How to Signal Canadianity

This question is particularly salient given the 2014 launch of another Canadian superhero—and another appropriation of Indigenous identity—by Marvel's competitor DC for their *Justice League United* series by Canadian comics creator Jeff Lemire (famous in Canada for his *Essex County* series) with art by British artist Mike McKone. The *JLU* relaunch was originally touted as *Justice League Canada*, but DC backed off from the idea and in the end only gave Lemire the green light to create one new superhero (though he was allowed to retcon—comics lingo for "retroactive continuity"—two others to give them Canadian backstories). In only having the opportunity to develop one new character, Lemire needed to signal the "Canadianness" of this relaunch as effectively as possible, and here we see history repeating itself as once again, we see mainstream American comic representations of Canadian identity coded through the appropriation of Indigenous culture. This time, the character in question is Equinox (birth name: Miiyahbin "Mii" Marten), a Cree teenager who gathers her powers from the Seven Generations.

It's worth noting that Equinox is a literal appropriation of a real woman, the late Shannen Koostachin of Attawapiskat. Koostachin was a teenage activist, leading the Attawapiskat School Campaign to lobby for proper academic spaces for her own and other reserve communities in Canada.[12] Koostachin died in a car accident in 2010, just before her sixteenth birthday, and in 2013 Lemire told the CBC, "I think if I can capture some of that heart and some of that essence in this character, perhaps she'll almost be a guiding spirit in the creation of this character" ("New DC Comics superhero inspired by young Cree activist"). Lemire has since distanced himself from the angle the CBC took on the story and perhaps from his own early comments. In an interview for *Maisonneuve Magazine*, Lemire notes:

> I actually want to clarify that. When I did the first interview for this project months ago, they asked me about Shannen Koostachin and if she was an inspiration and I

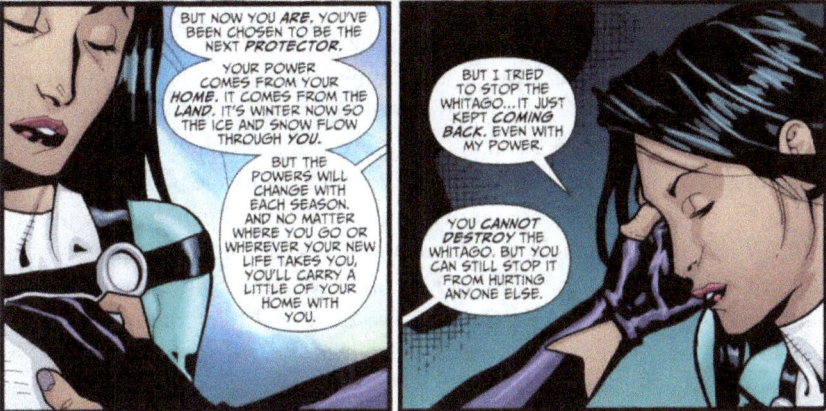

Equinox. From *Justice League United* #5 (2015): 14.

said, "Oh yeah, that's a very inspiring story," and from that it sort of turned into, as the story was re-presented online, as though the character was inspired by Shannen. But she actually isn't, for all the reasons you just said. I would never presume to appropriate a story that is so real and then turn it into a cartoon, especially without her parents', her family's, awareness or approval. That's something I would never do. So when I said she was an inspiration for me in creating a teenage character, definitely, but it's no way based on her or drawn from her story, much for that reason. As much as I take pride in my work I would never belittle or exploit a story just to tell people some pop culture or popcorn story. Her story is much more important than that so I'm glad you brought it up. (Sy)

Lemire's careful language here is important in clarifying the origin of the character, but there is no evidence in any of the original coverage from very reputable sources, from the CBC to the *Hollywood Reporter*, that Lemire ever asked for a correction to this misrepresentation be published. Indeed, as late as 2014, when the book was first released, media stories were still linking Koostachin to Equinox, and in the interviews at that time he does not make an effort to correct the misconception. Whether by intent or by omission, then, at least some of the marketing of this character occurred on the assumption or assertion of a connection to a real Cree girl. When we consider the ways in which Indigenous women's bodies are appropriated, abused, and disappeared by mainstream Canadian society, the use of Koostachin, even if (perhaps especially if) in an accidental way, to sell a comic as Canadian seems both particularly distasteful and particularly apt.

I want to acknowledge here that Lemire's attempt is certainly more delicate and nuanced than Adrian Dingle or John Byrne before him, and Lemire has partnered this project with some work in Northern Ontario Cree communities to encourage Northern children, Indigenous and non-Indigenous, to create comics.[13] But the construction of Equinox still engages in appropriation to make a thematic connection between the land and Indigenous cultures as a means of distinguishing this Justice League from its American counterpart. Equinox, we are told, is a Midayo, meaning that she can use the seven pillars of Cree life to defeat darkness, and her powers are unveiled to her when she first attempts to speak Cree, something she had no idea she had a capacity for. While Equinox is much more carefully connected to Indigenous land and territory than the *Alpha Flight* characters were—her Cree identity and her community in Moose Factory are explicitly and deeply intertwined, and she is not rendered as generically rural Canadian—we are still told somewhat vaguely that her powers come from the earth and change with the seasons, and Lemire has remarked of his setting that using Moose Factory seemed "more Canadian" than a more cosmopolitan city.

Further, the appropriation still involves the use of a superficially defined understanding of Indigenous spirituality: both *Alpha Flight* and the new *Justice League United* team have to fight Wendigo as a primary villain of the Canadian territory. Indigeneity again stands in as a shorthand for Canadianness when a superficially developed distinction between Canada and the United States is needed. Again, this reflects something of a pan-Indigenous mythology at play in both comics: Wendigo is the cannibal monster common to Indigenous nations of Algonquin-speaking lineage, such as Ojibwe or Cree, but in Marvel Comics—where Wendigo has also had to fight the Hulk, and other heroes, even outside of the nation-inscribing Canadian figures that make up the focus of this paper—it is a curse regional to the woods of Northern Canada, again reflecting a use of Indigeneity to reflect a generalized Canadianness; indeed, in Marvel comics Wendigo has appeared in Hope, British Columbia, and Regina, Saskatchewan, as well as in more traditional Algonquin-speaking territories. In the *Justice League United* run, the figure is called Whitago, but he seems to be connected to the same legend; in this case, he has taken over the body of Equinox's father, and in confronting him she accepts her powers and role in the Justice League.

In the end, Equinox was not a sales driver (perhaps because the comics in the *Justice League United* series rarely focused on her to the extent the media coverage primed readers for) and the series lasted only nineteen issues. When *Justice League United* folded in December 2015, so too did Equinox: while she remains a DC character—like all Big-2 creations, she is not owned by Jeff Lemire but instead by DC Comics—she has yet to be revived by another title. It is worth, perhaps, playing the thought game of considering what Equinox could look like as a character if she was not being used thematically to signal nationalism, and instead developed fully and empathetically, perhaps (dare one hope) by an Indigenous comics artist.

When the Nationalism Is Coming from Outside the Country: Brian K. Vaughan's *We Stand on Guard*

We Stand on Guard is a six-issue creator-owned comic written by Brian K. Vaughan and published by Image Comics from July to December of 2015. It sold very well in North America, with sales of 78,000 for the first issue and 35,000 for the last; even at its lowest sales, then, *We Stand on Guard* was in the top 75 of books sold in a month, significant for an independent series in an industry that releases between 300 and 400 individual issues each month through the central distributor, Diamond Comics Distributors. The premise of the comics is an old chestnut of Canada-US relations: 200 years in the future, Canada has been invaded by the US (spoiler alert: they want our water, and they're probably going to win) and scrappy Canadian freedom fighters are fighting to take it back. Conveniently, this is the aftermath of a war that began in 2112, making all the predictable and easy War of 1812 references ripe for the picking in this context. Vaughan's position as an American comics creator without even John Byrne's accidental citizenship (though artist Steve Skroce is Canadian) offers an interesting final example for this conversation about the exploitation of Indigeneity as inherently Canadian. In many ways, *We Stand on Guard* is a nationalist comic, for all the reasons *Alpha Flight* never was. Vaughan's comic setting is not postcolonial or post-settler, but instead shifts Canada's colonial position from the Commonwealth—as both colonizer and colonized—to the concerns of American colonialism and power and the erasure of Canada.

Of our protagonists, it is the Indigenous characters whose identities are most explicitly connected to rebellion in Canada. Like other American-published comics situated in Canada, Indigeneity is used as markers for authentic Canadianness, made more explicit in this case by the lack of Indigenous characters on the American side of the battle: as cities are obliterated, the landscape and land become the defining characteristics of nationhood in a fight that is ultimately over the most essential natural resource, water. Two characters in the series are coded Indigenous. One, known only as Mr. Pittialuk, is an Inuit man and greenhouse farmer in Nunavut who gets arrested by the Americans for allegedly sabotaging the water supply. The other, Highway, is one of the group of freedom fighters known as the Two-Four, the Canadian slang term for a case of beer; his Cree identity is discussed in relation to who will lead the next stage of the revolt. The discussion here is about who is more essentially Canadian: the Indigenous man or the grandchild of Syrian refugees. Both Indigenous characters are portrayed in opposition to the United States and essentially connected to the Canadian landscape. There is no mention of Indigenous people south of the border and what their relationship might be to this invasion or the crisis of water shortage; indeed, Indigeneity, like immigration, somehow becomes

Highway. From *We Stand on Guard* #4 (2015): 8.

a uniquely Canadian experience within the frame of *We Stand on Guard* and is used as an unproblematically embraced component of the Canadian identity. The Americans in the narrative cannot make sense of any Indigeneity they come into contact with. For example, the American leader can't keep the "fucked up names" of the places in the Northwest Territories straight and doesn't understand the derivation of Great Slave Lake, thinking Canadians have named themselves after their subservient cultural positioning. (It's worth noting that despite the commitment to a diverse cast of characters, the central figure and primary hero of the story is a white woman, and the final image of the series—depicting a moment of calm before the events of the war destroy the Canadian experience—is of that protagonist's white, nuclear family.) The messaging is that, on these issues, Canada is *good* in contrast to America's *evil*, thus eliding any significant problems with Canada's history and identity.

Vaughan's Canada is idealized through its reliance on largely stereotyped constructions of Canadianness. Because the team faces a more immediate colonizing force to contend with in the shape of a full-powered American invasion, all memory of or reference to Canada's colonial past vis-à-vis the Indigenous characters is effectively erased, as is any racist or homophobic history. This allows for the Canadians to be the unambiguous good guys, but it empties the Canadian community in the text of context and history; as such, it is reminiscent of 1990s "Beer Ad" nationalism typified by the Molson Canadian "I Am Canadian" ads of the late 1990s and early 2000s. Of course, the most famous of these ad spots was "The Rant," a beer ad so ubiquitous and so beloved it was played at antiseparation rallies in Quebec, performed live on Parliament Hill as part of that year's Canada Day concert, and found its way into the Penguin Treasury of Popular Poems and Songs. "The Rant" makes a lot of comforting assertions about Canada, all constructed in opposition to the United States: we're nicer, we're bilingual, we're world-respected, we're peacekeepers, we're multicultural. There is no space for critique of this definition of Canadianness in "The Rant" and, by positioning each assertion against an American other, the ad spot explicitly defines Canada as better than America. *We Stand on Guard* does the same thing, making it comfortable reading for settler Canadians, but again the Indigenous characters are used for thematic ends, standing in to define an easily anti-American Canada that feels neither authentic nor meaningful.

Systemic Issues: #OwnVoices,[14] Comics, and Representation

As I have suggested throughout, one of the most significant concerns I have with the ongoing appropriation of Indigenous identity in these mainstream Marvel/DC comics is the fact that Indigenous comics artists are rarely employed by the Big-2. In a thoughtful essay on this topic for *Comics Alliance*, critic James Leask writes about the experience of growing up Indigenous without very many well-constructed representations of Indigenous life in his comic books. Leask writes about the importance of Indigenous people telling their own stories and constructing their own representation, noting:

> If aboriginal people were more involved, a few things might change. Someone might let Marvel know that, given that Snowbird is an Inuit demigoddess, having her guardian be Shaman, a Tsuu T'ina man from a Nation a thousand miles away from the Inuit, is kind of problematic. (Leask)

Of all the examples Leask runs through in his piece, I was most grateful to this one for reflecting back at me my own settler-scholar ignorance; even in thinking through how connection to the land for Indigenous characters in *Alpha Flight* is rendered through a generically "Canadian" representation, I missed this idea of the kinship of Snowbird and Shaman that is completely divorced from their respective nations and geography. Instead, Snowbird is mentored by Shaman because they are both Indigenous, which suggests the larger issue of pan-Indigeneity in comics I referenced earlier. Leask's article gives an excellent overview of the paucity of Indigenous creators in mainstream comics, and he reflects on the tension of wanting to see accurate representation without asserting that Indigenous creators—or indeed Indigenous characters—can or should only be one thing.[15]

This paucity is why the thematic and nation-inscribing use of Indigenous characters, especially by settler-creators, is so problematic. In this moment of a national conversation in Canada about reconciliation, both in the wake of the Truth and Reconciliation Commission and the focus on decolonization that followed Canada's 150th birthday celebrations, would we expect a #OwnVoices Indigenous Marvel or DC Comics hero to unproblematically stand in for the colonial nation-state, to be used as metaphorical fodder for a distinction between Canada and the United States that many Indigenous nations themselves do not recognize? The use of Indigenous characters as symbols is galling precisely because there are not enough other options to counter this representation.

There are excellent comics being created by Indigenous artists and writers outside of the confines of Big-2 publishing. The recently Kickstarted *Moonshot: The Indigenous Comics Collection* now has two successful volumes showcasing the work of Indigenous creators, making it easier for readers to find and support their work. And significant contributions to the field by Michael Nicoll Yahgulanaas, David Alexander Robertson, Katherena Vermette, Scott B. Henderson, Patti LaBoucane-Benson, with more developing every day, demonstrate the breadth of possibility for Indigenous storytelling in the comics medium. And there are good reasons for Indigenous creators not to choose to work at Marvel and DC Comics: Big-2 comics publishing means giving up control of your characters, potentially perpetuating the kinds of representation issues discussed in this paper. But creator-owned comics distribution comes with its own pitfalls, including cost (a single issue of Katherena Vermette and Scott B. Henderson's *A Girl Called Echo* series costs $13.95 in Canada, compared with a typical Big-2 floppy priced closer to $4.95) and accessibility (because those comics are less likely to be found in mainstream comic shops and more likely to need to be purchased at bookstores or online, following a different discoverability path than mainstream comics). It would be nice to see the robust creator-owned world of Indigenous comics supported by a more successfully diverse and inclusive Big-2 ecosystem.

It's worth noting that Alpha Flight's later incarnations have made more explicit attempts to deal with Canada's actual problems, like the 2012 run that sees Alpha Flight fighting a Conservative government and the threat of climate change. But the appropriation of Indigenous identities and practices in each of these contexts is primarily about selling a version of Canadian identity to non-Canadians, and to attempt to remarket historically oppressed and restricted practices as somehow inherently Canadian. This is a convenient mythology that inherently restricts the rights of Indigenous people to represent themselves and their own history, and again further imposes a colonial boundary around and against Indigenous populations. The Big-2 remains a space absent of Indigenous #OwnVoices creators, and creator-owned Indigenous comics represent a tiny percentage of the comics sold annually. It is no secret that mainstream comics have a diversity problem, but when combined with the practice of using appropriative imagery to define Canadianness for international audiences, free of Canada's historical colonial context, the problem of representation is compounded. "We the North" is a comforting way of defining the dominant

Canadian culture as different from the US, but it also appropriates and elides Indigenous Northern communities to serve a national mythology in denial of its deeply colonial roots.

Notes

1. This chapter uses "America" as a short-hand for the United States of America, as is typical of discourse in Canada where the US functions often as a discursive foil. It is rare to hear Canadian citizens refer to themselves as American, in reference to their continental citizenship, and much of the scholarly criticism and fan discussion on the comics referenced in this paper (as well as, indeed, the content of the comics themselves) follow the popular convention of delineating "Canada" and "America" as the two states sharing the northern two-thirds of North America. I make use of this convention within this chapter without supposing to argue for its correctness in other areas of border and/or hemispheric studies.

2. It is important to acknowledge that there are Indigenous characters in the Marvel universe who are not Canadian or intended to signal Canadianness. This chapter does not examine that history, instead focusing on the ways in which Indigeneity is frequently used—problematically, given Canada's colonial context—in mainstream comics (and, indeed, culture writ large) to signal Canadianness.

3. John Bell is a historian and archivist with Library and Archives Canada. He deserves much credit for uncovering and archiving Canada's comic book history, and particularly his sustained interest in superhero comics. That said, as someone deeply invested in narrating the national story of comics, his assessments regarding comic quality are often undeservedly generous and should always be read critically; further, he has a tendency to ascribe his own nationalist aims to all Canadian-affiliated comics artists.

4. Byrne posted these comments in a forum he runs on his website for fans to talk to him about his art and also about cultural/political issues. This post was made in a thread Byrne started about birthright citizenship, a concept he argues against at some length vis-à-vis a fear of "anchor babies." Political cringe aside, Byrne's comments here make clear that he sees nationality as a conscious, active choice. Making a play for him as someone enacting Canadian nationalism on the page, then, seems particularly unfounded.

5. For a productive discussion of how queerness functions in Dean and Dan Caten's work, see Jennifer Andrews's discussion of the coverage of DSquared² in Canadian fashion media, "Queer(y)Ing Fur: Reading Fashion Television's Border Crossings."

6. At the time, the Catens did not respond to the controversy. A year later, when DSquared² was chosen to design the Olympic team uniforms, public outrage intensified at this national validation of the brand; in a move that looked a lot more like image management than contrition, the Catens did issue a formal apology and scrubbed all reference to the DSquaw collection from their website. But even in their apology they assert that all of their work—even DSquaw—is intended to proudly wave the Canadian flag ("We Are Truly Sorry").

7. There is complexity to the Oopik story. The federal government trademarked the Oopik on behalf of the Fort Chimo craft collective where it originated, and its brief popularity in the 1960s provided a steady income stream for those artists at the time. But it was also deeply commodified and typically sold to support a notion of the primitiveness of the Inuit and the consequent benefits of colonization to them (Colombo).

8. Interestingly, Pierre Trudeau's son, current PM Justin Trudeau, would himself be featured in a Marvel Comic in 2016, again shown in control of Alpha Flight. See *Civil War: Choosing Sides* #5.

9. See, for example, Ian Mosby's work on the nutrition experimentation done on Indigenous children in Canadian residential schools.

10. In the story, the mother and her son are not permitted to cross the Canada-US border because the mother refuses to declare herself as either Canadian or American. When asked for her nationality or citizenship, she asserts repeatedly, "Blackfoot." In King's story, the border guards eventually relent and let her through, but it's probably worth noting that the story was written pre-9/11.

11. Talisman is Shaman's daughter—her birth name is Elizabeth Twoyoungmen—but he abandoned her in his grief after the death of his wife, leaving her to be raised by a white family who eventually help her to reconnect with her father and discover her own role as a superhero. In my reading, this raises echoes of the official narrative of the 60s Scoop: that Indigenous children were raised by white foster families because their birth families could not care for them. Of course, we now recognize the 60s Scoop as part of a larger project of assimilation and cultural genocide, reframing white families from benevolent caregivers to, at best, unwitting pawns complicit in colonialism. The echoes of that history—uncritically, given the time of publication—are clear here.

12. The campaign built allyship between Indigenous and non-Indigenous youth by encouraging children across the country to write to the government demanded better academic resources on reserves. The school in Attawapiskat had been closed because of a diesel spill that contaminated the earth, and in her short life Koostachin never attended a proper school. You can read more about and contribute to Koostachin's legacy here: https://fncaringsociety.com/shannens-dream.

13. I do think Lemire generally means well. This is, however, not his only project of appropriation. Jeff Lemire was the comics artist on Gord Downie's *Secret Path*, a project that effectively involved a group of white men getting together to tell the storie of Chanie Wenjack, a boy who died in 1966 while trying to escape from his residential school. *Secret Path* has been praised by some and condemned by others, and it's important to acknowledge that the project has the support of Wenjack's family and the Assembly of First Nations. But it's also worth remembering that Lemire took the job of telling Wenjack's story through his white gaze even as he knows he works in an industry with a paucity of Indigenous artists and storytellers being employed on these kinds of large-scale mainstream popular publications. The general project of reconciliation requires that settlers—especially ones like Lemire with well-established careers—step aside, on occasion, and amplify Indigenous voices instead.

14. #OwnVoices is an online movement, primarily on Twitter, that seeks to encourage, celebrate, and amplify stories about marginalized communities written from within that community. It was launched by Corinne Duyvis in September of 2015, and she defines it as a text wherein "the protagonist and the author share a marginalized identity." More here: http://www.corinneduyvis.net/ownvoices/.

15. In an interesting turn in the comments section, Nathan Fairbairn (a mainstream comics creator who has worked with DC Comics and once penned a special story about Indigenous heroes Raven Red and Man-of-Bats) popped in to thank Leask for referencing one of his story lines and letting Leask and his readers know that he considers himself métis, his grandmother having been "a full-blooded Mi'kmaq" and himself having "lived on a reservation for a short while." He is careful not to use this revelation as a shield for discussions of the limitations in his own Indigenous-centered story lines, noting that he doesn't expect people to know a heritage he rarely discloses. Indeed, the purpose of his post seems primarily to be to alert Leask to the existence of Indigenous-identifying creators in mainstream comics. It would be interesting and productive to amass a complete list of Indigenous-identifying creators who had worked on Indigenous-centered Marvel or DC Comics titles. By both my and Leask's reckoning, Fairbairn is the only one.

Works Cited

Andrews, Jennifer. "Queer(y)Ing Fur: Reading Fashion Television's Border Crossings." *Parallel Encounters: Culture at the Canada-US Border*, edited by Gillian Roberts and David Stirrup, 27–46. Waterloo, ON: Wilfrid Laurier University Press, 2013.
Beaty, Bart. "The Fighting Civil Servant: Making Sense of the Canadian Superhero." *American Review of Canadian Studies* 36, no. 3 (September 2006): 427–39.
Byrne, John. *Alpha Flight #1–7*. New York: Marvel Comics, 1983–1984.
Byrne, John. "Birthright Citizenship." *Byrne Robotics*, August 19, 2015. http://www.byrnerobotics.com/forum/forum_posts.asp?TID=49180&PN=1&totPosts=45.
"Canadian Fashion Label Dsquared² under Fire for #Dsquaw Collection." *CBC News*, March 4, 2015, http://www.cbc.ca/news/Indigenous/dsquared2-under-fire-for-dsquaw-women-s-fashion-collection-1.2980136.
Colombo, John Robert. "Ookpik." *The Canadian Encyclopedia*. Toronto: Historica Canada, 2006. Web. February 8, 2006.
Comely, Richard. *Captain Canuck #1* (1974). Reprint. Toronto: Chapterhouse Archive, 2016.
Coupland, Douglas. *Souvenir of Canada*. Vancouver: Douglas & McIntyre, 2002.
Dittmer, Jason, and Soren Larsen. "Aboriginality and the Arctic North in Canadian Nationalist Superhero Comics, 1940–2004." *Historical Geography* 38 (2010): 52–69.
Edwardson, Ryan. "The Many Lives of Captain Canuck: Nationalism, Culture, and the Creation of a Canadian Comic Book Superhero." *Journal of Popular Culture* 37, no. 2 (Fall 2003): 184–201.
"Every G20 Nation Wants to Be Canada, Insists PM." *Reuters*, September 26, 2009. www.reuters.com, https://www.reuters.com/article/columns-us-g20-canada-advantages/every-g20-nation-wants-to-be-canada-insists-pm-idUSTRE58P05Z20090926. Accessed June 12, 2018.
Fontaine, Tim. "What Did Justin Trudeau Say about Canada's History of Colonialism?" *CBC News*, April 22, 2016. http://www.cbc.ca/news/Indigenous/trudeau-colonialism-comments-1.3549405. Accessed June 12, 2018.
Grace, Sherrill E. *Canada and the Idea of North*. Montreal: McGill-Queen's University Press, 2002.
Hirsh, Michael, and Patrick Loubert. *The Great Canadian Comic Books*. Toronto: Peter Martin Associates, 1971.
King, Thomas. "Borders." *One Good Story, That One*. Toronto: HarperCollins, 1993.
Leask, James. "Indigenous Representation in Superhero Comics." *ComicsAlliance*, March 31, 2015. http://comicsalliance.com/Indigenous-representation-superhero-comics/.
Lemire, Jeff, and Mike McKone. *Justice League United: Volume 1: Justice League Canada*. New York: DC Comics, 2015.
Mosby, Ian. "Administering Colonial Science: Nutrition Research and Human Biomedical Experimentation in Aboriginal Communities and Residential Schools, 1942–1952." *Social History* 46 (2013): 145–72.
"New DC Comics Superhero Inspired by Young Cree Activist." *CBC News*, October 30, 2013. http://www.cbc.ca/news/canada/sudbury/new-dc-comics-superhero-inspired-by-young-cree-activist-1.2288680.
"ReMatriate Wants to Take Back 'Visual Identity' of First Nations." *CBC News*, April 12, 2015. http://www.cbc.ca/news/canada/north/rematriate-wants-to-take-back-visual-identity-of-first-nations-1.3029833.
Smith, Will. "Cree, Canadian and American: Negotiating Sovereignties with Jeff Lemire's Equinox and 'Justice League Canada.'" *The Luminary*, no. 6: Visualizing Fantastika, 2015. https://www.lancaster.ac.uk/luminary/issue6/issue6article2.htm.

Sy, Waaseyaa'sin Christine. "An Interview with Jeff Lemire." *Maisonneuve: A Quarterly of Arts, Opinion & Ideas*, May 12, 2014. http://maisonneuve.org/article/2014/05/12/interview-jeff-lemire/.

Vaughan, Brian K., and Steve Skroce. *We Stand on Guard*. New York: Image Comics, 2017.

"'We Are Truly Sorry': Dsquared2 Apologizes for Dsquaw Collection." *CBC News*, February 26, 2016. http://www.cbc.ca/news/canada/north/dsquared2-dsquaw-apology-letter-1.3466472.

Jack Jackson, Native Representation, and Underground Comix

Chad A. Barbour

From November 1969 to June 1971, the Indians of All Tribes occupied Alcatraz Island. Less than two years later, from February 27, 1973, to May 8, 1973, the American Indian Movement led an occupation of Wounded Knee, engaging in a stand-off with the US government. While not the first or only examples of Native activism in the United States, these events are commonly remembered as hallmarks of the Native civil rights movement. Paul Chaat Smith and Robert Allen Warrior designate this span of years as "the most remarkable period of activism carried out by Indians in the twentieth century" (269). These actions, among many others, conveyed a clear call for recognition of the sovereignty and agency of Native peoples.[1]

In late 1970, while the Alcatraz action was occurring, Dennis O'Neil's *Green Lantern / Green Arrow* features a story line in which the two heroes aid a Native tribe in Washington state in protecting their land claims from a lumber company ("Ulysses Star is Alive," #79: September 1970). This comic evinced an awareness of its contemporary social and political issues.[2] O'Neil's engagement with such issues was an outlier in mainstream comics, though. While popular comics of the 1960s and 1970s demonstrated relatively little engagement with the political and social issues of their day, underground comix fully embraced politics and oftentimes radicalism in their pages.[3]

The willingness and freedom to engage with serious political commentary and activism, sometimes in earnest but many times through satire and humor, is a hallmark of underground comix. This freedom arises in one aspect from rejection of the Comics Code and thus freedom from institutional censorship and restrictions on free speech. As well, underground comix were relatively free from an economic system driven by corporate profit-making and shareholders' interests. Along with these factors, underground comix thrived in a cultural and social environment that encouraged experimentation and rejection of established norms and decorum. Thus, comix creators were able to confront and portray US history and culture in a manner that sought to challenge and correct the rosy, idealized image continually endorsed by official representations of the nation in expressions such as history textbooks and political officials' speeches, expressions largely driven by a white, male perspective. Underground comix present a complicated and sometimes problematic expression of political activism and social engagement. Although commonly associated with a progressive countercultural movement that advanced advocacy for civil rights and gender equality, underground comix were also the home for art that could be perceived as or actually was racist and misogynistic.

In the late seventies, Jack Jackson (originally publishing under the name Jaxon), one of the artists associated with the beginnings of underground comix, produced work that represents an intersection between the strand of political critique in comix and the groundswell of Native activism of the early seventies. While Jackson had previously been best known for the satirical *God Nose*, in the wake of the events at Alcatraz and Wounded Knee, he produced two significant works grappling with Native history in the United States. This chapter will examine Jackson's depiction of Native American subjects in his history comics. Two texts that will receive particular focus are "Nits Make Lice" (original appearance: *Slow Death* #7, Winter 1976–1977), which details the Sand Creek Massacre, and *Comanche Moon* (1979; original appearance: a trilogy of comic books, 1977–1978), which depicts the life of Cynthia Ann Parker, a white captive, and her son, Quanah, whom Jackson designates as "the last chief of the Comanches." Jackson's historical accounts demonstrate a departure from the typical representation of Native peoples found in comics, and in popular culture as a whole, while interrogating the parameters of historical recollection and nationalistic mythology in the United States. Joseph Witek frames the dynamic I am examining here succinctly when he argues, "Comic books have long been one of the places where America shows itself what it looks like, and Jackson's historical comics thus comprise in their very narrative form an intervention in the process of cultural mythmaking" (61).[4] This chapter aims to examine how Jackson's work intervenes, successfully and not, in the mythmaking that arises from the interlocution of Native representations and a recounting of US history that celebrates national expansion as noble, righteous, and heroic.

Native Representation in Comic Books

Representations and depictions of Native peoples in US popular culture constitute a complicated and expansive history that exceeds the space available here, so a thumbnail sketch will have to suffice. While one might trace this history as far back as European descriptions of Indigenous peoples primarily beginning with Columbus, of most immediate relevance to this study are the depictions found in US popular culture of the twentieth century. Film, television, and comics count as probably the most pervasive media in the United States circulating images and stereotypes of Native peoples during the twentieth century and after. A number of scholars have examined this area and a dominant theme in these analyses is that Native peoples exist in the white American imagination as either romanticized or exoticized figures of heroism and strength or as demonic or bestial wraths of bloodlust and violence (and sometimes a combination of these extremes).[5] Whatever the nature of the depiction, Indians in popular culture are rarely presented as autonomous human beings with legitimate and authentic desires, motivations, and existences independent of and apart from white desires. Popular culture Indians largely exist as reflections of white self-imaging and aspirations, mere tools of white fictions regarding national identity, racial hierarchy, and political mythology.

US comics are a prime locus of such representations, especially during the midcentury period when the Western genre was at its height of popularity in the United States.[6] The depictions in comics ran the gamut from admirable to savage to cartoonish caricature. The comic form possesses a potency of representation: the visual depictions or caricatures embodying complexes of symbolism and associations. For instance, the opening panel of "Red Fawn" (from *Indians* #1) depicts an idyllic and pastoral scene: Indian men, women, and children at home in their village, performing the mundane and quotidian tasks of their daily life (fig. 2.1). In contrast to the other two examples, the skin color of these Indians is a lighter color, perhaps a shade darker than what might be conventionally viewed as "white," thus not conveying a noticeable racialized difference between Indians and whites. This depiction conveys admiration and respect for the Native subjects, although it freezes them in the past.

The cover of *Fighting Indians of the West* #1, however, depicts the Indians as significantly darker than the white characters in the scene (fig. 2.2). This contrast is most visible between the Indian marauders carrying the unconscious blonde, white woman whose skin nearly glows in its whiteness.[7] This cover further contrasts the "Red Fawn" representation in casting these Indians as savages attacking whites, as enemies of white expansion and of white domesticity. The white woman as victim is a particularly powerful propagandistic device that emphasizes these Indians' savagery.

Big Chief Wahoo #7 engages in cartoonish caricature that exaggerates racial signifiers of difference (the nose, the skin color) of the male Indian while presenting the female Indian in a more standard depiction of female beauty (fig. 2.3). The racial distance between the presumably male audience and the male is widened while the distance between the presumably male audience and the

Figure 2.1. Opening panel of "Red Fawn." *Indians: Picture Stories of the First Americans* #1 (1950). Fiction House Magazines.

female is collapsed. Although Big Chief Wahoo is presented as a harmless buffoon, this depiction engages in racist caricature, a reduction of a people to a trope. Interestingly, too, is the possible influence this character had in the creation of the Cleveland Indians mascot. Brad Ricca notes the possible connection between the comic strip and the mascot. Whatever that connection might be, the fact remains that this third example demonstrates that cartoonish strand of popular representations of Native peoples.

These three examples provide, then, a glimpse of Native representation in comics, a representation that reflects and shapes the perceptions and depictions found in US culture as a whole in the twentieth century. While these particular examples are not in themselves inherently significant, they are indicative of the styles and tropes widely circulated in comics and in popular culture of the United States. With these representations in mind, one can appreciate how Jackson departs from them, working to represent Native peoples in a way that attempts to convey perceived notions of authenticity and sympathy, while recognizing how these representations still resonate in his work.

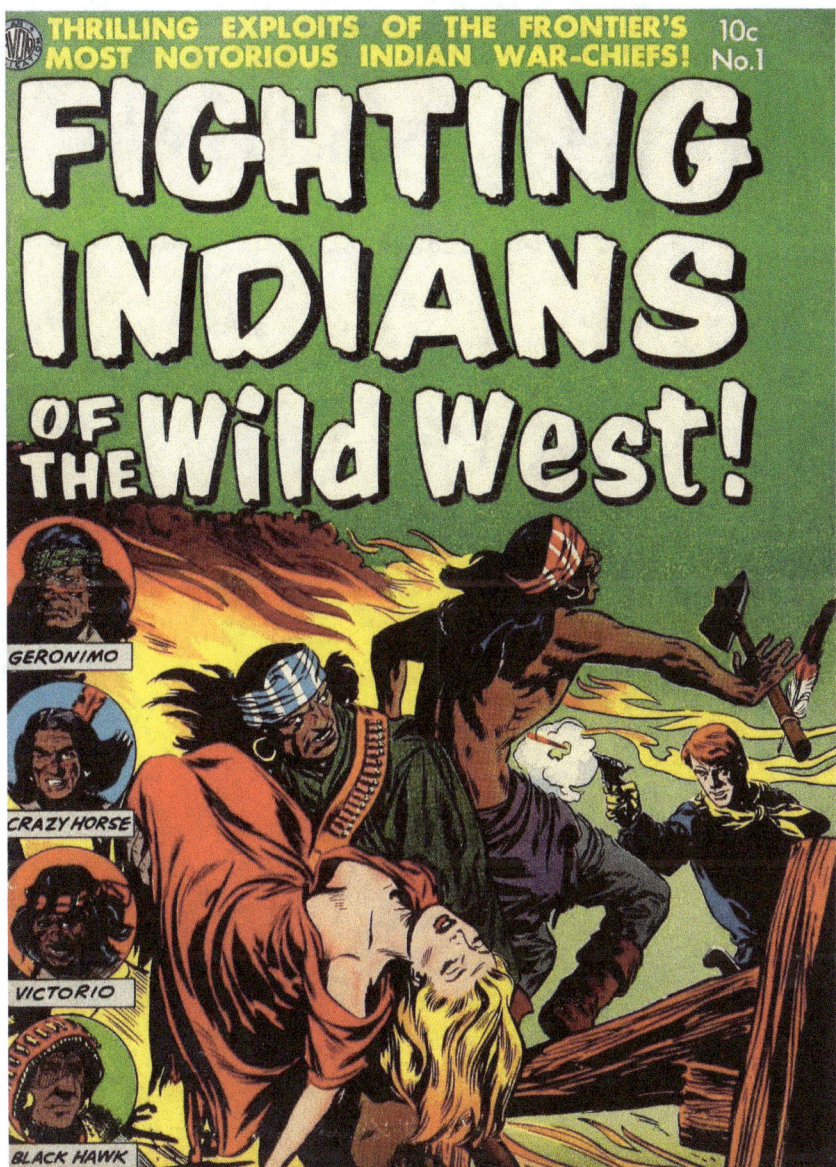

Figure 2.2. Cover of *Fighting Indians of the Wild West* #1 (March 1952). Avon Periodicals.

Jackson: Underground Comix and Native History

In "Nits Make Lice" and *Comanche Moon*, Jackson endeavors to present Native history accurately. While these stories largely avoid the typical tropes and stereotypes of popular culture representations of Native peoples, they are not perfect in their depictions. Nonetheless, Jackson has made a good faith effort to present his Native subjects as real individuals with human complexity.

Figure 2.3. Cover of *Big Chief Wahoo* #7 (Winter 1943). Famous Funnies.

If one aspect of the underground comix mission was to be completely honest and to confront the reader with unsparing realism, then Jackson follows that mission fully in "Nits Make Lice." This story carries an element of shock value and it may be debatable to what extent this desire to shock, even offend, perhaps defies expectations of historical objectivity. Yet, the event that Jackson depicts is offensive in itself and so if a true portrayal offends, then that is the nature of the subject matter and not of the author's intent. Historical objectivity becomes interrogated, as well, as an ideal that might muddle rather than clarify a complete understanding and assessment of US history. If Jackson is allowing his own anger to influence and drive this portrayal, then that potentially proves more effective in conveying the true horror of the event, a horror that might be mitigated by the desire to appear neutral in recounting the incident. As well, Jackson could also be seen to be turning the tables of what had been typical historical treatments of white-Native conflicts in which the Indians are treated as animals and savages against the noble humanity of the whites. In "Nits Make Lice," Jackson reverses this paradigm, showing the whites as bloodthirsty savages attacking a peaceful Cheyenne village.

"Nits Make Lice" recounts the Sand Creek massacre that occurred on November 29, 1864. Colonel John Chivington led seven hundred men in an attack on a Cheyenne village led by Black Kettle. In this unprovoked attack, men acting under the order of the US colonel killed one hundred five women and children and twenty-eight men. Jackson's choice of this historical moment provides a compelling example with which to interrogate and complicate perceptions of the nobility of US history and progress. Jackson's story indicts the expansion of the United States as a colonialist project, especially with centering the story upon the metaphor, "Nits make lice." Richard Drinnon traces the usage of this statement in the US context through various instances in nineteenth-century westward expansion (502). Katie Kane connects the phrase's usage further back to seventeenth-century English violence against the Irish, demonstrating how these words dehumanize their subjects, portraying them as parasites and an infestation of the colonizer (90).[8] Kane argues that the phrase "is at the center of the histories of colonial violence" and is a "figure of speech [that] turns up to justify military depredation and settlement" (86). Jackson's title places this colonizing rhetoric front and center and his story is unrelenting in conveying the horror of colonial violence.

In fact, what Jackson presents in the pages of "Nits Make Lice" is a horror story, an implication made more evident by the inclusion of a Crypt-Keeper style narrator in *God's Bosom* to introduce the two stories on westward US expansion which pairs "Nits Make Lice" with "The Colt Revolver and the Texas Rangers" (fig. 2.4). Witek notes the debt of "Nits Make Lice" to the EC horror comics, also citing Jackson's stated influence of these comics upon him (70).[9] The reference to the Crypt-Keeper invokes the horror comics of EC and thus

Figure 2.4. EC-style skeleton narrator: Jack Jackson, *God's Bosom and Other Stories*. Fantagraphics Books, 1995.

frames Jackson's accounts of western expansion as horror stories themselves. Jackson refers to the cultural memory of the EC comics, especially in their perceived transgression of social norms and moral code. The implied commentary here is that the true horror existed in actual American history rather than in the perceived menace of a comic book's fictional stories. The EC horror comics provide a visual vocabulary for Jackson in his deploying a skeletal narrator to introduce the two stories of US expansion.

Jackson presents an Indianized version of the Crypt-Keeper who sits in what appears to be a cave on a throne (84). Items and detritus associated with conquest surround him: gold, a cannon, a crucifix, the Texas flag, conquistador helmet, armor, swords, guns, a brand, a cowboy hat with an arrow through it, and so on. These items represent various facets of the European invasion of North America, especially the area that would become Texas. Spanish and Anglo-American objects litter the floor: the imposition of Christianity, cattle brands, and gold indicate an imperialism often dressed in religion but actually driven by material gain, whether it be land or money. The narrator's dress possesses potent connotations, as well. The outfit is meant to be read as "Indian." Most strikingly, perhaps, is the presence of a swastika on the left shoulder. While the swastika design is present in cultures around the world, including North American Indigenous cultures, long predating Nazi usage, the swastika's association with fascism, hatred, and genocide is the prevalent meaning here. The skeletal narrator declares: "Yikes! Things were brutal in the American West before the guys in white hats arrived! Indians, Spaniards—hacking away at one another. Let's revisit the place after folks became . . . uh, more sophisticated and turned genocide into a fine art!! He he" (84). The irony is quite evident here: as the succeeding stories demonstrate, "the guys in white hats" (the supposedly good and heroic white Americans) are as brutal, if not more so, than those figures that Jackson has depicted in the preceding stories. The presence of the swastika design references the perversion of the symbol by Nazi usage: an icon of hate and genocide that reverberates through the succeeding stories.

This point on the violent brutality of the white Americans, the depiction of their savagery, is highlighted in "Nits Make Lice." Jackson depicts Chivington's political ambitions as the impetus for his decision to attack the village. Chivington aims to improve his political standing and, in his words, "there's no way to do that like killing Indians" (93).[10] The point that Jackson expresses here reflects a larger trend in US history, especially in the nineteenth century. Numerous examples of white men running political campaigns based on their prowess in fighting Indians abound at this time, including figures such as William Henry Harrison and Andrew Jackson.[11]

Chivington's naked political ambition is abetted by the type of men being recruited to join the attacking force. Jackson presents a one-page prologue to the story that shows a recruiter for Chivington rounding up two hungover men in a bar (92). The recruiter greets them with the invitation: "Say, how'd you boys like to kill a few Indians?" He then initially appeals to the men's sense of justice with claims about white women and children being killed by Indians (although Black Kettle's band was not involved). This supposedly noble appeal quickly turns to one more gruesome and lascivious with offers of money, horses, and Cheyenne women. In the prologue, Jackson immediately frames the attack as one ostensibly motivated by a sense of justice but at its heart is driven by greed and violent desire. If these two men are representative of the volunteers who joined Chivington's troops, then they represent the worst of the worst: drunkards drawn into the mission by the likelihood of being able to rape Cheyenne women.

The one-page prologue consists of six panels of the same size. Jackson adheres to the typical look of a comic book but depicts content that is clearly not "comic book" material. The first panel presents a close-up of two men sitting at a bar, resting on their elbows, their grimaces expressing their hungover state. Panel two shifts the perspective to the side of the men (they are in the bottom left corner now) and to their right stands a man in US military uniform, a second soldier behind him. In the third panel, the composition echoes that of the first panel except the recruiter is between the two men, stoking their hatred with stories of Indian attacks on women and children. Panel four shifts focus to the recruiter, his face and upper chest fill the right side of the panel while the top of a flyer calling for "Indian fighters" fills the bottom left quarter. Above that, the recruiter's word balloon explains details of the assignment. This panel echoes the one above it with the recruiter on the right side except the flyer replaces the two drunks. The fifth panel reverses the point of view of the previous four panels: the view is now from behind the men, the angle from which the recruiter initially approached them. He has placed his hand on the shoulder of one of the drunks; the recruiter has convinced these men to join the volunteer unit.

This panel's deviation from the previous one's perspective emphasizes this moment along with the recruiter's vulgar offer of loot and women ("Cheyenne wimmen jest loves white stuff"). The final panel returns the perspective to the front of the men illustrating their camaraderie as the recruiter buys drinks for the men. These panels convey the idiom in which these men comprehend what they perceive to be their right and privilege: to kill Indians, to rape and pillage with impunity. In his artistic choices, Jackson fully displays the degradation and evil of these men in this prologue and thus his viewpoint is clearly not beholden to some ideal of neutral objectivity in depicting history.

While Jackson provides the basic facts of the incident's historical context, his depiction is not a neutral, objective attempt to convey historical events. The massacre itself occurs over the course of five pages (out of eight pages for the entire story). Two pages in particular require further scrutiny for Jackson's choice to depict the massacre in unrelenting, graphic detail. The narration for this sequence is as follows:

> Then the carnage begins . . . and lasts . . . without sympathy for the maimed . . . or the mutilated. Without mercy for the dead . . . much less the living . . . until they have

Figure 2.5. Recruiting drunks in "Nits Make Lice": Jack Jackson, *Slow Death* #7 (Winter 1976–77). Last Gasp Funnies.

served their cruel purpose . . . and rendered up grisly mementos to the valor of the Third Colorado Volunteers. Some soldiers, like Capt. Soule, powerless to stop the butchery, wander about in a daze . . . unable to believe the inhumanity that assaults their senses. Sad day this, warriors of the Cheyenne, for you to be away, hunting the buffalo . . . as the scalping knives reap their grim harvest among your elders, your women, your children. . . . (97–99)

Jackson levels condemning prose at the soldiers that becomes elegiac by the end of the passage, commiserating with the absent Cheyenne men who were not present to defend their home and families. The language of this passage emphasizes the violence inflicted upon the Cheyenne, although in a general way: "the maimed," "the mutilated," and "grisly mementos" frame the Cheyenne as victims of a savage rampage, yet do not convey the specificity of the violence; the narration's abstraction contrasts with the concrete specificity of the dialogue and the images.

The diegetic elements of the comic (dialogue and visuals) are unflinching in their depiction of the massacre, presenting the violence in uncensored detail (fig. 2.6). Not only does Jackson show the violence, he focuses particularly on the sexualized violence. In one panel ("without mercy for the dead") the bottom half presents a close-up of a soldier preparing to castrate a male victim; the soldier announcing to his companions, "Boys, I'm agonna' make me a tobacco pouch outta old White Antelope's go-nads!" (98). The horrid vulgarity of the dialogue juxtaposes sharply with the abstract platitude of the narration. The dialogue and image present actuality while the narration presents historical detachment. This dynamic continues throughout the comic. The next two panels depict the gang rape and murder of a woman; also depicted in close-up and

Figure 2.6. Scenes from the massacre in "Nits Make Lice": Jack Jackson, *Slow Death* #7 (Winter 1976–77). Last Gasp Funnies.

detail (98). The next page begins with the panel depicting the "grisly mementos." This panel shows a soldier gripping a severed breast in his hand while from the right side a hand holds up a severed vagina: both parts of the female anatomy shown with blood dripping.[12] Here the gruesome images clearly contradict the narration's assignment of these "mementos" to "the valor of the Third Colorado Volunteers" (99). The panel immediately below this one presents a pregnant woman who has been disemboweled, the fetus on the ground beside her; in the background Captain Silas Soule looks on in terror, hands clasped to the sides of his head. Soule functions as a rational and sympathetic figure in the story in contrast to the violence around him, even his name obtaining to additional significance within the narrative. Jackson shows him before the attack urging Chivington not to attack Black Kettle's band, but he has no power to stop the attack and his horror as witness of the carnage amplifies the impotence of his opposition. As Witek shows, Soule is "[a] moral center by which to judge the outrages" (73). He is representative of a small contingent of soldiers who are disgusted by the attack, yet impotent against its brutality, as Jackson describes them: "powerless to stop the butchery . . . unable to believe the inhumanity that assaults their senses" (99). In this way, Soule acts as a surrogate or anchor, on the US side, for the reader. His outrage channels ours. Yet, he is clearly outnumbered by the murderous and malicious forces of the rest of the soldiers. The assault on his senses embodies the assault on ours, and like him, we can only watch in horror.

Jackson's extreme detail in depicting the massacre raises some questions regarding the artistic choices. What do we make of Jackson's graphic depiction? This is a question that Witek raises, too, regarding, as he says, "the ethics of historical representation in visual media: can the truth be too awful to be seen?

Is there an aesthetics of atrocity?" (67).[13] An immediate response might be to point to the unflinching detail as an uncensored exposure of the truth that confronts the reader with the brutality of US expansion. Contrary to the typically bloodless stories of official accounts of US expansion, "Nits Make Lice" forces the reader to see the bloody and sadistic violence of conquest. Intertwined with this purpose would also be Jackson's roots in underground comix. If a major driving force of the underground comix movement was to shock, to defy decorum and censorship, to be honest and frank, and at times present the worst of the worst, then this motivation might play some role in Jackson's choices here.[14] Especially in regard to the sexualized violence and gore, there is an element here of tweaking the nose of mainstream society, both in the presentation of graphic violence and in rejecting official ideologies of American history. The instinct to shock can be problematic though. These scenes might also read as exploitative of the female body and of the Native body as objects of violence and degradation. Images of violence against women outnumber those against men. Although this fact reflects the actual circumstances, since women were the main victims of the massacre, one might question Jackson's choice to depict the violence against women in such graphic detail: the images of the rape, the severed female anatomy, and the dying pregnant woman are disturbing. Moreover, the women are generally nude and while female nudity in itself is not shameful, according to dominant social norms in the United States, it is. Perhaps complicating the utilization of the female body in this story is Jackson's depiction of the female body as voluptuous: typically, the nude women here are presented with features that are conventionally perceived to be as attractive. The supposed attractiveness of these women's bodies juxtaposes to the violence that is visited upon those bodies and thus might make them even more sympathetic figures (assuming typical conventions of attractiveness in US culture). On this point, though, one might also recognize Jackson's indictment of misogyny in American culture; that historically it has been predominately women who have suffered the brunt of male violence and assault.[15]

The element of Native suffering is a contingent issue here, as well. While Jackson puts forth a good faith effort to draw our attention to the atrocities of US expansion, to shine a light on the violence committed against Native Americans, Jackson's whiteness must be contended with in his position as author. The basic fact of the dynamic is this: a white author is reproducing and depicting white violence upon Native bodies. This fact cannot be ignored. That is not to say that as a white male, Jackson has no right to tell this story, and the obligation to be truthful in its telling impels him to show the violence. Yet, one cannot ignore the fundamentals of the interaction in play here. Jackson's whiteness implicates him in the colonial system that his story seeks to indict. Yet, implication does not necessarily equal complicity. The fact that he presents the story as an effort to remove the rose-colored glasses from perceptions of US history indicates that, though implicated, he is not complicit in a blind repetition of historical propaganda.

On this point, it may be helpful to situate Jackson's depiction of Sand Creek with those of two Native writers: Simon Ortiz (Acoma Pueblo) and Tommy Orange (Cheyenne and Arapaho). In *from Sand Creek* (1981), Ortiz considers the process of victimization and erasure of Native peoples from US history. Ortiz's poetry does not delve into graphic details of the massacre, but connects it to the tendency of US history to erase and forget its casualties, especially those of Natives, as he asserts in the preface, "the United States insulates itself within an amnesia that doesn't acknowledge that kind of history" (6). The poem beginning "In 1969 . . ." lists redacted statistics for Vietnam casualties and highway deaths of Coloradoans, with imperatives to remember My Lai and Sand Creek, stating that "In fifty years / nobody knew / what happened" and that "In 1864, / there were no Indians killed" (15). This latter statement is an obvious lie speaking to the poem's theme of erasure and amnesia in US history. More recently, Orange describes the massacre in his novel *There There* (2018). Unlike Ortiz and like Jackson, Orange depicts the atrocity in its graphic horror: "They did more than kill us. They tore us up. Mutilated us. Broke our fingers to take our rings, cut off our ears to take our silver, scalped us for our hair . . . Then they took our body parts as trophies and displayed them on a stage in downtown Denver. Colonel Chivington danced with dismembered parts of us in his hands, with women's pubic hair, drunk, he danced . . ." (8). Orange, writing in the first-person plural, speaks as an insider, providing an unblinking portrait of the vicious inhumanity of the massacre that contrasts with Ortiz's focus on the aftereffects of the massacre in US history and culture. Ortiz and Orange, then, present two possible options for treating the Sand Creek massacre: one that eschews a direct portrayal of the violence and one that does not, displaying the violence in full detail. Jackson's tack definitely falls into the latter course. The distinction is that Orange speaks for his people while Jackson speaks as an outside observer.

This distinction further reminds us that in Jackson's comic the representation of violence against Native peoples calls our attention to the colonialist system that produced the original event, just as Jackson's attempt to indict US treachery via the violation of women's bodies also participates in a visual subjugation of women's bodies. On one level, then, of the comic as material object and artistic document, it exists within the same racialized and gendered system of dominance that provided the ways and means to carry out the massacre. On the level of the story itself, of the narrative's meaning, it resists that system, delivering a graphic and vivid portrait of the dissonance between official versions of history and what actually happened.

This dissonance is most vivid in the final panels of the story. The concluding four panels (two rows of two panels each) presents Chivington in his tent after the massacre, daydreaming about what he believes will be his political reward and glory: "Exulting in the gore, J.M. Chivington spins political dreams, already in his mind receiving the accolades of a grateful constituency back in Denver" (100). This reverie is interrupted by a soldier asking for orders on prisoners from the attack. Jackson shows Chivington angered at this news; there are to be no prisoners. Chivington asks the soldier, "Don't you know nits make lice?" (100). In the final panel, the narration describes the off-panel execution of the prisoners while in the panel one sees Chivington's hand signing his report. One sentence is highlighted in the panel: "All did nobly" (100). In what Witek names "visual irony" (73), the diegetic words upon the page of the report directly contradict the narration's words that describe the cries of the prisoners gone quiet with the sound of gunfire. The narration conveys an auditory experience (conveyed through the non-diegetic voice of the narrator) in contrast with the visual experience of reading Chivington's actual words presented on the physical page of the report. This contrast within the reader's perceptual experience of the panel parallels the reader's conceptual experience of the dissonance between Chivington and his men's actions and his assessment of those actions as being noble. The words—"All did nobly"—are the focal point of the panel while the reader is left to imagine the murder of the women and children seen previously in the panel directly above this one. Furthermore, Chivington's hand is the sole human element in the panel, thus implicating to some degree the reader as he or she sits in the same position as Chivington looking down on the report. Chivington's hand also implicates Jackson as artist and writer of the comic; the drawn hand in the panel is an echo of the drawing hand that produced the visual. The comic continually links artist, audience, and subject, recognizing the inescapable interrelationship of past and present, how the way we imagine and understand history influences current behaviors and decisions in our present.

Jackson's *Comanche Moon: A Picture Narrative About Cynthia Ann Parker, Her Twenty-Five Year Captivity Among the Comanche Indians—and Her Son, Quanah Parker, The Last Chief of the Comanches* follows in the line of the historical work seen in "Nits Make Lice" while moving away from the underground ethos of shock and awe. As the lengthy subtitle indicates, this narrative details the lives of Cynthia Ann Parker and her son Quanah. *Comanche Moon* maintains Jackson's interest in Native history as seen in "Nits Make Lice," but this narrative noticeably departs from the underground aesthetic evident in the latter work. While Jackson's style remains consistent between these two works, the art in *Comanche Moon* leans more toward accuracy of detail and representation. In regard to Jackson's stylistic choices in *Comanche Moon*, he cites in the references the influence of Western art, the "Old Masters," as he calls them, specifically naming "Charles Russell, Frederic Remington, Harold von Schmidt, Nick Eggenhofer, and John Clymer" (121). In this regard, Jackson follows in a long line of artistic renderings of the frontier that played an influential role in shaping popular perceptions and cultural myths of the West.[16]

While Jackson acknowledges the aesthetic debt of *Comanche Moon*, his work also follows in two major traditions of American frontier stories: the captivity narrative and the vanishing Indian. The captivity narrative told the story of, usually, a white European who has been taken captive by an Indigenous group and, usually, is "redeemed," or ransomed and returns home. The narrative typically followed that of a religious or conversion experience. The height of its popularity was between the seventeenth and nineteenth centuries and among the many narratives published, Mary Rowlandson's is perhaps the best known; as well, James Fenimore Cooper's *The Last of the Mohicans* incorporates elements of the captivity narrative. One strain of the captivity narrative was the "unredeemed captive," that individual who assimilated and refused to return (Eunice Williams is perhaps one of the better-known examples of this phenomenon). Cynthia Ann Parker follows this model.[17]

The vanishing Indian myth rose in popularity in the early nineteenth century and romanticized what was seen to be the inevitable disappearance of Native cultures. The vanishing Indian was a noble, heroic figure whose time was done; frequently figured as male, his way of life was not compatible with the modern world and so rather than submit or assimilate into white society, he resists and usually dies in a blaze of glory, his passing mourned as a tragic, though necessary, loss.[18] *The Last of the Mohicans* serves as an example of this kind of story, while John Augustus Stone's *Metamora, or, The Last of the Wampanoags* (1829) was a popular play depicting the life and end of Metacom. In art, one might consider such sculptures as Ferdinand Pettrich's *The Dying Tecumseh* (1856), Thomas Crawford's *The Indian: Dying Chief Contemplating the Progress of Civilization* (1856), or, attesting to the power of the trope into the twentieth century, James Earle Fraser's *The End of the Trail* (1918). The vanishing Indian provided an object of admiration for white audiences while also assuaging their guilt connected to the removal, dispossession, and extermination of Native peoples.

While these archetypal narratives are present in his story, Jackson resists to some extent the propagandistic purposes these kinds of stories usually served. Cynthia Ann's captivity is not of the type of a Mary Rowlandson or Hannah Dustan in which the story aims to relate the savagery of the captors, conveying the captive's journey from capture to freedom as an allegory of God's blessing upon white settlers. Likewise, while there is some degree of romanticization and nostalgia in the designation of Quanah as the "last chief of the Comanches," Jackson presents this account more in terms of historical actuality that departs from the tone of such nineteenth-century depictions of "last Indians" as *Metamora* and *The Last of the Mohicans*. Unlike the majority of the precedents in these two strands of American mythology, Jackson's depiction of Native Americans seeks to humanize them, present them as individuals living in and responding to their changing world in the best way that they can. Jackson does

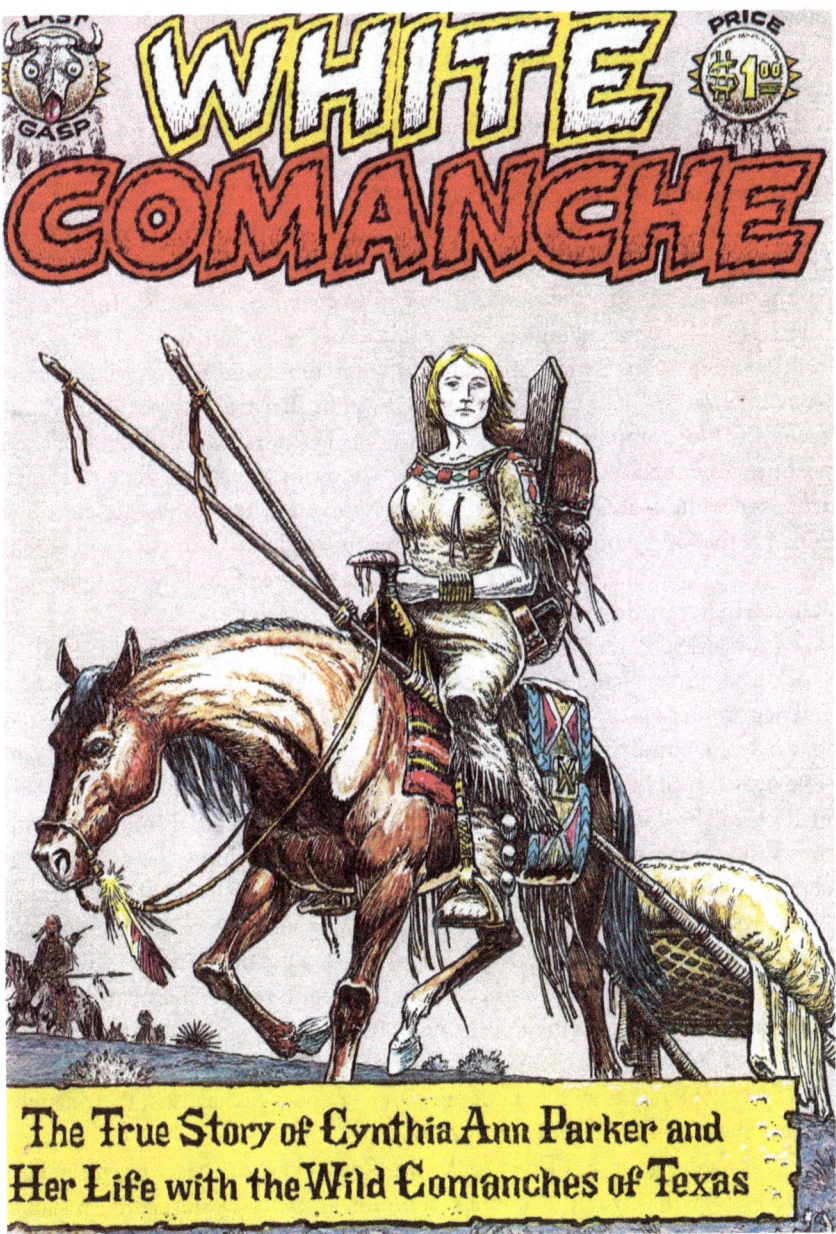

Figure 2.7. Cover: Jack Jackson, *White Comanche*. Last Gasp Funnies, 1977.

not dehumanize or objectify Native peoples: they are central to the story rather than being forces which only serve to progress a white person's narrative.

In *Comanche Moon*, the title page is a two-page spread that features Cynthia Ann Parker on the right page, framed on top and bottom by the title and subtitle. On the left page is her Comanche husband, Peta Nocona. This spread is derived from the wrap-around cover of *White Comanche* (1977) in which Cynthia Ann appears by herself on the front so that, along with the title, she is the central focus of this story. The subtitle in the original issue also focuses on Cynthia Ann: "The True Story of Cynthia Ann Parker and Her Life with the Wild Comanches of Texas!"

In *Comanche Moon*, this subtitle includes Quanah thus expanding the focus to encompass the lives of mother and son. In both versions of this subtitle, the ending clause remains the same: "the Wild Comanches of Texas." This phrase partakes in the typical language often associated with Indians in US culture: "wild" both indicating admiration and differentiation; wild as free, wild as apart from "civilization." Peta Nocona and Parker both sit astride horses in the foreground of the composition. Parker sits upon her horse with straight-backed posture, confidence evident in her pose as she looks directly at the viewer (fig. 2.7). Her white skin is evident while she is dressed in Comanche clothing. Parker is the focal point. Context clues allow the reader to correctly assume that this figure is Cynthia Ann Parker and her image is one of pride and confidence, at home in her world.

As for Jackson's depiction of her captivity, he conveys the expected initial shock and terror of the experience. In one panel, a close-up of Parker's face and her brother's is captioned with Jackson's narration: "The children are forced to watch the humiliation of Elizabeth Kellogg and Rachel Plummer, time and time again" (14). In contrast to Jackson's direct and graphic approach in "Nits Make Lice," he conveys the incident through implication and innuendo with the visuals being of Cynthia Ann and her brother watching, the girl's face in obvious distress. The bottom two panels of this page keep the focus on Cynthia Ann: two shots of her on horseback behind one of her captors. The second bottom panel portrays her determination to be strong. The narration describes her "fight[ing] off her tears" while a thought balloon reveals her own thinking: "Mamma always said crying doesn't help" (14). Although a captive and a child, Jackson depicts Cynthia Ann with some degree of agency and individuality. This first chapter ends with her adoption by a couple who have lost their daughter, and thus Cynthia Ann becomes Naduah.

Jackson's designation of her as "White Comanche" echoes a phenomenon of US history that would become a common trope in westerns and popular depictions of the frontier: the "unredeemed captive" or the "white Indian." A number of comics, especially in the 1950s, employ this trope with titles or characters such as *White Boy* (1933–1936), *Golden Arrow* (1940–1953), Fiction House's *Firehair* (1945–1952), *The Apache Kid* (1950), Manzar the White Indian in *Indians* (1950–1953), *White Indian* (1949–1954), *White Chief of the Pawnee Indians* (1953), *Cheyenne Kid* (1957–1973), DC's *Firehair* (first appearance 1969), and *Scalphunter* (1977–1980). These comics reflect a common plotline regarding the "white Indian": typically, a white child who loses their family and is adopted into a Native tribe. The child fully assimilates, ultimately identifying completely with their adopted family and people. In most instances, this type of story, particularly as found in comics and other popular media, expresses an exoticism of Native peoples associated with adventure and wildness. Common associations of freedom from rules and connection with nature also abound in these stories.

Jackson's designating Cynthia Ann as "white Comanche" echoes the language often found in the comics of the mid-twentieth century. His depiction of Cynthia Ann's assimilation into Comanche culture proceeds quite smoothly; her adopted parents treat her with kindness, displaying full parental love and care for her. As Jackson narrates, "And so begins Cynthia Ann Parker's new life as a white Comanche. Her adopted parents, Tabby-Nocca and Chatua, are not cruel to her, as is the case with many older captives. They give her the name of the lost daughter whose place she is to take" (16). She grows into adulthood, fully assimilating into Comanche culture: "Her memories of the lost family and her childhood at Parker's fort fade to a mere glimmer as time slips away. Except for her pale skin, blue eyes, and blonde, grease-smeared hair, she is nothing but pure Comanche!" (19). She then marries and gives birth to a son, Quanah.

Her return to white society is, as Jackson calls it, a "second captivity" (42). She is "more Indian than white" and when she follows Comanche tradition to grieve, she does so "to the horror of her civilized relatives" (43). In contrast to her first captivity, her second one is filled with sadness and anguish. Jackson describes her passing: "Finally she dies of a broken heart . . ." (45). She does not assimilate back into white culture; her home, her love being with her Comanche tribe.

On the one hand, Cynthia Ann Parker's assimilation into Comanche culture and uneasy resettling into white culture demonstrates the inability of whiteness to accommodate differing identities. Parker's persistent connection to her Comanche upbringing, even years after being reunited with her white family, is met with horror by her white relatives. On the other hand, Jackson depicts her son as being able to incorporate his originating heritage with adaptation to white ways. Cynthia Ann's and Quanah's movements between different cultures bookends Jackson's narrative. Their experiences of this cultural movement ends in strikingly different ways. The mother dies heartbroken, away from the people and loved ones with whom she would rather be. Her son, though, finds himself with some degree of fame and respect, preserving aspects of his Comanche culture while adopting white ways and norms as suits him. Quanah accepts the challenge of assimilation by citing his mother's example: "If my mother could learn the ways of the Indians, I can learn the ways of the whites" (104). He integrates into white society on his own terms. He turns down an offer to appear in a Wild West Show and successfully fights for the recognition of peyote as a religious sacrament (118).

Figure 2.8. Quanah's peyote vision: Jack Jackson, *Comanche Moon*. Reed Press, 1979.

While Jackson's attention to Parker's use of peyote adheres to the latter's history, there also may be an element of the counterculture informing this aspect of the narrative. Jackson maintains throughout the biography a realistic style except for two places: during Parker's vision quest (50–51) and in a panel regarding Parker's peyote usage as a religious ritual (112). This latter example occurs in one panel that occupies over half the page.

In this image, Parker sits cross-legged with eyes closed, his long hair floating upward, behind him the shape of a buffalo encompasses him, rising from the horizon. This panel stands out given its surreal style, contrasting sharply with the realism of the rest of the book. This panel, along with the vision-quest sequence, invite two observations. On one level, these images invoke the trope of the mystical Indian, that idea of the Indian as being attuned to some heightened state of spirituality or consciousness. On another level, this attention to peyote recalls the countercultural fascination with and copious usage of psychedelic drugs, an element also present in many underground comix. Thus, Parker's use and defense of peyote as part of his religion stays true to his biography, but one cannot ignore the contextual elements of the popular image of the mystic Indian and Jackson's roots in the counterculture world of underground comix.[19]

As the example above shows, Jackson's narrative strives to depict an accurate portrayal of the subject, but in doing so must contend with the preconceived notions and stereotypes that consume much of US culture regarding Native Americans. If he presents things as they were, he risks invoking certain tropes and misrepresentations. Overall, he is able to steer clear of perpetuating such misrepresentations. While Jackson's narrative touches upon some of these tropes, his work also departs from those reductive representations to create a more authentic and genuine representation of the history and of the Comanche people. He does not idealize or romanticize the Native figures in a way that strips them of their individuality and humanity (granted, some idealization is present, but that is to be expected in a biography that intends to celebrate someone's life). Jackson often features Native characters conversing among themselves about subjects beyond their interaction with whites (one might think of this as an Indian version of the Bechdel Test). They have agency and exist independently of white people. Importantly, too, Jackson writes their language as standard English, using idiomatic expressions and slang thus rejecting the typical pidgin English/Indian-speak often found in popular culture and westerns. Witek notes this feature of the language, observing that "the characters often generally speak as if they were modern Americans, with a few blatant anachronisms" (80). Jackson's linguistic choices, according to Witek, "subvert our generic expectations" (80). Jackson rejects that convention of Indian-speak so as to depict the Native characters as actual human beings to which a modern audience can relate. In *Comanche Moon*, Quanah Parker is not some exotic, primitive relic of a long-gone past. Instead, Jackson presents Parker as a complicated and real human being.

Preceding his work on the material that would become *Comanche Moon*, Jackson had drawn up art for a book on Native leaders (Rosenkranz 206). This work was eventually published in 1985 under the title *Long Shadows*. In his introduction to *Long Shadows*, Jackson attacks the concept of Manifest Destiny, calling it "a dogma of supreme self-assurance and ambition" (11). He concludes his introduction by aligning the Native leaders who resisted white expansion with the American spirit: "Though the Indians' great losses may sadden many readers . . . all freedom-loving Americans can indeed be proud of the Native people's determined fight to remain free" (11). *Long Shadows*, then, might be seen as an encapsulation of Jackson's approach toward Native subject matter. The Indian figures he illustrates are embodiments of freedom, resisting the encroachment of government upon their peoples and lands. While an element of the romantic is present in this depiction, there also seems to be a genuine admiration and respect present, too.

While Jackson's work retains some traces of negative representations, we see a departure from the predominant caricature and stereotype found in most popular representations of Native peoples. Jackson's comics may not be completely free of the tropes of popular culture Indians, but they assert an alternative to those tropes. Perhaps the vibrant Native activism of the early seventies modified to some degree the public perception of Native peoples. For Jackson in particular, his involvement with underground comix, along with the climate of the counterculture, would have encouraged a skepticism about official versions of US history. Such skepticism combined with the underground's attacks on mainstream dogma and decorum and the increased awareness of Native rights opened up an avenue of Native representation that could be more realistic, accurate, and human.

Notes

1. See Smith and Warrior for an in-depth history of this period of Native activism. Also see Dean Rader for his analysis of the aesthetics and cultural expressions of the Alcatraz action, 7–46.

2. See Jesse T. Moore's article on Green Lantern and Bradford Wright, 228–34.

3. For scholarship on underground comix, see James Danky and Denis Kitchen; Randy Duncan, Matthew J. Smith, and Paul Levitz, 39–49; Mark James Estren; Jean-Paul Gabilliet, 61–67, 80–83, 360n; Robert C. Harvey, 140–41; Charles Hatfield, 6–20; Leonard Rifas; Trina Robbins, 124–38; Patrick Rosenkranz; Roger Sabin, 36–51; Clinton R. Sanders; Dez Skinn; and Joseph Witek, 58–95.

4. Witek delivers an insightful chapter devoted to Jackson's historical comics. Witek's analysis is significant in his findings and in it being perhaps the only extended, scholarly examination of this work. My analysis parallels Witek's to some degree although he and I work toward different ends. Witek centers his discussion upon considering and assessing comics as a medium of history while my focus centers upon representation in Jackson's treatment of Native history. Nonetheless, Witek's scholarship is an important antecedent for my work here.

5. For scholarship on Native representations and appropriations in US culture, see Sierra Adare, Renee Bergland, Robert Berkhofer, S. Elizabeth Bird, Philip Deloria, Richard Drinnon, Joanna Hearne, Shari Huhndorf, Jacquelyn Kilpatrick, Elise Marienstras, Devon Mihesuah, Roy Harvey Pearce, Armando Prats, Paul Lester Robertson, Susan Scheckel, Michael Sheyahshe, and Richard Slotkin.

6. Maurice Horn shows that western comic strips began appearing in the 1900s, with an increase in number in the 1920s (18–23). Slotkin identifies 1947 to 1972 as a particularly fertile period (*Gunfighter* 347–49). Michelle Nolan determines that the number of western comics was 3,478 in 1959, climbing to 5,000 later (23).

7. This contrast, in fact, recalls a similar one in John Vanderlyn's *The Death of Jane McCrea* (1804) in which two Indian males attack Jane McCrea, a white woman. See Robert Sheardy for further analysis of this painting.

8. Sadly, the rhetoric of infestation is still with us in our national discourse today.

9. In the introduction to *Optimism of Youth*, Kim Thompson and Gary Groth note the influence of EC on the generation of underground comix artists (5). Throughout *Rebel Visions*, Rosenkranz documents the influence, as well. S. Clay Wilson perhaps best encapsulates the

relationship of the underground to EC: "I always saw the underground comix movement as a sort of extension of the ECs" (qtd. in Rosenkranz 145). Not all of the underground were in the EC camp, though, as can be seen in Bill Griffith's fierce criticism in "A Sour Look at the Comix Scene" (1973) (Rosenkranz 186–88). See also Estren on the EC influence, 33–40.

10. Page references for "Nits Make Lice" are from *God's Bosom*.

11. John Sugden argues that the Battle of Thames (that resulted in the death of Tecumseh) "helped create one president, one vice president, three state governors of Kentucky, three lieutenant-governors, four United States senators, and a score of congressmen" (396–97). See also Thomas G. Mitchell, 45–68, for the influence of Indian fighting in the War of 1812 on subsequent US politics.

12. This imagery of sexual mutilation also appears in Jackson's "The Savage Within" (1990: in *God's Bosom*, 62–72) While the subject matter of this story and "Nits Make Lice" is different, the similarity of the imagery bears noting.

13. In his 1981 interview with Bill Sherman, Jackson expresses his awareness of the brutality of these scenes and the effect on the reader (109). Jackson also addresses these concerns in his 1984 interview with Bruce Sweeney in *Comics Interview*. See also Witek's citation of and commentary on this portion of the interview (76).

14. In a similar vein, *Bicentennial Gross-Outs* (July 1976) features a preface by William Stout. The introductory page depicts a skeletal Uncle Sam, hat in hands in front of him, a wall behind him and to the left, a city skyline, smokestacks pumping smog into the air, in the background. Uncle Sam states, "We feel the United States' 200th anniversary of its birth is the perfect time to make a careful, critical, and severe (where necessary) examination of our country's past and present! We feel democracy thrives in an atmosphere of truth and free thought! So, let us see ourselves honestly—let's view not only our highlights, but our dark side; our painful and sometimes shameful misdeeds whose stains we have often sought to cover up!" The first story in the comic, "Filipino Massacre," also by Stout, relates the US conflict with the Moro of the Philippines and offers an intriguing parallel (and possible antecedent) to "Nits Make Lice" in depicting US aggression against an Indigenous people. Stout also drew the cover and inside front cover of *Slow Death* #7; this inside cover has a composition similar to his Uncle Sam art, except this one features a skeletal soldier.

15. See also Witek's insightful analysis of this aspect of the story (71–73).

16. For scholarship on the influence of western art on US culture, see Edward Buscombe and Dawn Glanz.

17. A few starting points for scholarship on the captivity narrative would be Christopher Castiglia, John Demos, Kathryn Zabelle Derounian-Stodola, June Namias, and Gordon Sayre.

18. See Renee Bergland, Brian Dippie, Lora Romero, Gordon Sayre, and Julie Schimmel.

19. The use of peyote and other related psychedelics possesses a well-known popularity among the counterculture of the sixties. This popularity dovetails with a perception of Native cultures as being more mystically inclined than white culture. The valid usage of peyote as a religious sacrament would have made for an attractive prospect for white seekers of mystical or altered states of consciousness. Such a phenomenon is visible in other underground comix, as well. For example, Gilbert Shelton's "The Indian that Came to Dinner" (1968) tells the story of a middle-class white couple who get turned on to peyote by their Indian guest. For further analysis of the relationship between the counterculture and Native appropriation, see Deloria's chapter on the topic, 154–80. Furthermore, Jackson was aware of this attraction of religious peyote use to the counterculture: "I know it was very fashionable back in the hippie days for people to try and go out to become a member of the Native American Church. If they were card-carrying members, see, they could take peyote and buy peyote, transport peyote without having to get busted for it" (1981: 107).

Bibliography

Adare, Sierra S. *"Indian" Stereotypes in TV Science Fiction: First Nations' Voices Speak Out*. Austin: University of Texas Press, 2005.
Bergland, Renee. *The National Uncanny: Indian Ghosts and American Subjects*. Hanover: University Press of New England, 2000.
Berkhofer, Robert. *The White Man's Indian: Images of the American Indian from Columbus to the Present*. New York: Alfred A. Knopf, 1978.
Bicentennial Gross-Outs #1 (July 1976), Yentzer and Gonif.
Big Chief Wahoo #7 (Winter 1943), Famous Funnies. Digital.
Bird, S. Elizabeth, ed. *Dressing in Feathers: The Construction of the Indian in American Popular Culture*. New York: Westview Press, 1996.
Buscombe, Edward. "Painting the Legend: Frederic Remington and the Western." *Cinema Journal* 23, no. 4 (Summer 1984): 12–27. JSTOR. Web. July 19, 2018.
Castiglia, Christopher. *Bound and Determined: Captivity, Culture-Crossing, and White Womanhood from Mary Rowlandson to Patty Hearst*. Chicago: University of Chicago Press, 1996.
Clifton, James, ed. *The Invented Indian*. New Brunswick: Transaction Publishers, 1990.
Cooper, James Fenimore. *The Last of the Mohicans: A Narrative of 1757*. 1826. New York: Signet Classic, 1962.
Danky, James, and Denis Kitchen. *Underground Classics: The Transformation of Comics into Comix*. New York: Abrams ComicArts, 2009.
Deloria, Philip J. *Playing Indian*. New Haven: Yale University Press, 1998.
Demos, John. *The Unredeemed Captive: A Family Story from Early America*. New York: Vintage Books, 1995.
Derounian-Stodola, Kathryn Zabelle, ed. *Women's Indian Captivity Narratives*. New York: Penguin Books, 1998.
Dippie, Brian. *The Vanishing American: White Attitudes and U.S. Indian Policy*. Middletown: Wesleyan University Press, 1982.
Drinnon, Richard. *Facing West: The Metaphysics of Indian-Hating and Empire Building*. Minneapolis: University of Minnesota Press, 1980.
Duncan, Randy, Matthew J. Smith, and Paul Levitz. *The Power of Comics: History, Form, and Culture*. 2nd ed. London: Bloomsbury, 2015.
Estren, Mark James. *A History of Underground Comics*. 1974. Oakland: Ronin Publishing, 2012.
Fighting Indians of the Wild West #1 (March 1952), Avon Periodicals. Digital.
Gabilliet, Jean-Paul. *Of Comics and Men: A Cultural History of American Comic Books*. Trans. Bart Beaty and Nick Nguyen. Jackson: University Press of Mississippi, 2010.
Glanz, Dawn. *How the West Was Drawn: American Art and the Settling of the Frontier*. Ann Arbor: UMI Research Press, 1982.
Harvey, Robert C. *The Art of the Comic Book: An Aesthetic History*. Jackson: University Press of Mississippi, 1996.
Hatfield, Charles. *Alternative Comics: An Emerging Literature*. Jackson: University Press of Mississippi, 2005.
Hearne, Joanna. *Native Recognition: Indigenous Cinema and the Western*. Albany: State University of New York Press, 2012.
Horn, Maurice. *Comics of the American West*. New York: Winchester Press, 1977.
Huhndorf, Shari M. *Going Native: Indians in the American Cultural Imagination*. Ithaca: Cornell University Press, 2001.
Jackson, Jack (Jaxon) (w and a). *Blood on the Moon*. Berkeley: Last Gasp Eco-Funnies, 1978.
———. *Comanche Moon*. New York: Reed Press, 1979.

———. *God's Bosom and Other Stories: The Historical Strips of Jack Jackson*. Seattle: Fantagraphics Books, 1995.
———. "Jack Jackson." *Comics Journal* 100 (July 1985): 111–14. Web. July 30, 2018.
———. "Jack Jackson on His Work in the Underground and His New Book *Los Tejanos*." *Comics Journal* 75 (September 1982): 75–84. Web. July 30, 2018.
———. "Jaxon." *Comics Interview* 39 (March 1984): 40–49. Web. July 30, 2018.
———. *The Last of the Mohicans*. Adapted from James Fenimore Cooper. (1992), Dark Horse Comics.
———. "Learning Texas History the Painless Way." *Comics Journal* 119 (January 1988): 97–100. Web. July 30, 2018.
———. *Long Shadows: Indian Leaders Standing in the Path of Manifest Destiny 1600–1900*. Amarillo: Paramount Publishing Company, 1985.
———. *Los Tejanos and Lost Cause*. Seattle: Fantagraphics Books, 2012.
———. "Nits Make Lice." *Slow Death #7* (Winter 1976–1977), Last Gasp Eco-Funnies.
———. *Optimism of Youth: The Underground Work of Jack Jackson*. Seattle: Fantagraphics Books, 1991.
———. *Red Raider*. Berkeley: Last Gasp Eco-Funnies, 1977.
———. "Tejano Cartoonist: An Interview with Jack Jackson." *Comics Journal* 61 (Winter 1981): 100–111. Web. July 30, 2018.
———. *White Comanche*. Berkeley: Last Gasp Eco-Funnies, 1977.
Kilpatrick, Jacquelyn. *Celluloid Indians: Native Americans and Film*. Lincoln: University of Nebraska Press, 1999.
Marienstras, Elise. "The Common Man's Indian: The Image of the Indian as Promoter of National Identity in the Early National Era." In *Native Americans and the Early Republic*, edited by Frederick Hoxie, Ronald Hoffman, and Peter Albert. Charlottesville: University Press of Virginia, 1999.
Mihesuah, Devon A. *American Indians: Stereotypes and Realities*. Atlanta: Clarity Press, 1996.
Mitchell, Thomas G. *Indian Fighters Turned American Politicians: From Military Service to Public Office*. Westport: Praeger, 2003.
Moore, Jesse T. "The Education of Green Lantern: Culture and Ideology." *Journal of American Culture* 26, no. 2 (June 2003): 263–78. ProQuest Direct. Web. May 14, 2013.
Namias, June. *White Captives: Gender and Ethnicity on the American Frontier*. Chapel Hill: University of North Carolina Press, 1993.
Nolan, Michelle. "Collecting the Western Genre!" *Comic Book Marketplace* 2, no. 61 (July 1998): 23–26.
O'Neil, Dennis (w), and Neal Adams (p). *The Green Lantern / Green Arrow Collection*. Vol. 1. New York: DC Comics, 2004.
Orange, Tommy. *There There*. New York: Alfred A. Knopf, 2018.
Ortiz, Simon. *from Sand Creek*. Tucson: University of Arizona Press, 2000.
Pearce, Roy Harvey. *Savagism and Civilization*. Baltimore: Johns Hopkins University Press, 1965.
Prats, Armando José. *Invisible Natives: Myth and Identity in the American Western*. Ithaca: Cornell University Press, 2002.
Rader, Dean. *Engaged Resistance: American Indian Art, Literature, and Film from Alcatraz to the NMAI*. Austin: University of Texas Press, 2011.
"Red Fawn." *Indians: Picture Stories of the First Americans #1* (1950). Wings Publishing Co. [Fiction House Magazines]. Digital.
Ricca, Brad. "The Secret History of Chief Wahoo." *Belt Magazine*. June 19, 2014. Web. July 27, 2018.
Rifas, Leonard. "Race and Comix." *Multicultural Comics: From Zap to Blue Beetle*, edited by Frederick Luis Aldama, 27–38. Austin: University of Texas Press, 2010.

———. "Racial Imagery, Racism, Individualism, and Underground Comix." *ImageTexT: Interdisciplinary Comics Studies* 1, no. 1 (2004). Web. December 17, 2017.

Robbins, Trina. *Pretty in Ink: North American Women Cartoonists 1896–2013*. Seattle: Fantagraphics Books, 2013.

Robertson, Paul Lester. "Indians of the Apocalypse: Native Appropriation and Representation in 1980s Dystopic Films and Comic Books." *Journal of Popular Culture* 51, no. 1 (2018): 68–90. Digital.

Romero, Lora. "Vanishing Americans: Gender, Empire, and New Historicism." *Subjects and Citizens*, edited by Michael Moon and Cathy N. Davidson, 87–105. Durham: Duke University Press, 1995.

Rosenkranz, Patrick. *Rebel Visions: The Underground Comix Revolution—1963–1975*. Seattle: Fantagraphics Books, 2008.

Sabin, Roger. *Adult Comics: An Introduction*. London: Routledge, 1993.

Sanders, Clinton R. "Icons of the Alternate Culture: The Themes and Functions of Underground Comix." *Journal of Popular Culture* 8, no. 4 (Spring 1975): 836–52.

Sayre, Gordon M., ed. *American Captivity Narratives*. Boston: Houghton Mifflin Company, 2000.

———. *The Indian Chief as Tragic Hero: Native Resistance and the Literatures of America, from Moctezuma to Tecumseh*. Chapel Hill: University of North Carolina Press, 2005.

Scheckel, Susan. *The Insistence of the Indian: Race and Nationalism in Nineteenth-Century American Culture*. Princeton: Princeton University Press, 1998.

Schimmel, Julie. "Inventing the 'Indian.'" *The West as America: Reinterpreting Images of the Frontier, 1820–1920*, edited by William Truettner, 149–89. Washington, DC: Smithsonian Institution Press, 1991.

Sheardy, Robert. "The White Woman and the Native Male Body in Vanderlyn's *Death of Jane McCrea*." *Journal of American Culture* 22, no. 1 (Spring 1999): 93–100.

Shelton, Gilbert. "The Indian that Came to Dinner." *Feds 'n' Heads* (1968). Digital.

Sherman, Bill. "Panels of History." Rev. of *Comanche Moon*, by Jack Jackson. *Comics Journal* 53 (Winter 1980): 42–43. Web. July 30, 2018.

Sheyahshe, Michael A. *Native Americans in Comic Books: A Critical Study*. Jefferson: McFarland, 2008.

Skinn, Dez. *Comix: The Underground Revolution*. New York: Thunder's Mouth Press, 2004.

Slotkin, Richard. *Gunfighter Nation: The Myth of the Frontier in Twentieth-Century America*. 1992. Norman: University of Oklahoma Press, 1998.

———. *Regeneration through Violence: The Mythology of the American Frontier 1600–1860*. Norman: University of Oklahoma Press, 1973.

Smith, Paul Chaat, and Robert Allen Warrior. *Like a Hurricane: The Indian Movement from Alcatraz to Wounded Knee*. New York: New Press, 1996.

Sugden, John. *Tecumseh: A Life*. New York: Henry Holt, 1997.

Witek, Joseph. *Comic Books as History: The Narrative Art of Jack Johnson, Art Spiegelman, and Harvey Pekar*. Jackson: University Press of Mississippi, 1989.

Wright, Bradford W. *Comic Book Nation: The Transformation of Youth Culture in America*. Baltimore: Johns Hopkins University Press, 2001.

"Goin' Native!": Depictions of the First Peoples from "Down Under"

Jack Ford and Philip Cass

Depictions of Australia and Aoteoroa, New Zealand's Indigenous peoples, in comics, followed paths as divergent as the relationship between their Indigenous and European-settler cultures. Neither Australia nor New Zealand have experienced the accepted Golden, Silver, or Bronze Ages of comics that have occurred elsewhere. Both have been subject to periods of almost complete US dominance of the local market and intermittent attempts to revive local production. The presence of Indigenous characters reflects the broader development of both nations' comics. Little academic research has been conducted on this topic, which is an indication of the underestimation of this media-form within Antipodean universities. The development of Indigenous characterizations can be drawn from the history of these comics.

Australia

Australia's first comic *Vumps* lasted one issue in 1908, being unable to compete with British imports such as *The Boy's Own Paper*, with its tales of imperial derring-do. During the 1920s, the comic strip's arrival in newspapers influenced the restart of Australian comics. While individual, graphic illustrations or political cartoons had previously existed in newspapers and journals, the first Australian strip was not published until August 1920, when artist Stan Cross drew *You and Me* for *Smith's Weekly*. This strip would later develop into *Mr and Mrs Potts*, one of Australia's longest running strips. Other newspapers followed suit, providing employment and exposure for a flourishing local cartoonist trade. The strips were inserted into a weekly supplement format, giving Australians the comics concept. With funny stories, aimed at children, this section became known as "The Funnies." During the 1920s, the weekly strip page(s) provided the foundations of the future Australian comic book industry through the creation of such iconic characters: *Ginger Meggs* (1921), *Fatty Finn* (1923). In 1924, the first *Ginger Meggs Annual* comic book was published.

Despite the Great Depression, the 1930s saw an expansion of the variety of newspaper strip titles plus their spread into magazines like the *Australian Woman's Weekly*. Some characters, such as May Gibb's *Bib and Bub* were drawn from children's literature. Others were sourced from adult-humor literature; for example, C. J. Dennis's *Ben Bowyang*, Steele Rudd's *Dad and Dave*. In 1934, *Fatty Finn Weekly* appeared in the format that is now defined as a comic rather than a strip. By 1936, syndicated US strips like *Mandrake the Magician* had infiltrated Australian publications. This prompted Australian illustrators to start strips aimed at adults such as *Out of the Silence*.

During these strips first two decades, Indigenous depictions were almost non-existent. Two factors led to this image absence. First, these strips were drawn for urban newspapers, where Australians were increasingly residing. Aborigines or Torres Strait Islanders were rarely seen or reported upon in the major cities so the absence of Indigenous characters in strips reflected their invisibility to their readership and, therefore, their market. Even where strips were set in "the Bush," Indigenous characters were not included, reflecting that these peoples were forced to live on the fringes of even rural communities. Second, most strips were set, either in towns or in exotic locations (e.g., outer space), where Indigenous characters were thought out of place. This latter factor applied equally to the imported, syndicated US comic strips plus the cheap US comics imports entering Australia in the 1930s, hindering local comics development. The imports contained no Australian Indigenous images. Popular titles such as *Tarzan* or *Sheena, Queen of the Jungle* did feature Indigenous depictions, but of Africans.

Two minor examples of indigenous depictions were found from this period. In 1934, *Argus* began *Out of the Silence*. Drawn by Reg Hicks, it was a science-fiction strip based on Eric Cox's 1919 novel. Alan Dundas discovers a buried sphere on his property. The sphere holds records of an ancient white civilization that was destroyed by its nonwhite tribal neighbors. Unsurprisingly, this story line had *Out of the Silence* reflect the then "popularly held racial bias" such that its racism "has seen publishers and other media avoid the property [strip] since it was last published in 1947" (Ryan 38). The tribe, who destroyed this ancient white civilization were drawn as dark skinned but not, obviously, as Indigenous Australians. Rather they are drawn to type, being pseudo-African in appearance, with bald heads, mirroring the Bengali tribesmen drawn, from 1936, in *The Phantom* strip. Then there was Aboriginal boy "Tuckonie." He was a supporting character in the short-lived children's strip *David and Dawn* that was produced for *Smith's Weekly* between 1938 and 1939.

From 1939 to 1945, the Antipodes were fully occupied with World War II. With paper rationing and a need for war artists for propaganda illustrators, the War, ironically, had a positive effect on Australian comics. In July 1940, the

Menzies government banned both the import of US comics and syndicated comic proofs, leading to a boom in the local comics industry's production. Thus, two months after the war began in September 1939, the *Sunday Telegraph* issued a new, sixteen-page *Color Comics* supplement. It featured syndicated US comic strips printed there. Five previously printed issues were later bound together into a soft-cover comic and sold by newsagents. Just nine months later, in 1940, it was reduced to eight pages, with no US strips. The ban's result saw artists being paid to both draw plus write the text for Australian comics, which often contained multiple strips plus stories. Newsprint rationing regulations allowed only the publication of new titles in one-off issues. So, wartime publishers like O.P.C., F.J.P., and Syd Williams printed Australian-drawn comics that continued from issue to issue, with only the banner renamed for each "new" title. This rise in Australian comics saw a corresponding increase in Indigenous imagery. Jim Colt was possibly the first to depict Torres Strait Islanders, when he drew Koloona, shipmate of *Gus of the Gulf*, in O.P.C.'s *Pep Comics*. In O.P.C.'s *Jim Grey* strip *The Secret of the Wreck* (1942) Aborigines are drawn as warlike, attacking and capturing white aviators (Foster 1991, 72). For J.P.C., Unk White produced *Blue Hardy and the Diamond Eyed Pygmies* that featured Aboriginal tracker Jacky as Hardy's sidekick. In late 1942, Rhys Williams turned Aboriginal "Dreamtime" stories into comics for J.P.C. This series included *Thugine the Green Serpent*, *The Sacred Bullroarer*, and *The Sacred Frog*. In 1943, Syd Miller's *The Coming of Molo the Mighty* saw the arrival of the first notable Australian superhero. Like *Superman*, *Molo* was an alien, except that he had a companion in Aboriginal orphan Willy-Willy. This small boy taught Molo "Pidgin English" to converse with Aborigines they encountered.

The war produced two iconic strips, Stan Cross's *Wally and the Major* and Alex Gurney's *Bluey and Curley*. Whereas *Bluey and Curley* is set in a combat unit, *Wally and the Major* is set in Australia, where they are "base-wallahs." Each depicted ridiculous aspects of military life, rather than action, with both put into compilations sold as annuals. Wartime issues of *Wally and the Major*, being set in the Australian bush, could have included Aboriginal depictions, but did not appear to do so. *Bluey and Curley* did include background Indigenous characters but they were Papuans. They were drawn as "types," wearing skirts with "Fuzzy-Wuzzy Angels" hair-dos. Given that *Bluey and Curley* were stereotypes of the "true-blue" Aussie digger then Gurney's "native" caricatures fitted the tone of his comic. Other wartime strips such as *Wanda the War Girl*, *Alec the Airman*, *Tightrope Tim*, and *Adolf, Hermann, and Musso* had story lines, where Indigenous Australians did not fit. Still, the first strip to depict Aboriginal art and legends was launched just two weeks after Singapore's surrender in 1942. This was *Nungalla and Jungalla* in the *Sunday Telegraph* comic section (*Nungalla and Jungalla* comic strip, Web). Sisters Mary and Elizabeth Durack, members of a prominent Australian grazier family, used their familiarity with indigenous culture to present Aboriginal stories, for the first time in comic form. It was a text-heavy, story-time strip. Mary wrote the text, while Elizabeth was the illustrator. This unique strip only lasted a year before it was replaced by *Superman* in 1943.

The decade 1946–1956 saw a rise in Australian comic sales plus the return of US comics via local reprints. New strips arrived, while a few WWII strips like *Wally and the Major* and *Bluey and Curley* were "demobbed" into peacetime stories, with both strips lasting for over thirty years. Gurney's *Bluey and Curley* became laborers who "went bush" and met Aborigines. Gurney drew Aborigines, not as background stereotypes, but as individual characters participating in his comedy. Gurney poked fun at white Australia's ignorance of Aboriginal culture. He even had his Aboriginal characters belittling his cartoonist art (Gurney 10).

Wally and the Major worked in a North Queensland sugar mill. This location for *Wally and the Major* meant Aborigines not only appeared in this strip, but some became regular characters. Cross also drew Aborigines as participants in the comical situations surrounding the strip's two characters. They were part of the fun and not the butt of the joke. Others followed. Bart Barlock drew *Stockwhip Sam* with his Aboriginal sidekick Fergus in the *Telegraph Playtime* section from 1946 (Ryan 570). In *Playtime* (1946) was a comedy strip from Eric Jolliffe, who had the largest impact upon the drawing of Aborigines. British child migrant Jolliffe worked in shearing sheds, as a boundary rider or rabbit-shooter, where he mixed with Northern Territory Aborigines. His WWII service in the RAAF, brought experiences with Western Australian Aborigines. Jolliffe became a *Smith's Weekly* caricaturist but he resigned after learning that the newspaper's "management was not in sympathy with his approach to the Aborigines" (Ryan 59). His first strip was *Tom Flynn Stockman*. While Flynn was the central character, the Pultara people were a vital part of the story lines. They had to deal with cattle stations encroaching upon their traditional lands in an early land rights tale. Jolliffe's portrayal of the Aborigines was respectful, realistic, and it showed what he had learned about differing Indigenous cultures and customs. *Tom Flynn Stockman* did not demean Aborigines. Jolliffe was able to present comic's first realistic portrayal of the impact of European civilization on the Indigenous population. Except for the rare moments of comedy relief, Jolliffe showed the Aborigines in a very sympathetic manner and from the Aboriginal point of view (Ryan 59). By 1949, *Tom Flynn Stockman* had relocated to the *Sunday Herald*, with Tom and his Aboriginal boy, off-sider Nim, now working on Western Australian pearling luggers.

Jolliffe became a successful freelance, black and white, cartoonist drawing *Saltbush Bill* and *Witchetty's Tribe* cartoons for *Pix* (later *Pix/People*) magazine and the *Sandy Blight* strip for the *Sun-Herald* (1950–ca. 1973). While there were no Aborigines in *Saltbush Bill*, Jolliffe drew them in *Sandy Blight*, where they

"Abo-Original," *BLUEY and CURLEY*, 1955.

poked fun at white Australian ignorance about Aboriginal culture. He particularly enjoyed showing that Aborigines were often smarter and more worldly than white Australians presumed. In *Sandy Blight*, a tourist approaches an Aborigine for a weather forecast. He replies, "Big Rains Coming Boss," and the astounded tourist asks, "How d'you Native rainmakers work it out? Some inborn instinct?" The Aborigine smugly replies, "Dunno about that, but it was in all the papers and on the radio" (Jolliffe 1979, 73). Underestimation was a continuous comic theme explored in *Witchetty's Tribe*, which was unique in that all its characters were Aborigines, with only the odd European drawn into the background, for a punchline. A criticism of Jolliffe's artwork was that he drew young Aboriginal women voluptuously. Certainly, some of his images looked like they were meant to be Aboriginal versions of Marilyn Monroe, Jayne Mansfield, or Raquel Welch but that was his joke aimed at Australian wowsers (i.e., moralists). Jolliffe recalled:

> A couple of bureaucrats reckoned my art was an insult to the Aboriginal race. They just wanted to draw attention to themselves and reckoned to have a piece of me was the way to go. They fell flat on their faces, of course. The drawing they seized on was of a lubra. She was wearing a bra and a couple of lubras in the foreground were saying, "It's a white man's garment she got from a missionary's wife" but she's got it on the backside instead of the boobs. They picked that out as the insult to all Aboriginal women and the joke was, I'd just been invited as guest of honour to the Aboriginal Olympic Games in Arnhem Land. It was around 1971 and it was a big deal. [. . .] I went and took with me an exhibition of cartoons of Saltbush Bill and Witchetty's Tribe and right in the middle of them was the cartoon that was supposed to be an insult to all Aborigines. (M. Jolliffe, Web)

Postwar, the US imports ban remained, which aided the further growth of Australian comics. But continued rationing of newsprint caused titles to have brief, uncertain print runs. *Pacific Pictorial Comic*, *Tex Moreton Western Comics*, and others, came and went. *Pacific Pictorial Comic* (1947) featured the strip

"She got it from the missionary's wife — it's for figure control."

Witchetty's Tribe, n.d. (Jolliffe (b), E. 22).

Pogol, Namja & The Dragon Goanna. Drawn by Rosamond Stoked, it featured an Aboriginal boy and girl, who lived within an Outback mission, as main characters. It was unusual, being aimed at a younger market. But while "Stokes had an appealing way of drawing animals and Aboriginal children . . . the storylines were too simplistic and below the interest of the average reader" (Ryan 1960). It lasted but two years. Country singer Tex Morton's few comics included his Aboriginal mate Jacky. Some local comics thrived. *The Lone Avenger* (1946–1959), *The Adventures of Devil Doone* (1946–1969), *Tim Valour* (1948–1957), *The Crimson Comet* (1948–ca. 1957), and *Captain Atom* (1948–1952). Being variants of US-influenced adventure comics, there was no room for Indigenous characters in their plots.

As the 1950s progressed, Australian strips and comics evolved. Jim Russell reinvigorated *Mr & Mrs Potts*, adding new characters to become the more family-friendly *The Potts* in 1951 and achieved international syndication as *The Potts and Uncle Dick*. Gurney died in 1955, with *Bluey and Curley*, with its Aboriginal support cast, continued by Norm Rice; then by Les Dixon. More US strips appeared, while the Australian comics industry thrived, mainly issuing black-and-white reprints of US titles with Australian-drawn color covers. K. G. Murray Comics reprinted DC comics titles. Horwitz reprinted Atlas and Marvel stories, while Wogan had, from 1946, a deal to reprint Disney titles. On September 9, 1948, a new company, Frew, published an Australian version of *The Phantom*, which is now the world's longest-running comic. (See Kevin Patrick's chapter in this volume.) Frew issued two Australian titles that thrived, the cowboy *The Phantom Ranger* in 1949 and crime fighter *The Shadow* in 1950. Frew's comics did not accommodate Indigenous roles but bizarrely, *The Shadow* was white millionaire Jimmy Gray, who, when he became "The Shadow," was drawn with a black face, but still with white arms. By 1957, reprint comics sold well and were replacing strips, as Australia's primary comic source. In 1955, DC's *Detective Comics* No. 215 introduced bushranger costume-clad Aboriginal superhero "Ranger" to readers in the United States (Marvel database, Web). In 1956, television arrived; then in 1959 the US imports ban lifted, and everything changed.

The period 1957–1970 saw the gradual extinction of Australian strips and comics, though, initially, the future looked bright. During 1957, Jolliffe drew his first two-page comic *Callaghan's Kids* for the *Australian Chuckler's Weekly*. It was peppered with Jolliffe backgrounds, including Aboriginal bark humpies. Concurrently, Paul Wheelahan introduced his popular *The Panther* set in the Congo. Horwitz produced its first Australian title in 1959. The short-lived *Carter Brown Comics* was based on its profitable pulp, crime novels. Horwitz's most successful comic was next. Aviation enthusiast John Dixon, who had drawn for aircraft comic *Tim Valour*, began a WWII and Korean War comic *The Phantom Commando* in 1960. Yaffa created Page Comics in 1965. It reprinted US titles. Horwitz and Page did put Aborigines in a shared comic title. Dixon began the long-lasting strip *Air Hawk and the Flying Doctors* in 1959. WWII veteran Jim Hawk flew charter-craft from Alice Springs in the Northern Territory. He worked with the Royal Flying Doctor Service and the Australian Inland Mission, both servicing Aboriginal communities. Dixon regularly inserted Aborigines as important and active participants into his dramas. The Outback backdrop for the strip *Air Hawk and the Flying Doctors* gave Dixon the opportunity to explore its landscape through his drawings such that its "setting allows for the introduction of Native fauna, Aborigines and their way of life and Dixon captures these all with graphic authenticity" (Ryan 85). Horwitz issued it as a three-issue comic in 1962. Page revived it in 1966 (three issues) but retitled as *The Hawk and the Flying Doctors* in Issue 22.

The 1960s saw Australian comics decline due to the dominance of US (e.g., Dell, Gold Key) or UK comics (e.g., Fleetway, *Commando*) and television. It was rare to have overseas imports contain stories set in Australia. In 1961, Dell published *Marge's Lulu and Tubby in Australia*, No. 42. Its only Indigenous imagery was Aboriginal "stick-figures" drawn onto *A-Maze-In' Australia* on the inside-back cover. *The Panther* ended in 1963, *The Phantom Commando* in 1966, *The Phantom Ranger* in 1967, *The Shadow* in ca. 1968. One attempt at a new Australian crime comic was *Napoleon Bonaparte*. Based on Arthur Upfield's 1950s detective novels, it centered on half-caste Aboriginal police inspector "Bony" (Upfield 1970) and drawn in 1961 by Paul Wheelahan. He could not find a publisher. Another country singer was celebrated in the eleven issues of *The Adventures of Smoky Dawson*. Smoky imitated an American cowboy, but in the Australian bush, so his comic got a limited run. New strips were few and finished. In 1969,

Ralph Peverill's *The Didgeridoos* appeared in the *Sun-News Pictorial*. Peverill, from Alice Springs, drew Northern Territory fauna that dealt with adult comical situations. Animal characters were no longer seen as being targeted at children. This strip did have one human, the Aborigine "Munga." Apart from strips, newspapers occasionally printed political cartoons about an Indigenous issue, as in the 1967 Constitutional Referendum to recognize Aboriginal and Torres Strait Islander rights. The 1960s saw the development of Aboriginal characters in children's literature. In 1963, June and Bruce Macpherson produced *The Magic Boomerang*. No artist drew its characters, who were depicted in photographs using plastic dolls. The "Kinjiwa" character was the "Spirit of the Never Never" (the Outback). In 1968, Bernard Tate and Joan Watson Smith produced *Jindi's Australian ABC, The Mopoke and the Necklace, The Rosella and the Rain Cloud*, and *Jindi the Picanniny Fairy*. "Picanniny" was white Australian slang term for an Aboriginal toddler. "Jindi," the main character, with her Aboriginal mother "Queen Jindina" were drawn with European features and olive complexions, mirroring the familiar "Disney princess" animation style. In comparison, "Kinjiwa," in *The Magic Boomerang*, looked Aboriginal, with dark skin and tribal body-markings.

During the 1970s, many strips such as *Bluey and Curley, Wally and the Major* (retitled *Pudden*), and *The Potts* were dropped as old strips were deemed outdated. New strips were tried, but canceled. In 1973, Jolliffe followed the norm of publishing his art in annuals, under the title *Jolliffe's Outback*. Aboriginal imagery appeared in *Witchetty's Tribe* and *Sandy Blight*. *Jolliffe's Outback* featured portrait sketches of individual Aborigines plus reissues of Aboriginal depictions from *Saltbush Bill* or *Witchetty's Tribe*. In 1975, the *Sun-News Pictorial* replaced *Bluey and Curley* with a strip that proved a winner. Allan ("Sols") Salisbury drew *The Old Timer*, set in the Bush. It started with a few cartoon characters including two Aborigines, "The Lost Tribesman" and his unnamed wife. The joke was that the "Tribesman" was hopeless at all he tried—the perennial Loser. Another Aborigine, "The Witch Doctor," was added. They interacted with other animal and human cartoon characters. As a jibe at Australia's military weakness, Salisbury made "The Tribesman" the lone sentry for the "Northern Defence Force Headquarters" (Salisbury 11). In 1976, Salisbury added a lovelorn snake to his strip. "Snake" soon became the central character so that the strip's title was changed to *Snake Tales* in 1978. It is now known simply as *Snake*.

K. G. Murray, Rosnock, Newton, and Yaffa published black-and-white reprints of Warren, Marvel, DC, or Gold Key American comics across the 1970s. After thirty-two years, Wogan published its last color Disney comic in 1978. In 1976, Wogan finally released a Disney comic, set in Australia. *Uncle Scrooge* No. G652 featured a story, where Scrooge, Donald Duck, and nephews Huey, Dewey, and Louie fly to the Outback to solve a wild dogs (dingoes) problem. They encounter a wild-girl, leader of the pack attacking the sheep. She is not drawn as Aboriginal but rather as a white girl (duck) dressed in fur with kangaroo-feet slippers. New Australian comics were launched without Indigenous characters. In 1970, two issues of Junior Readers Press's comic *Skippy the Bush Kangaroo*, based on the famous television show, were drawn by Keith Chato. Set in Waratah National Park, issue No. 1 did depict Aboriginal rock art. In 1975, actor Fred Cullen drew *The Adventures of the Jolly Swagman*, an AMPOL fuel promotion, single comic. Aborigines appeared in a 1971 British comic, Peter O'Donnell's *Modesty Blaise: The Stone Age Caper*. Its sexualized heroine and friends hide among Outback Aborigines, where she "goes Native," drawn bare-breasted and disguised with ash and grease. However, the Aborigines are drawn with 1970s "Afro" hairstyles. They reuse white-racist slang by telling Modesty that "Miss Blaise—you and the lady make fine Abo girls!" (O'Donnell & Romero panels 296–98). Australian children's literature provided one image, when an Aboriginal corroboree was drawn in the animated film tie-in *Dot and the Kangaroo Meet Mr. Playtpus* in 1977.

The 1980s marked the demise of Australian comics plus the common usage of the term "graphic novel" for designated comics. K. G. Murray issued reprints of Hanna-Barbera cartoons (color) plus DC comics (black and white). Government-commissioned Streetwize comics (1984–2007) was youth oriented and included Aboriginal issues. It was inadequately resourced and so poorly received. Chris Lopez and John Bredent put an Aboriginal male superhero in self-published *Forerunners* No. 1, 1987 (Foster 2009, 170). Budget cuts made newspapers downsize the "Funnies." Their cartoonists such as Bruce Petty, Bill Mitchell, Alan Moir, Donald Greenfield, and Larry Pickering issued compilations in paperback books or additionally, as calendars (Pickering). Aborigines and Torres Strait Islanders were drawn, if the cartoon of that day involved Indigenous issues (e.g., land rights). In 1988, political cartoonist Sean Leahy began the *Beyond the Black Stump* strip, which, had Outback animal, not human, characters, reflecting rising sensitivity about Indigenous cartoons: "Over recent years community attitudes . . . have resulted in a changed editorial response. It is a question, too, that has divided cartoonists, for many today admit to avoiding deliberately the depiction of Aborigines in any comic-ridicule situation" (Vane 63).

The most popular 1980s strip, later paperback comic book, came from New Zealand. Murray Ball's *Footrot Flats* did highlight Māori characters. From overseas, came Marvel's first Aboriginal superhero "Gateway." He appeared in 1988 in *Uncanny X-Men* #229. His special powers were telepathy and teleportation via a bullroarer musical instrument. Marvel's description of "Gateway" renders a mishmash of Aboriginal beliefs.

"Nothing has been revealed about the origins of the Indigenous Australian known only as Gateway prior to his forced servitude to the Reavers, a band of criminal cyborgs. The Reavers held him hostage by threatening to irretrievably destroy one of his people's sacred places, forcing his ancestral spirits to become demonically enslaved and walk forever lost in other-dimensional 'Dreamtime'" (Marvel database Web). In this volume, Dennin Ellis goes into greater detail about the Reavers.

The mutant "Bishop" (1991) was another Aborigine, except his Marvel-drawn image varied from Australian to black American (Cleverman Web). Aborigines appeared in the Scottish *Commando* comics in 1989. Issue No. 3976 *Outback Army* featured a multiracial force defending northwestern Australia from Japanese invasion. While the Aborigines were well drawn, the plot included implausible concepts like Australian recognition of Aboriginal sacred sites back in 1942 (Cass & Ford Web). In Australia, the most successful use of a comics character came during the AIDS crisis. Aunty Gracelyn Smallwood and some Townsville Aboriginal health workers designed "Condoman," in 1987, to promote the safe-sex message in Indigenous communities. Based on *The Phantom* comic, familiar to these communities, it was successful because "Condoman was created by Aboriginal and Torres Strait Islander people, and for Aboriginal and Torres Strait Islander people" (Condoman/History Web).

During the 1990s, most comics disappeared suddenly throughout Australia. Blame was laid on video games, a comics collection investment portfolio strategy, or on steep rises in comic prices. Self-published *Southern Cross Comics* featured some Aboriginal heroes (Cleverman Web). In contrast, Aboriginal stories bloomed within children's literature. Dick Roughsey produced *The Rainbow Serpent*, while Aborigines poet Oodgeroo Nunukul and artist Brownyn Bancroft produced *Dreamtime: Aboriginal Stories* in 1994. Bancroft illustrated *The Outback* (author Annaliese Porter) in 2008 and *Ready to Dream* (authors Donna Joan Napoli, Elena Furrow) in 2009. James Vance Marshall wrote, and Francis Firebrace illustrated, *Stories from the Billabong* in 2010. Bancroft produced *Why I Love Australia* (2016) and *Colors of Australia* in 2017.

Comic output was sporadic after 2000. Jolliffe continued drawing until his death in 2001. *Witchetty's Tribe*, *Saltbush Bill*, and *Jolliffe's Outback* remain popular, attracting high prices online. In 2009, the *Condoman* campaign was relaunched with superhero partner "Luberlicious" added.

In 2009, Marvel developed teleporter "Eden Fesi / Manifold" as a "Gateway" stories link (Marvel database Web). In 2008, DC added Melbourne tattooist "Dark Ranger" as Batman's urban, Aboriginal ally. DC created (2014) "Thunderer," a Mowanjum weather god (DC Database Web). Japan had an Aboriginal character, redhead "Kiddy Ensil" in the 2012 manga series *Silent Möbius* (Cleverman Web). The World War I Centenary prompted a limited Australian comics revival. Hugh Dolan created Z Beach True Comics in 2012. It managed two issues: *Gallipoli: The Landing* and *Kokoda: That Bloody Track*. A graphic novel featuring Indigenous characters was published in 2015. Dolan and Adrian Threlfall produced *Reg Saunders: An Indigenous War Hero*. Saunders

Condoman & Lubelicious poster, 2018. (Condoman images Web)

fought in the Australian army in World War II and Korea. He was the first Aboriginal commissioned officer, occurring when Aborigines were not citizens.

New Zealand

In the early twentieth century, New Zealand imported British illustrated humor magazines, but by the 1930s many newspapers were printing full-color weekly comic supplements. While these chiefly comprised American content, they also contained locally produced material like the *Tee Wees Adventures*, which appeared in the *Christchurch Star* (Bollinger 1). The advent of American adventure strips led to fears about the effect of comics on children, and New Zealand, no stranger to moral panics, introduced import controls in 1938. "Several comics were banned for placing 'undue emphasis' on horror, crime, sex, obscenity and cruelty" (Kinnaird 15). The official view was:

> British comics were considered culturally, morally and artistically "superior" by the state authorities, teachers and librarians alike. Those with fewer speech balloons and more explanatory text, as in the British style, were considered more sophisticated and thus more "beneficial" to younger readers. (Bollinger 2)

The blocking of American imports led to the development of a small local comic industry. New Zealand printers produced collections of American or Australian newspaper strips. Local artists were often used to produce the cover art for these publications (Bollinger 3). Historians list forty-seven titles published in New Zealand during the 1940s and 1950s by Feature Productions in Lower Hutt and the Times Printing Co. in Auckland (Bollinger 3). These included Eric Resetar's *Crash Carson of the Future*, Jack Raeburn's *Sparkles*, and Harry W. Bennett's *Supreme Feature Comic*. The import ban meant that what Bollinger called "American comic culture" did not penetrate New Zealand until the 1950s. Even then comic fans faced an additional crisis with the publication of Frederick

Wertham's *The Seduction of the Innocent*, which claimed comics warped young minds. Despite the fact that none of the comics Wertham listed were available in New Zealand, a government-appointed committee had prohibited as many as 260 comics by 1958. As a result, the only American comic available in New Zealand for a long time was *Classic Comics* that featured stodgy adaptations of famous novels (Bollinger 5). Because of the ban on US comics, the main influences in New Zealand were British and European comics such as the Fleetway picture libraries (*War Picture Library*, etc.), *2000AD*, *Eagle*, *Look and Learn* (particularly *The Trigan Empire*), *Tintin* (Belgian), *Blake and Mortimer*, and *Asterix* (French). Horrocks depicts this lovingly in the introduction to his magnum opus, *Hicksville* (Horrocks, *Hicksville* i–vii). Japanese manga was also influential, as was the French magazine *Metal Hurlant*. The British war comic *Commando* also had a decisive effect upon New Zealand comics (Cass and Ford, "What Are You Waiting For, Diggers?").

The defining aspect of the New Zealand comics industry has always been its size. New Zealand has a small population and anybody who wanted—or wants—to make a living from their artistic skills had to leave. In the twentieth century, this meant artists moved across the Tasman to Sydney or even farther afield to London. Thus, David Low became London's *Daily Mail's* cartoonist and was on Hitler's death list. New Zealand's market has always been too small to sustain more than a handful of artists making and selling their own comics:

> New Zealand cartoonists were more likely to be employed as local caricaturists, editorial satirists or commercial illustrators. Others made a living overseas, in the growing comic book industries of Australia and Britain. Early expatriate pioneers in the Australian scene of the 1930s and '40s [included] Noel Cook, "Unk" White and Ted Brodie—Mack drew genre western, sci-fi, romance and jungle adventure comics for both the Australian and New Zealand markets. Cook is said by some to have "invented" the sci-fi comic idiom with his "Peter" strip for the Australian *Sunday Times* in 1924. (Horrocks, *NZ Comics* 2)

A small number have found both local and international fame. New Zealand's best-known comic artist—at least to a general audience—was the late Murray Ball, whose long-running strip *Footrot Flats* focused on the enduring relationships of "The Dog," "Wal," "Cooch," and a dozen other characters on a wet, windswept, sheep farm. Kinnaird said he left *Footrot Flats* out of New Zealand's best-known comics history, *From Earth's End*, because it did not have a narrative, but in fact one can sense a very long story arc, the coming and going of the seasons and the cycles of birth and death that run beneath the day-to-day lives of the main characters (Bamber; Kinnaird 435).

Even in the twenty-first century, New Zealand comics—at least those produced for local consumption—remain essentially a cottage industry, produced

Hicksville by Horrocks, 2012 (Horrocks, 233).

in small numbers, printed on photocopiers, sold at comics or science fiction conventions, or in a small number of comic shops. The advent of digital distribution has meant artists can market their work online but this does not necessarily generate an income. The other outlet for comics is in anthologies and the histories of comics that have appeared in recent years. While acting as a showcase for local work, they have exposed fractures in the local scene, with one anthology, *Three Words*, being published as an angry response to the almost complete absence of women artists in Kinnaird's *From Earth's End*. If women were conspicuous by their almost complete absence from Horrocks's and Kinnaird's histories, then Māori artists are equally absent from the dominant narrative. It may not be insignificant that Māori artists are only identified as such in *Three Words* where they represent a doubly excluded group—artists who are both women and Indigenous. Beyond a simple enumeration of Māori artists, this further raises the question of the presence of Māori as Tangatā Whenuā (people of the land), of Tikanga Māori (Māori culture), and Te Reo Māori (Māori language) in New Zealand comics.

Māori have been a constant presence in New Zealand art—at least the western variety—since the nineteenth century. Lindauer and Goldies' portraits of Māori are well known—respectful, heroic, even glamorous within their formal painterly confines (Auckland Art Gallery). Representations of Māori were often westernized, so that, for instance, Steele and Goldie's painting *The Arrival of the Māoris in New Zealand* is really just a local version of Gericault's *Raft of the Medusa* (Auckland Art Gallery). Elsewhere, pākehā and Māori fought, warred, competed, and intertwined with each other's cultures in unexpected and often uncomfortable ways. Māori artistic expressions and language became a part of everyday New Zealand life, from the koru on the tail of Air New Zealand aeroplanes to the absorption of Te Reo words into pākehā English. Yet, relations between pākehā and Māori or portrayals of Māori were never straightforward. Local political cartoonists were capable of depicting Māori as lazy, comical, and child-like figures (Diamond). They appeared in comics from the 1940s, with a family discovering a lost tribe of Māori in *The Secret Valley* (Kinnaird 21). George F. H. Taylor created *Little Hongi: Adventures in Māoriland* for Auckland publisher John G. Helleur. One story shows Hongi hearing the story of how Maui drew-up the North Island of New Zealand, Te Ika ā Māui. He then goes fishing and when his line snags on a reef the little boy is convinced he has drawn-up his own island (Emery). In the 1970s, comic artist Dick Frizzell was commissioned to produce a rather more sanguinary version of the Maui story for the *New Zealand School Journal*. He said the journal's editors hated it. Not only was it in Te Reo, but the retired teachers in charge of the journal, which was supplied free to schoolchildren throughout the country, were wary of the artwork:

> They were very nervous about the whole project. Because I was really going for it in the artwork—there was bodies flying, blood splattering everywhere [. . .] in that superhero style everything was rampant, totally erect the whole time, veins popping and all that. (Kinnaird 416)

The violence of Frizzell's comic may have been at odds with what had long been perceived to be the ideal of peaceful race relations in New Zealand, in which Māori had been elevated under British rule almost to the status of "honorary members of the white tribe" (Loveridge 63). In 1956, the minister of Māori Affairs had declared that Māori and pākehā were "a homogeneous people united in the common purpose of individual welfare and national stability" (Diamond 5). However, in the same decade, visiting Fulbright scholar David Ausubel warned that this apparently happy state of affairs was a delusion and that "the only realistic prospect for the future [was] the emergence of a brown proletariat segregated in the urban slums and living in a state of chronic tension with their white neighbours" (Diamond 5). By the 1980s, Māori were facing precisely the situation predicted by Ausubel and began to demand that they be accorded the rights and respect due to them under the Treaty of Waitangi, regarded as New Zealand's founding document. Decades of struggle led to greater political and cultural accommodation and an official recognition of New Zealand as a bicultural community. The revival of Te Reo Māori has been one of the more prominent markers of this period, as has the re-emphasis on Māori artistic expression. However, the reality is that predominant depictions of Māori myths, stories, people, language, and culture have come from pākehā artists. It could be argued that the absorption of Māori culture into mainstream pākehā life—uneven and incomplete as it is—has meant that pākehā artists have been able to depict Māori with a reasonable degree of sympathy, accuracy, and confidence. How people react to those depictions will, however, vary enormously. For instance, the only recurring Māori character in *Footrot Flats* is young "Rangi Wiremu Waka Jones" known simply as "Rangi." He is described by "The Dog" as

> Rangi Jones from up Mad Martha's line. His old bloke is a slaughterman at The Works and his mum teaches standard 3 and 4 at Raupa School. She's the tough sheila with moko who shot old Jack McGregor with a slug gun for drivin' his cows through an old burial ground. She also bucketed the contents of her septic tank onto the steps of the council office because they had refused to move the town sewerage outlet away from the Pawai Point mussel beds. She was suspended from school for a term for organising a petition calling for a boycott of the Olympic Games unless the British withdrew from the occupied islands of the South Pacific. (Corballis and Small 188)

While Corbiss and Small find this a depiction of "troublesome Māori" the description, then again, could be interpreted as meaning that Rangi's whanau are simply advocating for their rights.

The twenty-first century has seen the appearance of a number of works aimed at mainstream audiences, in which Māori are central characters. In Horrocks's 2010 reworking of *Hicksville*, for instance, there is a subplot which becomes the key to everything the other characters are doing. In the book, the Māori leader Hōne Heke and the British explorer Captain Cook wander the landscape, trying to chart where the country is going and finding new ways to tell the story of the land and its people. Depicted in the role of Kaitiaki o te Whenua, Heke asks: "The land has never been still like a corpse. How do you map a man's life? The earth is playing a joke on you" (Horrocks, *Hicksville* 156). While the comics-obsessed residents of Hicksville struggle with their lives, it is Hōne Heke who ensures that the story comes to a proper conclusion. Historically, Captain Cook sighted New Zealand on October 6, 1769, landing at Poverty Bay on October 8. During his first encounter, he saw several Māori were killed, but he established friendly contact thereafter. Ngāpuhi chief Hōne Wiremu Heke Pōkai supported the signing of the Treaty of Waitangi. However, he became disillusioned by the encroachment of British authority. As a sign of unhappiness, he hewed a British flagpole and flag. This led to war between the British and some northern Māori. In real life a scourge of the British colonists, in *Hicksville,* Hōne Heke simply laughs at the foolishness of the pākehā and leads them in the right direction. He may appear on only a few pages, but he is actually the central driver of the larger, metaphysical aspect of the story. What is significant about Hōne Heke's depiction in *Hicksville* is that, like Rangi in *Footrot Flats*, he is one of the few Māori figures not to fit into one of the stereotypes listed above. It might be easy to dismiss him as a simple shamanistic figure, but his sense of humor and endless patience with his pākehā companions make him a fully rounded human being. Chris Grozs's *Kimble Bent Malcontent*, which appeared the following year, is set during the Taranaki War, which erupted in 1860 as resistance to British purchase of Māori land. Grozs tells the story of an army deserter, who became a pākehā Māori, a white man living as a Māori. Bent is essentially a slave, a pākehā chattel to be passed around from owner to owner and never fully trusted. *Kimble Bent* owes a debt to the kinds of comics that formed the bulk of so many New Zealand children's reading. While the pictures look like woodcuts, the text-heavy pages and narrative blocks are a clear link to *Commando* comics and the didactic, scene-setting introduction is reminiscent of the "educational" *Classic Comics*.

Neither Horrocks nor Kinnaird list any artists who identify as Māori. Joyce et al. identify four women Māori artists. These include artist, musician, and performer Coco Solid (real name Jessica Hansell), who is of Ngapuhi, Samoan, and German ancestry. She produced *This is not a Comic* from 2005 to 2008, an annual 'zine *Philosophygirl* and *Hook Ups*. Other artists include Susan Te Kahurangi King, Maiangi Waitai (Nga Wairiki, Ngati Apa, Ngati Tuwhaeretoa, Rangitane), and Adele Jackson, who is of Ngati Raukawa descent. Her short comic *Minnie's Story* is a painful evocation of what could happen to Māori women living on the fringes of pākehā society in the nineteenth century (Joyce et al. 53–55). The fact that an artist appears in a collection does not mean other artists do not exist, of course, simply that they have not come to the attention of the particular editor.

The desire to revive Te Reo Māori and create a new generation fluent in the language, led, earlier this century, to the New Zealand Education Department supporting the publication of a number of graphic novels dealing with the experiences of Māori during the Second World War. *Hautipua Rerarangi / Born to Fly* (Arahanga 2012) and *Ngarimu Te Tohu Toa / Victory at Point 209* (Burdan 2012) are in Te Reo and English and are about the achievements of Māori servicemen. In *Ngarimu Te Tohu Toa*, Māori deities appear over the North African battlefield as the Māori Battalion advances on the German lines. A similar image of Māori war deities appearing behind the Māori Battalion can be found in a World War One cartoon published in the *New Zealand Observer* in December 1915. This shows a Māori soldier attacking the Turkish lines at Gallipoli with semi-divine support (Loveridge 66). Burdan also drew *Haka / Whiti Te Ra* (2015), which tells how New Zealand's best-known haka, *Ka Mate*, was composed by the Ngāti Toa chief Te Rauparaha and *Ngarara*

Māori surrounding Kimble Bent (Grozs, 33).

Huarau (2018) about a taniwha (water monster) that travels from Hawke's Bay to Wairarapa in search of his sister, Pari-kawhiti, and its battle with local warriors. Elsewhere, Chilean-born New Zealand artist Gonzalo Novaro has published, in English and Te Reo, *Aotearoa Whispers*, combining "historical fact, traditional mythology and modern concepts" (Horrocks, *NZ Comics* 74). Chris Slane, one of New Zealand's best-known artists, has published a number of graphic novels depicting Māori stories in Te Reo with the support of the Ministry of Education. From 2008 to 2009 he produced *Huria Matanga, Kahe Te Rauoterangi, Hine Poupou, No Hea Te Hau, Ko Wai hokitera Mauka*, and *Tukuna Aku Waikano*. The last three have online interactive versions (Chris Slane Comics). More recently, Sid Marsh has turned to the battle between British forces and Te Kooti Arikirangi te Turuki, founder of the Ringatu religion in *Crow of Whareatua*, the art of which can best be described as manga meets Aubrey Beardsley.

Some graphic novels telling Māori stories or drawing on Māori mythology depict their characters in something closely resembling standard, western, superhero mould. The illustrations in *Arohanui: Revenge of the Fey*, for instance, are described as "a well-drawn fusion of contemporary super-natural comic book characters and Māori warriors" (Tau 47). Yet, some Māori artists specifically reject the western model. Te Arawa artist Chaz Mikaere is launching a collection of works in the form of a comic book that depicts eight Te Arawa women who are kappa haka performers and who are descended from particular Māori-ancestor figures. The western model rejection is encapsulated as: "We don't have to look at the likes of Marvel for ways of living, for ways of being Māori now, for ways of being leaders and understanding pressure" (McLean).

As with Mikaere's projects, much of the work being done by Māori artists has an educational, social, or cultural purpose. For educators trying to reach younger readers, digital technology has become increasingly important. The Māori Language Commission / Te Taura Whiri i te Reo Māori commissioned a number of comics and graphic stories from Kiwi Digital to encourage reading fluency in Te Reo. A collection of Māori myths, *Ngā Atua Māori*, was created for schools. The series of graphic novels tells the story of Māori gods beginning with *Te Orokotīmatanga o te Ao*. It can be downloaded for free in Te Reo and English and can be watched, read, and listened to on a range of devices or on You Tube (Gillies). Elsewhere, Christchurch-based Maui Studios is working with writer Maia Tapsell, whose ancestry includes Ngati Whakaue and Ngati Pikiao, on the story of Tametekapua, who led the canoe Te Arawa from Hawaiki to New Zealand. The comic will be published in Te Reo and English for appeal: "For young people who are struggling with their literacy or their Te Reo, they can maybe benefit from reading stories like this which are based in a visual way" (Guy; Hurihanganui).

It should be unsurprising that depictions of Indigenous New Zealanders spill over into comics produced by other countries. Concern over depictions of Indigenous people is not uncommon and frequently justified. Too often Indigenous characters in popular culture are confined to a set number of stereotypes: Noble savage, warrior, shaman, tracker, "natural" man or woman, or semi-divine heroes. Sheyahshe, author of *Native Americans in Comic Books*, argues:

> Whether it's the whooping, attacking horde of Indians in the early "cowboy" movies, the notion of Native American as a crack-shot and/or expert tracker in comics [...] pop culture media serves to mirror the emotional consensus of how mainstream America sees us. (Henzi 23–38)

There was considerable apprehension among Pasifika peoples before the launch of Disney's *Moana* in 2017, with many expressions of concern about how it would depict Polynesian culture (Cass 2016). At the other end of the scale Māori director Taika Waititi turned *Thor: Ragnorak* into a celebration of Māori and Aboriginal culture, with the character Valkyrie being given a quasi-Māori identity and turning up in a spaceship painted in the colors of the Aboriginal land rights flag (Taipua). Marvel comics have often created figures to represent different Indigenous cultures. Māori have been used in minor roles but they hardly seem to be anything other than exotic background characters. The Māori character "Kiwi Black" first appeared in *Uncanny X Men* No. 429 in 2003 but eventually disappeared (Marvel Universe). Elsewhere Marvel has appropriated a range of Hawai'ian and Pasifika deities as characters as well.

Depictions of the First Peoples from "Down Under"   71

Māori "horse-whisperer" (Low, 227).

The WWII Māori Battalion was depicted in the *Fleetway* war comics. Another example of depictions of Māori people from nonlocal sources comes from British *Commando* comics, which has long dominated the image of Australians and New Zealanders at war. Because they are single-issue stories, they provide succinct studies of how Indigenous people have been depicted. One of *Commando*'s earliest stories, *The Māori Challenge*, described the New Zealand land wars and has been dealt with at some length elsewhere by the authors (Cass and Ford "What Are You Waiting For, Diggers?"). In a later story, *Trial by Battle*, we meet Willie "Wing Heels" Taonea, who is fighting German *fallschirmjaeger* during the battle for Crete. Willie is a "full blooded Māori" and "one of his country's top athletes" who was expected to run at London's White City athletics ground. Despite this we are told that before the war he was a student at "a leading British university" (Low 211). Somehow Willie's intellectual skills are not put to the test during the story. Instead, he is the archetypal, cunning Māori warrior, slipping through the bush and outwitting the German paratroopers. Perhaps because he is a "full blooded Māori," Willie has an instinctive affinity with wildlife and can calm a horse he has rescued from a burning stable. When asked by his incredulous companion how he did this he replies: "I sang an old Māori song to him. Animals seem to like it" (Low 227).

Realistically, the limited Australian and New Zealand comics markets means that they remain small-scale industries, where Indigenous depictions have been intermittent. White-men artists drew Māoris as warriors or Aborigines as

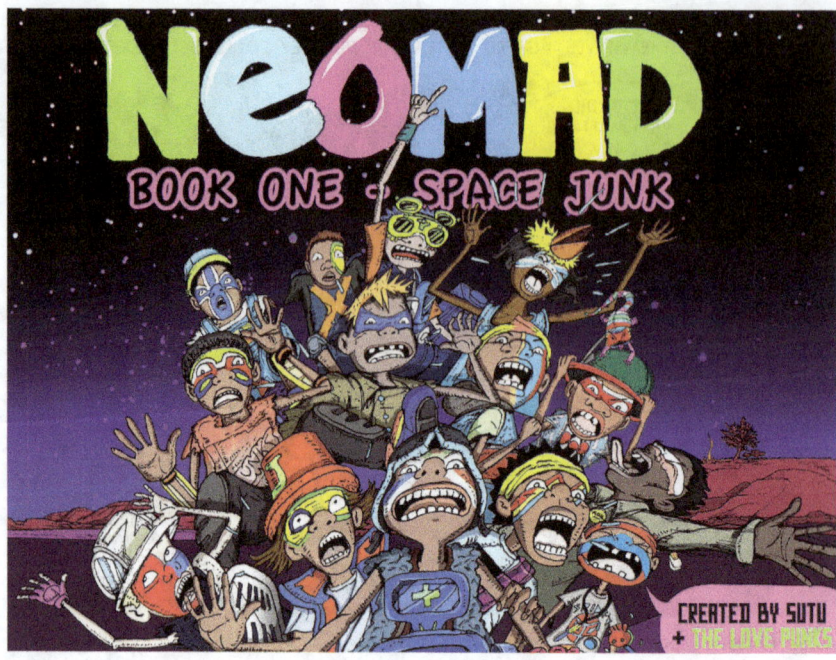

Neomad opening page, 2016. (Gestalt Web)

bushmen. In both countries, depictions by non-Indigenous comic artists have been in the hands of those who have been sympathetic toward and knowledgeable on their subjects. The worst excesses of Indigenous imagery have been largely avoided in both countries, although it is clear that depictions by overseas artists have left much to be desired. This is changing. The recent phenomena of Indigenous artists creating comics containing their own culture and characters appears to be much stronger in New Zealand than Australia. Yet, in 2016, a group of young, remote, Ieramugadu Aborigines won the Gold LEDGER award for their *NEOMAD* digital comic (*The Guardian* Web). With online publishing, graphic novels produced by Māori, Aborigines, or Torres Strait Islanders may yet overtake children's literature's Indigenous imagery.

Works Cited

Arahanga, Julian. *Hautipua Rerarangi / Born to Fly*. Wellington: Huia Publishers, 2012.
"The Arrival of the Māoris in New Zealand." *Auckland Art Gallery*. Web. June 2, 2018.
Bamber, Shaun. *Footrot Flats: Murray Ball's Enduring Gift to New Zealand*. Web. June 12, 2018.
Bollinger, Tim. "Comics in the Antipodes: A Low Art in a High Place." *Nga Pakiwaituhi o Aoeteoroa / New Zealand Comics*. Auckland: Horrocks, D & Hicksville Press, 1998.
Burdan, Andrew. *Te Tohu Toa / Victory at Point 209*. Wellington: Huia Publishers, 2012.
Burdan, Andrew, and Grace Phaka. *Haka / Whiti Te Ra*. Wellington: Huia Publishers, 2015.
Cass, Phil. "Disney Withdraws Moana Costume." *Kaniva News*, 2016. Web. June 12, 2018.

Cass, Philip, and Jack Ford. "What Are You Waiting For, Diggers? The ANZAC Image in Commando Comics." *Pacific Journalism Review* 56, no. 2 (2017): 197–215.

———. "New Guinea Gold: Commando Comics in the Pacific." 8th International Graphic Novel and Comics Conference, University of Dunedin, June 27, 2017. Web. June 15, 2018.

"Cleverman: The First Aboriginal Superhero?" *Koori History.com—Aboriginal History & Culture of South Eastern Australia*. Web. June 5, 2016.

"Condoman." *Campaign in Australia Images*, 2018. Web. July 26, 2018.

"Condoman." *History*, 2018. Web. July 26, 2018.

Cook, James. *Teara: The Encyclopaedia of New Zealand*. Web. June 4, 2018.

Corballis, Richard, and Vernon Small. "New Zealand Cartoon Strips." *Journal of Popular Culture* 2, no. 19 (1975): 175–89.

"David Low: New Zealand Cartoonist on Hitler's Blacklist." Christchurch Art Gallery, 1996. Web. June 6, 2018.

Diamond, Paul. "A Window into Race Relations: Using Cartoons as a Historical Source." *New Zealand Cartoon Archive*. Web. June 7, 2018.

Dittmer, Jason, and Soren Larsen. "Aboriginality and the Arctic North in Canadian Nationalist Superhero Comics, 1940–2004." *Historical Geography* 38 (2010): 52–69.

Duff, Michelle. "Coco Solid: 'It's time for a switch-up.'" *Stuff*, July 26, 2015. Web. June 7, 2018.

"Eden Fesi (Earth-616)." *Marvel Database*. Web. July 26, 2018.

Emery, Matt. "Little Hongi—George F H Taylor." Pikitia Press. March 5, 2012. Web. June 7, 2018.

"Eric Jolliffe." Interview with Mick Jolliffe, Web. July 2, 2018.

"Explore Art and Ideas." *Auckland Art Gallery*. Web. June 1, 2018.

Foster, John. "A Social History of Australia as Seen through Its Children's Comic Books." *Journal of Australian Studies* 22, no. 59 (May 2009): 165–72.

Foster, John. "From 'Ulla Dulla Moggo' to 'Serene Azure Vault of Heaven': Literary Style in Australian Children's Comic Books." *Journal of Popular Culture* 25, no. 3 (Winter 1991): 63–77.

"Gateway (Earth 616)." *Marvel database*. Web. July 10, 2018.

Gillies, Shannon. "Māori Myths Hit the Digital Age." *Radio New Zealand*. June 25, 2005. Web. March 30, 2018.

Grozs, Chris. *Kimble Bent, Malcontent*. Auckland: Random House, 2011.

Gurney, Alex. *Bluey and Curley*. Melbourne: Sun-News Pictorial, 1955.

Guy, Alice. "Comic Book Writer Maia Tapsell Telling Traditional Te Arawa Stories." *New Zealand Herald*. Web. March 20, 2018.

Heke Hōne. *Teara: The Encyclopaedia of New Zealand*. Web. July 1, 2018.

Henzi, Sarah. "A Necessary Antidote: Graphic Novels, Comics and Indigenous Writing." *Canadian Review of Comparative Literature* 43, no. 1 (2016): 23–28.

Horrocks, Dylan. *Nga Pakiwaituhi o Aoeteoroa / New Zealand Comics*. Auckland: Hicksville Press, 1998.

———. *Hicksville*. Wellington: Victoria University Press, 2010.

———. *New Zealand Comics and Graphic Novels*. Wellington: Hicksville Press, 2012.

Hurihanganui, T. "Māori Designers: From Traditional to Contemporary." *RNZ*, September 12, 2017. Web. June 13, 2018.

"Indigenous Australia Timeline: 1901 to 1969." *Australian Museum*. Web. June 2, 2018.

Jolliffe, Eric. *Jolliffe's Outback: Cartoons & Australiana Study to Frame*, No. 104. Dee Why: Jolliffe Publications, 1979.

———. *The Best of Witchetty's Tribe by Joliffe*. Dee Why: Jolliffe Publications, 1980.

Joyce, Rae, Sarah Laing, and Indira Neville, eds. *Three Words: An Anthology of Aotearoa / NZ Women's Comics*. Auckland: Beatnik Publishing, 2016.

Kinnaird, Adrian. *From Earth's End: The Best of New Zealand Comics*. Auckland: Godwit, 2013.

"Kiwi Black." *Marvel Universe*. Web. July 9, 2018.

Lindsay, Vane. *The Inked-in Image: A Social and Historical Survey of Australian Comic Art*. Richmond: Hutchinson Group, 1979.

Loveridge, Steven. "Sentimental Equipment: New Zealand, the Great War and Cultural Mobilisation." PhD thesis, Victoria University, Wellington, 2013. Web. June 25, 2018.

Low, George. *50 Years: A Home for Heroes*. London: Carlton, 2011.

———. "Outback Army." *Anzacs at War*. Sydney: HarperCollins, 2007.

———. "Test by Battle." *Anzacs at War*. Sydney: HarperCollins, 2007.

Marsh, Sid. *Crow of Whareatua*. Auckland: Lasavia Publishing, 2017.

McLean, M. "Artist releases works of Te Arawa superheroes." May 8, 2018. *Māori Television*. Web. March 29, 2018.

"Neomad Wins Gold at the 2016 Ledger Award." *Gestalt*, 2016. Web. July 26, 2018.

"Ngā Atua Māori Playlist." *YouTube*. Web. July 9, 2018.

Nungalla and Jungalla comic strip, 1942. Web. July 4, 2018.

O'Donnell, Peter, and Enric Romero. "Modesty Blaise: The Stone Age Caper." *Modesty Blaise: The Puppet Master*. London: Titan, 2006.

"The Origins of Ka Mate." *NgatiToa Rangitara*. Web. July 10, 2018.

"Ranger (New Earth)." *DC Database*. Web. July 10, 2018.

Ryan, John. *Panel by Panel, An Illustrated History of Australian Comics*. Stanmore: Cassell, 1979.

Salisbury, Alan. *Snake Too!!: Selected Strips from the Snake Tales Cartoon*. Elsternwick: Boomer, 1978.

Sheyahshe, Michael. *Native Americans in Comic Books: A Critical Study*. Jefferson, NC: McFarland, 2008.

Slane Chris. *Maui*. Wellington: New Zealand Ministry of Education, 2008.

———. "Comics and Graphic Novels Bibliography." *Chris Slane Comics*. Web. July 10, 2018.

"Snowbird." *Marvel Universe*. Web. July 12, 2018.

Taipua, Dan. "Thor and His Magic Patu: Notes on a Very Māori Marvel Movie." *The Spinoff*. October 31, 2017. Web. June 16, 2018.

Tan, Monica. "Aboriginal Sci-Fi Neomad Wins Australia's Top Comic Book Award." *Guardian*; Australian edition. April 18, 2016. Web. April 19, 2016.

"Taranaki War." *New Zealand History*. Web. June 16, 2018.

Tau, Te Rakitaunuku. "Review of Arohanui: Revenge of the Fey." *Te Karaka*, Spring 2015.

«Te Orokotīmatanga o te Ao». *Kiwa Digital*. Web. July 10, 2018.

"Thunderer (Earth 7)." *DC Database*. Web. July 27, 2018.

Upfield, Arthur. *Bony and the Mouse*. London: PAN, 1970.

Wertham, Frederic. *Seduction of the Innocent*. New York: Rinehart, 1954.

Wilson, Bill, and Justin O'Brien. "'To Infuse a Universal Terror': A Reappraisal of the Coniston Killings." *Aboriginal History* 17 (2003): 59–78.

Representations of Indigenous Australians in Marvel Comics

Dennin Ellis

As the medium of comics continues to evolve, becoming not only more mainstream but a focus of serious study, the necessity of examining its ability to be inclusive becomes more apparent. Likewise, as the medium moves increasingly from being focused almost purely on (white) male power fantasies to one of social critique and inquiry, there is likewise a necessity for having the world on the printed page come to resemble that of the reader. Marvel Comics in particular has always prided itself on realism ("the world outside your window" being an oft-used tagline), but this endeavor has always been successful to highly variable degrees, even when it comes to supposed bastions of inclusion, diversity, and cultural sensitivity such as the X-Men.

In the annals of comic books, the X-Men have long been known as a metaphor for civil rights—a team of people who were born different (i.e., super-powered) and therefore subject to bigotry, a highly relevant topic during their initial appearance in 1963. Despite the tone-deafness of their beginnings (five white teenagers living in an exclusive boarding school in Westchester, owned by their ultra-rich WASP headmaster, serving as an analogue for African Americans being subjected to segregation), the team did eventually become far more inclusive, serving in some capacity as symbols of every persecuted minority (a premise best explored in Ramzi Fawaz's *The New Mutants: Superheroes and the Radical Imagination of American Comics*).

In their second classic incarnation, the team incorporated characters from all over the world, and in doing so embraced the downtrodden of every nation. However, the tone-deafness was still present. Across all media, when looking to other nations for inspiration, stereotypes tend to determine character traits. Perhaps this hinges on ignorance, especially in the pre-Internet age, when information about other cultures was not so readily available. Thus, the *X-Men* writers were in a tricky place of having to write characters who came from parts of the world they knew nothing about. As a result, they tended to mine character traits from history, mythology, and stereotypes. Hence, the "new," international X-Men who appeared in *Giant-Size X-Men* issue 1 were largely based on these scant and often inaccurate sources of information.

The new characters included Colossus, a Russian strongman whose skin could turn into organic metal (keep in mind Josef Stalin's adopted surname roughly translated to "man of steel"); Thunderbird, a Native American whose enhanced strength and durability made him the ultimate outdoorsman (his costume incorporated elements of stereotypical Native American garb); and Storm, an African princess whose weather powers caused her to be worshipped as an actual goddess by Native Kenyans. Also joining were earlier characters: Banshee, a green-clad Irishman with a superhuman sonic scream, inspired by the mythological creature that shares his namesake; and Sunfire, a Japanese man with destructive radiation powers whose mother died of radiation exposure from Hiroshima.[1] In addition, each of these characters engage in gratuitous use of their Native languages and/or slang: rarely does an issue pass without Colossus exclaiming, "Bozshe Moi!" Banshee referring to someone as "boyo," or both.

This idea of mining what little knowledge was available rarely applied to American characters (especially white Americans). Instead, they (being the most populous of the Marvel Universe) are allowed the true breadth of personalities, backgrounds, and abilities, avoiding stereotypes at all measures. However, such stereotypes do seem to exist. In other parts of the world, Captain America could rightly be seen as a stereotype of Americans, being an ultrapatriotic super-soldier, as could Iron Man, a heavily armed propagator of the military-industrial complex. However, the difference between Captain America and the aforementioned X-Men is that the former, being created *by* Americans, is free to embody not the things America is internationally known for, but the things it *wishes* to be known for. After all, the other important aspects of Cap's character are his unwavering determination and sense of morality, and Iron Man, originally a free-market capitalist (to counter communism), evolved into a technological innovator. The X-Men characters, however, were based on whatever random bits of knowledge happen to be in the public canon. True characterization came later, if at all.

While incoming X-Men writer Chris Claremont was certainly able to define these characters beyond their roots in stereotype, he was only able to do so because they were now the stars of the series rather than ancillary characters. The greater Marvel Universe still employed often crude, half-baked characters in supporting roles. The "new" X-Men were arguably a truly international team, and in that sense better fit the original notion of being stands-in for (and champions of) the oppressed. However, the international team of X-Men still leaned heavily toward traditional Western civilization, with three characters from Europe (Banshee, Nightcrawler, and Colossus) and two from North

America (Wolverine and Thunderbird), while even the African character (Storm) was born in the United States. This left only Sunfire, who abandoned the team after their first adventure.

This trend of featuring occidental characters would continue unabated for much of the ensuing decades, with Africa, South America, and Australia being particularly underrepresented even to this day.[2] And in the case of the latter, the few Australian characters who did appear were white rather than Aboriginal. Ironically, this did not prevent them from being defined by an American writer's limited knowledge of Australian culture.

The first Australian character in the Marvel Universe was Spider-Man villain Frederick Myers, also known as Boomerang, an Australian man who can throw things with near-superhuman accuracy. He commits crimes using a variety of boomerangs rigged with blades, explosives, and tear gas. A later Spider-Man story introduced Frank Oliver, the Kangaroo. As a young man, Oliver had studied and lived with kangaroos in his Native Australia. Somehow, this led him to developing the ability to jump very high, which he put to use first as a boxer, then as a criminal. Later on, he was given cybernetic enhancements in his legs that granted him superhuman leaping powers. As if this weren't enough, there was a second villain who took the name Kangaroo, Brian Hibbs, who wore an armored suit that allowed him to leap great distances (complete with a prehensile tail, large ears, and a pouch-cannon). In a small subversion of the trope, while Hibbs was from Australia, his occupation before super-villainy was interior decorating. One character avoids this trope by way of a continuity error. In X-Men villain Pyro's first appearance, he is twice referred to as an Englishman. However, writer Chris Claremont later decided to make the character Australian. Hence, the trope was avoided only because he was not intended to be Australian in the first place. It remains unclear why the change was made, but making the character Australian after the fact seems to be the reason Pyro is not saddled with some other super-villain identity hinged on his nationality. However, the greater rule of basing non-American characters on stereotypes remained in place.

Nowhere is this more evident than in the 1982 mini-series *Contest of Champions*, which pitted heroes against one another in an epic tournament executed by cosmic forces. Originally envisioned as a tie-in to the 1980 Olympics, the series included a number of international heroes, some previously established, all of whom, like the X-Men, fell back on stereotypes; Sabra, an Israeli woman with a head of curly hair and whose costume incorporates the Star of David; the Arabian Knight, who is aided in battle by his scimitar and flying carpet; and the Russian superhuman Vanguard, whose weapons of choice are a hammer and sickle. Because there was a dearth of such heroes at the time, many were created especially for this series. And while it is admirable that Marvel wanted to be more inclusive in this way, they fell back on creating characters based on national/ethnic stereotypes.

These new characters included Shamrock, an Irish woman with luck powers dressed entirely in green spandex; Defensor, an Argentinian man in conquistador armor; the Collective Man, actually five Chinese brothers who could merge into one and "summon the collective might of their race"; and German superhero Blitzkrieg, who had electricity-based powers. Like with the X-Men, these new characters' dialogue is full of gratuitous use of the Native tongues, as if to emphasize their otherness from the American characters. In fact, the only instance of an American character's national identity being referenced is when Darkstar, a Russian superheroine, asks Daredevil for confirmation that he is from the United States. Elsewhere, many other international characters remark on their own non-American origins or that of others. In fact, at several points as characters are introducing themselves, the international heroes refer to their home countries while the American heroes simply state their names.[3]

Among these new characters is Talisman, the first Aboriginal Australian character in the Marvel Universe. He is not exempt from being weighed down by bits and pieces of his culture being integrated into his powers, personality, and manner of speech.

His powers, enabled by entering "dream-time," are ill defined, described as being able to "pass through objects and teleport short distances" as well as "[separating] his astral form from his physical body." Furthermore, he is able to "open up a portal into 'dream-time' large enough to engulf others." What this last power actually means is not well established; when seen in action it is described as a distortion of reality that warps the senses. "Dream-time" is likewise ill defined as a "swirling altered-state . . . a myth-realm of the eternal past adjacent to real-time." Talisman's powers are based on broad strokes of knowledge about Aboriginal culture, as is his appearance: incredibly dark skin, a totally bald head, gold armlets, a loincloth, and a gold cross on his face, likely some kind of tribal marking or makeup. In addition, he carries a bull-roarer, a simple musical instrument used in traditional Aboriginal ceremonies, which enables him to open portals to the dream-time.

Talisman's demeanor and dialogue also fall into the realm of gratuity in his use of linguistic and cultural touchstones. Beyond his constant references to the dream-time (he also refers to it as the "altjeringa") and discussing the use of his "tjurunga," his "sacred weapon," Talisman has, like Colossus, Nightcrawler, and others, an exclamation that indisputably marks his identity, in the form of "By the eternal Numbakulla!" All of these are broad references to Aboriginal beliefs. First, "altjeringa" is an alternate spelling for "alcheringa," also known as "altjira" or "alchira." It is used by the Aranda people to describe a concept for which there is no easy English equivalent, although the term "the dreaming" was determined to be the closest approximation by the Aborigines who worked with Australian anthropologist W. E. H. Stanner. Second, Talisman's weapon is called a "churinga," an object of religious significance, passed from

Talisman, Marvel's first Aboriginal character.

generation to generation to be used in religious rituals. Those with strings attached were categorized as bull-roarers by European settlers due to their resemblance to objects fashioned in a similar way in Europe. Last, the god he invokes is known as "Numakulla," or "Nambakala," one of the supreme creator deities of the Aranda religion. Furthermore, his dialogue suggests more vague, spiritual abilities rooted in the shamanistic customs and practices of various Aboriginal peoples. In response to danger, he remarks, "The spirits of my ancestors bid me beware," suggesting some ability to communicate with the dead. When asked for his name, he instead responds, "To give one's name is to risk one's soul . . . But I may be called Talisman," implying further mystical knowledge. His moniker, therefore, is an alias, and we never learn his actual name. Talisman has only appeared in three issues since *Contest of Champions*, and then only in a largely nonspeaking role as a background character among a group of other magical superheroes.

However, Talisman was arguably a dry run for a character that later appeared in the X-Men's divisive "Outback era." During an epic conflict with a Native American trickster god known as the Adversary, the team is forced to sacrifice their lives, only to be resurrected by a different, benevolent god.[4] With the world now believing them to be dead, the X-Men choose to let that untruth lie in order to strike back at their enemies with the element of surprise. In order to facilitate this, they choose an incredibly remote location as their new base of operations: the Australian Outback. It is here that they meet the man they call Gateway.

This new character has a lot in common with Talisman. They are both Aboriginal men who live in some indeterminate location in the Outback. They both have vaguely defined mystical powers based in being able to enter and manipulate the "dream-time," which is facilitated through the use of their bull-roarer. They are both nameless, Talisman choosing his own name whereas Gateway is given his due to his abilities skewing most heavily toward teleportation. And most of all, they both serve as ancillary characters who make it possible for the main characters to act, rather than acting themselves.

The main difference between Talisman and Gateway is that the latter seems to have even less agency than the former, as he is mute, given a name rather than adopting one of his own accord, and spends the majority of his appearances in the service of others. This does not change over time and, like Talisman, denies the character the opportunity to grow.

It is important to note that, at this time, the lineup of the X-Men had significantly changed. Wolverine, Colossus, and Storm remained, along with four newer members and one long-absent member. Among these five are three Americans (Rogue, Havok, and Dazzler) and one British character (Psylocke). The final new member is Longshot, who despite hailing from a parallel dimension full of aliens of all shapes, sizes, and colors, has the appearance of a white, blond-haired, blue-eyed man who speaks with an American accent. For all

The X-Men of the "Outback era": Longshot, Storm, Rogue (*top row*), Colossus (*center*), Dazzler, Psylocke, Havok (*middle row*), Wolverine (*foreground*).

intents and purposes, the X-Men continue to be stands-in for Western civilization despite the posturing as an all-inclusive group.

Which makes their relationship with this new character very odd. Issue 229 serves as the X-Men's introduction to Australia, here described as "A wild, desolate land . . . A place that in many ways appears as the world did when it was young, raw and untempered by either elements . . . or man." We are also introduced to Gateway, "This thin, wizened man as weathered as the hills, and, some joke (but never in his presence) probably as old." Throughout his tenure in the book, Gateway remains mostly passive, or as Rogue describes him, "Never says a word, just sits there an' watches the world go by." Little further description is given.

Gateway's muteness seems to serve two purposes in a sociopolitical context. The first, obviously, is that his muteness constitutes a lack of agency. Whereas the Indigenous population has been figuratively silenced, this manifests in Gateway in a literal sense. Second, and oddly enough, Gateway's silence may be a means of walking the thin line of creating an "Aboriginal" character while preventing him from lapsing completely into stereotype and, therefore, complete ethnic parody. Chris Claremont, being a British-born American, is himself a representation of the oppressive class, a fact he was likely somewhat aware of. He had to tread carefully in creating a character like this, not only to avoid stereotypes but because he was writing about a character whose background was largely an unknown factor, even for many contemporaneous scholars. The question of how this character would speak and interact left little other option than to fall back upon the stereotypical language that plagued Talisman. And one of Claremont's own writing follies was to fall back on such language. So, would it have been better to give Gateway a voice with which he could shout, "By the eternal Numbakullah!" once per issue (as Colossus, Nightcrawler, and Banshee, and the others, have their own frequent dialogic markers of ethnicity), or to just make him mute? From a narrative perspective, having limited knowledge of one's subject at hand, the character's muteness does indeed help avoid stereotyping to some degree, while also adding a sense of mystique and sageness to the character (which, unfortunately, come with their own trappings of stereotype).

Gateway's exact abilities are difficult to pin down. By spinning his bull-roarer, he opens up portals that can transport people anywhere in the world, as well as opening portals for them to return. Since Gateway is a mute, it's difficult to know how he is aware of a passenger's desired location, or when they want to return. X-Men member Psylocke communicates with him telepathically, but there are others without such powers, and it remains a mystery how Gateway communicates with them. It is implied that he has some sort of extrasensory perception that allows him to, through the Dreaming, see great distances, even into other dimensions: "This waking world is merely one of many the ancient aborigine perceives . . . and far from the most important." He also seems to be able to manipulate reality while within the Dreaming. In issue 233, he appears in another person's dream for the first time, and uses his bull-roarer in a different way: "In our waking reality, this opens a teleportal gateway. Here, it has other abilities." The exact reason he manipulates the dreams of others, as he does several more times, is not clear. He is neither benevolent nor malevolent in this regard, "for that is not his purpose in the scheme of things." His purpose, it seems, is to facilitate events for the main characters rather than have his own story explored. There is indeed a backstory to be explored, but we are never given more than hints. In *X-Men* issue 229, it is implied that Gateway can never leave his dwelling place because he is protecting the spirits of his people. In issue 269, there is talk of a "geas," or a mystical curse that implies some obligation, described only as "both debt and task . . . binding [him] to this place and the Reavers' service."

In his first appearance, Gateway is in the service of the Reavers, criminals who use his teleportation abilities to rob and loot across the entire world and make a quick getaway to their hideout, an abandoned mining town in the Outback, where Gateway keeps his "eternal vigil." His service is involuntary, as the Reavers threaten "any funny stuff, an' the Reavers'll trash your place

Gateway, the X-Men's silent Aboriginal ally/servant.

beyond any hope o' reconsecration—an' then your people will never know peace. They'll wander the dreamlands, slave to the outsign spirits, to the end o' time an' beyond!" There are conflicting reports about precisely where this town is, but the most likely location is Central Australia in the Northern Territory, as that is the location shown on a map in *X-Men* issue 249, and is also where Uluru (or Ayers Rock) is located, where Gateway appears in *X-Treme X-Men* issue 4. This location, as well as the use of the tjuringa/bull-roarer, would suggest that Gateway is of the Aranda people.

Gateway's subservient role to a group of white criminals is a simplified, and yet oddly appropriate microcosm of European imperialism. Little to no respect is given to Gateway, his land, or his people. Instead, he, they, and it are mined for usefulness, presumably to be discarded when used up. What is truly odd, though, is that when the Reavers are defeated by the X-Men, they do not do the noble thing and release Gateway from servitude. Instead, they continue to use him for an almost identical purpose. As stated above, the X-Men at this time were largely white and Western, meaning Gateway's subjugation continues, albeit under a slightly different group. And though Gateway distinguishes between the two groups (as the narrator states, "Those intruders were enemies and he served them because he had no choice. The ones who replaced them, however, who dwell here now, have earned his friendship"), the fact remains that he is a prop who is sometimes chastised by members of the X-Men for stepping outside his role as a means of transportation, and for manipulating things while the team stays on his land. In other words, the X-Men are bad guests who seem to merely tolerate his presence on his own home turf. The only exception is Rogue, who at one point finds a whistle among the Reavers' stash of treasure and gives it to Gateway as a gift. He, in return, plays it for her. His kindness at allowing them to stay, and transporting them wherever they want to go, is ultimately not reciprocated. The Reavers return and Psylocke, having a premonition of the X-Men's demise in the battle, forces the team to escape and leave Gateway behind, where he once more falls under the thrall of the Reavers.

It is unlikely that there was any malice intended in the actions of the X-Men, just like there is probably not any malice in the actions of the writers who conjure up these characters. Instead, perhaps there is simply a dearth of information available on Indigenous Australians, meaning there is less material to mine for story and character ideas. After all, this is a group of people who largely orally passed down their history and traditions, meaning written records are scant. Because of the severe population decline in the wake of imperialism, the number of information sources also declined. Perhaps this is why, at least in the case of Indigenous Australians, writers paint them with such broad strokes: they feel they have no alternatives.

But this speaks to a fundamental difference in how various peoples view history. For Western civilization, the story of the the people is the history. In contrast, many Aboriginal tribes view history as the story of the land. People are secondary. However, in the wake of a near-extinction level event, there aren't many people left to tell that history, and it instead gets told by someone else. And those new authors can pick and choose what parts they want to use. For comic book writers who employ ideas of astral planes and multiple dimensions, something like "the Dreaming" proves irresistible, even if they are misinterpreting what the Dreaming is. Then again, in Aboriginal beliefs one's relationship to the Dreaming is highly personal, and thus somewhat open to individual interpretation. In the face of this, perhaps it is not *quite* so strange for outsiders to put their own spin on it, seeing it as something akin to a dimension of thought, which, in a way, it is. In fact, in certain tribes such as the Pintupi, the entirety of history is formed and dictated by the Dreaming.

Although there are hundreds of distinct tribes of Aboriginal peoples in Australia, it is impossible to know with any certainty to which Gateway belongs. For writers, it is likely that no distinction is made and all tribes are grouped together into a pan-Australian or even pan-Oceanic entity. This would not be unheard of, as American and European portrayals of distant parts of the world blend various ethnic and national groups together. In the Far East, there may be a distinction between China and Japan (perhaps even Korea), but rarely will there be any mention of the several other countries making up Southeast Asia, or of the various ethnic groups within China alone. There is a similar blurring of the various peoples of Africa, all of whom could be exchanged with one another in a pan-African union often based on outdated ideas of the continent being wracked by near-constant famine and disease, as well as a lack of modern technology or urbanization. Likewise, there is the lumping together of Native American peoples across North America, with certain touchstones that are presumed to be present in each tribe, such as feathered headdresses and vague mysticism. The peoples of Australia and its outlying areas become a pan-Aboriginal archetype that encompasses not just "the Outback" but Tasmania and the Māori of New Zealand as well.[5] No attempt is made to highlight the specific aspects of culture that would distinguish one group from another, and instead the greater area is painted with broad strokes. This obviously carries over to how the characters from that area are built. Hence, the extraordinary similarity in Marvel's characters of Aboriginal descent.

Strangely, Native American depictions often share traits with that of Aborigines in that they lean on the noble savage archetype. Perhaps noncoincidentally, there are also similarities in the history of both groups, having their lands invaded by European imperialists, and their population subsequently decimated. As far as many media are concerned, they are groups that time forgot, and their stories tend to lean into characters living traditionally. The trouble is that these traditions are being interpreted, and often misunderstood, by outside writers, leading to the propagation of such noble savage stereotypes that simultaneously elevate a character by praising their unique communion with nature while devaluing them for their simple, out-of-date beliefs and ways that posit them as an obstacle to human progress. Gateway is simply one more example of this, a soon-to-be-extinct relic of a bygone era. Their environments are often contrasted with civilization: the Outback is barren and devoid of life except for nameless shamans, compared to the thriving metropolis of Sydney. Therefore, even more than Talisman before him, Gateway is a stand-in for the countless dead and dispossessed of Australia, and though the beliefs of his people are given passing lip service, the troubled history of his people is never addressed in the slightest.

The inability, or perhaps the unwillingness of superhero comics to directly address the painful process of assimilation, and its varying degrees of success, speaks not to a limitation of the medium but to a broader cultural disengagement from confronting this process. Often, Indigenous peoples are given a dangerous choice when attempting to integrate into "normal" society; give up one's ancestry, and therefore a significant part of one's identity (which also includes a sort of forgiving any historical trespasses) or remain outside of the mainstream. Oftentimes, the latter choice results not just in social but physical segregation, as is the case with many Native Americans throughout the United States. A third option, and the most preferable, having a genuine voice in social and political matters, has long eluded Indigenous populations. This remains true for Indigenous Australians as well as Native Americans. In fifteen years, Australia's Aboriginal and Torres Strait Islander Commission (ATSIC) went from being a bold new undertaking and a promise to give voice to the voiceless to being completely dismantled and labeled a failure by the right-leaning Howard administration.

The choice most often adopted, then, is the first, which largely results in a combination of personal, political, and social compromises in order to simultaneously hold onto one's ancestry while being a part of mainstream society. As Indigenous scholar MaryAnn Bin-Sallik puts it: "Sadly and unfairly, many Aboriginal people begin to identify with, and behave in accord with the label, and this continued negativity prevents any real chance of challenging such a formidable and consistent portrayal of who we really are. That, and over time, it is simply easier to conform to these toxic labels."

Indigenous populations, on a personal and collective level, are given the option of conforming to what mainstream society believes about them, or foregoing mainstream society entirely. What they get in exchange is not the chance to shape public policy, but mere access to it. This process is not a true compromise at all, in that only one side is really giving up anything, and in exchange, Indigenous culture is further minimized, commodified, simplified, and made vulnerable. This only continues the process. Further choices must be made to continue to allow one's culture to be appropriated and misused by largely disinterested parties, or to become a defender of it. Once again, this seems to be a universal truth for Indigenous populations. As Native American scholar Elizabeth Lynn-Cook writes, "The journey through another world, beyond bad dreams beyond / the memories of a murdered generation, / cartographed in captivity by bare survivors / makes sacristans of us all" (62). This experience of being given the unenviable task of constantly serving as a protector of one's culture is yet another part that is so often glossed over by most depictions of Indigenous peoples, as they instead choose to embrace stereotypes and "toxic labels."

On one hand, having Aboriginal characters in the Marvel Universe is something to be applauded. On the other hand, the initial, stereotypical representations like Talisman and Gateway only serve to reinforce those stereotypes and therefore offset whatever good comes from inclusion. The problem appears when stereotypical representations are the only ones present. A minor story in *Marvel Comics Presents* issue 16 has Longshot wandering through the Outback when he literally bumps into an unnamed Aboriginal man who, like Talisman and Gateway, also has indeterminate abilities associated with the Dreaming. Captain America is arguably a stereotype of Americans, but this isn't a problem because comics as a medium has more than enough American characters who don't fit any American stereotype; Cap becomes an outlier rather than a trope codifier. This is not the case for most non-American characters, especially Aboriginal Australians.

In fact, the list of Marvel characters who identify as such is very short, comprising only seven characters out of tens of thousands. This level of representation, purely by number, could be interpreted as somewhat accurate due to the Aboriginal people constituting only 3 percent of the total population of Australia, and less than one ten-thousandth of a percent of the global population. However, numerical accuracy does not account for shoehorning these characters into stereotypical roles.

Two other characters are largely rehashes of Talisman and Gateway. First is Willie Walkaway, a hero known as Dreamguard, who possesses the ability of "dream-sight," which allows him to interact with spirits. Willie was originally an integrated citizen, but upon discovering the legends his grandfather used to tell him were true, he adopted his superhero alias (as well as a costume consisting of white paint, a loincloth, and a giant boomerang) and voluntarily became the latest in a long line of ancestral "dreamguards." The unfortunate implication here is that Willie, an Aboriginal man who has successfully assimilated in Australian culture, will forever be bound and drawn back to his ancestry, which marks him as different, making permanent and voluntary assimilation impossible. Instead, his ancestry bears the burden of inevitable regression.

Then there is Eden Fesi, also known as Manifold, first introduced in 2009. Certainly the outlier of the group, Eden bucks the trend not only by being a nuanced, fleshed-out character, but by having a far greater number of appearances with a speaking role. However, there are a number of traits that link him to previous Aboriginal characters, not least of which is that Gateway serves as his tutor in the use of his abilities. And those abilities, like Gateway's, involve being able to open portals between space and time. Furthermore, like Gateway, Eden carries an object typically associated with less-civilized peoples, in this case a spear. Taken as a whole, his character seems more like an attempt to take the core traits of Gateway and turn him into a superhero, a feat that simply wouldn't be credible using Gateway himself due to his advanced age, muteness, and having been dead on more than one occasion (as have most Marvel characters who have stuck around long enough).

This makes five out of eight, or 62.5 percent of the Aboriginal characters in the Marvel Universe, based on outdated, imperialist stereotypes. One of the remaining three characters, Jack Mead (also known as Jack-in-the-Box) instead had basic telepathy and a radar sense, the latter of which could arguably be based on the stereotype of Aborigines being good at tracking things through the wild. Despite not adhering to the tropes of Aboriginal characters, Jack Mead was never given the opportunity to develop, as he made three brief appearances before fading into obscurity. The other two characters were retroactively considered Aboriginal by descent, these being longtime X-Men member Bishop and his sister Shard. In *X-Treme X-Men* issue 4, Gateway himself reveals, via the imagery of the Dreaming, that Bishop and Shard, who have traveled back in time from one of the X-Men's many dystopian futures, are his great-grandchildren.

At first, this can be viewed as trying to adhere to one of the most prevalent X-Men story tropes, that of characters secretly being related to each other, especially well after they have been around for a while. This trope is harder to pull off with nonwhite characters for the simple fact that there are fewer mutants of color running around the Marvel Universe, and connecting characters who shared an ethnicity was an instance of lazy writing for the sake of conforming to this trope. However, the idea that Gateway is the ancestor of these characters leads to an inadvertent, yet fascinating implication about Gateway's character.

First, the issue in question presents Bishop being transported to the Dreaming by Gateway and encountering the spirit of a recently deceased teammate, who informs him that despite his trepidation and seeming ignorance of how to navigate the Dreaming, that ability is "in [his] blood." This means Bishop is yet another Aboriginal character with abilities connected to the Dreaming and, by virtue of this being a genetic trait, so is his sister. This means six of the eight, or 75 percent, of Aboriginal characters in the Marvel Universe are connected to the Dreaming.

Secondly, Bishop and Shard grew up in North America in the future. As Bishop says, "Australia was gone, nuked during the Gene War. Our home was Brooklyn . . . My folks barely got out of 'Oz' alive. No photos, no mementos, nothing of their life there. We started over from scratch." At no point do we ever meet Gateway's wife, companion, or his children. However, with this revelation, we *do* know that his descendants are integrated into Western society. The implication, then, is that Gateway's children were taken from him to be assimilated into white, colonial Australia, making them part of the so-called stolen generations.

Gateway's own story, and the fact that it is missing so many parts as to make it whole, is itself analogous to how the story of the treatment of Indigenous Australians remained unknown for decades, and the full truth has yet to be completely uncovered. Supposedly prompted by the latter dying off in great numbers, the British Empire saw fit to seize Aboriginal children for forced integration to prevent a "race-wide extinction." This practice was in effect for the majority of Australia's history. Rather than actually protecting aborigines, it seems more likely that this stemmed from an inability to understand how Indigenous peoples can survive and even thrive without the hallmarks of modern culture. Furthermore, this was, like blackbirding and slavery, another form of erasing an undesired culture to make room for colonies. However, these actions effectively erased large swaths of Australia's history, further creating a mystique of an unknowable land.

And despite this period of X-Men history being referred to as "the Outback era," very little of it actually takes place in Australia. Gateway serves as a sort of deus ex machina that allows the team to remain in seclusion, plotting against their enemies, while also having adventures around the world, thereby circumventing the necessity of exploring an unknown land. Over the course of the Outback era, stories take place in Denver, New York, Los Angeles, Chile, Poland, India, and Mexico, as well as the fictional locations of Limbo (a demonic alternate dimension), the Savage Land (a chunk of Antarctica with a tropical climate populated by dinosaurs and Native peoples), Madripoor (a crime-ridden island nation modeled off Singapore, and located in the same part of the world), and Genosha (another island nation, to be discussed later).

Very little of Australia is seen. As such, very little of typical European-descended Australians are actually seen. In issue 235, the X-Men are pursuing a foe through Sydney and the final page shows the aftermath of a battle, with local police assessing the scene. Their speech patterns, like those of Colossus, Nightcrawler, and the others, are peppered with diction that makes explicit their nationality to an absurd degree, calling each other "mate," referring to "super-blokes," and describing the scene as something out of *Mad Max*. The cherry on top is the lead officer, Inspector Mick Dundee, who shares his name with the titular star of the *Crocodile Dundee* films, the second of which was released just months prior to the publication of this issue.

The depiction of white Australians therefore follows the pattern established by non-American characters. They lean heavily into stereotype and have very little personality outside of that. In issue 239, Dazzler takes some time off to visit

A "typical" white Australian reacting to an alien invasion.

a local bar and sit in with the house band. She arrives in media res, finding a violent brawl taking place among the regulars. In *Marvel Comics Presents* issue 24, Havok takes off for an adventure on his own and twice is accosted by heavily armed white Australians who look as though they're on safari. One of them refers to Havok and his new lady-friend as "stray wallabies." In issue 26, Havok enters a completely different bar, where he finds a third gang of fighting mercenaries, whom he dispatches. Considering that these are the only Australians appearing in these stories, it establishes a pattern of white Australians being naturally inclined to violence.

There is also the stereotype of white Australians being stupid, which is on full display in *X-Men* issue 245, a humorous issue that sees Sydney being invaded by completely inept aliens.

However, the underlying joke is that the citizens of Sydney are likewise so inept they don't even realize their city is being invaded. For instance, a tremendous alien tank rolls down the street and a man shouts, "Move that crate over, ya Bruce! . . . Flippin' foreigners!" Elsewhere, a hulking alien soldier is distracted by a barfly who, seemingly unaware of his new friend being an extraterrestrial, introduces him to beer, saying, "Mother's milk, to some! Drink up, mate, drink up! Y'know, I was inna army myself! Had the worst pig of a sergeant—!" Another alien soldier enters the bar where the X-Men are relaxing and gets no response from the locals besides a man who greets him with "G'day, cobber!" When the alien overlord blasts the Sydney Opera House (the only Australian landmark most people know), a local onlooker remarks, "Been wanting to do that myself for years! But . . . it is on all the postcards and brochures . . . so I'm afraid you'll have to put it back the way it was." In a brief Superman parody, the scene shifts to an unnamed "metropolitan" news station where an excited journalist reports that Australia is being invaded by aliens, to which the chief responds, "What, more tourists? Japanese, I'll bet." When the journalist protests the chief's indifference, the chief says, "Big deal. Place is mostly desert," and says the invasion is news "Only to the Ozzies, kid."

It could be argued that, since this entire issue is played for laughs, these depictions are not meant to be representative of Australians as a group. However, such an analysis ignores two things. First, these depictions must be taken with all others of the era, none of which contain non-stereotypical white Australians. Second, this particular issue ends with a single-page epilogue, meant to set up a future storyline, where one of the X-Men's foes comes across a massacre of her men by another foe. The scene, with blood-splattered walls and bodies strewn about, is most definitely not played for laughs and effectively deflates the humor of the rest of the issue, inadvertently making the humorous depictions take on an air of seriousness. Therefore, throughout the entirety of the X-Men's "Outback era," all portrayals of white Australians suggest they are violent, stupid alcoholics. At least in that regard the white Australians are treated the same as

Indigenous Australians. However, in depictions of both, the unfortunate history of Australia is not mentioned. What makes it so odd that it isn't addressed in the pages of *X-Men* (or any other comic of the time, for that matter) is that this was a period when comics were not only becoming more "mature" (see *Watchmen*, etc.) but were also more willing to tackle social problems. For instance, the four-issue mini-series *Havok & Wolverine: Meltdown*, produced concurrently with the "Outback era," addressed Cold War tensions in general and fear of nuclear power in the wake of the Chernobyl disaster.

Likewise, *Heroes for Hope Starring the X-Men* was a special one-shot collaboration featuring the talents of people like Stephen King and Harlan Ellison. All proceeds from the comic were donated to efforts for famine relief in Africa. The story, rather unfortunately, implies that famine is caused by an ancient demon rather than real-world forces. Famine relief was, in the mid-1980s, a popular social cause which resulted in the music industry's Band Aid record and Live Aid concerts. Like many social causes before and since, it turned into a sort of trend or even contest to see who could out-charity whom, leading to bizarre projects like Hear N' Aid (the equivalent of Band Aid formed by heavy metal singers who felt left out). *Heroes for Hope* was one such project. The efforts of white Americans and Europeans to outdo each other eventually branched off into other African issues, most notably apartheid in South Africa. There had long been a boycott of the country by Western musicians, but the movement amped up throughout the 1980s with further activism and charity songs, eventually culminating in 1988's "Nelson Mandela 70th Birthday Tribute" concert at Wembley Stadium.

The comic book world, as they did with *Heroes of Hope*, took on the popular social issue of the day in the form of *Uncanny X-Men* issues 235 through 238, which appeared on the stands a few months after the Nelson Mandela concert, falling early in the X-Men's Outback era. These issues marked the first appearance of the island nation of Genosha, a technologically advanced society that prospered due to enslaving its mutant population. The comparison between Genosha and South Africa is obvious, made more so by the fictional nation's location near Africa.

What follows is perhaps the most political story in the X-Men's canon. At least once per issue there is a lengthy discussion of the issues of slavery, with Genosha's Genegineer (the official in charge of the mutate process by which Native mutants are bonded to a suit marking them as slaves) debates the rights of the mutates with his son and son's girlfriend, who is to undergo the mutate process. He describes the enslavement as necessary so "Genosha can maintain its standard of living . . . This island is one of the most inhospitable rocks on the face of the planet. However, through our God-given intelligence and talent and skill—and yes, sacrifice—we've made Genosha a paradise on Earth." He goes on to justify the treatment of slaves, saying they "have a responsibility

Magistrates and a "mutate" in Genosha, Marvel's analogue for apartheid South Africa.

to the community that bore and nurtured" them, and that they are "well-fed, well-housed—most of the world's population would probably kill for such a life." More than this, he describes the absolute necessity of mutant enslavement: "Their power is sufficient to destroy us. That's why we have to impose such strict controls. Not slavery, child. Self-defense."

The truth, however, is that the mutates are ghettoized, living in what is essentially a prison camp, and the mutate process itself seems to not only affect their bodies but their minds, as they all speak in stilted, childlike language: "Fix real good, boss," "Do my work good, boss," and so on.

The speech patterns bear a slight resemblance to those of minstrel show characters, and to add insult to injury, the mutates must address everyone as boss, while a number of Genoshan civilians refer to them as "boy."

Obviously, this story line is an analogue for slavery and apartheid. However, there are some glaring omissions that make it a rather half-hearted commentary. First, it ignores the intersectionality of race and gender as points of oppression. Despite the enslavement of the mutant population, Genosha is a surprisingly equal society, with women serving in the military and holding a number of high-ranking positions in the government, including the presidency. Second, the entire population of Genosha is white, despite the fact that it is an island nation in between Madagascar and Seychelles, which leads to the third point: issue 237 shows a propaganda video that details Genoshan history, first as a haven for French pirates, then as a nation that grew rich thanks to deposits of iron and other precious metals. At no point is there any discussion of the island prior to white settlement. Further stories, as well as Marvel's encyclopedic sources, also fail to discuss pre-European history of Genosha. However, based on the part of the world it is in, and the fact that it is rich in precious metals, it is almost entirely likely that the island was previously inhabited by settlers who came from Africa thousands of years ago. All we need do is look at the similar history of its real-world neighbors, Madagascar and Seychelles, both of which had their Native populations enslaved upon settlement by Europeans.[6] That there are only white people left on Genosha suggests that at some point the Native population was completely wiped out, either by disease or a campaign of genocide. This implication is the most troubling part of the story because it is not at all addressed. Whichever is the cause of the Native population being destroyed, it suggests why mutants were enslaved in the first place: no other population was still available.

The story of Genosha, when viewed in context of the Outback era as a whole, makes it curious why Marvel was so willing to take on an issue like apartheid while avoiding the troubled history of Indigenous Australians. After all, slavery is itself often a byproduct of imperialism, as is the decimation of an Indigenous population, implied by the lack of nonwhite people in Genosha. These are the same things that happened during the European colonization of Australia. Why, then, is so much energy devoted to showcasing the ills of apartheid while none was given to injustices perpetrated against Indigenous Australians? The first and most obvious reason is that apartheid was the hot issue of the day. However, other factors prevented the same level of highly public calls for social change. First, the population of Aboriginal Australians is very low. Compare it to another country with an Indigenous, yet downtrodden minority: African Americans made up 12 percent of the US population in 1990 (roughly when the "Outback era" ceased), a percentage more than four times larger than that of aborigines in Australia, where the latter had roughly the same population as that of Chinese or Indian immigrants. Fewer people makes it more likely a population simply gets lost in the shuffle.

Second, the length of time in which both of these social injustices were being carried out played a part. The Victorian Aboriginal Protection Act of 1869 was the first such legislative measure carried out in Australia for the purposes of forcibly assimilating Indigenous Australians into the population of the British

Commonwealth. This policy continued in various forms for over a century. By 1988, the policy was simply a part of Australian culture. The effect of it being in place for so long was one of normalizing the practice. In comparison, South Africa formally instituted the policy of apartheid in 1948, meaning that by 1988, there were plenty of people still living who remembered a time before apartheid. Not enough time had passed for it to become completely normalized.

Third, Australia's geographic isolation afforded it a degree of privacy and the ability to carry out unsavory practices without neighboring countries getting in the way or even noticing. Add to this the uniqueness of modern-day Australia being a sort of European nation in practice, but being an island nation at the same time, and therefore not subject to making nice with its continental neighbors, because it has none. This further allowed injustices to be carried out unseen. South Africa, in contrast, was part of a continent, with plenty of neighbors.

The last reason has to do with Australia being a member of the Commonwealth. The history of the two nations provides a stark contrast. Whereas Australia has remained part of the Commonwealth, and therefore loyal to the crown of England (regardless of whether this is simply a symbolic allegiance or not), South Africa deliberately spurned the British Empire with a 1960 referendum on whether the Union of South Africa, as it was then known, should become a republic. The referendum passed and the country became the Republic of South Africa, leaving the Commonwealth and removing the Queen as the head of state. In doing so, South Africa drew a clear line between itself and the rest of the British Commonwealth, and by extension the rest of Western civilization. This, perhaps more than anything else, led to public pressure on South Africa to amend the ills of apartheid while no such call was made to Australia's racist policies.

And yet, there are hints within *X-Men*'s Genosha story line that a finger is clearly being pointed at imperialism being a source of great injustice. Issue 235 introduces the Press Gang, a group of Genoshan mutants who have traded their service and abilities to their government in exchange for relative freedom. Their primary task is recovering runaway mutate slaves as well as capturing mutants to be taken into slavery.

The group's name comes from a colloquial term for officers of the military engaged in "impressment," or the involuntary conscription into the armed forces. Often this practice was tantamount to kidnapping, as "the press gang" would round up able-bodied men with no prior notice and force them into service. The nation that employed this tactic the most was the British Empire, especially during the height of the Age of Exploration, when Great Britain was in a fierce war with other imperial powers to claim as much of the world as they could. Although the practice of impressment eventually waned in the years following the Napoleonic Wars, it was still very much alive during the years when the British Empire first established colonies on what would later be the nation of Australia, and while records are scant, it is highly likely that a great number of early colonists in Australia were impressed men. Beyond this was the practice of "blackbirding," in which people (in this case Indigenous people from Australia and neighboring islands) were recruited as laborers through coercion and trickery. It is a popular misconception that early laborers in Australian colonies were solely convicts. Impressment, blackbirding, and protectionism were highly lucrative practices during the first several decades of these colonies.

Marvel's willingness to cast impressment officers in the role of villains is to acknowledge the evils of the practice and by extension the evils of imperialism. What little is known about the character of Gateway likewise implies imperialism being villainous. However, Marvel did not go far enough by neither implicitly nor explicitly tying villains like the Reavers to the real-world evils of imperialism, or Gateway as one of its victims. This is a shame and a tremendous missed opportunity since, if there were ever to be a comic book that had placed itself in a position of condemning imperialism, it should be X-Men, as the preeminent champions of the downtrodden. But, as before, Marvel failed to grasp the intersectionality of forces of oppression. Aboriginal Australians were subject to this oppression not only due to race but because of their role as imperial subjects.

In the past few decades, Marvel Comics has made great strides to be more inclusive. There are now dozens of LGBTQ characters of all races and nationalities. And thankfully, more often than not, the creation of a character is no longer based upon stereotypes related to ethnicity or nationality. However, there is still an issue with underrepresentation due to the prevalence of older, more stereotypical characters outnumbering newer characters in certain parts of the world, Australia included. Until this is addressed, fans of Marvel Comics have to settle for depictions of Aboriginal Australians as a variation of outdated noble savages whose entire being is inextricably linked to a misunderstood aspect of their heritage, doomed to never grow beyond such a role. However, we are currently in a moment in which inclusivity and diversity are being demanded by creators and fans alike. The days of the superhero being a square-jawed, All-American white male are over. Despite the fact that only a few short decades separate a character like Talisman, rooted completely in stereotype, to one like Manifold who has a distinct personality and motivations, should be applauded. And while no Indigenous Australian character has thus far proven popular enough to stick around, the fact that Manifold was given that opportunity (he was briefly a member of the Avengers) should likewise be applauded. More and more, we are seeing the definition of "superhero" being expanded to include women and people of color. And while we are not there yet, it is only a matter of time before this definition includes Indigenous peoples.

Notes

1. Three other characters were present, all of whom avoided this trope; Cyclops, a holdover from the original team; Nightcrawler, a German man with a demonic appearance and the ability to teleport (created and adapted from an unused series by artist Dave Cockrum); and Wolverine, a Canadian man who, if anything, subverts stereotypes of the polite, laid-back Canadian by being a killer prone to bursts of "berserker rage."

2. Main writer of the X-books Chris Claremont later fixed the problem to a degree with the "junior X-Men" book *The New Mutants*, which counted two South American members; Roberto DaCosta (Sunspot) from Brazil; and Amara Aquilla (Magma), who hails from Nova Roma, a lost colony of the ancient Roman empire that has avoided contact with the outside world for thousands of years. This makes her a white, blonde-haired, and blue-eyed woman who is technically South American.

3. *Contest of Champions* is generally problematic in this regard, as often these differences in national identity are used pejoratively during combat. In the span of four pages, the Arabian Knight is referred to as "Turban-Top," "Arab," and "Sinbad." He, meanwhile, refers to Sabra as "Jewess" and Captain Britain as "English Swine."

4. The benevolent god in this case is known as Roma, and aspects of her character tie into British legend, such as living in the Arthurian Otherworld and being the daughter of Merlyn. This sets up the unfortunate conflict that the X-Men have involved themselves in a war between the gods of Indigenous Americans and the gods of imperial Britons, and have unhesitatingly chosen to support the latter, enhancing the idea that, despite being an international team, the X-Men are agents of Western civilization.

5. The only character in the Marvel Universe descended from the Māori appears to be Kiwi Black, an extremely minor X-Men character who, while avoiding the stereotypical teleportation powers, is named after "kiwis," a slang term for New Zealanders, and the All Blacks rugby team.

6. Only a few names are given for the citizens of Genosha, but they make it clear that they are descended from French and English settlers. Madame Renau, the president, and the Genegineer Dr. Moreau (obviously also named after H. G. Wells's mad scientist from *The Island of Dr. Moreau*) and his son Philip have French surnames while Jenny Ransome, Cormack Grimshaw, and Tam Anderson all have English surnames.

Works Cited

Abnett, Dan, Andy Lanning (w), Jim Calafiore (p), and Rey Garcia (i). "Dreamtime." *Force Work* #9 (March 1995), Marvel Comics.

Bendis, Brian M., Jonathan Hickman (w), and Stefano Caselli (a). "Nick Fury: Agent of Nothing, Part 4." *Secret Warriors* #4 (July 2009), Marvel Comics.

Brown, Audrey. "Rainbow Nation—Dream or Reality?" *BBC News*, July 18, 2008, news.bbc.co.uk/2/hi/africa/7512700.stm. Accessed August 10, 2013.

Campbell, Gwyn. *An Economic History of Imperial Madagascar, 1750–1895: The Rise and Fall of an Island Empire*. London: Cambridge University Press, 2005.

Christie, M. F. *Aboriginal People in Colonial Victoria, 1835–86*. Sydney University Press, 1979. 175–76.

Claremont, Chris (w), John Byrne (p), and Terry Austin (i). "Days of Future Past." *Uncanny X-Men* #141–42 (January–February 1981), Marvel Comics.

Claremont, Chris (w), Dave Cockrum (p), and Bob McLeod (i). "The Doomsmith Scenario!" *Uncanny X-Men* #94 (August 1975), Marvel Comics.

Claremont, Chris (w), and Salvador Larocca (a). "Dreamtime Serenade." *X-Treme X-Men* #4 (October 2001), Marvel Comics.
Claremont, Chris (w), Jim Lee (a), and Art Thibert (i). "Rogue Redux." *Uncanny X-Men* #269 (October 1990), Marvel Comics.
Claremont, Chris (w), Rick Leonardi (a), and Terry Austin (i). "Who's Human?" *Uncanny X-Men* #237 (November 1988), Marvel Comics.
Claremont, Chris (w), Rick Leonardi (a), P. Craig Russell (i).] "Welcome to Genosha." *Uncanny X-Men* #235 (October 1988), Marvel Comics.
Claremont, Chris (w), Rob Liefeld (a), and Dan Green (i). "Men!" *Uncanny X-Men* #245 (June 1989), Marvel Comics.
Claremont, Chris (w), Marc Silvestri (a), and Dan Green (i). "Busting Loose." *Uncanny X-Men* #236 (October 1988), Marvel Comics.
Claremont, Chris (w), Marc Silvestri (a), and Dan Green (i). "Dawn of Blood." *Uncanny X-Men* #233 (September 1988), Marvel Comics.
Claremont, Chris (w), Marc Silvestri (a), and Dan Green (i). "Down Under." *Uncanny X-Men* #229 (May 1988), Marvel Comics.
Claremont, Chris (w), Marc Silvestri (a), and Dan Green (i). "Gonna Be a Revolution." *Uncanny X-Men* #238 (November 1988), Marvel Comics.
Claremont, Chris (w), Marc Silvestri (a), and Dan Green (i). "Ladies' Night." *Uncanny X-Men* #244 (May 1989), Marvel Comics.
Claremont, Chris (w), Marc Silvestri (a), and Dan Green (i). "The Dane Curse." *Uncanny X-Men* #249 (October 1989), Marvel Comics.
Claremont, Chris (w), Marc Silvestri (a), and Dan Green (i). "'Twas the Night..." *Uncanny X-Men* #230 (June 1988), Marvel Comics.
Claremont, Chris, Ann Nocenti, Jim Starlin et al. (w), John Romita Jr., John Buscema, Brett Anderson et al. (p), and Al Gordon, Klaus Janson, Joe Sinnott et al. (i). "Heroes for Hope." *Heroes for Hope, Starring the X-Men* #1 (December 1985), Marvel Comics.
Copland, Mark Stephen. "Calculating Lives: The Numbers and Narratives of Forced Removals in Queensland 1859–1972." PhD thesis, Griffith University, 2005. Internet Archive, Accessed May 17, 2018.
Cowan, James G. *Myths of the Dreaming: Interpreting Aboriginal Legends*. Prism, 1994.
Cronin, Brian. "Comic Legends: Which X-Men Villain Was Originally Intended to Be Gay?" CBR.com, July 28, 2017, www.cbr.com/x-men-villain-originally-gay/.
DeFalco, Tom. "1980s." *Marvel Chronicle: A Year by Year History*, edited by Laura Gilbert, 22. DK Publishing, 2008.
Eliade, Mircea. "Australian Religions: An Introduction." *History of Religions* 6, no. 2 (1967): 50–53. JSTOR, www.jstor.org/stable/1061738. Accessed June 7, 2018.
Ennis, Daniel James. *Enter the Press-Gang: Naval Impressment in Eighteenth-Century British Literature*. University of Delaware Press, 2002.
Fawaz, Ramzi. *The New Mutants: Superheroes and the Radical Imagination of American Comics*. New York University Press, 2016.
Gibson, Campbell, and Kay Jung. "Historical Census Statistics on Population Totals By Race, 1790 to 1990, and By Hispanic Origin, 1970 to 1990, For The United States, Regions, Divisions, and States." Census.gov., 2005. https://www.census.gov/population/wwwdocumentation/twps0076/twps0076.pdf.
Gruenwald, Mark, Bill Mantlo, Steven Grant (w), John Romita Jr. (a), and Pablo Marcos (i). "Contest of Champions." *Contest of Champions* #1–3 (June–August 1982), Marvel Comics.
Haddon, Alfred C. *The Study of Man*. New York: G. P. Putnam's Sons, 1898. 225.

Harras, Bob (w), Ron Lim (p), and Jeff Albrecht (i). "Pharaoh's Legacy." *Marvel Comics Presents* #24–31 (July–November 1989), Marvel Comics.

"Hendrik Frensch Verwoerd." *South African History Online*, February 17, 2011. www.sahistory.org.za/people/hendrik-frensch-verwoerd. Accessed March 9, 2013.

Horton, David, ed. *The Encyclopedia of Aboriginal Australia: Aboriginal and Torres Strait Islander History, Society and Culture*. Canberra: Aboriginal Studies Press, 1994.

"Indigenous Australian." marvel.wikia.com/wikiCategory:Indigenous_Australian. Accessed June 7, 2018.

Isaacs, Jennifer. *Australian Dreaming: 40,000 Years of Aboriginal History*. Sydney: Lansdowne Press, 1980.

Kilborne, B. "On Classifying Dreams." *Dreaming: Anthropological and Psychological Interpretations*, edited by Barbara Tedlock, 171–93. Cambridge University Press, 1897.

Lee, Jim, Whilce Portacio, John Byrne (w), Whilce Portacio (p), and Art Thibert (i). "Fresh Upstart." *Uncanny X-Men* #281 (October 1991), Marvel Comics.

Lee, Stan (w), Gene Colan (p), and Dick Ayers (i). "When a Monarch Goes Mad!" *Tales to Astonish* #81 (July 1966), Marvel Comics.

Lynn-Cook, Elizabeth. "You May Consider Speaking about Your Art . . ." *I Tell You Now: Autobiographical Essays of Native American Writers*, edited by Brian Swann and Arnold Krupat. University of Nebraska Press, 1987.

MacKillop, James. *A Dictionary of Celtic Mythology*. Oxford University Press, 1998.

McAteer, William. *The History of Seychelles from Discovery to Independence*. Mahé: Pristine Books, 2000.

McLauren, Marc (w), Scott Benefiel (p), and Frank Turner (i). "Sudden Burning." *Cage* #13 (April 1993), Marvel Comics.

Nocenti, Ann (w), Larry Dixon (p), and Alfredo Alcala (i). "Dreamwalk." *Marvel Comics Presents* #16 (April 1989), Marvel Comics.

Ponniah, Kevin. "Australia census: Five Takeaways from a Changing Country." *BBC News*, June 27, 2017. www.bbc.com/news/world-australia-40416350.

Portman, Jamie. "G'day Again, 'Crocodile' Dundee Amiable Aussie Is Back in 'Crocodile' Dundee II." *Toronto Star*, May 21, 1988, p. J3. Accessed June 7, 2018.

Romita, John, Stan Lee (w), John Buscema (p), and Jim Mooney (i). "The Coming of the Kangaroo!" *The Amazing Spider-Man* #81 (February 1970), Marvel Comics.

Scalera, Buddy (w), and Karl Kerschl (a). "Falling to Pieces." *Weapon X: The Draft—Sauron* #1 (October 2002), Marvel Comics.

Shooter, Jim, ed. *Official Handbook of the Marvel Universe* #10 v2 (September 1986), Marvel Comics.

Simmonds, Alecia. "Australia Needs to Own up to Its Slave History." *Sydney Morning Herald*, April 28, 2015, www.smh.com.au/lifestyle/australia-needs-to-own-up-to-its-slavehistory-20150427-1muhg3.html.

Simonson, Louise and Walt (w), Jon J. Muth, and Kent Willams (a). "Meltdown." *Havok & Wolverine: Meltdown* #1–4 (May 1988), Marvel Comics.

Smith, W. Ramsay. *Myths and Legends of the Australian Aborigines*. Farrar & Rinehart, 1932.

Wein, Len (w), and Dave Cockrum (p/i). "Second Genesis!" *Giant-Size X-Men* #1 (May 1975), Marvel Comics.

Wein, Len (w), Herb Trimpe (p), and Jack Abel (i). "And Now . . . the Wolverine!" *Incredible Hulk* #181 (November 1974), Marvel Comics.

The Wisdom of the Phantom: The Secret Life of Australia's Indigenous Superhero

Kevin Patrick

The Pacific Art collection of the National Gallery of Victoria (Australia) contains hundreds of items, ranging from bowls and spatulas to carved figures and masks, gathered from different parts of Papua New Guinea, the vast island archipelago north of Australia. Nestled among these traditional handicrafts are a selection of wooden shields from the Wahgi Valley in the Western Highlands Province. Two shields, in particular, stand out from the others. The first depicts the American comic-strip character, the Phantom, and is adorned with a Papuan license plate and a metallic car badge. These, we are told, are symbols of pride and wealth, indicating that the clan that made this shield owned a car ("Phantom shield c. 1970"). The second shield also portrays the Phantom, his figure lit from below, casting him in a menacing glow, and bears the painted legend, "Black 1989 Civil War" ("Phantom shield c. 1989"). These wooden shields offer no protection against modern firearms that have supplanted "traditional" weapons, such as spears, bone daggers, and stone axes. Nevertheless, they are stark relics of the intertribal conflicts that have wracked the Highlands of Papua New Guinea for decades. Reports estimate that 20 percent of the nation's population is affected by these so-called micro-conflicts, which are responsible for hundreds of deaths each year (Reilly 15).

Putting their martial purpose to one side, these shields raise intriguing questions. Why did Papuan tribes choose the Phantom as decorative shield motif? And why would an Australian public art gallery select them as representative examples of contemporary Pacific art? The answers to these questions arise from the Phantom's unique cultural status in Australia and throughout the Oceanic region. The Phantom may be all but forgotten in his American homeland, but he has enjoyed an ardent following in Australia, which is home to the world's longest-running edition of *The Phantom* comic book, which celebrated its seventieth anniversary in 2018. In a country that prides itself on its egalitarian traditions, the Phantom transcends all barriers of race, class, and gender. His exploits are enjoyed by schoolchildren and the elderly, by blue-collar workers and merchant bankers. High-profile politicians and sporting figures are among the character's most devout fans. Brittle copies of the earliest Australian issues of *The Phantom* comic from the 1940s routinely fetch record sums at auctions.

The story behind the Phantom's journey "Down Under" offers fascinating historical insights about the production, circulation, and reception of American mass culture, which this author has documented at length elsewhere (Patrick 2017). This chapter, however, focuses on how the Phantom came to be venerated by Indigenous peoples, from the highlands of Papua New Guinea, to Aboriginal and Torres Strait Islander communities throughout Australia. The Phantom has, over many decades, been appropriated for maverick art projects and public education programs that speak to the political demands and cultural aspirations of Indigenous peoples in both countries.

To understand this remarkable phenomenon, this chapter will briefly discuss the circumstances surrounding the debut of *The Phantom* comic strip in Australia and Papua New Guinea, and how they helped cement the series' success for decades to come. It will consider the intrinsic appeal of the Phantom himself, together with his fantastic jungle world, and why these resonate so strongly with antipodean audiences. This will lead us to address the fundamental paradox of the Phantom. How can a hero, whose very existence hinges on the basic tenets of colonialism, prove so popular with Indigenous people?

The answer to that question may be found in the many roles that the Phantom has played, as a political activist, tribal counselor, and cultural custodian, in vastly different contexts. These are glimpses into the secret life of the Phantom—a hero from the New World, reinvented to meet the needs of ancient cultures in faraway lands.

The Phantom's Australian Odyssey

Midway through 1936, American newspapers began carrying advertisements that spoke in excited tones about a "mysterious adventurer" and "strange personage" who was destined to bring a "thrilling novelty" to comic strips (Scandinavian chapter 35). Clad in a skin-tight costume and trunks, his face concealed by a cowl and mask, the Phantom looked like no other hero that had yet graced the "funny pages" of America's newspapers.

The Phantom, created by Lee Falk (author) and Ray Moore (illustrator), made its debut in the *New York Journal* on February 17, 1936. Even though his earliest adventures owed much to contemporary pulp-fiction magazines, the Phantom provided the visual template for the costumed superhero, two years before Superman graced the cover of *Action Comics* in 1938. However, the Man of Steel soon overshadowed the character that comics historian Maurice Horn dubbed "the granddaddy of all costumed superheroes" (242). As Superman took off, the Phantom gradually receded from America's popular consciousness, despite repeated efforts to relaunch the character in magazines, books, films, and television shows over successive decades. The Phantom may be all but forgotten in his American homeland, but he enjoyed astonishing success abroad. Even today, decades after its debut, King Features syndicates the comic strip to more than five hundred newspapers in forty countries and it is printed in fifteen languages ("History"). And nowhere does he enjoy a more ardent following than in Australia, where the Phantom has become an "adopted" national hero.

The Phantom's arrival in Australia was a consequence of a circulation war between Australia's leading women's magazines. The *Australian Woman's Mirror* had, by the mid-1920s, achieved the highest circulation of any weekly Australian periodical (Rolfe 290). Its commercial dominance was challenged by the arrival of the *Australian Women's Weekly* in 1933. This glossy, upmarket magazine began serializing Lee Falk's first comic-strip serial, *Mandrake the Magician*, in December 1934, which proved an instant hit with Australian readers (O'Brien 55). The *Australian Woman's Mirror* quickly snapped up local magazine rights to Falk's newest comic strip, *The Phantom*, which debuted as a full-page feature on September 1, 1936.

The magazine promoted *The Phantom*, not as a juvenile comic strip, but as an "exciting picture serial," intended for adult readers ("The Phantom," 1936). It deliberately marketed *The Phantom* as an Australian, rather than American, comic strip; American spelling and slang, along with references to American dollars, were replaced with their "correct" Australian equivalents. The Phantom's love interest, Diana Palmer, was no longer a New York socialite, but "a young Sydney girl" (Falk and Moore, "The Phantom"). Many of the character's early adventures were set throughout Southeast Asia, while the Phantom's secluded jungle home was initially located in Luntok, "a British protectorate off the coast of Sumatra" (Falk and Moore, "The Singh Brotherhood"). The character's geographic proximity to both Australia and Papua New Guinea, together with cosmetic changes made by the magazine's editors, reinforced the idea that the Phantom was a local, rather than imported hero.

The *Australian Woman's Mirror*, unlike metropolitan newspapers, enjoyed nationwide circulation, which ensured maximum exposure for *The Phantom* in a periodical that—like so many women's magazines of that era—were read and enjoyed by men and women alike. This proved beneficial for *The Phantom* comic book, which found a readymade audience when it was launched by Frew Publications (Sydney) in September 1948. *The Phantom* comic magazine was buoyed by the explosive postwar growth of Australia's comic book industry (Patrick, "Cultural Economy" 164–65), and was selling 90,000 copies per issue by 1950 (Snowden 6). Even as the local comics industry underwent commercial

Figure 5.1. *The Phantom*, No. 155, Frew Publications (Australia), 1959.

decline following the introduction of television broadcasting in 1956, *The Phantom* continued to exert a "phenomenal grip on the juvenile market" ("The Comics Business" 6) and shifted from a monthly to biweekly publishing schedule in the early 1960s, which Frew Publications maintains to this day (see fig. 5.1). Whereas imported American comics suffered from erratic distribution, *The Phantom* was ubiquitous—it could be purchased at newsagents and convenience stores, while giveaway copies were included in "show bags" sold at agricultural fairs held throughout the country. Thus, the character became an ever-present fixture in Australia's media landscape.

But these commercial factors alone cannot account for the Phantom's enduring popularity with Australian audiences. That he is not, as Coulton Waugh observed, a "superhero in the wild, modern meaning of the word" goes some way toward explaining his appeal (260). Reliant on his quick wits, mental ingenuity, and physical strength, the Phantom is an "ordinary" superhero that everyday readers can identify with. We will never be an orphan from the planet Krypton or be bitten by a radioactive spider—but with dedication and training, we could feasibly be just like the Phantom. Australians frequently single out his moral code and personal conduct as a reflection of their national self-image. As one fan remarked:

> Ironically, [The Phantom is] part of the Australian cultural image, [even though it isn't] written by an Aussie. I think it's his understated way of doing things, championing [the] weak and looking after a mate, that has appealed so much to Australians. (qtd. in Patrick, *Phantom Unmasked* 156–57)

This sense of identification also extends to the Phantom's physical realm. For years, Lee Falk set the Phantom's exploits in the fictional land of Bengali (later renamed "Bangalla"), which sometimes resembled sub-Saharan Africa, India, or Southeast Asia. These shifting geographical markers allowed readers to imagine the Phantom's world as their own world. For one Australian woman, growing up in Papua New Guinea—"very much like the jungle of Bengalla [sic]"—provided her with the perfect backdrop to imagine herself as the Phantom: "Even though I am a female, I could see myself being a do-gooder like the Phantom, and [fighting] crime, pirates, and baddies" (qtd. in Patrick, *Phantom Unmasked* 155).

Perhaps the most baffling aspect of the Phantom's popularity in this context is the most troubling. During the strip's formative years, Lee Falk initially portrayed the Phantom as a god-like figure who ruled the jungle with an iron fist, striking fear among superstitious Natives. Richard F. Patteson suggests that comic strips like *The Phantom* are modern-day continuations of imperialist romances, popularized by the likes of H. Rider Haggard, which expressed the need for "white civilization" to establish "European authority over Native peoples" (115).

Falk subsequently downplayed this theme and recast the Phantom as an unofficial peacekeeper and arbitrator of tribal disputes, while successive illustrators toned down the crude racial caricatures that were all too common during the strip's early years. Yet as Fredrik Strömberg observes, the strip's basic premise—wherein "a white man in the jungle protects simple savages by spreading law and order"—remains problematic in today's postcolonial environment (81). The quasi-imperialist scenario of *The Phantom* invites parallels with Britain's colonization of Australia, and its legacy of frontier violence and the dispossession of Aboriginal lands. Russell Marks, however, believes that the Phantom's commercial longevity cannot be attributed solely to some "lingering colonial [fantasy] in the minds of white Australians" (2013). As Russell McGregor points out, white Australians' attitudes toward Aboriginals throughout the twentieth century "was more commonly apathy than malevolence," because they did not pose a threat to Australia's national existence in the same way that fears of unchecked Asian migration excited political debate and public imagination (2011, xviii). Instead, Marks argues that many non-Indigenous Australians would like to imagine their contact with Aboriginal society in accordance with the Phantom's "sanitized" jungle realm, where the Native populace embraces the benefits of modernity, while remaining "cultural villagers" (2013).

"Bai Yu Kamap Strong Olsem Phantom"

The colonial fantasy of *The Phantom* stands at odds with Australia's imperial designs for New Guinea. This mountainous archipelago became one of the last arenas for the "great game" played between Europe's imperial powers. Britain annexed southeast New Guinea in 1884, while Germany added northeast New Guinea—renamed Kaiser Wilhelm Land—to its Pacific possessions that same year. In 1906, control of British New Guinea was transferred to the Commonwealth of Australia and was now known as the Territory of Papua (Mair 10–11).

The political future of New Guinea for much of the twentieth century was decided during the First World War. Soon after Britain declared war on Germany in August 1914, an Australian naval and military expeditionary force—at Britain's request—occupied German New Guinea, after swiftly overcoming the small German garrison stationed there (Nelson 25–28). It remained under Australian military government control until 1921, when the League of Nations designated it an Australian Mandated Territory. The dual Australian administrations in the north- and south-east were formally amalgamated as the Territory of Papua and New Guinea in 1949 and remained under Australian control until 1975 (Mair 34–41).

The idea that Australia was ever a colonial power ran counter to the egalitarian spirit and humanitarian traditions "in which Australians wished to see themselves" (Nelson 13). New Guinea, after all, was Australia's "external territory," not a "colony." These semantic exercises, however, could not disguise the fact that it was largely governed to serve Australia's political, economic, and strategic interests. Contemporary juvenile literature painted Papua New Guinea as Australia's last true frontier, "where any boy could imagine playing the deeds that won an empire" (Nelson 14). *The Phantom*, therefore, can be read as a modern, updated version of the frontier fantasies that once filled the pages of British and Australian children's magazines during the interwar decades. As Makarand Paranjape points out, the Phantom was an "undying white patriarch," whose jungle realm furnished the West with "new playing fields to enact its dramas of domination," where British imperialism gave way to the "newer, incipient imperialism" of the United States (2008, 12). The Phantom's reception in Papua New Guinea, however, suggests that ostensibly "colonized" audiences bypass such critical objections, and choose to interpret the series in ways that reflects and reaffirms their own cultural experiences and belief systems.

The Phantom frequently reached international audiences through unconventional channels that had little in common with the metropolitan newspapers that were the main conduit for comic strips in the United States during the first half of the twentieth century. This was certainly true of Papua New Guinea, where *The Phantom* first appeared in the pages of a Catholic newspaper printed in Tok Pisin, a widely spoken Creole language that is now one of the country's three official languages, alongside English and Hiri Motu.

Wantok ("One Talk") was a biweekly newspaper sponsored by the Society of the Divine Word, a Catholic order that adopted Tok Pisin as a language of religious service ("Tok Lotu") in the 1920s (Cass, "Fr Francis Mihalic" 213). Under the guidance of its American-born editor, Fr Francis ("Frank") Mihalic, *Wantok* adopted an ecumenical, apolitical outlook to appeal to a broader (non-Catholic) readership, as well as attract advertisers (219). The first issue of *Wantok* was published on August 5, 1970, with a modest print run of just 7,000 copies. However, the newspaper's deliberate appeal to "grassruts" audiences in remote areas, ensured that even single copies would be passed around an entire village, thus boosting its overall circulation figures (Cass, *Press Politics and People* 140).

Mihalic constantly tested new ways to broaden the newspaper's appeal and extend its geographic reach. *Wantok* reproduced photos supplied by the Department of Information and Extension Services, which documented everyday life throughout the country. The newspaper invited government departments, churches, local businesses, and sports groups to submit stories about their activities (Cass, *Press Politics and People* 131–32). It ran a regular column, "Political Edukesen," to inform readers about the country's changing political landscape, as it made the transition from parliamentary self-government under Australian administration, to achieving political independence in 1975 (133). *Wantok* published readers' letters from across the country, and its letters page became a popular forum for public debate about local issues (142).

Figure 5.2. "The Phantom," *Wantok* (Papua New Guinea), April 2, 1977, p. 18.

Mihalic bought the Papuan newspaper serial rights to *The Phantom* comic strip from Yaffa Syndicate (Australia), which was King Features' sales representative for the Australasian / South Pacific region. The strip, translated into Tok Pisin, debuted in 1973 and was an immediate hit with readers (see fig. 5.2). Government officials sought permission to use the Phantom to encourage the public to eat protein-rich peanuts instead of starch. The Phantom soon appeared on posters throughout the country. "Sapos yu kaikai planti pinat," he declared, "bai yu kamap strong olsem phantom" ("If you eat many peanuts, you will become strong like the Phantom") ("Fantom, Yu Pren Tru Bilong Mi" 16).

Wantok published a Tok Pisin edition of *The Phantom* comic book in the mid-1970s, in response to reader demand, which have become sought-after collectors' items. But why did the Phantom prove so popular? Alan Spanos, a nutritionist based in the Chimbu Province, said the character connected with Papuan readers on many levels:

> He succeeds here because his image strikes deep chords. He is big and strong and white, like the much-admired and envied Europeans. He is generous and fair and helps the weak, like the government in the colonial era. He has magical powers and is solitary and of mysterious origin, so he may well be really a returned ancestor. After all, the first European explorers were often taken for returned ancestors, partly because of the common belief that the spirits of the dead are white. (qtd. in Gill 14)

If anything, the Phantom proved too successful for *Wantok*. The *Post-Courier*, Papua New Guinea's largest-selling English-language newspaper, was now publishing daily episodes of *The Phantom*, and asked King Features to revoke *Wantok*'s rights to the comic strip. While the newspaper's biweekly circulation had risen to 9,500 by this time, it was hardly a serious commercial rival to the *Post-Courier*, which had a daily circulation of 17,000. Mihalic, however, suspected that *Wantok* posed a subtler threat to its larger competitor:

> *The Post-Courier* actually gave *Wantok* more credit than it deserved. It felt that . . . *Wantok* had the psychological edge in knowing how local customers were thinking and what they liked and disliked. (qtd. in Cass, *Press, Politics and People* 145)

The matter was taken up by Papuan government officials, who, together with the Australian Religious Press Association, lobbied King Features to ask that *Wantok* be allowed to retain Tok Pisin language rights to *The Phantom*. The matter became a cause célèbre in the Australian press, but the *Post Courier* eventually secured exclusive Papuan publication rights to the series ("The Ghost Who Walks" 18). Yet the legacy of the Phantom remains visible throughout the Highlands of Papua New Guinea, long after the comic strip ceased appearing in *Wantok*. The Phantom became a popular motif on tribal shields throughout the 1970s and 1980s, especially among younger warriors who identified with the Phantom's role as tribal protector ("Fighting Shield"). Kaipel Ka, a Papuan sign-writer and painter from the Western Highlands Province, grew up reading *Phantom* comics, and frequently depicts the character on shields intended for his tribe's fiercest warriors. "Because those who led the battle are the toughest fighters," he explained, "just like the Phantom" (qtd. in Eby 2014).

Defining Aboriginal Identity

The Skull Cave boasts treasure rooms filled with coins, gold, and priceless artifacts seized from pirates, thieves, and brigands. But its greatest prize is the Phantom Chronicles, a vast library containing firsthand accounts of every Phantom's exploits, dating back nearly five hundred years. It was from one such volume that the present-day Phantom learned that his ancestor—the 14th Phantom—undertook a perilous voyage to Australia in the early 1800s. Searching for a missing heiress rumored to be living in the central Australian desert, the Phantom and his companions are rescued from a sandstorm by members of the Wuluti tribe. Recording his experiences in the chronicles, the 14th Phantom wrote that he learned some of their language, observed their ceremonies, and "listened to their mysterious music played on a didgeridoo" (Worker and Cruz 31). This story, originally produced for the Swedish *Fantomen* comic, was published with considerable fanfare by Frew Publications in 1989. The cover blared: "History is made! The Phantom in Australia!"

This episode from the Phantom Chronicles doesn't shy away from the reality of frontier violence between Aboriginals and British colonists, but it does present an undeniably romanticized portrayal of Indigenous Australians. The inclusion of the fictitious "Wuluti" tribe only hints at the diversity and complexity of Aboriginal society and culture. These are, of course, unrealistic expectations to have of what is essentially a work of escapist literature. But it nevertheless provides us with the opportunity to briefly consider, if only for the purposes of this chapter, the very notion of "Aboriginal identity," and how this has influenced the appropriation of the Phantom as an "Indigenous" superhero.

In the early 1980s, the Commonwealth Department of Aboriginal Affairs proposed a tripartite definition of "Aboriginal" that was based on descent, self-identification, and community recognition: "An Aboriginal or Torres Strait Islander is a person of Aboriginal or Torres Strait Islander descent who identifies as an Aboriginal or Torres Strait Islander and is accepted as such by the community in which he (she) lives" (Gardiner-Garden 4).

This definition, subsequently adopted by all federal government departments, draws crucial distinctions between mainland Aboriginals and Torres Strait Islanders, who inhabit several islands in the waterway that separates Australia and Papua New Guinea, as well as parts of Cape York Peninsula in northern Australia ("Torres Strait Islander Flag" 2017). The term "Indigenous Australians" is often used to encompass both Aboriginal and Torres Strait Islander people. However, Aboriginal people frequently use self-designations, such as "Koori" ("person"), that identify them with a specific language group, or geographic region (Heath 2005). Torres Strait Islanders, too, use the name of their home island to describe themselves to outsiders ("Indigenous Australians" 2018).

Based on the latest available census figures, 649,200 people reported being of Aboriginal and/or Torres Strait Islander origin, representing 2.8 percent of Australia's total population (23.4 million) in 2016 ("Aboriginal and Torres Strait Islander Population" 2018). The census reported that 10 percent of Aboriginal and Torres Strait Islander people spoke an Indigenous language in their homes (2018). However, the second National Indigenous Languages Survey paints a more complex picture. It found that of 250 known Indigenous Australian languages, only 120 were still spoken, down from 145 languages reported in the previous 2004–2005 survey. Of these 120 languages, only 13 were considered "strong," still spoken by all age groups, and being passed on to children (Marmion et al. xii). Despite these discouraging statistics, the overwhelming majority of survey participants said the use of traditional language formed a "strong part of their identity" and was crucial to maintaining the well-being of Aboriginal and Torres Strait Islander people (Marmion et al. 29–30).

Australian educators have long recognized comic books' value as an instructional medium that appeals to younger readers. Pioneering educational comics include the *Pictorial Social Studies* series from the 1950s, and *Falcon Comics*, a series of remedial-level "graphic novels" issued in the 1970s (Patrick, "In Search of" 59–61). It is therefore not surprising to learn that *The Phantom* could be adapted for similar pedagogical purposes. Nick Thieberger, an instructor at the Batchelor College School of Australian Linguistics in the Northern Territory, used *The Phantom* to help Aboriginal students develop their own vernacular-format literacy materials:

Some students were reading *The Phantom* comic ... [so] I figured it was good to start with something they wanted to read anyway. It just so happened that the [issue] they were reading had the Phantom freeing black slaves in chains, so it was pretty topical for Indigenous students. (Thieberger 2018)

The story, "Black Ivory," originally produced for the Swedish *Fantomen* comic in 1983, was subsequently translated into English by Frew Publications for the Australian market (Guaraz and Bess 1985). Thieberger and his students translated the English version into the Walpiri language and developed a "blank" template version (with all captions and dialogue removed), so it could be used by others. Thieberger subsequently produced a Manyjilyjarra language version of the same story in collaboration with the Punmu community in the Great Sandy Desert. This was made available through the Wangka Maya Pilbara Aboriginal Language Centre in Western Australia. This ersatz version of *The Phantom* comic is indicative of the small-scale projects developed to teach and preserve Indigenous languages that are undertaken in collaboration with Aboriginal communities in regional and remote areas of Australia.

The Agitprop Superhero

The legend of the Phantom begins, not in America, but on the distant shores of an uncharted continent. In 1525, Sir Christopher Standish, an English nobleman, was sailing to the Americas with his father, when the notorious Singh Brotherhood attacked their ship. Sir Christopher saw his father slain by this vicious pirate gang moments before he was tossed overboard during a violent storm that swamped their vessel. He was washed ashore on a remote beach, where he was found unconscious by members of the Bandar pygmy tribe, who nursed him back to health. Sometime later, he discovered the body of a Singh pirate on a distant stretch of the same rugged coastline. Swearing an oath on the skull of his father's murderer, Sir Christopher vowed to fight "against all piracy, greed, and cruelty," and pledged that "as long as my descendants walk the earth, the eldest male of my family shall carry out my work" (Falk and Moore, "The Singh Brotherhood" 115). This unbroken succession from father to son, kept secret for centuries, led many to believe that the Phantom was immortal. Thus began the legend of "The Ghost Who Walks—Man Who Cannot Die."

To some observers, the origins of the Phantom dynasty shares similarities with the British colonization of Australia, when the First Fleet disgorged its human cargo of convicts, marines, and civil administrators upon the shores of Botany Bay, Sydney, in 1788. David Dale, seeking to explain the Phantom's historical appeal among Australians, recast the character's origins as an idealized version of Australia's "founding myth" as a distant land of exile:

[The first Phantom] was an innocent, cast away on a fatal shore, far from his home and loved ones, and forced to carve out a new life. He made friends with the local wildlife, adapted to the ecology, and earned the respect of the Natives. Then he proceeded to fight for the underdog, wherever he saw injustice. Isn't that exactly the story of Australia? (Dale 74)

The British colonization of Australia, celebrated annually as "Australia Day" on January 26, is frequently denounced by Aboriginal activists as "Invasion Day." Nevertheless, echoes of this romanticized version of Australia's "founding myth" can be found in contemporary artistic tributes to the Phantom. Euan MacLeod, a New Zealand-born painter known for dramatic works depicting lone figures set against harsh landscapes, touches on this theme in "Father of the first Phantom." MacLeod's work retells the origin of the Phantom in an ethereal, multi-layered fashion, juxtaposing the dual figures of Sir Christopher Standish and the Phantom against a split-level seascape, depicting a landing party from a distant ship holding aloft a naval ensign as they stride ashore. It was one of many works featured in The Phantom Show, cocurated by artists (and lifelong Phantom fans) Peter Kingston and Dietmar Lederwasch, which toured Australia throughout 2014–2017 (Bevan 2017).

Other Australian artists, however, have used the racial premise of *The Phantom* comic strip to comment on the historical legacy of conflict between British settlers and Australia's Indigenous people. Franck Gohier, a French-born painter, sculptor, and printmaker, has lived in Darwin since his parents migrated to Australia's Northern Territory in 1975. Gohier describes his work as a "form of urban archaeology," which incorporates found objects and ephemera that reflect on his experience of living in Darwin, which he describes as "an often harsh, outpost, frontier town" (Macleod 2018). The Phantom is a frequent subject of his work, as Gohier explains: "Lee Falk's comic book creation 'The Phantom' has always been my favorite comic. It is very popular on Australian Indigenous communities, as it is in Papua New Guinea" (2010). Gohier claims that the Phantom's story is simply about a "white fella" being rescued and adopted by the local Indigenous tribe, who establishes himself as "the boss" by imposing his ethics and morals on a tribal society "that was doing quite fine without him prior to his intrusion" (2010). This was, according to Gohier, a "familiar pattern" he witnessed growing up in Darwin, and later when he was conducting printmaking workshops in remote Indigenous communities throughout the Northern Territory (2010).

The Phantom's ambivalent status as a "benevolent ruler" is a central theme to Gohier's work. *It's for Your Own Good* (2009) depicts the Phantom as a menacing, gun-toting figure, looming over a group of "native" children, huddled together in fear ("Out of the Studio" 2016). But other works, like *Big Boss* (2012), undercuts the Phantom's moral authority, portraying him as the victim of his own brand of "rough justice," mortally wounded by a giant hunting boomerang hurled by an unseen (Aboriginal) opponent (Gohier 2012).

But the Phantom has also been reimagined as a friend and ally of Indigenous peoples, prepared to defend their rights against the encroachments of mainstream (white) society. Without Authority, a printmaking studio established by Joanne Horniman and Tony Chinnery, created a poster titled "Phantom (Hawke)" depicting the character against a lush, jungle backdrop. The skull emblem on his gun belt now replaced with an anarchist symbol, the Phantom recites a radicalized version of the "oath of the skull": "I swear on the skull of my anti-uranium badge to devote myself to the overthrow of Hawke and to spend my life in the destruction of capitalism and the state" ("Without Authority"). The Phantom was situated at the forefront of environmentalist and left-wing political groups' opposition to the decision made by the Australian Labor Party (led by Prime Minister Robert Hawke) to allow uranium mining in the Northern Territory. The poster, produced for Sydney's anarchist bookstore, Jura Books, freely appropriated Frew Publications' "Phantom Comics" poster, which was intended for in-store display at newsstands/stationers, comic shops, and other retailers. Without Authority can be likened to "textual poachers" who, according to Henry Jenkins, "appropriate popular texts and reread them in a fashion that serves different interests" (23). Jenkins initially applied this term to science-fiction fans whose creative endeavors—circulated via fanzines and other amateur media outlets—were characterized by their shared enjoyment of popular media texts, such as *Star Trek* or *Doctor Who*. However, the appropriation of the Phantom by Australian artists has often (but not always) had less to do with sentimental affinity with the character and arose from more diffuse creative and political impulses.

Vote 1 Phantom

The steadfast morality of the Phantom, sworn to fight all forms of "piracy, greed and cruelty," has allowed the character to be claimed as champion of Aboriginal people by both antiauthoritarian political activists and government agencies responsible for Indigenous affairs. Different branches of Australia's federal government and judiciary have recruited the Phantom for public information campaigns intended for Aboriginal communities. Their decision to use the Phantom, ahead of other American comic book heroes, acknowledges the character's long-standing popularity among Indigenous Australians. As Aboriginal lawyer and land rights activist Noel Pearson recalled: "When I was a kid, the old and . . . young read comic books, cowboy stories and magazines . . . [which] would make their way around the village . . . *The Phantom* was, of course, premium" (37–38).

Figure 5.3. *The Phantom Enrols & Votes*, Garage Graphix, 1988.

Paradoxically, the Phantom is portrayed as a champion of Indigenous Australians, but one who nevertheless advocates engagement with political processes and institutions which, some have argued, promote assimilationist policies, instead of advancing political self-determination for Aboriginal people.

The Australian Electoral Commission (AEC) was established in 1984 as an independent statutory authority, responsible for conducting federal elections and referendums and maintaining the Commonwealth electoral roll (it previously operated as a branch of the Department of Home Affairs). Although voting in Australian federal elections has been compulsory since 1924, the AEC has, since its inception, produced a large body of educational material that explain the workings of Australia's parliamentary electoral system, and to inform Australians about their voting rights and responsibilities. The AEC's decision to commission educational comic books featuring the Phantom can thus be seen as part of its ongoing public outreach program.

The Phantom Enrols & Votes, produced by Garage Graphix on behalf of the AEC, was the first of two educational comics intended for Aboriginal audiences. The Phantom, fresh from "banging heads" and fighting crime, returns to his home in a remote Aboriginal community, where he learns that his neighbor, Aunt Jess, is running for federal parliament (Garage Graphix 1–2). When one woman, Dot, asks him if he's enrolled to vote, the Phantom confesses that he's forgotten to do so. She takes him to meet Bill, the AEC community electoral assistant, who helps the Phantom complete and submit his electoral enrollment form. The Phantom visits the polling booth on election day, but again turns to Dot for help with filling out his ballot paper correctly (see fig. 5.3). Dot muses that "Phantoms are all the same, big on muscle, small on brains" (5). Bill, in turn, explains how the Phantom can lodge a postal vote before the election, especially if he was "going to be away fighting crime on election day" (6). The Phantom, impressed by the AEC's efforts to reach Aboriginal voters in remote areas, promises Dot that he's "gonna' spread the word about this voting business" (7).

The second AEC comic, *Vote 1 Phantom*, addresses political issues of vital concern to Indigenous voters that seldom trouble the "mainstream" electorate. Disillusioned by local councilors' apparent willingness to let "outsiders" destroy their land, the community urges the Phantom to stand as their candidate. "You know the area and we trust you, Phantom," urges one woman (Garage Graphix and Legge 4). The Phantom agrees to be their candidate, but seeks advice from Aunt Jess, who previously stood for parliament, about running a political campaign. "You've got to get support," she tells him. "Put up posters. Get on the radio. Talk to people" (5). Hitting the outback campaign trail, the Phantom—astride his white stallion, Hero—addresses a public gathering: "Are you sick of people destroying your land? Are you tired of outsiders ripping you off? Then do something about it! Vote for me and I'll do my best to put it right" (5). Meanwhile, Dot encourages her friends to visit Bill, the AEC community electoral assistant, to discuss their concerns about the election, and ensure they're enrolled to vote. Bill explains that the election is about choosing someone to speak on your behalf in parliament: "That's called representation" (8). There is a huge turn-out on election day, and the Phantom is eventually declared "the new member of the Skull Cave Shire Council" (12). The Phantom confesses to Aunt Jess that he's "dirt scared of council meetings." Aunt Jess dismisses his concerns: "Oh, Phantom. After all those crooks you have to deal with, you're scared of a few men in suits? You'll be right. Anyway, the council needs a bit of color to liven it up" (13). The Phantom attends his first council meeting and warns the other (white) councilors that the days of "business as usual" are over. "The people are tired of not being looked after," he says. "We've got to give them what they want" (14).

Garage Graphix, which produced both of these comics, was a community arts collective established in western Sydney in 1981. It made a concerted effort to employ and train Aboriginal women in both administrative and creative roles, which led to the production of posters and public art projects that reflected "cultural significance and identity for urban Aboriginal people" (Hall 12). It is difficult to tell whether their educational comics resonated with their intended audience, not least because they are crudely drawn when compared to *The Phantom* comics available to Aboriginal readers (the images of the Phantom himself appear to be copied directly from the "official" comic magazine). Nevertheless, these comics reflect Australian governments' historical reliance on visual aids to disseminate voter education information to Indigenous communities. The first of these was *Franchise for Aborigines*, a filmstrip that explained Australia's parliamentary system and voting procedures, and could be exhibited on projection screens, as well as on the walls of public buildings in remote areas ("My Voice for My Country" 2016). The filmstrip was circulated by the Commonwealth Electoral Office (forerunner of the AEC), after the *Commonwealth Electoral Act* was amended in 1962 to give all Aboriginal and Torres Strait Islander adults the right to vote in federal elections. But as Paul Daley points out, these materials rarely discussed how voting might affect the lives of Indigenous Australians. Nor did they challenge the "assimilationist ideology" that underpinned these electoral reforms, which encouraged Aboriginal voters to forego links to their own culture and integrate with mainstream Australian society (2016).

The Family Court of Australia (FCA) was established in 1975 to resolve complex legal family disputes arising from divorce and separation, such as financial settlements and child custody arrangements. In 1997, the FCA produced an educational comic book, *The Wisdom of the Phantom*, to provide counseling information for Aboriginal and Torres Strait Islander communities. Herein the Phantom returns "home"—now situated somewhere in northern Australia—and learns from his wife, Diana Palmer, that their friends Pug and Ruby have separated and are in dispute over custody rights to their children. The Phantom urges Pug and Ruby to seek advice from the Family Court's counselors, reassuring them that the Court employs people "who know us and our ways" and who will "respect our traditions" (Family Court of Australia 6–7) (see fig. 5.4). With the help of Family Court counselors, Pug and Ruby eventually negotiate a shared custody arrangement, so their children can absorb the cultural traditions of each parent's extended community and retain their links to the land. The Phantom's refusal to intervene directly in Pug and Ruby's marital dispute is vindicated by the counselors' ability to address their concerns without taking sides and help them arrive at a mutually beneficial decision. While the Phantom is saddened by Pug and Ruby's separation, he acknowledges that the counselors have helped them keep their family and their community traditions strong (15).

The Wisdom of the Phantom is a far more visually appealing comic, thanks largely to the artwork of Antonio Lemos, a Uruguayan illustrator who by this time had become the resident cover artist for the Australian edition of *The Phantom* comic magazine. His sensitive portrayals of Aboriginal people and everyday life on Indigenous communities greatly enhance the narrative, and avoids the visual chaos commonly associated with superhero comics. These educational comics produced by the AEC and the FCA are undoubtedly different from one another, in terms of their subject matter and creative execution. What is remarkable about each of these comics is how easily they transplanted the Phantom (along with his Skull Cave) to outback Australia, where he is portrayed as a respected participant in the affairs of Indigenous Australians. Although they depart from the "official" narrative of the American comic strip, these comics acknowledge the Phantom's enduring status as a champion of the oppressed among Aboriginal and Torres Strait Islander communities.

Figure 5.4. *The Wisdom of the Phantom*, Family Court of Australia, 1997.

Don't Be Shame, Be Game

The Phantom dynasty relies on the eldest male of each generation fathering an heir to continue the crusade against piracy, greed, and cruelty. This runs counter to the practice of sexual renunciation evident with other comic book superheroes, such as Superman, who must devise strategies for "segmenting the element of sexual need out of their personalities" (Lawrence and Jewett 42–43). By contrast, the Phantom's earliest adventures fairly crackled with erotic energy. When he wasn't locked in a passionate embrace with his then-girlfriend, Diana Palmer, the Phantom was often confronted by femme fatales, who demanded his undying love, under threat of death. (Naturally, he spurned their advances, and eventually married Diana Palmer, who bore him two children, thus ensuring the Phantom dynasty would continue.) To celebrate the character's fifty-fifth anniversary, a Sydney art exhibition featured several works that "[explored] the Phantom's sexuality" ("Phan-tastic!" 1991). One painting depicted him being flayed with a riding crop by a buxom dominatrix, while another showed the Phantom kissing a man in front of his bewildered pet wolf, Devil.

Indigenous health organizations have tapped into the Phantom's sexual mystique and have used him to convey the importance of safe sex to Indigenous Australians. Aboriginal and Torres Strait Islanders have been overrepresented in sexual disease statistics, contracting sexually transmitted infections (STIs) such as chlamydia, gonorrhea, and syphilis at substantially higher rates than non-Indigenous Australians, especially in rural and remote areas (Davidson

2018). This situation is compounded by the understandable reticence among young Indigenous Australians to openly seek treatment for STIs, especially in areas where local community members employed at health clinics may be known to them, thus raising concerns about confidentiality of patient information (Brady 10–11).

The need for culturally appropriate sex education materials that would appeal to Indigenous Australians became more urgent during the late 1980s, when the spread of AIDS pushed the issues of sexually transmitted diseases and safe-sex practices to the forefront of public debate. The federal government's controversial 1987 "Grim Reaper" television commercial warned that AIDS was no longer confined to the gay community and intravenous drug users, and now posed a significant health risk to the general public (Padula 2007). This campaign undeniably raised public awareness about AIDS, but there were concerns among Aboriginal health workers that it did not resonate with Indigenous communities and failed to provide them with the resources they needed to make informed decisions about sexual health issues.

The Kimberley Aboriginal Medical Services Council (Western Australia) launched its own AIDS information campaign in 1987, aimed at local Indigenous communities. The Phantom and his "girlfriend" (rather than his wife, Diana Palmer) were featured in a fold-out pamphlet, *Why Wanda said "No" in Broome*, which promoted safe sex. The comic-strip brochure capitalized on the fact that young people in surrounding communities were avid *Phantom* comic book readers (Brady 12), and used colloquial humor to stress the importance of condom use, while dispelling the myth that AIDS was an exclusively "gay disease" (O'Riordan 1998).

In 1987, a group of Aboriginal sexual health workers (led by Gracelyn Smallwood) gathered in Townsville, Queensland, to develop an HIV/AIDS awareness campaign to encourage condom use. They came up with the idea for an Indigenous superhero, Condoman, and commissioned Redback Graphix, a Sydney arts studio known for producing politically charged posters and prints, to develop the concept further. Their poster design showed Condoman, a black superhero dressed in the colors of the Aboriginal flag (red, black, and yellow), holding a pack of condoms. "Don't be shame, be game," he says. "Use Frenchies!" (see fig. 5.5). Alison Alder, a former Redback Graphix artist, said the character was based on the Phantom, "which was a really popular comic in north Queensland at the time" (Walmsley 2015). The poster campaign was successful, and Condoman soon became a nationwide "cult figure," after the Commonwealth Department of Community Services and Health commissioned a modified version of the poster for national distribution. "The line 'Use Frenchies' was vernacular from north Queensland at the time," according to Alder. "Then it was changed to 'Wear Condoms' for broader distribution" (Walmsley 2015).

Figure 5.5. Condoman poster, Redback Graphix, 1987.

The character was redesigned and relaunched by the Queensland Association for Healthy Communities (QAHC) and the 2 Spirits Program in 2009. Condoman appeared in a self-titled comic book, as well as in videos distributed via the HITnet touchscreen network. In 2013, he acquired a female compatriot, Lubelicious, dressed in the colors of the Torres Strait Islander flag (green, blue, and black). The safe-sex superheroes were granted a second comic book, and actors portraying the characters regularly give live performances at Aboriginal and Torres Strait Islander events staged throughout Queensland (Dempsey 2015). Condoman's appearance has been modified so that the character—now owned by QAHC—no longer resembles "The Ghost Who Walks." But there is no denying that the Phantom greatly influenced the original version of Condoman, whose message successfully encouraged responsible sexual behavior and helped overcome the stigma and embarrassment once associated with condom use.

The Phantom, on many levels, subverts the popular definition of a "superhero." He has no special powers or abilities, nor is he impervious to injury and pain. He can, in fact, be killed. Aside from his Colt .45 pistols, which he never uses to kill, he possesses no special equipment or advanced technologies. He inhabits a remote jungle, instead of a bustling metropolis. Accompanied by his loyal wolf, and astride a white stallion, the Phantom is as much a knight errant as he is a costumed crimefighter.

It is perhaps for these reasons that the Phantom is a more universal hero, who enjoys greater international acclaim than the likes of Superman or Spider-Man, who are inextricably linked with modern American society and culture. As one Australian reader observed, even the Phantom's costume sets him apart from other comic book superheroes:

> [The Phantom] is more like a persona that the reader can wear . . . his simple, bland costume, and his [mask] that lacks pupils help to give this feeling in the reader . . . He's unspecific, so "he could be me, if I was as good as I could be." (qtd in Patrick, *Phantom Unmasked* 203)

Thus, generations of Australian readers have come to see the Phantom as the embodiment of their defining national characteristics—his understated persona, his subtle sense of humor, his affinity with nature, and his compassion for the underdog. This process of self-identification was also made possible by deliberate attempts to promote *The Phantom* as an Australian, rather than American comic strip.

But this only goes some way toward explaining the character's popular status among Indigenous peoples—not least because the Phantom's status as an unelected "ruler" of African tribes is rooted in the historical imperatives of British imperialism and colonialism. Yet just as white Australia can identify with this transplanted American hero, so too can Papuans and Indigenous

Australians express affinity with the Phantom in ways that reflect their respective cultures and historical experience.

Garry Kinnane remarks on this when recalling his encounters with Aboriginal stockmen (cowhands) in Queensland during the early 1960s. Kinnane, a folk musician, tries to teach them old Australian ballads, but without success:

> A number of the Aborigine [sic] guys play guitar, sing cowboy songs. I wish they would learn some Australian folk songs, but they don't seem interested in that kind of music, it doesn't speak to them as much as . . . Country and Western music does, which . . . being American, has nothing to do with the white Australian culture that they feel excluded from. With this non-Australian material, they feel free to make the sentiments in them their own. (2012, 186)

The Phantom's malleable persona has made it possible for religious groups, government agencies, and Indigenous organizations to adapt him for their own needs, in ways that speak to the needs and aspirations of Indigenous people throughout Australia and Papua New Guinea. The Phantom may be the product of modern American society, but his heroic, almost universal qualities are what make it possible for others to see him as a uniquely "Indigenous" superhero.

Works Cited

"Aboriginal and Torres Strait Islander Population: 2016 Census Data Summary." Australian Bureau of Statistics, July 11, 2018, www.abs.gov.au/ausstats/abs@.nsf/Lookup/by%20Subject/2071.0~2016~Main%20Features~Aboriginal%20and%20Torres%20Strait%20Islander%20Population%20Data%20Summary~10. Accessed August 4, 2018.

Bevan, Scott. "Comic aficionado Dietmar Lederwasch curates return of The Phantom to Newcastle Art Gallery." *Newcastle Herald* [Australia], June 12, 2017, www.theherald.com.au/story/4716708/the-phantom-child-in-all-of-us/. Accessed August 1, 2018.

Brady, Maggie. *The Health of Young Aboriginals*. National Clearinghouse for Youth Studies/Department of Education, University of Tasmania, 1992.

Cass, Philip. "Fr Francis Mihalic and *Wantok* niuspepa." *Pacific Journalism Review* 17, no. 1 (2011): 208–24.

———. *Press, Politics and People in Papua New Guinea 1950–1975*. Unitec ePress [Auckland], 2014.

"The Comics Business." *Observer* (Australia), 3, no. 25, December 10, 1960, 5–6.

Dale, David. "How Swede Is Our Love Affair with the Ghost Who Walks." *Sun-Herald* [Sydney], October 1, 2006, 74.

Daley, Paul. "Only 58% of Indigenous Australians Are Registered to Vote. We Should Be Asking Why." *Guardian*, June 29, 2016, www.theguardian.com/commentisfree/2016/jun/30/only-58-of-Indigenous-australians-are-registered-to-vote-we-should-be-asking-why. Accessed August 1, 2018.

Davidson, Helen. "Indigenous STI Rates Sign of Government Failure Rather Than Child Abuse, Experts Say." *Guardian*, March 24, 2018, www.theguardian.com/australia-news/2018/mar/25/Indigenous-sti-rates-sign-of-government-failure-rather-than-child-abuse-experts-say. Accessed August 5, 2018.

Dempsey, James. "Condoman and Lubelicious: The Superheroes Designed to Teach Children Safe Sex." *Newstalk.com*, March 19, 2015, www.newstalk.com/Condoman-and-Lubelicious-the-superheroes-designed-to-teach-children-safe-sex. Accessed August 25, 2018.

Eby, Mark, dir. "The Man Who Cannot Die—Featuring Kaipel Ka." *Bruno Classens*, uploaded December 14, 2014, http://brunoclaessens.com/2014/12/the-story-of-a-comic-heros-appearance-on-new-guinea-war-shields/#.W2-Ir-hKjIV. Accessed August 11, 2018.

Falk, Lee, and Ray Moore. "The Phantom." *The Phantom*, no. 1, 1938 [Australia], 3–58.

———. "The Singh Brotherhood." *The Phantom: The Complete Dailies—Volume 1, 1936–1937*, 15–128. Hermes, 2010.

Family Court of Australia. *The Wisdom of the Phantom*. Publications Office of the Family Court of Australia, 1997.

"Fantom, Yu Pren Tru Bilong Mi." *Time*, September 26, 1977, 16.

"Fighting Shield 'kumba reipi' Phantom Design." *Michael Reid Sydney*, michaelreid.com.au/artwork/private-sales/. Accessed August 11, 2018.

Garage Graphix. *The Phantom Enrols & Votes*. Australian Electoral Commission, 1988.

Garage Graphix and Alistair Legge. *Vote 1 Phantom*. Australian Electoral Commission, 1990.

Gardiner-Garden, John. *Defining Aboriginality in Australia*. Department of the Parliamentary Library [Australia], 2003.

"The Ghost Who Walks Has Troubles in Jungle." *Sunday Sun* [Sydney], May 22, 1977, 18.

Gill, Alan. "The Phantom—He'll Make or Break the Pidgin Press." *Sydney Morning Herald*, May 28, 1977, 14.

Gohier, Franck. "The Phillip . . . More True Tales from the Far North." February 24, 2010, franckgohier.blogspot.com/2010/02/phillipmore-true-tales-from-far-north.html?q=true+tales. Accessed August 1, 2018.

———. "Big Boss." June 4, 2012, franckgohier.blogspot.com/2012/06/big-boss.html. Accessed August 1, 2018.

Guaraz, Layla, and Georges Bess. "Black Ivory." *The Phantom*, no. 825A [Australia], 1985.

Hall, Lee-Anne. "Garage Graphix." *Caper*, no. 27 (1988): 12–13.

Heath, Geoffrey G. "Australian Aboriginal Languages." *Encyclopedia Britannica*, February 10, 2005, www.britannica.com/topic/Australian-Aboriginal-languages. Accessed August 4, 2018.

"History." *The Phantom*, thephantomcomics.com/history/. Accessed August 1, 2018.

Horn, Maurice. *100 Years of American Newspaper Comics: An Illustrated Encyclopedia*. Gramercy Books, 1996.

"Indigenous Australians: Aboriginal and Torres Strait Islander People." Australian Institute of Aboriginal and Torres Strait Islander Studies, March 21, 2018, aiatsis.gov.au/explore/articles/Indigenous-australians-aboriginal-and-torres-strait-islander-people. Accessed August 4, 2018.

Jenkins, Henry. *Textual Poachers: Television Fans and Participatory Culture*, 1992. Routledge, 2013.

Kinnane, Garry. *Fare Thee Well, Hoddle Grid*. Clouds of Magellan [Melbourne], 2012.

Lawrence, John Shelton, and Robert Jewett. *The Myth of the American Superhero*. William B. Eerdmans Publishing Company, 2002.

MacLeod, Bridget. "Franck Gohier: Artist Profile." *PressReader*, March 1, 2018, www.pressreader.com/australia/artist-profile/20180301/282879436234444. Accessed August 1, 2018.

Mair, L. P. *Australia in New Guinea*, 1948. Melbourne University Press, 1970.

Marks, Russell. "The Legend and the Phantom." *Overland*, June 14, 2013, overland.org.au/2013/06/the-legend-and-the-phantom/. Accessed August 2, 2018.

Marmion, Doug, et al. *Community, Identity, Wellbeing: The Report of the Second National Indigenous Languages Survey*. Australian Institute of Aboriginal and Torres Strait Islander Studies, 2014.

McGregor, Russell. *Indifferent Inclusion: Aboriginal People and the Australian Nation*. Aboriginal Studies Press, 2011.

"My Voice for My Country." Australian Institute of Aboriginal and Torres Strait Islander Studies, 2016, aiatsis.gov.au/exhibitions/my-voice-my-country. Accessed August 1, 2018.

Nelson, Hank. *Taim Bilong Masta: The Australian Involvement with Papua New Guinea*. Australian Broadcasting Commission, 1982.

O'Brien, Denis, *The Weekly*. Penguin Books Australia, 1982.

O'Riordan, Maurice. "Everyone's Business: Love, Magic and the Art of Resistance." *National AIDS Bulletin* 12, no. 3 (1998), reconciliation.tripod.com/nab_everyone.htm. Accessed August 2, 2018.

"Out of the Studio—Paintings from 2006 to the Present." *Outstation*, 2016, www.outstation.com.au/exhibitions/2012/out-of-the-studio-paintings-from-2006-to-the-present/. Accessed August 1, 2018.

Padula, Marinella. *The AIDS Grim Reaper Campaign*. The Australia New Zealand School of Government, May 27, 2007.

Paranjape, Makarand. "Cultural Flows in Asia: Australian Locations, Asian Identities and Bombay Dreams." *Situations* 2 (2008): 1–28.

Patrick, Kevin. "The Cultural Economy of the Australian Comic Book Industry, 1950–1985." In *Sold by the Millions: Australia's Bestsellers*, edited by Toni Johnson-Woods and Amit Sarwal, 162–81. Cambridge Scholars Publishing, 2012.

———. "In Search of the Great Australian (Graphic) Novel." *Australasian Journal of Popular Culture* 1, no. 1 (2011): 51–66.

———. *The Phantom Unmasked: America's First Superhero*. University of Iowa Press, 2017.

Patteson, Richard F. "King Solomon's Mines: Imperialism and Narrative Structure." *Journal of Narrative Technique* 8, no. 2 (1978): 112–23.

Pearson, Noel. "Radical Hope: Education and Equality in Australia." *Quarterly Essay* 35 (2009): 1–105.

"Phan-tastic!" *Australasian Post*, March 30, 1991.

"The Phantom." *Australian Woman's Mirror*, September 1, 1936, 49.

"Phantom shield c. 1970." National Gallery of Victoria, https://www.ngv.vic.gov.au/explore/collection/work/80356/. Accessed August 10, 2018.

"Phantom shield c. 1989." National Gallery of Victoria, https://www.ngv.vic.gov.au/explore/collection/work/80358/. Accessed August 10, 2018.

Reilly, Benjamin. "Ethnic Conflict in Papua New Guinea." *Asia Pacific Viewpoint* 49, no. 1 (April 2008): 12–22.

Rolfe, Patricia. *The Journalistic Javelin: An Illustrated History of The Bulletin*. Wildcat Press [Sydney], 1979.

Scandinavian Chapter. *Lee Falk, Storyteller*. The Scandinavian Chapter of the Lee Falk Memorial Bengali Explorers Club / GML Förlag [Sweden], 2011.

Snowden, John. "Frew Publications Checklist: Part One." *Cooee* [Australia] 7 (1973): 2–19.

Strömberg, Fredrik. *Black Images in the Comics: A Visual History*. Fantagraphics Books, 2003.

Thieberger, Nick. "Re. The Phantom comic (Manyjilyjarra language edition)." Received by Kevin Patrick, July 23, 2018.

"Torres Strait Islander Flag." Australian Institute of Aboriginal and Torres Strait Islander Studies, July 27, 2017, aiatsis.gov.au/explore/articles/torres-strait-islander-flag. Accessed August 4, 2018.

Walmsley, Hannah. "Condoman: Indigenous Sexual Health Campaign Collection on Show in Canberra." *ABC News* [Australia], March 26, 2015, www.abc.net.au/news/2015-03-26/Indigenous-sexual-health-condoman-campaign-collection-on-show/6349320. Accessed August 2, 2018.

Waugh, Coulton. *The Comics*, 1947. Luna Press, 1974.
"Without Authority." *Australian Prints + Printmaking*, www.printsandprintmaking.gov.au/explore/works-and-networks/?artistid=5816. Accessed August 1, 2018.
Worker, Norman, and Carlos Cruz. "Wuluti's Secret." *The Phantom* [Australia], no. 1755, June 16, 2016, 6–37.

PART II
DECOLONIAL IMAGINARIES
TERRA SOUTH

Outsmarting the Lords of Death: An Amerindian Cognitive Script in Comics

Arij Ouweneel

Rhode Montijo's little Pablo in *Pablo's Inferno* (USA, 1999–2000) travels the different levels of the Aztec Underworld guided by the Aztec god Quetzal, discovering his lost Mexica (or: Aztec) heritage. For Jorge Santos, the journey questions the established vision on the Colonial Divide, this "troubling binary that pits European/Catholic and Indigenous/Aztec cultural heritages against one another in the context of Mexican American resistance to cultural assimilation" (Santos 3). Santos notes that Pablo and Quetzal explore a kind of Anzaldúan "new *mestiza* consciousness" (Anzaldúa 99–113) that integrates elements from both sides of the Divide, but without truly building bridges between these two very antagonistic positions; repetitively including rather than excluding. This *crosspollenization* (Anzaldúa 99) is an activity that the Nahuas understand as *nepantla* or torn between ways *and* placed outside them at the same time. The Bolivian sociologist Silvia Rivera Cusicanqui speaks of *ch'ixi*, an Aymara word pointing at a similar type of *in-betweenness and outsideness* (Gago 13). Of course, Pablo's quest is for his lost or inarticulate *nepantla-ch'ixi* identity.

The psychologist David Moshman says: "An identity is an explicit theory of oneself as a person" (4). A theory as a body of knowledge is built with building stones called *cognitive schemas* (among others: Arbib and Hesse 42–62; Ouweneel, *Freudian Fadeout* 217–24, and, *Resilient Memories* 6–11, 19–20; Shore 24, and passim; Solso 223–58). Cognitive schemas contain all our encoded knowledge of the world, of our body, our self and others, and they motor our actions, performances, behaviors, and responses to the world around us. The activation of cognitive schemas works outside of consciousness and fills therefore the content of our unconscious (memory). This unconscious is open and not closed off or "repressed," as the followers of Sigmund Freud would have it (Ouweneel, *Freudian Fadeout*, and *Resilient Memories*). There are many types of cognitive schemas. Any human being works with thousands and thousands of specific "special-purpose" cognitive schemas. Some of them are very tiny—a mailbox schema, for example—whereas others may have enormous dimensions. The latter should not discourage us. As political scientist Katja Michalak summarizes: "Examples of schemata include rubrics, social roles, stereotypes, and worldviews" (VII, 2362). All this means that "identity" is the sum of one's cognitive schemas.

Usually, our cognitive schemas are based on personal or social experiences—by learning in daily life, deduction, and the interpretation of the senses—or by experiences shared with others, told to us in stories. We also learn from printed work, still images, and moving images on the silver screen, television screens, and computer screens. This includes fiction. In fact, fiction can be understood as the mind's flight simulator (Oatley, Mar, and Djikic). Fiction transports us into simulations of situations we may normally not be, including unnatural dangers, in order to allow us this way to think them through and how to respond to them. This is why ideas, values, and behavioral and conversational solutions presented in stories, books, films, and comics root in our brains as potential simulations to influence behavior. For example, violent and frightening films help us manage danger by thinking about it; by improving the "fear schemas," which means for example developing better survival skills. In short, because cognitive schemas are encoded to be used in real life, their basic building stones are information for *doing* things. Therefore, humans dive into narratives; we are hardwired to be transported into storyworlds.

Also building an explicit theory of oneself as a person rests on encoded scripts, simulations, stereotypes, attitudes, and other schemas. Both Pablo's idea to start his quest and the conclusion he reached could be encoded in the brain of the reader of *Pablo's Inferno* as a personal Cognitive Identity Schema. It would usually include simulations of cognitive scripts of how to deal with certain situations. This means that the actions and doings—or passivity—of protagonists in stories can be analyzed as clues to such simulations. In fact, because reading comics and "decoding" them may reveal schemas, scholars should use this feature of our thinking. Among many, many possible cognitive schemas to be identified in comics, this chapter is about one quintessentially Amerindian cognitive schema that can be decoded from a series of Latin American comics: the simulations that point at the Outsmarting Schema. In what follows I try to demonstrate that the actions of the protagonists in a small corpus of Latin American comics may create simulations about escaping the Underworld by outsmarting the Lords of that Underworld. These simulations suggest that the Underworld for the Aztecs, the Maya, or the Amerindians in general is similar to what the Europeans and the Christians understand as Purgatory and that the protagonists in comics may serve as its memory device. Stories taking place in the Underworld, Hell, or Purgatory may be, as the historian David Carrasco reiterates, "meaningful ways of overcoming death in symbolic and psychological ways" (Carrasco 140). However, I believe that they are basically about creating simulation scripts to deal with daily life in the Upperworld.

The choice for the word "Amerindian" requires some clarification. Because Schema Theory is not a personality theory, I will not look at *who* is Amerindian—authors, artists, characters—but *what* is: actions, performances, behaviors, and responses to the world around us. It is here that we may map Pablo's quest, for example: What *doings* can we recognize in comics written by authors interested in the *in-betweenness and outsideness* of the *nepantla / ch'ixi* (or of *cholificación*, as this is called in Peru; see Ouweneel, *Resilient Memories* 209, 220, 234–38), Latin American indigeneity, and mestizaje in general?

The focus of this chapter is not on the work of Indigenous creators but on *indigeneity* in cultural products as discussed by Arturo Aldama mentioned in the introduction to this volume. As we all know, the Europeans wounded the peoples of the world deeply, but, as Frederick Luis Aldama writes above: "From these violent wounds we have survived. We are *mestizos*. We are Mexipinos. We are Asiatic and Indigenous admixtures. We are Canadian *métis*. We are Taíno, African, Latinx *métissage*. And from these wondrous new spaces we have been able (against the odds) to create dynamic, syncretistic cultural phenomena, comics included." This sounds like a *transnational mnemonic community*. We may call it "Indigenous" of course, but I met many Andeans and Maya who genuinely did not like the word; they saw it as excluding again. Therefore, over decades of research, I have come to the conclusion that this transnational mnemonic community—to which, I think, also Pablo's actions belong—may be addressed as *Amerindian* (Ouweneel, *Resilient Memories*), precisely because they share this joint history of colonization and internal colonization.[1]

Mnemonic communities share common memories, a common past, a common heritage. They are classified as "mnemonic" because the identities are triggered by encounters with mnemonic aids in the world, like specific artifacts, types of behavior, cultural expressions, and the recognition of being with other members of a mnemonic community. The concept of mnemonic communities brings together the individual and the collective, the cognitive and the group, in identity and community-building. The *doings* of the Amerindian mnemonic community should be understood as being confined to cognitive schemas and especially scripts and simulations. For example, to empower his mnemonic community, Pablo sets out with Quetzal to reconstruct his *nepantla* memory and through his presence in this comic he reconstructs that of his mnemonic community—his and his community's *nepantla* cognitive schemas.

Purgatory

Pablo's descent into the Underworld is neither limited to pre-Hispanic stories, nor to fiction. Over two decades ago, I read a file stored in the Archivo de Indias in Sevila about a person who—in 1761—descended into what he called *purgatorio* (Ouweneel, *Flight of the Shepherd*). Later I learned that Amerindians in Central Mexico believed in the 1970s, at least, that their souls would always go to Purgatory and that because of their cyclical thinking that would only be temporary—eventually, their Purgatory would turn into an "Upperworld" of the Glory or Heaven on Earth (Iwańska). Also several churches built and illustrated by *indios*—as the Amerindian colonized were classified under Spanish rule—all over Central and South Mexico and Guatemala contain murals in two layers: below the Purgatory (sometimes painted in an almost Maya-like style as in the sixteenth-century church of Ixmiquilpan), and above the Saints the Spaniards preferred, seen as in Heaven. In a way, I believe the *indios* regarded the *república de indios* of the sixteenth to eighteenth centuries—and to which their municipalities (*pueblos de indios*) belonged—as purgatorial; and therefore as the *antechamber* to await the turnover from social inferior to social dominant (see the documentation discussed in Ouweneel, *Flight of the Shepherd*). This must be the link between how to perform in daily life and the grand cosmic scheme of Creation and the Afterlife that delivers the simulation scripts.

As said, the Outsmarting Cognitive Schema figures among the important Amerindian cognitive schemas. Amerindian storytelling is full of meetings with Lords and other characters in the Underworld—Down Below—to build simulations in the minds of their audience. From this perspective, Pablo's descent into the Underworld is no exception. The Underworld Down Below versus the World Up Above is set within a cyclical time frame of large cycles in which different groups dominate or are in some way subordinate. This is the Amerindian Time Schema. The consequence of the cyclical view is that the Down Below will one moment turn again into the Up Above and later on, perhaps, vice versa. Because in *Pablo's Inferno* the protagonist and Quetzal are navigating "a mystical Mexican landscape in order to restore Azteca presence and influence in the modern world" (Santos 2), Montijo's sequential art story is an instrument in creating a simulation script of how to bring the Down Below of the *Chicano/a nepantla* to some kind of Up Above. Furthermore, the Amerindian Time Schema suggests that the Down Below and the Up Above belong to one cosmic unit that impedes the idea of a Christian-typed Hell detached from the life of the living; and "Purgatory" seems to be the proper metaphor for this cosmic unit. *Pablo's Inferno* is about Purgatory, not Hell. First, at the end of his story, in Book Five entitled "Soul Harvest," Pablo liberates the tormented souls and paves the way to find their "final destination"—in the direction of the Light (#5, 46–47). In the final panel (#5, 52–53), Pablo himself, carried by Quetzal, follows them.

Leaving Hell for Heaven is impossible in Christian teaching. In Amerindian belief it was not. From the wide variety of research into this topic Mary E. Miller and Karl Taube conclude:

But unlike hell in the Christian world, the Mesoamerican Underworld was not the preserve of sinners, but rather the destination of all those who escaped violent death, for it was only these latter who went directly to one of the heavens. In their preaching [to the Nahuas], the Spanish friars generally translated the word for the Christian hell as Mictlan, but threats of an eternity in Mictlan had little effect, since the audience already knew that all souls, whether rich or poor, good or evil, must go there. (Miller and Taube 177)

Nevertheless, it was no pleasant stay in Mictlan. For the Nahuas (Aztec) it was what Xibalbá was for the Maya: a Place of Fright (in K'iche') where the souls had to overthrow the forces of death if they wanted to have a pleasant afterlife in the heavens.

Xibalbá

A group of Mexican comic artists adapted the creation story of the K'iche' Maya of Santo Tomás Chichicastenango (Chuilá), the *Popol Wuj—The Book of the People* (Christenson 64; van Akkeren). Reading studies on the *Popol Wuj*, talking with archaeologists, anthropologists, and Maya shamans, Manuel de Santiago Bouchez, Edgar Álvarez Estrada (both script writers), and José Luis Manzour (artist) found a way through the stories recorded in the mid-sixteenth-century story, transcribed by the Dominican Fray Francisco Ximénez in 1701–1702, and published several times in different languages in our own times. The narrative is a creation story about the beginning of time, set on the moment the Sun and the Moon appear at the heavens to give light to the world. To be able to do this, the Sun and the Moon had to wander the dark earth as hero twins and eventually descend into the Underworld Xibalba to defeat the Lords of Xibalba.

What would be the desired simulation script here? Although the *Popol Wuj* also tells a history of the K'iche' empire and its defeat during the Spanish Invasion, Santiago Bouchez, Álvarez Estrada, and Manzour limit themselves to a six-volume series *Popol Vuh*.[2] In the classic *Popol Wuj*, Xibalbá is the place where the dead reside but also where life could be regenerated (Carrasco 140–41), if only the Lords of Death could be defeated. This was precisely what these "hero twins," Hunahpu and Ixbalanqué, set out to do. The Classic Maya name for Hunahpu was One-Ahaw or One-Lord; for Ixbalanqué it was Yax-Balam or Snakejaguar (Freidel et al. 108). These were calendar dates, the first and the last, as a kind of α and ω (alpha and omega). A major event in their struggle was to win a ball game. Note that the ball court is to be understood as the entrance to the Underworld—as if losing a game would mean to be transferred Down Below. In all, after having turned their world from Down Below into Up Above by creating time, creating a new cycle, the reader realizes—encodes a simulation script—that the proper way to do this is by being an able player and a cunning trickster at the same time.

Although I am aware of the problems with adaptations—in this case from a "classic" into a comic (see, for example, Perret; Beineke; or, Mitaine)—for a discussion of simulations this is not relevant. As an adaptation, the *Popol Vuh* comic should be seen as a stand-alone project. The Fundación Rafael Dondé in Mexico City distributed the series freely among at least one million children; and later digitally to an unknown number of online readers. The reader follows the adventures of the "cosmic" twins Junajpú and Ishbalanke, first in the "Upperworld"—the world "above" the Underworld (not necessarily "the respectable law-abiding part of society" as Merriam-Webster calls it)—where they had to eradicate three giants. Next, they descended into the Underworld, where they faced more ordeals. At the end of the episode, a rabbit told them the story of their father and uncle, another twin couple: Junjún and Junvucub, the two best players of *pok-ta-pok*, the Mesoamerican ball game. They were their ancestors. Back in time, playing ball the elderly twins Junjún and Junvucub had made so much noise that the Lords of Xibalbá wanted to punish them. They ordered them to come to Xibalbá. The twins had realized that if they would not accept the invitation, the Lords would bring disasters to the Upperworld. In good spirits, they left (see fig. 6.1).

Entering Xibalbá, the Lords lured the elderly twins into one trap after another. Don't be too naïve upon entering the Underworld! Never underestimate your opponents. Junjún and Junvucub did. Soon they realized that they would not be able to leave Xibalbá—and eventually died. However, in order to save their spirits and look for continuity of their existence, they had revived an old tree. One of its fruits contained the head and power of Junjún. When the girl Ishkík approached, the head spew in her hands, impregnating her with Junajpú and Ishbalanke as reincarnations of Junjún and Junvucub. The twins had outsmarted the Lords of Xibalbá after all. A newborn life in the House of Death! To avoid this shameful event, Ishkík was sent to the home of Junjún and Junvucub in the Upperworld to give birth. Now the modern reader would realize that for girls, the comic—and the original story—carries a strange message: although Ishkík is happy and cooperates fully, Junjún's impregnation of the girl was beyond her free will of course. She thought she could eat the head as a fruit. As a true trickster, Junjún had deceived her. His spitting looks like rape. Women have a secondary role in the *Popol Vuh*, also in this contemporary version. Nevertheless, although the Upperworld battles of Junajpú and Ishbalanke and the ball game by Junjún and Junvucub had been demonstrations of skills and force, beating the Lords of Xibalbá demanded outsmarting, chicanery, and very clever thinking indeed.

For the newborn twins Junajpú and Ishbalanke the Upper- and Underworlds were male playgrounds to demonstrate their power and above all, their smartness. Strangely enough, it was also allowed to deceive disloyal family members

Figure 6.1. Junjún and Junvucub on their way to Xibalba. Source: de Santiago Bochez, Álvarez Estrada et al. *Popol Vuh*. #3 (2012).

as, for example, the jealous half-brothers Batz and Chuen, who wanted to chase the twins away from the homes. Junajpú and Ishbalanke transformed them into monkeys and told their family at home that it had been their own fault. Eventually, the twins became very good players of *pok-ta-pok* and were also invited to play in Xibalbá. Finally, they outsmarted the Lords and defeated them in a few ball games—although they opted for a draw during the first of the games in order to be able to find out about the fate of Junjún and Junvucub (see fig. 6.2). Eventually, after many games and fighting, and a final *pok-ta-pok* game, the Lords were imprisoned in some sort of pit and the twins condemned them to eat garbage for all eternity. Next, the inhabitants of Xibalbá were liberated, both from the yoke of some violent dictatorship but also from darkness in general, because—after bringing Junjún and Junvucub back to life—Junajpú and Ishbalanke entered the Heavens as the Sun and the Moon and Time began, "giving the Maya an experience of regeneration" (Carrasco 145).

As in *Pablo's Inferno*, Xibalbá was a world ruled by Lords of Darkness who had been capable of coercing an entire population of the dead. The situation required a kind of superheroes, the hero twins as community or people's representatives, to free this incarcerated population and bring prosperity (Light) on Earth. A new cycle could begin. In addition, this new cycle was "germinated" by the ancestors (Junjún and Junvucub), evidence of the enduring influence of the ancestors and the Underworld in general on daily life in the Upperworld. Under- and Upperworlds were now united by the cycles of the Sun and the Moon: when the Sun illuminated the Upperworld, the Moon did so Down Below, and vice versa. The ancestors reside in the Underworld also to "achieve control over its moist forces for the benefit of the living" (Read and González 260; also, Miller and Taube 177–78). In short, the *Popol Vuh* creates simulations of developing good skills—*Be Good in What You Do*—and a spirited resistance based on cleverness and a practice of outsmarting; and, when necessary, the end justified the means.

Figure 6.2. Junajpú and Ishbalanke defeat the Lords of Xibalbá during a *pok-ta-pok* game—but they have more plans. Source: de Santiago Bochez, Álvarez Estrada, et al. *Popol Vuh*. #5 (2012).

Andean

It is not difficult to recognize many elements of the previous story in the one recorded by Peruvian writer José María Arguedas in 1965,[3] recently adapted by the Peruvian illustrator and cartoonist César Aguilar Peña. Different from the transcendental and mythical creation narrative of the *Popol Wuj*, Aguilar Peña takes the Outsmarting Schema closer to home. He is a bilingual artist (Spanish-Quechua), living in Cusco. In a local television interview, he said that the Andeans today seem to have the wind in their sails: "We have taken Lima, and soon we'll take over the State." He said it with a smile. He added that his work is "painted in Quechua [. . . by . . .] an Andean mind" (Telecultura Ayaviri). He referred to a "deep" culture, to what was called *profundo* in Peru and Mexico; a cultural memory that goes back centuries and which still actively triggers life today in shared and contested cognitive schemas, constantly being reproduced and renegotiated. Retelling Arguedas's tale Aguilar Peña pictured a humble man of small, frail stature, who was one of the hacienda servants in the Paucartambo area in Cusco. The humble man had to perform the obligation of *pongo* or household service in the hacienda house—the *casco* or *casa-hacienda*. He did so silently and loyal, although the hacendado, a devilish character, humiliated him regularly in front of all the other workers, especially at dusk around the daily religious service. We may regard the hacienda as the pongo's Underworld; he is clearly in a Down Below position vis-à-vis the hacendado (see fig. 6.3, left).

However, one afternoon the pongo unexpectedly asked permission to speak. He told the hacendado that he had dreamed that the two of them had died. They had been standing naked before Saint Francis, next to each other. The saint had observed them closely and intensively. It was clear that the saint knew that the hacendado had been rich and powerful. Next, one angel entered with a golden cup filled with the most delicate and translucent honey and another

Figure 6.3. The pongo and the hacendado: on the hacienda (*left*) and in Heaven (*right*). Source: Aguilar Peña, *El sueño del pongo*.

one covered the hacendado with it. "In the splendor of the heavens," the pongo told the hacendado, "your body shone as if made of transparent gold." Now, the most ordinary angel brought a gasoline can filled with human excrement and another humble, old angel covered the pongo with it. "In the midst of the heavenly light," the pongo continued, "I stank and was filled with shame." "Just as it should be!" crowed the master. For a very long time, Saint Francis looked at the two men before him and finally said, "Now, lick each other's bodies slowly, for all eternity." And an angel was entrusted to make sure that the saint's will was carried out, forever and ever (see fig. 6.3, right).

The Andeans have adopted and assimilated—*amerindianized*, I would say—into their cognitive schemas many symbols and customs from other cultures around the world—"Sin perder su esencia" ("Without losing its essence"), Aguilar Peña said. This included, for example, Catholic rituals and symbols; in fact, Christianity in the Amerindian world should therefore be labeled Colonial Catholicism and not Roman. However, the new scenery still was the battleground between Lords of Death—and the hacendado certainly was one—and smart mortals who fought to regain their life back; and perhaps in better circumstances than before. Although Aguilar Peña portrays a hacendado from European descent, confirming the colonial cognitive schema of the European sweater, reading his Arguedas adaptation the reader still encodes scripts on how to outsmart much powerful opponents; as in the *Popol Vuh* comic.

Another amerindianization can be recognized in the last version of *Supercholo*. In this Marvel-inspired tale, the protagonist acted again as the Amerindian hero to redeem the inhabitants of Other Worlds. (There were earlier versions: see Ouweneel, *Resilient Memories* 14–15; for more background about the recent version 15n50.) Supercholo did so in the company of a kind of twin brother as well: Juanito Pumasoncco, also known as Capitán Intrépido or Captain Fearless. Although Supercholo had begun his life as another version of the pongo in 1957, the writer Francisco Miro Quesada Cantuarias a.k.a. Diodoros Kronos, his creator, and Carlos Castellanos Casanova, the new illustrator, transformed Supercholo into a smart, powerful, and self-confident Andean warrior (fifty-one pages, one page a week, in *El Dominical* between October 1995 and November 1998, see Castellanos Casanova, "Reencuentro/ Regreso"; also: Ledgard, *De Supercholo a Teodosio*). The Peruvian readers could be proud of them, and their "race." The world of Supercholo had become a multicultural Peru, with a prominent role for the Andean hero.

Playing the quena (an Andean flute), Supercholo has been traveling with llamas, vicuñas, a puma, and a condor through the highlands, until the inhabitants of the multicultural alien planet Geos requested him and his friend Captain Fearless to help them out. The two *Supercholo* heroes were fighting an appalling dictator called Deinos, the ruler of the planet Megas. Of course, Supercholo and Captain Fearless triumph in the end. Geos and the entire universe are saved. The fate of Geos, and our own planet Earth of course, had been in their capable and valiant hands. Courage, cleverness, and wisdom had been their major assets. This, again, the reader encodes as simulation scripts. The rewards could be great. In Cosmopolis, the capital city of Geos, a multicultural and well-developed Western type of city, Supercholo is given a hero's reception (see fig. 6.4). Interestingly, the entrance to Outer Space and the cosmic road to Geos is through a cave—as in any Underworld—and the people of Geos are oppressed the same way as the people of Xibalbá and in *Pablo's Inferno*. And next to strength, outsmarting was Supercholo's and Captain Fearless's major asset in defeating Deinos, this Lord of Death of Outer Space.

As Aguilar Peña said, an Andean spirit is taking over Lima. Superheroes in the more classical (Marvel) style begin to combat evil. A good example is *Turbochaski, The Messenger of Peace*, developed and made by Ricardo Walter Rodríguez a decade ago. A pilot version of the comic won an honorable mention at the Second Peruvian Superhero Contest, organized by the daily *Peru.21* in Lima. Rodríguez's protagonist Pedro Paucar is an Andean immigrant—born in Cusco—who had received an ancient golden Inca amulet from the shaman Apu-Machu. The piece provided him with extraordinary powers (see fig. 6.5). However, he is not alone in Lima. For a few years the villains are punished violently by La Chola Power. This female superhero is created by Martín Espinoza Díaz, who won the *Peru.21* contest of 2008. Like Pedro Paucar, Elisa La Chola Power is a migrant from the Andes, born in the poor region of Andahuaylas. At this moment, I have seen five booklets and about eight adventures published separately in the series *Seminario de MedComics*, all in the late 2000s and early 2010s. In Peru, she defends the Peruvian state against superhero villains. One

Amerindian Cognitive Script in Comics 137

Figure 6.4. Supercholo and Captain Fearless return victoriously to their friends in Cosmopolis. *Source:* Castellanos Casanova, "Return of Supercholo."

day, coincidentally working as a stewardess on a flight to Cusco, she even saves the presidential couple, flying in the plane as passengers, from being killed by one of these super villains (see fig. 6.6). In the third booklet, *La Chola Power 3: Demonio en la tierra*, we learn about her history as the daughter of the Sun; which was also revealed, by the way, in a more modest way, in the first issue (*La Chola Power 1: Horror en Cusco*, 13).

In Roman Catholic eyes, the Lord of the Underworld was the Devil. In Colonial Catholic terms, the Devil was the Lord of the Underworld, and that is not the same thing. Because in the Amerindian cognitive schema of the afterlife, the Underworld was much more a kind of Purgatory, the Amerindian Underworld/Upperworld Schema mapped the eternal danger of the Lord(s) of the Underworld or the Devil of Purgatory. For sure, the Lord(s) of the Underworld, the Devil, could be outsmarted, tricked, and defeated—which also finally occurs, by the way, in the last issue of *Pablo's Inferno*. And although there is no single Devil among the Lords of Xibalbá in the *Popol Wuj*, Deinos in *Supercholo* surely is diabolic, as is the Sun's enemy in *La Chola Power*—a demon called Wichama (as stated in panel 1, fig. 6.7). This could make the circle round here, as we connect La Chola Power's adventures with the *Popol Wuj*. The comic may produce the same simulation script of dealing on Earth with the cosmic powers of evil: the performance has the blessing of the Inca Sun. However, La Chola Power and Turbochaski differ on one point deeply from the Maya hero twins or Supercholo: they only fistfight—as if there is no need for outsmarting the opponent.

Devil

This brings me to another Andean comic, compiled by writer Jorge Siles and artist Óscar Zalles, both from Bolivia, entitled *Supay* or *Devil* (2015). The book is a collection of four connected "graphic short stories" staged in different periods

Figure 6.5. Pedro Paucar receives an Inca medallion from Apu-Machu (*above*) and transforms into Turbochaski. *Source:* Rodríguez, *Turbochaski*.

and different places. The connection is the presence of the Devil, the Lord in the Earth, who cannot be defeated. The book was published in August 2015, which is for the Bolivian Amerindians the month the Earth opens her mouth—the Earth is female, Pachamama—to be fed in order to recuperate the fertility of her soil. This "food" she consumes can include human flesh (blood). For the rulers and "victors" Up Above versus Down Below means "to feed and be fed," as historian Susan Ramírez once explained the crux of pre-Hispanic—and post-Conquest—Andean culture (*To Feed and Be Fed*). In *Supay*, the Devil outsmarts the humans. Or better, he lures them into his traps. In the first story, "5UP4Y," the Devil inhabits a magical portal between a crater on the Moon and a dangerous curve in one of Bolivia's treacherous provincial roads. Two moon voyagers in a distant future fall in that trap. One of them, called Reyes, recognizes road tombs, erected for traffic victims, with their name written on it in Quechua. They also fall victim to the Devil, who resides in this portal as the well-known Tío or Uncle in the Cerro Rico, Potosí's Silver Mountain. In "Agua negra," the Devil has taken possession of a prizefighter who fails to comply his duties—who cannot "feed" in order that his world be "fed"—and unwillingly causes the 2002 mudflow in La Paz. In "Todos Santos" a partygoer enters a bar and has sex with the Devil—and disappears from the Earth. All victims here can be seen as a kind of losers. They are either unknowing of the Devil's presence, or are not capable of outsmarting him on time.

In the last story, "El asombroso Niño Sikimira," the protagonist cannot succeed either. He is a Roman Catholic exorcist who arrives in the Bolivian

Figure 6.7. Attacker comes running toward the priests in "El asombroso Niño de Sikimura." *Source:* Siles, Jorge, and Óscar Zalles. *Supay* (47) (panels 3 and 4).

altiplano town of K'uchu Muela, near Punata in the Cochabamba region, during the times of Spanish rule, to save a girl from the Devil. He is informed by the local priest and is at the spot when a demon—as it later appears to be—attacks one of the priests (figs. 6.7 and 6.8). The priests bring the exorcist to the spot of a ruined church and open the trapdoor to the crypt where the possessed girl is housed. The exorcist is unexpectedly unable to do his job, basically because the girl *is* the Devil in flesh—and not just in spirit. The exorcist tries to escape, but his colleagues have blocked the trapdoor with stones. The Devil explains to the exorcist that he should not blame him but his colleagues; this was a typical case of "with malice aforethought," he says. The exorcist is "fed" to the Devil, in order, perhaps, to secure peace and fertility to the Upperworld. Interestingly, this story is set to explain the popularity of the Christ Child of Sik'imira, not far from K'uchu Muela (Morom). Many towns in Latin America have their own shrines of miraculous appearances of Christ or the Virgin. This one, retold in the short story as well, is about a Christ Child, whose small image is kept in the church of K'uchu Muela. Due to his experience in the crypt, the exorcist's conclusion is that the Christ Child must be the Devil himself, and in the last pages we read that the local priest seems to be aware of this.

We can now recapitulate the basics of the Amerindian Outsmarting Schema, a major cognitive schema of their cultural memory. When Sunset really is Dawn, someone has outsmarted the Devil and that person will be a hero, perhaps part of a couple of hero twins. In many cases, the hero is good in fistfighting but even better in setting traps for the Devil. This Devil does not reign in Hell but in Purgatory; people can be liberated from Purgatory and either return on Earth—from Down Below to Up Above—or travel directly to the Heavens. Despite the many similarities to Christian teachings, this is an Amerindian worldview, which includes a series of Amerindianized recreations. Both worlds,

Figure 6.8. Person who attacked priest appears to be a demon in "El asombroso Niño de Sikimura." *Source:* Siles, Jorge, and Óscar Zalles. *Supay* (50) (panels 5 and 7).

Under (Down Below) and Upper (Up Above), are made one by cyclical advancing time; from chaos to order and back again in the Upperworld, or in larger cycles when Sunset needs to become Dawn again.

The schema is built with visions on Upperworld(s) and Underworld(s), cyclical time, Lords and Heroes. It also contains cognitive scripts on what to do in certain cases; and what not. This has been told over and over again, generation after generation by people who have been ethnotyped in the past as *indios* and today as *indígenas*, *cholos*, or *mestizos*—among several others. In our new media times, we find the continuous regeneration of the schema and its scripts encoded in simulations in short stories, novels, comics, short fiction films, feature films, documentaries, and even video games. The protagonists are doing what the readers and film viewers decode as part of their schemas, and subsequently encode again in an adapted version (also about lessons to be learned: Peterson and Park 15). This explains why Pablo, the pongo, Supercholo, Turbochaski, and La Chola Power do the things they do; and why *Supay*'s protagonists fail. By keeping the Amerindian cognitive schema's alive, comics like *Pablo's Inferno, Supercholo, La Chola Power, Turbochaski*, and *Supay* are key mediators of Amerindian memory.

Notes

I would like to thank my colleague Christien Klaufus for a reading of a first draft. The text is much better thanks to her constructive criticism. Also I would like to thank my talented Bolivian student Tania Montes Eguino, who bought *Supay* for me in La Paz.

1. In fact, based on its wider transnational genealogy, I believe the *cholos* and *mestizos* are in the majority; although in many cases some anthropologists may speak of *indígenas* where others ethnotype them as *mestizos* or *cholos*, or even as *Indigenous mestizos*; De la Cadena, *Indigenous Mestizos*.

2. The comic was commissioned by the Fundación Rafael Dondé to be distributed free of charge among at least one million children. Also videos were produced by Mawizoa Multimedia and Planeta Anawak TV in Mexico in cooperation with HM Studios (José Luis Manzour). The project was directed and researched by Manuel de Santiago Bochez and Frank Díaz, and produced by de Santiago Bochez and Edgar Álvarez Estrada (script) and José Luis Manzour (artist). Interestingly, Xibalbá is also the topic of one of the few novels written by a Maya writer, *Time Commences in Xibalbá* by Luis de Lión (2012), the English translation of *Tiempo principia en Xibalbá* (1984).

3. Original story based on Arguedas, *Sueño del pongo*, and "Pongoq mosqoynin." After the first publication in 1965, the story was reprinted in Chile in 1969; and in Arguedas's *Obras Completas* in 1983. Several editions followed, including the well-known translated version published in *The Peru Reader* by Orin Starn, Carlos Iván Degregori, and Robin Kirk in 1995 and 2005; English quotes are from the 2005 version. See: Arguedas, "Pongo's," 273.

Works Cited

Aguilar Peña, César. *El sueño del pongo. José María Arguedas*. Adaptación a historieta de César Aguilar Peña (Ch'illico). Cusco: Lluvia editores, 2016.
Akkeren, Ruud van. "Authors of the Popol Vuh." *Ancient Mesoamerica* 14 (2003): 237–56.
Anzaldúa, Gloria. *Borderlands/La Frontera. The New Mestiza*. 3rd ed. San Francisco, CA: Aunt Lute Books, 2007.
Arbib, Michael A., and Mary B. Hesse. *The Construction of Reality*. Cambridge: Cambridge University Press, 1986.
Arguedas, José María. "The Pongo's Dream." In *The Peru Reader: History, Culture, Politics*, edited by Orin Starn, Carlos Iván Degregori, and Robin Kirk, 258–63. Durham, NC: Duke University Press, 1995; repr. in *The Peru Reader: History, Culture, Politics*. 2nd ed., revised and updated. Durham, NC: Duke University Press, 2005. 273–78.
———. *El sueño del pongo: cuento Quechua*. Lima: Ediciones Salqantay, 1965; reprinted as "Pongoq mosqoynin (Qatqa runapa willakusqan). El sueño del pongo (cuento quechua) (1965)." In *Obras Completas I*, 249–58. Lima: Editorial Horizonte, 1983.
Beineke, Colin. "Towards a Theory of Comic Book Adaptation." Lincoln: PhD thesis, University of Nebraska, May 2011.

Carrasco, Davíd. *Religions of Mesoamerica*. 2nd ed. Long Grove, IL: Waveland Press, 2014 (1990).
Castellanos Casanova, Carlos. "El reencuentro con el Supercholo / A Reunion with Supercholo." *Etiqueta Negra* 6, no. 79 (2009) (written in 1996).
Christenson, Allen J. *Popol Vuh: The Sacred Book of the Maya*. Norman: University of Oklahoma Press, 2007.
De la Cadena, Marisol. *Indigenous Mestizos: The Politics of Race and Culture in Cuzco, Peru, 1919–1991*. Durham, NC: Duke University Press, 2000.
de Lión, Luis. *Time Commences in Xibalbá*. Translated by Nathan C. Henne, Afterword by Arturo Arias. Tucson: University of Arizona Press, 2012.
de Santiago Bochez, Manuel, Edgar Álvarez Estrada, et al. *Popol Vuh. Cómic de la saga de los gemelos del Popol Wuj 1. Los Gemelos Cósmicos: la lucha contra los gigantes, parte 1*. Mexico City: Fundación Rafael Dondé, Dondé Educarte, 2012.
de Santiago Bochez, Manuel, Edgar Álvarez Estrada, et al. *Popol Vuh. Cómic de la saga de los gemelos del Popol Wuj 2. Los Gemelos Cósmicos: la lucha contra los gigantes, parte 2*. Mexico City: Fundación Rafael Dondé, Dondé Educarte, 2012.
de Santiago Bochez, Manuel, Edgar Álvarez Estrada, et al. *Popol Vuh. Cómic de la saga de los gemelos del Popol Wuj 3. Los Gemelos Cósmicos: el origen, parte 1*. Mexico City: Fundación Rafael Dondé, Dondé Educarte, 2012.
de Santiago Bochez, Manuel, Edgar Álvarez Estrada, et al. *Popol Vuh. Cómic de la saga de los gemelos del Popol Wuj 4. Los Gemelos Cósmicos: el origen, parte 2*. Mexico City: Fundación Rafael Dondé, Dondé Educarte, 2012.
de Santiago Bochez, Manuel, Edgar Álvarez Estrada, et al. *Popol Vuh. Cómic de la saga de los gemelos del Popol Wuj 5*. Mexico City: Fundación Rafael Dondé, Dondé Educarte, 2012.
de Santiago Bochez, Manuel, Edgar Álvarez Estrada, et al. *Popol Vuh. Cómic de la saga de los gemelos del Popol Wuj 6*. Mexico City: Fundación Rafael Dondé, Dondé Educarte, 2012.
Espinoza Díaz, Martín. *La Chola Power 1. Horror en Cusco*. Lima: Grupo MedComics, 2013.
———. *La Chola Power 3. Demonio en la tierra*. Lima: Grupo MedComics, 2015.
Freidel, David, Linda Schele, and Joy Parker. *Maya Cosmos. Three Thousand Years on the Shaman's Path*. New York: Quill and William Morrow, 1993.
Gago, Verónica. "Entrevista: Orgullo de ser mestiza." *LAS 12 Página 12* (July 30, 2010), https://www.pagina12.com.ar/diario/suplementos/las12/13-5889-2010-08-03.html (accessed February 28, 2018). Web.
Iwańska, Alicja. *Purgatory and Utopia. A Mazahua Indian Village of Mexico*. Cambridge, MA: Schenkman Publishing Company, 1971.
Ledgard, Melvin R. *De Supercholo a Teodosio. Historietas peruanas de los sesentas y setentas: junio–julio 2004*. Lima: Instituto Cultural Peruano Norteamericano ICPNA, Galería ICPNA San Miguel, 2004.
Michalak, Katja. "Schema." In *International Encyclopedia of Political Science*, vol. 7, edited by Bertrand Badie, Dirk Berg-Schlosser, and Morlino Leonardo, 2362–64. Thousand Oaks, CA: Sage Publications, 2011.
Miller, Mary E., and Karl Taube. *The Gods and Symbols of Ancient Mexico and the Maya: An Illustrated Dictionary of Mesoamerican Religion*. London: Thames and Hudson, 1997.
Mitaine, Benoît. *Bande dessinée et adaptation: littérature, cinéma, tv*. Clermont-Ferrand, France: Presses Universitaire Blaise Pascal, 2015.
Mitchell, W. J. Thomas. *Picture Theory: Essays on Verbal and Visual Representation*. Chicago: University of Chicago Press, 1994.
Montijo, Rhode. *Pablo's Inferno*. 5 vols. Stockton, CA: ABISMO, 1999–2000.
Morom, María. "Mito del ninño Sik'imira." Cochabamba, Bolivia: Tesis de Licenciatura en antropología, Universidad Catolica Boliviana San Pablo, 1991.

Moshman, David. "Identity as a Theory of Oneself." *The Genetic Epistemologist: Journal of the Jean Piaget Society* 26, no. 3 (1998): 1–9, also at http://www.piaget.org/GE/1998/GE-26-3.html (accessed February 28, 2018). Web.
Nugent, José Guillermo. *El laberinto de la choledad*. Lima: Fundación Friedrich Ebert, 1992.
Oatley, Keith, Raymond A. Mar, and Maja Djikic. "The Mind's Flight Simulator." *Psychologist* 21 (2008): 1030–32.
Ouweneel, Arij. *The Flight of the Shepherd: Microhistory and the Psychology of Cultural Resilience in Bourbon Central Mexico*. Amsterdam: Aksant & Cedla, 2005.
———. *Freudian Fadeout: The Failings of Psychoanalysis in Film Criticism*. Jefferson, NC: McFarland, 2012.
———. *Resilient Memories. Amerindian Cognitive Schemas in Latin American Art*. Columbus: The Ohio State University Press, 2018.
Perret, Marion D. "Not Just Condensation: How Comic Books Interpret Shakespeare." *College Literature* 31 (2004): 72–93.
Peterson, Christopher, and Nansook Park. "The Positive Psychology of Superheroes." In *The Psychology of Superheroes: An Unauthorized Exploration*, edited by Robin S. Rosenberg with Jennifer Canzoneri, 5–18. Dallas, TX: Smart Pop, 2008.
Ramírez, Susan E. *To Feed and Be Fed: The Cosmological Bases of Authority and Identity in the Andes*. Stanford, CA: Stanford University Press, 2005.
Read, Kay Almere, and Jason J. González. *Mesoamerican Mythology: A Guide to the Gods, Heroes, Rituals, and Beliefs of Mexico and Central America*. Oxford: Oxford University Press, 2000.
Rivera Cusicanqui, Silvia. *Ch'ixinakax utxiwa. Una reflexión sobre prácticas y discursos descolonizadores*. Buenos Aires: Tinta Limón, 2010.
Rodríguez, Ricardo W. *Turbochaski: el mensajero de la paz*. Turbochaski.Blogspot.com, 2016, at http://turbochaski.blogspot.com/feeds/posts/default (accessed March 15, 2018). Web.
Santos, Jorge. "Ambulatory Identities: Montijo's Revision of Chicano/a Hybridity in *Pablo's Inferno*." *ImageTexT. Interdisciplinary Comics Studies* 8, no. 3 (2016): 1–33.
Shore, Bradd. *Culture in Mind. Cognition, Culture, and the Problem of Meaning*. New York: Oxford University Press, 1996.
Siles, Jorge, and Óscar Zalles. *Supay*. La Paz: Pseudogente Editores, 2015.
Solso, Robert L. *The Psychology of Art and the Evolution of the Conscious Brain*. Cambridge, MA: MIT Press, 2003.
Starn, Orin, Carlos Iván Degregori, and Robin Kirk, eds. *The Peru Reader: History, Culture, Politics*. Durham, NC: Duke University Press, 1995.
———. *The Peru Reader: History, Culture, Politics*. 2nd ed.; revised and updated. Durham, NC: Duke University Press, 2005.
Telecultura, Ayaviri. "Connotado Caricaturista César Aguilar visitó Ayaviri." Published at YouTube December 20, 2015, at https://www.youtube.com/watch?v=bXluim5nsb8 (accessed March 15, 2018). Web.

Memory in Pieces: Chola Power's Origin Story and the Quest for Memory in Peru

Javier García Liendo

This chapter examines a recent Peruvian comic book that reflects on the role of memory in times of neoliberalism and globalization. *Nuestros Muertos* [Our Dead] (2017) is a five-part comic series that narrates the origin story of Chola Power, a superhero created in 2008 by graphic artist Martín Espinoza. In 2015, at the initiative of the now-defunct publishing label Comics21, Espinoza invited comic writer César Santiváñez to create an origin story for this superhero. Chola Power is the daughter of the Inca sun god and has been sent by her father to fight a wave of criminality that has taken over Peruvian society. This mission is evident throughout *Nuestros Muertos*, but the series also informs *La Chola Power* followers that their superhero has a second mission, one perhaps more important for explaining her origins: that of safeguarding the memory of a past that neoliberal society seems intent on burying forever. The series is really about two types of memory: cultural memory associated with the Indigenous societies of the Andes and political memory in reference to the internal war waged between the insurrectionary group Shining Path [*Sendero Luminoso*] and the Peruvian state from 1980 to the mid-1990s. These memories have no place in the fictional Lima that is portrayed in *Nuestros Muertos*: a dystopian megacity governed by authoritarianism, corruption, technology, unchecked consumption, and the promotion of individualism as the exclusive route to success and social mobility.

In *Nuestros Muertos* memories of the nation's violent recent past and of Indigenous traditions are not evoked through coherent and explicit narratives that would allow readers to identify them with real events. Instead, this memory is fractured, and the pieces are reassembled and confusedly put into relation through a single, multidimensional narrative, thereby generating what could be characterized as an aesthetic experience of defamiliarization for the series' readers. I read this obscurantist effect as the series' aesthetic stance with regard

Figure 7.1. Chola Power vs. Pachamac in the cover of *Nuestros Muertos*, vol. 5.

to the difficulty of producing and transmitting memory and its opposition to the notion of communicational transparency that seems to have spread with the rise of social media. In *Nuestros Muertos* the process of memory-decoding demands a detective-reader capable not only of connecting and reconstructing the pieces and narratives of memory, but also of putting down the comic book in order to research Peru's political and cultural past. This commitment to the reader's agency encourages what Frederick Aldama has called the "co-creating process," which designates the comic book reader's emotional and cognitive involvement with a work to the point of becoming its coauthor in the creation of a story world in which meaning is negotiated and exceeds the limits of visual and textual discourse (90–91).

My reading of the multidimensional narrative of memory in *Nuestros Muertos* will seek to reconstruct and analyze the three main themes that comprise it: (a) the history of Peru's violent recent past, in relation to which the series mixes fiction and reality, deliberately confusing names and events; (b) the use of categories of Indigenous thought as a way to introduce forms of the production of meaning that serve as alternatives to the linear discourse of History, as well as the use of dialogues in Quechua without Spanish translation; and (c) the presence in the superhero's own name—Chola Power—of different layers of significance that refer to changes in popular ethnicity in Peru resulting from the context of urbanization and mass migration from countryside to city over the last century. The analysis will treat these themes separately, although in the series itself they overlap and blend together. Their combination in a single narrative yields a challenging visual and textual object, one that therefore shows interesting strengths but also includes aspects that elicit critical evaluation.

One clarification must be made at the outset of this chapter. Chola Power's origin story is not authored by Indigenous comic book creators, but by pop culture artists working in a Global South country shaped by the effects of political violence and a rapid process of ethnic change. These artists do not seek to represent contemporary indigeneity in Peru, nor do they aim to depict Indigenous knowledge as a counter-perspective to challenge or resist dominant discourses and structures of power. They employ epistemic categories, characters, and stories from Quechua culture as part of a broader discussion on public memory in Peru. Intervening in the sphere of mass consumption, they seek to open a public discussion on both the trauma of a recent violent past, and a long-lasting dynamic of marginalization of Indigenous cultures and heritage from national narratives and citizenship. In the sphere of mainstream cultural production, topics such as violence and indigeneity are treated as spectacle, when not completely ignored. Finally, the amalgam of stories and characters from Indigenous, national, and global cultures in Chola Power's origin story is intended for a young contemporary national audience that is adept at decoding global fluxes of cultural hybridity.

Before proceeding with my analysis, I will offer a synthetic contextualization of *Nuestros Muertos* in relation to recent Peruvian comic book production. Unlike other countries such as Argentina or Mexico, Peru has not been known for having a significant comics industry. However, as Mario Lucioni has observed, Peruvian comics have sought, since their inception, to "narrate with images a poor and divided country," thereby applying a political and critical orientation to history and daily life. With the expansion of readership in the second half of the twentieth century—the emblematic event of which was the appearance of the tabloid *Última hora* in 1950—there appeared new graphic artists and writers who saw comic books as a form of popular visualization for conducting political or social criticism, even in repressive contexts of dictatorship.[1] The rise of a mass audience for newspaper comic strips also coincided with a movement of cultural nationalism that rejected foreign comics—especially from the United States—in an international context defined by the Cold War and global movements of decolonization. A key moment in this regard was the *Última hora* issue of September 12, 1952, in which a celebrated new Peruvian character, Sampietri, appeared in the comics section to inform Donald Duck, Brick Bradford, and Roy Rogers that starting the following day the tabloid would only be publishing comics featuring Peruvian characters (fig. 7.2). In Peru, comics have also been used as an alternative means of visual expression for popular groups historically excluded from the lettered city of intellectuals and political society.[2]

The first two decades of the twenty-first century have seen greater numbers of comic book publishing ventures both in Lima and in the provinces.[3] These publications feature many themes, but for the purposes of this chapter it is essential to highlight the importance among them of Indigenous memory and the memory of political violence. With regard to the former, several productions have adapted a variety of prehispanic and regional stories to the language of the comic book; others have created superhero stories based on Quechua and Aymara mythology.[4] The idea of a Peruvian superhero had been around since the publication of *Supercholo* (1957–1962), about a peasant who migrates from the countryside to the city accompanied by his llama. Condescendingly represented with coarse physical features and a weak body, the character nonetheless demonstrated impressive strength in facing the dangers and villains of the city (Ledgard 16–18). With the appearance of the "new" superheroes of Andean origin, particularly Chola Power, these stereotypical representations were transformed into images that celebrate Indigenous roots and the empowerment of the descendants of the Native populations. However, in these new representations "the Indigenous" is no longer associated with rural life nor with the recent experience of migration, but is instead portrayed within the dynamics of cultural change or hybridity, in which local traditions coexist with global identities and technological flows.

The topic of the internal war also generated particular interest among Peruvian comic book writers following the publication in 2003 of the *Informe Final* [Final

Figure 7.2. Donald Duck fired from the comic page by Peruvian character Sampietri in *Última Hora*, September 12, 1952.

Report] of the Peruvian Truth and Reconciliation Commission (known as CVR, based on its Spanish acronym), with various graphic artists and screenwriters subsequently conducting important work on the construction of public memory of the internal armed conflict using comics as a more democratic means of expression than that of the *Informe*'s written and academic discourse.[5] This comic book production was—and continues to be—carried out in the delicate context of the tensions generated by memory disputes among the different points of view of the actors involved in the conflict as well as in the face of the difficulty of achieving consensus on questions related to culpability and victimhood.[6] In her analysis of the graphic novel *Rupay: Historias de la violencia política en el Perú*, Cynthia E. Milton examines the importance of comic books not only for fostering debate over the armed conflict and its public memory, but also for serving as a medium that gives voice—thanks to its mixture of fiction and historical documentation—to survivors, soldiers, and murdered persons, who had no such voice in the *Informe Final* or in other historical accounts of the conflict (Milton 177). *Nuestros Muertos* is part of this line of exploration of public memory. However, in the collective work of Martín Espinoza and César Santiváñez fiction devours documented history and at times modifies the latter to the point of unrecognizability. Operating in a space of mass circulation (thanks to the distribution of Comics21), *Nuestros Muertos* competes in newspaper kiosks for popular readers of sensationalist journalism and foreign comic books. The series appeals to these readers' thirst for superheroes and entertainment as a lure to attract their attention and—without failing to satisfy that thirst—introduces themes of cultural memory and the memory of the internal war in a story that continually traverses the boundaries between fiction and reality.

Political Violence: The Contamination of the Historical Record

In *Nuestros Muertos* the history of Peru's internal war is narrated like a work of detective fiction, in which a journalist and a group of young anarchists—known as Colectivo Vichama—seek the truth about certain recent and past events linked to political violence and its effects in contemporary Peru. They alone are interested in seeking the truth in a society bombarded by sensationalist television news and social media. The story is set in 2016, a year doubly associated with events of political violence and their aftereffects. First, the year marks the thirty-third anniversary of the Uchuyanay massacre perpetrated by the bloodthirsty terrorist group Senda de Luz [Path of Light]. Second, the story is set on the eve of presidential elections. The leading candidate is a man named Badenheimer, but the leader of the Senda de Luz, a certain Gálvez Rendón, has also just announced his candidacy from his prison cell and is running second place in the polls. No one knows how his candidacy has been approved, and suspicions of collusion between Gálvez Rendón, politicians, and the state create the foreground of the detective fiction narrative. The entirety of Peruvian society is characterized as a conspiracy woven around widespread corruption and the absence of memory about the political violence initiated by Senda de Luz.

For Peruvian readers these references bear an uncomfortably familiar relation to reality. The names are too similar to those of the real history of Peru's internal conflict, but at the same time their fictional status contaminates the historical record and the pact of plausibility with the reader. Senda de Luz bears practically the same name as Sendero Luminoso [Shining Path], and Gálvez Rendón could not be other than the group's infamous leader, Abimael Guzmán Reynoso. Since 2009 the MOVADEF Collective has sought to turn Shining Path into an official political party and has repeatedly demanded the release of Guzmán Reynoso.[7] Likewise, Uchuyanay is an obvious reference to the massacre of Uchuraccay, perhaps the best-known event of Peru's internal conflict, in which eight journalists, a guide, and a peasant were murdered in this community in the province of Huanta (Ayacucho region) under circumstances and for reasons that continue to be in dispute. The CVR's *Informe Final* calls the Uchuraccay massacre an "emblematic referent of violence and pain in the country's collective memory as well as of the demands for justice and truth that were made throughout those years" (121). News of the massacre was met with immediate shock on the part of many Peruvians, but it was not until 2002 that the true scope of the tragedy was revealed, thanks to testimonies given by the town's surviving residents to the CVR: 135 inhabitants out of a total population of approximately 470 were murdered in the months following the killing of the journalists, due to Shining Path incursions, the army's antisubversive measures, and the actions of *rondas campesinas* (communal self-defense organizations). In little more than a year, Uchuraccay ceased to exist, as survivors fled to take refuge in other towns and cities (123).

The historical similarity of names and events in *Nuestros Muertos* makes it impossible not to relate its fictional references to events in the nation's violent recent past, yet any such similarity is immediately contradicted by the comic book's character as artifice, which the reader is unable to overlook at any time.⁸ The sheer dimensions of the Uchuraccay tragedy might have led other artists to privilege a realist aesthetic in order to avoid sowing confusion among young audiences born after the events in question. However, *Nuestros Muertos* opts for an aesthetic of shock that aims to break the reader's familiarity with names that are in continuous circulation in the public sphere. In his famous essay "Art as Technique," Viktor Shkolvsky designated this artistic operation the technique of defamiliarization [*ostranenie*], through which art seeks to make the familiar appear strange and thereby counteract the automation of perception that occurs through habit or through repeated exposure to the same object, speech, or event. Defamiliarization interrupts the gaze and forces the perceiver to see the object in question as something new, thereby encouraging an active mode of cognition. The words "internal war," "Shining Path," or "Uchuraccay" are repeated continuously in the Peruvian media, in schools, and in the speeches of politicians and government officials. For this reason, the use of made-up names that are similar to historical references encourages the reader to examine the level of truth or fiction of *Nuestros Muertos*. Names that circulate continuously in the public sphere are deautomated and draw the audience's attention. The reader seems to be invited to complete or correct that which the fiction elides or tends to obscure.

The clash between fictional discourse and the historical record also traverses the series' story line focused on the investigations carried out by a journalist and by Colectivo Vichama. The journalist, Julián Gayoso, the son of one of the journalists killed in the Uchuyanay massacre, is obsessed with uncovering the truth and identifying the perpetrators of the crime. His prior investigations have led him to suspect that responsibility for the massacre is shared between Gálvez Rendón and a certain General Monroy, but he has no proof. The former's presidential campaign presents Gayoso with the opportunity to interview him, but the encounter fails to uncover anything new about Uchuyanay. For its part, the Vichama Collective has unearthed documents that not only definitively prove Gálvez Rendón's intellectual authorship of the massacre but also establish that the state was involved. At this point, the plot becomes more complex.⁹ Gálvez Rendón escapes from prison thanks to a bomb that explodes during a protest against his candidacy organized by Colectivo Vichama. The candidate Badenheimer arranges a secret meeting with Gayoso under the pretext of divulging to him a plan to defeat Senda de Luz, but Badenheimer has previously hidden the fugitive Gálvez Rendón in the cemetery, since the two of them have been working as allies to win the presidency. In a moment of oversight, Gayoso kills the leader of Senda de Luz, at which point Elisa—Chola Power in disguise—appears. Gayoso and Elisa had met hours earlier in the prison, when she saved his life following the explosion. In desperation, Gayoso informs Elisa that he has just killed the only person who could have told him the truth about

Uchuyanay. Elisa decides to use her superpowers to communicate with the dead man, thereby transmitting his memories to Gayoso. The transmission, much like a movie, reveals what really happened in Uchuyanay: the eight journalists were taken captive by Gálvez Rendón and General Monroy while the latter two were in Uchuyanay on "business." The frightened journalists tell their captors that they have not been pursuing these affairs and have only come to the town to investigate a story about the reincarnation of a pre-Inca god in the community. Gálvez Rendón refuses to believe them and delivers them over to the peasants, telling them: "they have come to destroy your god in the name of progress. Don't hold back. Finish what you started" (Vol. 3).[10]

By this point, the storytelling is characterized less by the resemblance between real and fictional names and events and more by the mixture of the story of the massacre with fantastic elements—for example, the appearance of Chola Power and her ability to communicate with the dead. However, the overwhelming certainty of Gálvez Rendón's and General Monroy's guilt in the story line forces the reader—who has been keyed into the use of historically evocative names for characters and events—to contrast the comic book story with information from outside the work. That effort reveals motives and events that differ from the story line. For example, neither the historical leader of Shining Path nor any army generals were present at the massacre. According to the CVR, the peasants killed the journalists after mistaking them for members of the terrorist group, because the army had previously notified them that military personnel would be arriving by air and Shining Path members by land—which is how the eight journalists traveled to Uchuraccay (*Informe Final* 134). In addition, the reason for the journalists' trip was to confirm the truth of the army's claim that the peasants had autonomously organized the defense against the guerrillas. For this reason, President Belaúnde Terry had praised the peasants as examples of patriotism, as well as seeking to use them as justification for not employing the army in the counterinsurgency offensive (131–33). However, the reader who finds this information will also discover that this version of the events is not accepted by everyone in Peru, and that the history of Uchuraccay is marked by rumors and "a plethora of versions and partial 'truths'" (Milton 173). Thus, the overwhelming certainty of the guilt of Gálvez Rendón and the state could be merely one more component of the rumors and stories circulating around the history of Uchuraccay. The discursive mechanism that mixes reality and fiction imposes a dynamic of hysterical significance.

One detail introduced in the comic book's detective story is particularly controversial: the idea that the peasants were motivated by a "primitive mentality" and are violent by nature. This perception is introduced in Gálvez Rendón's mandate to the peasants ("they have come to destroy your god in the name of progress. Don't hold back. Finish what you started"), but is also complemented in the visual discourse of the scene in which the peasants are about to kill the journalists (fig.

Figure 7.3. Campesinos are about to kill journalists in Uchuyanay in *Nuestros Muertos*, vol. 3.

7.3).¹¹ In the foreground, the image shows us Elisa—Chola Power—ending her mouth-to-mouth communication with the corpse of Gálvez Rendón. In the inset image Gálvez Rendón appears, with a cynical expression, along with a lost-looking General Monroy. In the background, several peasants wielding pickaxes and lamps head off to assassinate the journalists locked in a house. One of them looks at the reader with a sadistic smile and an expression of pleasure. The peasant is thereby represented as a "savage" and naturally violent subject. Does *Nuestros Muertos* thereby reproduce a stereotypical view of Indigenous populations?

The answer to this question could go in two different directions. The first would conclude that the series does, indeed, reproduce the stereotype in question and reinforce it among urban readers. In the visual portrayal of Indigenous cultures, their members have often been ascribed a "savage" and violent nature. Since the nineteenth century, Peru's Indigenous peoples have also been identified with archaic worlds that must be eliminated by modernity, and the survival of their ways of life has often resulted in their being blamed "for the failed or incomplete modernization of the nation" (Franco 4). *Nuestros Muertos* would thereby be reproducing this deeply rooted belief, perhaps unconsciously, via its images and dialogue.

A second reading would suggest that this comic book series does not seek to reproduce the stereotypes in question, but instead to show those stereotypes being *voiced* by specific social actors that have pronounced them with regard to Peru's Indigenous populations during and after the nation's internal conflict. First of all, it is important to bear in mind here that the character who refers to primitive gods and progress is the leader of the fictional counterpart of the "Shining Path" and that, historically, the latter group has expressed continuous contempt for Indigenous cultures. Carlos Iván Degregori observes that the "quasi-religious scientism of Shining Path," together with the personality cult of its leader, in whom that scientific truth is embodied as a divine spirit, sought to defeat the old Andean gods who—according to the members of the movement—"for centuries subjected [the peasants] to 'total domination'" (*Qué difícil* 240). To the extent that Shining Path was a modernizing movement, it saw Indigenous religion and culture as primitive and as obstacles to the movement's idea of communist modernity. However, this belief was also held on the other side of the political spectrum as well, as was made manifest by one of Peru's most recognized public writers and intellectuals, Mario Vargas Llosa,[12] who served as president of the first commission investigating the events of Uchuraccay (1983). In his report summarizing the commission's findings, Vargas Llosa blamed the massacre on a barbarian Peru that was resistant to modernity. The Andean peasants, he charged, still lived "in prehispanic times," in a "backward and . . . violent world" (cited in *Informe Final* 151). On another occasion, Vargas Llosa claimed that "the massacre had magical and religious as well as political and social overtones. The horrible wounds inflicted on the bodies seemed ritualistic. The eight [journalists] were buried in pairs and face down, a way the communities bury people they consider 'devils' or those like the scissors dancers whom they believe have made a pact with the devil."

In the scene in *Nuestros Muertos*, the face of the peasant who appears to be taking pleasure in the imminent mass murder could well be constructed either from the perspective of Shining Path or that of Vargas Llosa. Following Milton's idea (177), one could say that the use of fiction permits the introduction of perspectives such as those of Abimael Guzmán, of Peruvian intellectuals, or of the murdered journalists. The comic's work on memory creates a flow of mixed voices that the reader must attempt to identify. The most visible limitation of this aesthetic project is that it requires a reader willing to investigate the CVR's *Informe Final* or the literature on Shining Path. Perhaps too much is being demanded of this comic book reader. *Nuestros Muertos* runs the risk of reproducing the stereotype of the peasant as a savage and naturally violent subject.

The Birth of Chola Power and the Mythical

The introduction of mythological stories and categories of Indigenous thought in *Nuestros Muertos* has to do primarily with the theme of memory and the explanation of the superhero's powers. Examination of the latter leads progressively to an understanding of the former. Up to this point we know that Chola Power has the ability to communicate with the dead. The comic book will soon reveal that this superpower is not a convention of the fantastic genre but is related to the mythical origin of the superhero herself. That origin will reveal one of the most important of Chola Power's superpowers for fulfilling the mission of preserving cultural memory and the memory of violence: her ability to move through time by reincarnating herself in different characters and connecting present and past.

Chola Power's origin story refers to the prehispanic myth of Vichama, which Elisa retells to Gayoso. According to this myth, at the beginning of the world the god Pachacamac creates a human couple but neglects to give them food. When the man dies, the woman asks for help from the Sun god, father of Pachacamac. The Sun conceives a male child, Vichama, with this woman (thereby marking the first coming of Vichama). Enraged, Pachacamac rips his brother to pieces, but from the limbs of the latter sprout corn, yucca, and other agricultural products. However, the mother continues to grieve over the disappearance of Vichama, so the Sun resurrects him, allowing him triumph over death (this marks his second coming). Vichama departs to travel around the world, and on his return he learns that his mother has been killed by Pachacamac. He takes revenge by destroying the town of Pachacamac. Ever since, both brothers have fought cyclically in an ongoing struggle to establish their order.[13] The comic book reveals that Elisa is the latest incarnation of Vichama, and that to protect him from Pachacamac, the Sun god has "decided to hide him not in one single place, but throughout history, in the form of different incarnations" (Vol. 4).[14] This ability to move through historical periods allows the superhero to create relations between the past and the present that humans are unable to establish themselves.

The myth of Vichama introduces in the comic the Andean categories of *duality* and *pachacuti*. That of duality allows us to understand the world as an order constituted by parts that are both opposing and complementary; for example, *Hanan* (above) and *Hurin* (below); man and woman; or day and night. The complementarity of these elements guarantees cosmic and social equilibrium.[15] For the same reason, the destabilization of duality heralds a moment of crisis and transformation. *Pachacuti*, or "the turning of the earth," is one of these figures of crisis, because it creates a cosmic time in which the current civilizing order (Hanan) can be defeated by the civilizing order represented by the other element of the duality (Hurin).[16] One of the stories that receives the most attention in *Nuestros Muertos* is the confrontation between Vichama (Chola Power) and

Pachacamac, which can be understood as a struggle between two elements of a complementary duality but whose ritual confrontation opens the possibility of a pachacuti. While Elisa is engaged in helping Gayoso access the memories of Gálvez Rendón, Pachacamac appears, announcing himself in the form of an earthquake from the underworld (fig. 7.4).[17] This god has located Vichama in the present in his disguise as Elisa and is determined to destroy him. A complementary relationship is thereby established—in a mirror-like symmetry—between the struggle against Senda de Luz and the fight against Pachacamac. This double risk of pachacuti contributes to the overall aesthetics of the comic book by encouraging confusion or the proliferation of stories or information that require interpretation. However, as mentioned earlier, this operation also carries a risk, since it can lead to dehistoricizing readings of the Peruvian internal war, insofar as layering a cyclical logic over the story line contributes to identifying that war as part of an inevitable cosmic cycle of creation and destruction.

The discovery of the Vichama/Pachacamac duality is the key to understanding that in *Nuestros Muertos* all the characters are conceived in a logic of duality, which multiplies them as if they were facing mirrors. Of all the possible dualities in this regard, the most relevant to our purposes here is the one established between Elisa and Gayoso. I argue that the formation of this duality allows relationships to be established between past and present, connecting the prehispanic world (although here limited to the memory of the Incas) with contemporary Peru. Only when these relationships are established is Chola Power born, in her final form and in the fullness of her identity and her powers.

To explain this hypothesis, it is necessary to conduct a close reading and describe the most important details of the stories of each character in the comic. At the beginning of *Nuestros Muertos*, journalist Gayoso has a photo of the Uchuyanay massacre showing a blurred silhouette of Elisa, whom he initially identifies as a bloodthirsty demon guilty of the death of his father.[18] It is not until Elisa helps him to connect with the memory of Gálvez Rendón's corpse that Gayoso realizes that she/he is in fact a prehispanic god who has the gift of hiding in history. Starting at this moment, Gayoso becomes believer of Vichama. On his part, Vichama first appears at the beginning of the comic book series reincarnated in the form of a young archaeologist member of Colectivo Vichama. This archaeologist works at the National Museum of Archeology and Anthropology of Lima, a site he has made available as a meeting place for the Collective. When he is discovered and dismissed from his job, he is replaced by Elisa, who is of course none other than Vichama himself reincarnated as a woman. In his guise as Elisa, Vichama reveals himself to Gayoso in the cemetery, at which point Pachacamac arrives from the underworld having finally located his rival. The two figures engage in a violent struggle, but Pachacamac's power is much greater. Vichama/Elisa is on the verge of defeat when Gayoso finally realizes that in order for her to recharge her powers in the present she needs

Figure 7.4. Pachacamac emerging from the underground or *hanan pacha* in *Nuestros Muertos*, vol. 4.

him to sacrifice himself. He assents and is subsequently transformed into pure energy, which feeds the body of Elisa. Vichama/Elisa thus acquires an incomparable power, and Chola Power is born, finally defeating Pachacamac (fig. 7.5). The establishment of a complementary duality between Gayoso and Elisa is the condition of possibility of the hero's emergence.[19] Through the duality of the two characters, the past can be inserted into the present, thereby allowing the construction of a cultural memory. This duality allows the past to be made present, converting the ancient god Vichama into the superhero Chola Power.

The use of categories of Indigenous thought to create new layers of meaning is not an invention of *Nuestros Muertos*. On the contrary, there is a significant cultural production—particularly in literature—that has worked in the same direction. Central to this effort is writer-anthropologist José María Arguedas, who used these categories profusely in his literary works. Of special mention is his posthumous novel, *El zorro de arriba y el zorro de abajo* (1971) (*The Fox from up Above and the Fox from down Below*), in which he employed the categories of duality and pachacuti to describe—among other things—changes in the peasant population due to mass migration and industrialization.[20] At the end of the twentieth century, the writer Óscar Colchado Lucio also used categories of

Figure 7.5. Chola Power is born: "I am new life," in *Nuestros Muertos*, vol. 5.

Indigenous thought to narrate the memory of the Peruvian internal war from the peasant perspective in his novel *Rosa Cuchillo*.[21] *Nuestros Muertos* dialogues with this tradition of literary production that has vitality to this day.

If the defamiliarization procedure was already a serious challenge for the reading of *Nuestros Muertos*, the use of categories of Indigenous thought adds yet another layer of complexity. The latter superimposes new levels of meaning to the changes of names and the representation of different voices. To all this must be added, finally, the comic's use of the Quechua language without translation into Spanish, which is employed in two moments of the work. The first of these occurs when Colectivo Vichama is putting up posters announcing the demonstration in protest of the candidacy of Gálvez Rendón (Vol. 1). While the young people are being portrayed, a portable radio is playing the *huayno* song "Pin Chay Mana Allin Runakuna?" ("Who Are the Real Terrorists?"). The song is about the Andean populations, who are being accused of being terrorists by the state. In a denunciatory tone, the song claims that it is the rulers, the military, and the guerrillas that are killing off this population. The song is also clearly associated with the criminalization of protest in contemporary Peru, through which young university protesters are accused of being terrorists. The second time lines in Quechua appear in the work is in the numerous dialogues between Chola Power and Pachacamac. These dialogues are in fact conducted entirely in Quechua and refer to the ritual confrontation between the two gods as well as to Pachacamac's surprise upon seeing that his brother has become a beautiful woman.[22] Chola Power calls her brother a demon while presenting herself as the creator of life: "musuq kawsay kani" ("I am new life").[23] Her triumph over Pachacamac ultimately signifies the latter's failure to achieve the pachacuti he had sought.

It was César Santiváñez, the writer of the script of *Nuestros Muertos*, who made the decision to include Quechua in the work. When I asked him about this decision, he commented that he wanted to change the dynamics of cultural power between Spanish and Quechua. Speakers of the latter language are obliged to learn the language of the state and hegemonic society, while Spanish speakers usually do not need or want to learn Quechua or other Indigenous languages. For this reason, Santiváñez sought to propose a "change of roles": "This time it is the Quechua speaker who is able to access more information." Although the Vichama myth vindicates a prehispanic culture—specifically, the Incan past—the inclusion of Quechua in the comic leads to the revindication of a contemporary culture, drawing the attention of urban readers to the cultural tensions of the present. Obviously, a new risk that *Nuestros Muertos* takes with this mechanism is that Spanish-speaking readers might not make the effort to translate the Quechuan dialogues and will thereby fail to access the information communicated in this language.

The Female Superhero: Gender and Ethnicity

In general terms, female superheroes in comic books escape the more traditional roles that have been assigned to women in society and in the media, such as that of the helpful wife who unconditionally supports her husband or the beautiful princess who requires rescue by a hero. In this way, female superheroes transgress the heteronormative gender roles of motherhood or domesticity. However, as Jennifer K. Stuller has observed, the representation of the female superhero continues to be problematic, since in most cases these heroes skirt the line between "an oppressive stereotype or an empowering one—often [they are] simultaneously both" (22). For this reason, in analyzing any female superhero one inevitably confronts the question of whether the character in question is a progressive one or merely reaffirms the male gaze by once again objectifying the female body.

The portrayal of Chola Power does not escape this situation. On the one hand, the commonplaces of the genre are immediately evident on the visual level of the series. From the moment of her first appearance, Elisa wears revealing clothing that accentuate her curvy, exuberant, and sensual body, in a way that is reminiscent of the stereotype of Latina women frequently reproduced in the US media (Molina Guzmán and Valdivia).[24] According to the character's creator Martín Espinoza, this characterization of Chola Power is part of the series' interest in revalorizing "Peruvian beauty" by questioning the prevalence of white beauty models in the country: "Someone once wrote to me saying, Chola Power reminds me of Karen Dejo! I said: Perfect, don't expect her to remind you of Marilyn Monroe!"[25]

On the other hand, despite this sexualization on the visual level, on the narrative level of *Nuestros Muertos* there is no explicit reference to Chola Power's sexuality. On the contrary, there is no mention of her having a lover or a "love interest" (as is often common in the genre, e.g., Jessica Jones). She is a solitary and independent character who does not need any kind of masculine assistance. Although it is true that in the great battle at the end of the series Chola Power receives the help of journalist Gayoso, the relationship established between them is not a love relationship but that of a believer with his god. Gayoso surrenders to her not as a woman but as a divinity. His words are marked by a cosmic transformation: "Now I am an explosion, an idea unfolding into infinity. . . . I am transformed into life. Only life. And I pour myself in another container" (Vol. 5).

In addition to avoiding a direct mention of her sexuality, there is in *Nuestros Muertos* a plasticity in the representation of the protagonist's gender identity. First, Chola Power is the reincarnation of the prehispanic male god Vichama, a conceit introduced by the scriptwriter and not based on the original myth. When Vichama and Pachacamac are fighting and speaking in Quechua, the latter shows surprise that his brother has reincarnated as a woman, thereby suggesting his discomfort with not fighting another man. However, the struggle does not end at that point, thereby relegating the perceived gender identity of the combatants to a level of insignificance. Similarly, in the first volume of the series we are introduced to Chola Power first as a man—as an employee of the museum and member of the Vichama Collective. But almost immediately the character literally rips off his mask to reveal Elisa, who will eventually turn into Chola Power. From the perspective of a Peruvian reader, *Nuestros Muertos* changes a society marked by traditional gender roles into a space that welcomes a gender-fluid, empowered nonbinary character; but this space is of course fictional.

Equally interesting as the way in which Espinoza and Santiváñez position Chola Power at the center of ongoing debates over gender fluidity, female sexualization, and empowerment is the treatment of the character's ethnicity in the context of changes that have taken place in recent decades in Peru. The key to this connection lies in the female superhero's name. The term *cholo* has long been associated with a sense of inferiority and sociocultural discrimination. Although the term has been used since colonial times, with the rise of mass migrations in the second half of the twentieth century, it began to be used to refer to migrants and to the types of culture and ways of life they were creating in Peruvian society.[26] *Cholo* designated new forms of labor and cultural practices that were recognizably influenced by modern national and international culture but based on migrant Indigenous or mestizo culture.[27] To the extent that these changes involved the majority of the population, scholars began to speak of a process of *cholification* in Peru that put patrimonial society in crisis. By the same token, the process signified a potential change of hegemony (Quijano). From the perspective of traditional urban society, Chola culture was characterized as ugly, grotesque, poor, improvised, and inferior—as a failed attempt at modernization that would end up forming a new basis of discrimination. In the grammar of Peruvian racism, everyone could be more or less *cholo*, depending on the degree to which they deviated from Indigenous traits.

The use of the term *cholo* in the feminine adds another layer of meaning to previous tensions. Numerous anthropological studies have examined the complex figure of the chola in Andean countries (Ecuador, Bolivia, Peru), emphasizing the term's double valence between, on the one hand, its degrading sense in ethnic and gender terms, and on the other, its affirmation of economic and social agency on the part of women of Indigenous origin. In her classic book *Cholas and Pishtacos*, Mary Weismantel has analyzed the phenomenon of Indigenous women who have become merchants in the urban markets of Andean cities. Whether they wear traditional or modern clothing, these cholas are perceived as a disturbing presence for men because they are always out of place: they are supposed to stay in the peasant world but have instead settled in the city; they should remain in the private sphere but have decided to act in the public sphere, entering marketplaces and engaging with money and activities of mercantile exchange traditionally associated with masculinity. In the public space, the chola loses her purity and is associated with "scandalous behavior," a perception that is subsequently transferred to her female body, thereby sexualizing the work and agency of women in the public sphere (45–49). These observations allow us to perceive that the dynamic of sexualization/empowerment at work in the characterization of the female superhero also comes from the intersections of race, ethnicity, and class among Andean women identified as cholas. Both are figures of transgression, one of whose primary expressions is that of violating the restriction of women to the private sphere. The insertion of the chola and the female superhero in the public sphere sexualizes their agency, generating comments about their bodies and the objectives they are pursuing. This narrative of gender and ethnicity resonates in the term *Chola Power*.

However, Chola Power signifies, or seeks to signify, an important change with respect to the cholo narrative. In contemporary Peru, the term "chola power"—or "cholo power" in the masculine—refers to a person who can be identified phenotypically as "Peruvian" (thereby alluding to a long process of miscegenation—Indigenous, European, Afro-descendant, Asian) and who is perceived to possess power and success in accordance with hegemonic social standards. The subjective dynamics that intervene in the identification of chola/o power include the achievement of fame in popular culture, the acquisition of wealth, or the performance of an activity desired or admired by many (thereby also generating pride and identification from the public). The label is commonly ascribed to athletes, cumbia singers, or television actresses, in whom success is usually identified with a sexy body that is publicly celebrated without prejudice. In this sense, chola power—and it should be pointed out that the use of English is an important element in its definition—is a term that condenses the negotiation of popular identities in a neoliberal and global world, that exacerbates individualistic success, and that creates models of social mobility in figures of spectacle. The term is presented as a contradictory attempt to overcome discriminatory practice: on the one hand, the feeling of inferiority associated with *cholo* is rejected and is instead celebrated as a source of pride; on the other hand, *not* becoming cholo power is the fault of the individual for having failed to follow the rules of success and power as established by hegemonic neoliberal society. If one adheres to traditional ethnic attributes (those of dress, agricultural labor, and so on) one is affirming the *cholo* and impeding the *cholo power*.

Elisa does not like the name Chola Power. The nickname is given to her by the tabloid press after a video in which she is seen fighting on the street is broadcasted (fig. 7.6). She protests: "Chola Power? What a terrible name! What *chicha* people!" (Vol. 2). *Chicha* is inserted in the history of the term *cholo*, because it is used to refer—whether in a derogatory or vindicatory

Figure 7.6. "Chola Power is trending!" TV talk show mocks Chola Power's popularity in *Nuestros Muertos*, vol. 5.

fashion—to the hybrid cultural forms of migrants.[28] The scene is quite suggestive, as it shows Elisa clashing with contemporary Peruvian popular culture when one of her missions is precisely to prevent the cultural memory of the Incas from disappearing. The superhero will have to live with this tension, negotiating her hidden identity with the one ascribed to her by Peruvian contemporary popular culture.

War Zone Memory

At the beginning of this chapter I argued that the efforts of *Nuestros Muertos* to fill its pages with the aesthetic effects of obscurity and defamiliarization can be seen as a commentary on the difficulty of producing and transmitting memory. The sensation produced in reading *Nuestros Muertos* is that of encountering visual and auditory impressions that come from some unidentified place or from a broken or blurred memory. Past and present, fiction and reality mix, often to the point of becoming indistinguishable. The fragments appear and disappear, are repeated or are forgotten. I would suggest that these fragments emerge from a narrative voice that behaves as if affected by post-traumatic stress disorder. It is from this tenuous positionality that the textual and visual narrative of *Nuestros Muertos* is constructed. The work's enunciation is marked by flashbacks, cloudiness, anxiety, and mistrust, as if it were being forced to confront undesired and distressing memories. The subject remembers, but not in such a way that would provide an objective account of the traumatic event, and what we read is the work of this subject's discourse. Reality—or what this subject transmits to us as reality and that is experienced in reading the comic—is projected like a war zone. The fragments of this reality are the only indications the reader possesses for the task of reconstructing the memories and making the narrator's discourse intelligible.

This narrator's discourse also confronts a reader who must act like a detective. In Ricardo Piglia's typology of readers, the narrator works her or his narration as if hiding a crime in it, while the reader, for his or her part, must try to decipher the enigma, even if there is none (14–15). This detective operation is comparable to that of the psychoanalyst: as Carlo Ginzburg has observed, the two methods of interpretation are similar, insofar as both work with "discarded information, on marginal data, considered in some way insignificant." For Freud it is about reading symptoms; for Sherlock Holmes, it is about finding clues (101). The reader-detective suspects that the reality is impenetrable as a totality, but perceives clues that allow him or her to enter and to reconstruct—following the proposed analogy—the story of the crime. In this chapter I have discussed some of these clues: (a) the resemblance between made-up and real names in relation to Peru's internal war invites the reader to depart from the text in order to reconstruct the facts and contrast them with the information provided in the comic book; (b) the intersections between the fiction of the mythological discourse and the historical discourse connects past and present, establishing connections between the presidential candidacy of the Senda de Luz leader and the history of a forgotten violence; (c) the allusions to contemporary popular culture connect the neoliberal present with the history of migration (from chola to superchola). The narrator's main operation with regard to memory is to erase it, positing reality as a war zone. The reader-detective proceeds in reverse, under the assumption that behind that effect there are penetrable zones that allow one to renarrate the memory that has been scattered in fragments.

Notes

I am grateful to José Luis Guardia, director of the Comicteca Galilea Ramírez at the Peruvian National Library, for allowing me to work with the most complete public collection of Peruvian comics to date. I also thank Martín Espinoza and César Santiváñez for answering my questions, and Andrés Cano Mori for helping me navigate Lima's comic world.

1. On the history of comic strips in Peru, see Lucioni; Sagástegui; Ledgard; Villar.
2. An emblematic reference in this regard is the organization of comic workshops in Villa El Salvador (a working-class area of Lima created due to migration from the Andes) by graphic artist Juan Acevedo in the 1970s.
3. The duration of these comic books tends to be quite irregular. Some have managed to last several years, such as the magazine *DC Comics* created and published by Martín Espinoza, which includes the stories of *La Chola Power* as well as those of other Peruvian superheroes. However, many comics do not last more than a year. In Lima bookstores foreign comic

books—from DC or Marvel—dominate sales, but there are also other circuits of circulation, especially for manga and anime comics (Casallo Mesías).

4. In 2006 Juan Carlos Silva published the comic book *El origin de los Incas*, on the myth of Inkarri (the return of the Inca). In 2010 Martín Espinoza also published another version of Inkarri through MED Comics. Comics based on the adaptation of Indigenous regional memory include *Relatos del abuelo Atoc: Los Pururauca* (2014) by William Palomino Cahuana, as well as *Apumayta: El Génesis andino* (2013) by Mario Alonso Morales Vite. In 2015, Casa de la Literatura sponsored the publication of *Dioses y hombres de Huarochirí*, an important prehispanic chronicle of the Sierra de Lima. *Qosqomic* magazine (Cusco) has also been publishing stories of superheroes based on prehispanic mythology and influenced by science fiction and American comics. The comic *Super Condor* (2015), by Alejandro Nieto and Martín Espinoza, tells the stories of a crime-fighting superhero in Lima who takes on the identity of a condor, the sacred bird of the Incas. Finally, MED Comics magazine publishes the stories of three other superheroes besides Chola Power: (1) Descomunal: a gorilla-lion hybrid created through a mafia genetic experiment; (2) Xcorpiona: a superheroine who returns from the future to battle an alien that had been frozen in an Andean glacier for centuries and has now been released thanks to global warming; (3) Guachimán (a term used in Peru for a private security guard who works for neighborhoods or banks, derived from the English word watchman): a young immigrant from the Andes who arrives in the capital to study at the university, but decides to become a crime-fighting street watchman.

5. In 2008, L. Rossell, A. Villar, and J. Cossio published *Rupay: Historias gráficas de la violencia en el Perú, 1980–1984*. Cossio has continued to publish other comics on similar topics, including *Barbarie* and, more recently, *Los años del terror*. For an analysis of comics devoted to political violence, see Milton.

6. In current Peruvian politics, media, and public education, there is extensive debate over the historical significance of violence, victimhood, and state reparations. Some defend the need for the public discussion of memory and for the acknowledgment of violations of human rights committed by various actors in the conflict. Others argue that the past should be forgotten. Some in the latter group accuse the former group of justifying terrorism, claiming that it places the actions of Shining Path and the state on the same level (the latter position indirectly defends presidents Alan García and Alberto Fujimori). The tensions generated by these discussions can be seen in recent events at the Lugar de la Memoria (LUM), a Lima museum devoted to political violence.

7. In 2011 MOVADEF (Movement for Amnesty and Fundamental Rights) tried to formally register as a political party, but its request was rejected.

8. Another veiled reference to historical reality in the work is the fact that 2016 was an election year in Peru. The comic book makes several connections with the elections, although outlining them here would exceed the scope of this discussion.

9. In what follows, I will be selecting and discussing only those events in the story that are most relevant to my analysis. The plot has numerous complexities, and its chronology does not always follow the sequence suggested by my analysis.

10. Gayoso also thought that the massacre had been the work of a malevolent god; nevertheless, accessing the memories of Gálvez Rendón led him to see his error.

11. The notion that the journalists believed in the reincarnation of an evil god could be interpreted as part of their desperate attempt to save their lives.

12. Much has been written on this subject. I refer here to Enrique Mayer's study.

13. Here I am following the version of this myth that is featured in *Nuestros Muertos* (Vol. 2). However, this version is based—with a few exceptions—on colonial sources collected by Rostworowski (*Pachacamac, Estructuras*).

14. This explains, for example, why Chola Power was present at the Uchuyanay massacre. A photograph taken by one of the murdered journalists captures Elisa's (Chola Power's) silhouette, and Gayoso believes the figure is that of a demon who caused the slaughter.

15. On the concept of duality, see Rostworowski (*Estructuras*), particularly with regard to his discussion of the concept of *yanantin* as proposed by Tristan Platt (22–23).

16. On the concept of *pachacuti*, see McCormack 284–93.

17. *Pachacamac* can be translated as "earth-maker." He was a prominent god in the Peruvian central coast region, considered the creator of the people who lived in that part of Peru. Upon expanding their domain, the Incas incorporated Pachacamac in their religious system, establishing a duality between past/present and coastal region/Andean region.

18. This photo was discovered in the camera of one of the murdered reporters. The event actually took place in the Uchuraccay case.

19. In a complementary duality, there must be *reciprocity*, a category that requires an active exchange between the two poles. In *Nuestros Muertos* it is not just Gayoso who gives to Chola Power (i.e., his belief and his sacrifice); she also grants to him—through her connection with the corpse of Gálvez Rendón—the possibility of finding the perpetrators of the Uchuyanay massacre.

20. I have previously proposed a reading of this novel from this perspective ("El reflejo").

21. On *Rosa Cuchillo*, see Lambright.

22. In this chapter I do not discuss the representation of gender, because such discussion would require a lengthier analysis. However, gender is an important aspect of *Nuestros Muertos* that has many parallels to the topic of ethnicity that I will discuss further on.

23. I want to thank Franklin Espinoza Bustamante for his assistance in helping me translate the Quechua sections of the comic book.

24. This observation is of course also valid for other countries in Latin America.

25. Karen Dejo, a Peruvian actress and dancer, is an example of the "Peruvian beauty" that the comic seeks to celebrate.

26. In the colonial period, *cholo* was defined as an individual of mixed race born to one parent who was Indigenous and another who was of African descent. In the wake of the mass migration phenomenon of the twentieth century, the term came to be redefined in reference to the culture of migrant populations as well as to transformations in social life. For example, the term *cholo* stands in definitional contrast to the way of life of the rural peasants who labored for centuries in the Andean *haciendas*. Whereas these peasants endured conditions of semi-slavery, lacked access to education and other services, and were dependent on the will of the *hacendados*, *cholos* are defined as individuals who have been inserted in a process of social mobility, initially taking jobs in the services sector (as drivers, bakers, merchants, and so on).

27. I have discussed the formation of *cholo* culture as effect of mass migration and urbanization with regard to José María Arguedas's work (*El intelectual*).

28. The term *chicha* originally refers to a prehispanic drink made from fermented corn. During the final decades of the twentieth century, the term also came to define a type of popular music that combines the *huayno* (a genre of popular Andean music and dance) with cumbia (see Degregori "Huayno"). *Chicha* likewise came to designate sensationalist, low-cost tabloid newspapers featuring colorful front pages and frequent use of urban slang (Mejía Chiang). This double reference accounts for the chief attributes of chicha culture, which is associated with (a) the effects of mass migration to cities and the subsequent creation of a new mass-oriented culture that prominently features the mixing and fusion of Andean cultural traditions (mainly of Indigenous origin); and (b) that which is considered socially marginal (related to the urban periphery, the informal economy, and criminality) or culturally marginal (i.e., which fails to rise to the level of "good taste" established by traditional urban society or the accepted taste of models from the global cultural industry).

Works Cited

Acevedo, Juan. *Para hacer historietas*. Madrid: Editorial Popular, 1992.
Aldama, Frederick Luis. *Latinx Superheroes in Mainstream Comics*. Tucson: University of Arizona Press, 2017.
Arguedas, José María. *El zorro de arriba y el zorro de abajo*. Edited by Eve-Marie Fell. Paris: ALLCA XX, 1997.
Casa de la Literatura Peruana. *Dioses y Hombres de Huarochirí*. Lima: Casa de la Literatura Peruana, 2015.
Casallo Mesías, Víctor. "Nuevas mediaciones de la historieta: Texto, imagen e identidad juvenil entre cómics y mangas." *Escritura e imagen en Hispanoamérica: De la crónica ilustrada al cómic*, edited by Cécile Michaud. Lima: Pontificia Universidad Católica del Perú, 2015. pp. 285–300.
Colchado Lucio, Óscar. *Rosa Cuchillo*. Lima: San Marcos, 2009.
Comisión de la Verdad y Reconciliación. *Informe Final*. https://www.cverdad.org.pe/ingles/ifinal/index.php. Accessed May 13, 2018.
Cossio, Jesús. *Barbarie: Comics sobre violencia política en el Perú, 1985–1990*. Lima: Ediciones ContraCultura, 2010.
———. *Los años del terror: 50 preguntas sobre el conflicto armado en el Perú, 1980–2000*. Lima: Ediciones ContraCultura, 2016.
Cossio, Jesús, Luis Rossell, and Alfredo Villar. *Rupay: Historias gráficas de la violencia en el Perú, 1980–1984*. Lima: Ediciones ContraCultura, 2008.
Degregori, Carlos Iván. "Huayno, 'Chicha': El nuevo rostro de la música peruana." *Del Mito Del Inkarrí Al Mito Del Progreso: Migración y Cambios Culturales. Obras Escogidas* vol. 3. Lima: Instituto de Estudios Peruanos, 2013. 189–96.
———. *Qué difícil es ser Dios: El Partido Comunista Del Perú-Sendero Luminoso y el Conflicto Armado Interno en el Perú: 1980–1999. Obras Escogidas* vol. 1. Lima: Instituto de Estudios Peruanos, 2011.
Espinoza, Martín. *Inkarri. Medcomics*, vol. 5. Lima: MedComics, 2010.
Espinoza, Martín. Personal Interview (with Andrés Cano Mori). June 19, 2018.
Espinoza, Martín, and César Santiváñez. *Nuestros Muertos. La Chola Power*. 5 vols. Lima: Comics21, 2017.
Franco, Jean. "Alien to Modernity: The Rationalization of Discrimination." *A Contra Corriente* 3, no. 3 (2016): 1–16.
García Liendo, Javier. *El intelectual y la cultura de masas: Argumentos latinoamericanos en torno a Ángel Rama y José María Arguedas*. Lafayette, IN: Purdue University Press, 2017.
———. "El reflejo y la memoria: Los zorros en la última novela de José María Arguedas." *Palimpsestos de la antigua palabra: Inventario de Mitos Prehispánicos en la literatura latinoamericana*, Bern: Peter Lang, 2013. 137–71.
Ginzburg, Carlo. "Clues: Roots of an Evidential Paradigm." *Clues, Myths, and the Historical Method*, translated by John and Anne Tedeschi. Baltimore: Johns Hopkins University Press, 1992. 96–125.
Lambright, Anne. *Andean Truths: Transitional Justice, Ethnicity, and Cultural Production in Post-Shining Path Peru*. Liverpool: Liverpool University Press, 2015.
Ledgard, Melvin. *De Supercholo a Teodosio: Historietas peruanas de los sesentas y setentas*. Lima: Instituto Cultural Peruano Norteamericano, 2004.
Lucioni, Mario. "La historieta peruana." *Tebeosfera.com*, https://www.tebeosfera.com/documentos/la_historieta_peruana_1.html. Accessed July 27, 2018.
Mayer, Enrique. "Peru in Deep Trouble: Mario Vargas Llosa's 'Inquest in the Andes' Reexamined." *Cultural Anthropology* 6, no. 4 (November 1991): 466–504.

McCormack, Sabine G. *Religion in the Andes: Vision and Imagination in Early Colonial Peru*. Princeton, NJ: Princeton University Press, 1991.

Mejía Chiang, César. *Cultura popular limeña y prensa chicha*. Lima: Mesa Redonda, 2011.

Milton, Cynthia E. "Death in the Andes: Comics as Means to Broach Stories of Political Violence in Peru." *Comics and Memory in Latin America*, edited by Jorge Catalá Carrasco et al., 166–96. Pittsburgh: Pittsburgh University Press, 2017.

Molina Guzmán, Isabel, and Angharad Valdivia. "Brain, Brow, and Booty: Latina Iconicity in U.S. Popular Culture." *Communication Review* 7 (2004): 205–21.

Morales Vite, Mario Alonso. *Apumayta: El Génesis Andino*. Lima: Impacto Comics, 2013.

Nieto Polo, Alejandro, and Martín Espinoza. *Super Cóndor*. Vol. 1. Lima: Nima Producciones, 2015.

Palomino Cahuana, William. *Relatos del Abuelo: Atoc, Los Pururauca*. Lima: Perro Muerto Producciones, 2014.

Piglia, Ricardo. *Crítica y ficción*. Buenos Aires: Seix Barral, 2000.

Qosqomic. *Qosqomic: Revista de cómics y cultura de la narrativa gráfica*. Vol. 3. Qosqomic, 2013.

Quijano, Aníbal. *Dominación y cultura: lo cholo y el conflicto cultural en el Perú*. Lima: Mosca Azul, 1980.

Rostworowski, María. *Estructuras andinas del poder: Ideología religiosa y política. Obras Completas*. Vol. 7. Lima: Instituto de Estudios Peruanos, 2018.

———. *Pachacamac. Obras Completas*. Vol. 2. Lima: Instituto de Estudios Peruanos, 2014.

Sagástegui, Carla. *La historieta peruana 1: Los primeros 80 años, 1887–1967*. Lima: Instituto Cultural Peruano Norteamericano, 2003.

Santiváñez, César. Personal Interview. July 9, 2018.

Shklovsky, Viktor. "Art as Technique." *Russian Formalist Criticism: Four Essays*, edited by Lee Lemon and Marion Reiss, 3–24. Lincoln: University of Nebraska Press, 1965.

Silva, Juan Carlos. *El origen de los Incas. Incarry El Semidios, Incarry El Inca y Rey*. Lima: Art-Comics, 2006.

Stuller, Jennifer. "What Is a Female Superhero?" *What Is a Superhero?* edited by Robin Rosenberg and Peter Coogan, 19–23. New York: Oxford University Press, 2013.

Vargas Llosa, Mario. *Making Waves*. Edited and translated by John King. Kindle ed. Farrar, Straus and Giroux, 1996.

Villar, Alfredo. *Búmm! Historieta y humor gráfico en el Perú: 1978–1992*. Lima: Reservoir Books, 2016.

Weismantel, Mary. *Cholas and Pishtacos: Stories of Race and Sex in the Andes*. Chicago: University of Chicago Press, 2001

Visualizing an Alternative Mesoamerican Archive: Daniel Parada's Comic Series *Zotz* in Historical Perspective

Jessica Rutherford

This chapter explores how Daniel Parada—author-artist of *Zotz: Serpent and Shield* (2011–2016), a serial comic set in sixteenth-century Mesoamerica—engages with Indigenous subjects and experiences in a fictionalized historical context to reinscribe marginalized subjectivities into popular culture. Parada leaves little room for doubt with regard to the authorial intent behind his work; in the preface to issue 2, he tells the reader that

> This story is not meant to educate. I'll leave that to independent investigation and scholars. Zotz is meant to stir a conversation, to encourage others to learn more about Mesoamerican cultures ... or at least give readers a glimpse of this world, which is unfairly underrepresented in popular culture, including contemporary comics. (7)

Explicit in the publication of *Zotz* is the signaling of a lack of representation of Indigenous history and culture in Latin/x America, which is true not only of Latin/x American comics production but also of the larger historical archive, an issue that I take up in my analysis of the representation of pre-Columbian history and culture in Parada's work. In this series, with three issues published and a fourth in production, Parada reimagines colonial history to create a story-world in which Mesoamerican culture continues to unfold without the disruption of Spanish invasion in the region. Parada combines historical, social, and cultural elements from the pre-Columbian world to create an alternative space that continues these traditions in graphic narrative form.

The European and Christian bias in the historical record, largely narrated from a western-European perspective, is well documented in scholarship that represents the decolonial turn in Latin/x American studies.[1] Western historiographical discourse is ridden with archival silences, the result of various phases of conquest and colonization in the region (not only from European invaders but also from Amerindian imperial powers that rose and fell in the region prior to contact). Following the initial European encounter, in addition to the demographic devastation that Indigenous populations experienced,[2] Spanish conquistadors and missionaries worked ardently to destroy Indigenous history and culture. With the Spanish invasion of the Americas, Indigenous populations suffered not only physical violence but also epistemological violence.[3] For this reason, we have very few pre-Columbian materials that inform modern-day understandings of this period in Mesoamerican history. Utilizing pre-Columbian narrative elements to imagine a Mesoamerican world allowed to evolve in the absence of colonization, *Zotz* posits the comics medium and its graphic-narrative form as a potent archival space for the preservation of the foundational history that many Maya and Nahua cultures share. The medium is particularly apt given its combination of text and image, a core component that pre-Columbian historical narratives utilize, as well.[4]

Parada's self-ascribed project to write—both textually and visually—these silences in popular cultural production extends beyond its original intent and also serves as an alternative archive in which Mesoamerican religion and culture are both preserved and reproduced for a modern-day audience. In her well-known work *The Archive and the Repertoire*, Diana Taylor opens up the concept of the archive to include a larger cultural repertoire comprised of performance and other ritual memory acts to understand history. In the case of the colonial period, she asks, "How do populations and culture survive a crash [like that of the Euro-Amerindian encounter]? What happens when the populations themselves undergo change, and become the biological product of the 'encounter'?" (93–94). Taylor defines the encounter as a process of exchange that operates in a new space created from the "crash" of cultures. Taylor borrows a Nahuatl term to represent this exchange, calling it nepantla, "the space between the Indigenous and Spanish cultures. Nepantla reflected the cracks, the liminality zone that was no longer just Indigenous but that was not yet (and never would be) quite Spanish" (96). Gloria Anzaldúa also discusses the idea of the cultural "choque" that results from colonial encounters in her work on borderlands, in addition to incorporating the term nepantla into her cultural reflections in *Light in the Dark / Luz en lo oscuro*. As they reflect on the cultural clash inherent to the colonial encounter in the Americas, both Anzaldúa and Taylor bring attention to the pain and trauma that go along with the fragmentation/fracturing of Indigenous identities and experiences. In the interest of healing, Anzaldúa provides some solace, pointing out that "The creative process is an agency of transformation," asserting that "Using the creative process to heal or restructure the images/stories that shape a person's consciousness is a more effective way of healing" (*Light in the Dark / Luz en lo oscuro*, 35).[5] *Zotz* occupies/represents this space of nepantla—not only recognizing but also working to repair the epistemological damage suffered by Indigenous communities—to "heal or restructure the images/stories," using a hybrid/transcultural graphic form that combines oral, visual, and textual elements to reimagine this history.

Parada tells a story of two Maya Hero Twins, Kaan and Pakal, originally from the Chan village, located in the borderlands of sixteenth-century Maya and Nahua empires, a complex network of nation-states with an ancient shared history. The myth of the Hero Twins permeates Maya cultures in reference to the formation of the world, the creation of people, and the first sunrise for many Maya communities.[6] Oswaldo Chinchilla Mazariegos situates the myth as "an extended explanation about the origin of the sun, the moon, and the maize—the sowing and the dawning—that brought about the onset of a new era and its inhabitants, moral people who responded to the gods' demands and provided for them" (*Art and Myth of the Ancient Maya*, 57). The importance of the Maya Hero Twins in pre-Columbian culture cannot be overstated, evident in Parada's adaptation of the myth in his reproduction of this dynamic duo in *Zotz*. In Mesoamerican myths, the first set of Hero Twins, One Hunahpu and Seven Hunahpu, descend from Xpiyacoc (the divine father) and Xmucane (the divine mother). The second generation of Hero Twins, Hunahpu and Xbalanque, are fathered by both One and Seven Hunahpu, who spit into the hand of Blood Moon, the daughter of Blood Gatherer (lord of Xibalba, the underworld), to impregnate her.[7]

As is true of One Hunahpu and Seven Hunahpu and Hunahpu and Xbalanque, the story of Kaan and Pakal follows the same basic tropes of the spirit quest that befalls the Maya Hero Twins. Issue 1 opens with Kaan and Pakal playing the ball game, recognizing the ritual significance of the game in Mesoamerican culture. Then, Kaan and Pakal set off on their spirit quest to avenge the death of their father, a key mythological component in the larger story arc of the Hero Twins. They are also presented with a sacred medicine bundle, first in issue 1 after the death of their father and then again in issue 3, a gift from Tezcatlipoca (the Nahua trickster God) to aid them in their journey. Finally, the spirit quest of Kaan and Pakal mirrors that of the Hero Twins in that the duo gains warrior status and eventually come in to their own as tlatoani (a speaker/leader within the community). Suffice it to say, Parada did his homework in his recreation of a fictionalized historical narrative in which Maya and Nahua empires maintain their dominance in what is present-day Mexico and Central America, despite Spanish invasion of the region.

In terms of the historical dimension of the series, while the Tlacao Kingdom and Teotl Empire are fictional superpowers in *Zotz*, the comic also includes historically accurate events, such as the rise and fall of the Mexica Triple Alliance; the fall of cities like Teotihuacan; and the rise and dismantling of the Mayapan in the Yucatán. Beyond this, the food, clothing styles, religions, worldviews, architecture, economics, societal structures, specific rituals or idioms are historically based.⁸ For example, the comic consistently shows the presence of turkey and deer throughout the series, an echo of the Maya name for the Yucatán, The Land of Turkey and Deer, even referring to European horses as the "hornless deer." Cacao beans are used as currency in the series and the symbolic as well as nutritional significance of corn is central to the storyworld. Moreover, Parada incorporates Maya hieroglyphs into the graphic form that the narrative takes, particularly in his representations of sacred rituals dedicated to Mesoamerican deities. Although not the focus of the *Zotz* series, Castilians are still present in the series, along with a Turkish population that also operates at the margin of the Maya and Nahua empires that control the region in the context of Parada's storyworld. In reality, the Ottoman Empire, of course, did not extend into Mesoamerica, although the Spanish empire certainly did, which resulted in a tragic encounter for Amerindian societies in the hemisphere. Via his fictionalized (but historicized) storyworld, *Zotz* reimagines the well-paved trans-Amerindian sociocultural exchange networks that connected Nahua and Maya populations throughout Mexico and Central America.

Parada borrows heavily from the Popol Vuh,⁹ the Council Book of the Maya-Quiché, in his creation of the *Zotz* storyworld. The concept for *Zotz* (meaning bat in many Maya languages) is taken from Kamezotz, traditionally known as Maya death bats in the underworld of Xibalba, depicted in the Popol Vuh. Not only does understanding the connections between *Zotz* and the Popol Vuh help to elucidate the pre-Columbian elements in Parada's storyworld, such as the comic's title, but the comic also opens up a critical space to highlight the parallels between the oral, visual, and textual storytelling techniques that both texts implement, which are central to the narration of traditional Maya histories.¹⁰ In the face of demographic devastation due to Spanish invasion in Guatemala in the sixteenth century, the Quiché elders retreated to the highlands of the region to write the Popol Vuh to preserve their religion and culture.¹¹ The elders wrote their founding religious myths and histories in the Quiché language using the Roman alphabet—this use of the western-European writing system is a symptom of Spanish-dominated archival materials in that it demonstrates the elders' recognition that their traditional way of life was at stake, hence the need to write in the colonizers' writing system for fear that their traditional book might not be decipherable.¹²

Traditionally, Maya writing systems made use of logographic and phonetic signs to reproduce these narratives in hieroglyphic form. Logographic signs oftentimes include a pictorial connection with the word that the sign references while phonetic signs correspond to syllables: different phonetic signs can be combined with one another to represent a word and they can also combine with logographic signs to create meaning.¹³ This interplay between text and image is central to traditional storytelling in the region. In the introduction to his English translation/edition of the Popol Vuh, Dennis Tedlock explains, "In

Maya languages the terms for writing and painting were and are the same, the same artisans practiced both skills, and the patron deities of both skills were twin monkey gods bearing two different names for the same day, translatable as One Monkey and One Artisan" (27). He goes on to clarify,

> In the books made under the patronage of these twin gods there is a dialectical relationship between the writing and the pictures: the writing not only records words but sometimes offers pictorial clues to its meaning. As for the pictures, they not only depict what they mean but have elements that can be read as words. (27)

Just as the "pictorial clues" are important in Mesoamerican storytelling, they are also a central component to the way which readers engage with comics. Scott McCloud, well known for his work *Understanding Comics: The Invisible Art*, identifies comics as "juxtaposed pictorial and other images in deliberate sequence, intended to convey information and/or to produce an aesthetic response in the viewer" (9). In fact, McCloud cites Maya hieroglyphs and pre-Columbian codices as proto-comics (10–11). Given this connection between text and image, not only in Maya hieroglyphs but also in comics, *Zotz* is an apt form to document an alternative archive that works in the mode of nepantla, an in-between space in terms of the archive as well as the comic, given its hybrid form.[14]

In continued recognition of the oral and visual aspects of traditional Mesoamerican storytelling techniques, the initial tale of Kaan and Pakal begins around the fire with the tlatoani (a term for leader and/or speaker in Nahuatl) of the community orating that evening's story, an important role that the tlatoani assumes to preserve/reproduce the community's religious traditions and local histories. On this particular night, the last before Kaan and Pakal's world would be turned upside down as a result of the pending attack on their village, the story was that of "[t]he tale of our father the sun and our mother the moon" (issue 1, 30). The story of Xbalanque and Xt'actani (also known as Blood Moon) points to the belief that the "sowing and dawning movements of the heroes, along with those of their supporting cast, prefigure the present-day movements of the sun, moon, planets, and stars" (Tedlock, *Popol Vuh* 34). For example, Hunahpu, Xbalanque's twin brother, is linked to the star Venus and One Monkey and One Artisan reference the planet Mars.

The two panels that Parada constructs here represent the way in which the author-artist incorporates pre-Columbian style and shapes, modified for contemporary audiences. The quotations indicate the tlatoani's continued speech in the advancement of the narrative, grounding the reader in the communal scene around the fire while they simultaneously explore the story. The way in which the figures reach out across the space of the gutter to connect highlights not only the sacred bond between Xbalanque and Xt'actani but also the cyclical connection between the movements of the sun and the moon. As McCloud

Xbalanque and Xt'actani become the Sun and the Moon in *Zotz* #1. © 2011, Daniel Parada.

notes, the gutter is the space where closure takes place—the action that the reader creates in her/his own mind to complete the narrative arc.[15] Here, Parada makes that connection for us, in some ways solidifying and granting even more authority to this belief in the link between these two gods as well as the sun and the moon. This dimension of the comic series, and of traditional Mesoamerican cosmology, points to another archival layer at work, that of the sky itself.

The *Zotz* storyworld, in addition to the creation of an astral archive, also represents a spiritual archive for Amerindian religious traditions, another layer to the nepantla that the comic series offers. In addition to the appearance of Xbalanque and Xt'actani, other important Mesoamerican deities appear in *Zotz*, such as Quetzalcóatl (the deity that links the sky and the earth given its hybrid form as the bird and the serpent), who appears in issues 2 and 3, taking the form of the eagle, the serpent, and the spiritual adviser of the text. This spiritual adviser, referred to as "sorcerer" in *Zotz*, is detached from the action of the narrative, serving as an omen within the larger narratological structure. This is also true of the employment of Kamezotz (Maya death bat) in the third issue, which reveals the climax of the Hero Twins' spirit quest when Kaan assumes his new identity as Tzotz. Some of these Mesoamerican gods even make their way out of Parada's storyworld and into his own reality, as we see in his dedication to issue 3 in which, in addition to the special thanks that he gives to people that helped with the issue, he thanks "Xochiquetzal, Tlaloc, Tonatiuh, Zotz, Xochipilli, and Nanahuatzin." For those of us familiar with the pantheon at hand, it comes as no surprise that Parada gives, "No thanks to Tezcatlipoca and Itzpapalotl," presumably because of their infamously nefarious nature as the trickster god and warrior goddess (particularly for women who die in childbirth) respectively.[16]

While traditional Mesoamerican storytelling techniques (combining text and image to narrate foundational myths) are a central strategy in the reconstruction that the *Zotz* storyworld does, Parada's series also decenters colonial history geographically, linguistically, and culturally. Geographically, Parada begins each issue with a map that reinstitutes Maya and Nahua place-names in Anahuac (the Amerindian term for what we know today as Mexico and Central America). Linguistically, he incorporates different Indigenous languages in his character dialogue throughout the series, paying special attention to embed geographically accurate languages spoken in different regions, which include variations of Nahuatl and Maya languages. For example, in the borderland of the Tlacao and Teotl empires, Kaan and Pakal cross paths with a traveling warrior, who greets them in Nahuatl, "Cualli tonalli. Quen timetzica?" (Good morning. How are you?) (Issue 2, 39). Kaan and Pakal respond in shaky Nahuatl, noting among themselves that the traveling warrior is a "yaqui," a Maya term for speakers of Nahuatl. Parada also includes a pronunciation guide in issue two that urges readers to understand the sounds of these Indigenous languages.

In line with this same decolonial turn, Parada also embeds significant aspects from a traditional Mesoamerican soundscape in Anahuac, as we see in figure 8.2.[17] For example, to represent spoken words, Parada regularly implements speech glyphs. Additionally, Parada helps the reader visualize the acoustic dimension of the storyworld and it is this soundscape that binds together the different geographic spaces that this scene spans: Parada guides the reader to visualize the sounds of the conch and drum—in unison with the voices represented in the speech glyphs—in the frame via music notes, along with a bat-like instrument that lets out a loud "SHRIEK!": the speech glyphs that we see in the upper-right cell, the "SHRIEK!" and its reverberation throughout the valley represent a sequence that emphasizes how one moment flows into the next that binds these panels together temporally. Time seems to stand still in these longer panels, giving the reader the sense that what is represented here exists both in and outside of time, a key component in the liminality of ritual space. The size and layout of the three panels—the long, page-filling for—in addition to their production in color, changes the reader's perception of time, giving these moments more narrative weight, which contrasts with the panels that follow on the next page, paced differently to detail specific action; in this case, the ritualized production of war in Mesoamerican culture.

The panels provide multiple perspectives of the same moment: the warriors on the ground are set alongside a spiritual support network on top of the hill where we see a tlatoani working in unison with a group of musicians to summon Our Lady of Death, who answers the call. This call and response between

The Landscape, Soundscape, and Sacred Topography of Mesoamerican War Rituals in *Zotz* #3. © 2016, Daniel Parada.

humans on earth and the deities that guide them is key to Mesoamerican rituals, a central practice not only in war but in everyday life. Moreover, Parada's representation of Our Lady of Death in physical form points to the way in which the series also works to reconstruct the sacred landscape of Mesoamerica, a testament to the multicoded dimensions of the archival nepantla that the author-artist creates in the *Zotz* storyworld.

Parada also works to decenter Western representations of Mesoamerica culturally via his representation of historical time in the series. Just as many Mayas begin their own historical narrative with the primordial myth of the three hearthstones, as we see in the Popol Vuh, so does the storyworld of *Zotz*. At the beginning of issue 1 of *Zotz*, the reader is given a timeline: the story begins on 4 Lord (3114 BCE) when "the three hearthstones were placed. Marking the beginning of our world" (*Zotz*, 3). The three hearthstones are central to ancient/traditional Maya fireplaces, formed to make a triangle. As is true of many Mesoamerican myths/histories, the primordial hearthstones also have an astronomical referent. Tedlock links the three primordial hearthstones to the constellation Orion, writing that "we know that the contemporary Quiché have a hearthstone constellation consisting of a triangle of the three stars in Orion. The authors of the Popol Vuh might well be telling us the origin story of this constellation, but they never come right out and say so" (16). He goes on to explain, "Those writers [who worked at Palenque and Quiriguá many centuries before them] clearly state that at the end of the world before this one, three hearthstones marked out a new place for themselves in the sky" (*Popol Vuh*,

16). In the glossary of terms in issue 1, Parada unpacks the significance of the words "3 Hearth Stones were placed," noting that "The hearthstones were laid out during the creation of the world. They were also the center of every home. From these stones, the fire was lit to cook, warm, and give light" (57). In keeping with this ancient tradition, the three hearthstones that represent the creation of the Mesoamerican world are visible in the center of the homes and fire pits throughout *Zotz*, a sign of great reverence for this foundational ritual, well documented in Parada's comic series.

After establishing the primordial triangle of hearthstones and providing a chronology of other significant events, the first child of Zotz is born on 3 Lord (2000 BCE). In continuation of this ancestral lineage, Kaan and Pakal are born on 13 Lord (C 1561). And, it is on 7 Lord (C 1573) when Parada brings the reader into the *Zotz* storyworld by placing them inside a cave, looking onto the graphic narrative space in which the most recent incarnation of the Hero Twins will unravel. The cave represents a spiritual land formation in Mesoamerican history and culture, a sacred encounter solidified even further as the frame's anonymous narrator says, "Let's drink to them." This is a traditional Maya invitation to begin a tale that centers on the Maya mythical trope of the Hero Twins that echoes the beginning of part three of the Popol Vuh in which the Quiché elders write that, "And now we shall name the name of the father of Hunahpu and Xbalanque. Let's drink to him, and let's drink to the telling and accounting of the begetting of Hunahpu and Xbalanque" (91).[18]

Here, the text at the top of the panel serves as narration, in contrast to the dialogue-driven speech balloons, which also speaks to an impulse to create a historical archive in comics form. Issue 2 opens this same way—a page in black and white without clearly defined panels, an effect that further works to suspend the reader in time—but with more narrative context: a young Indigenous girl asks the tlatoani to continue the story of Kaan and Pakal. The tlatoani responds, saying, "Anxious to hear the rest, ey? Very well, get the musicians" (10). As the reader's eye moves down the page, the larger scene reveals itself, showing a group gathering around the fire with the "Tun! Tun! Tun!" of the drum almost reverberating off the page. These opening scenes in issues 1 and 2 serve as continued examples of the way in which the comic as a hybrid form, combining text and image to tell a story, opens up a space for the reader to experience Mesoamerican history in several dimensions simultaneously, via: the stories themselves; its visual aspects; as well as the soundscapes in which these communities operated.

While the comic series recreates a historical archive in which Mesoamerican culture maintains dominance after the "crash" that resulted from the Euro-Amerindian encounter, the pain and trauma is still present. For example, Parada represents a Chiapanec legend in which "[t]he people resisted the invaders to the bitter end, and when their stronghold gave way . . . the people jumped over

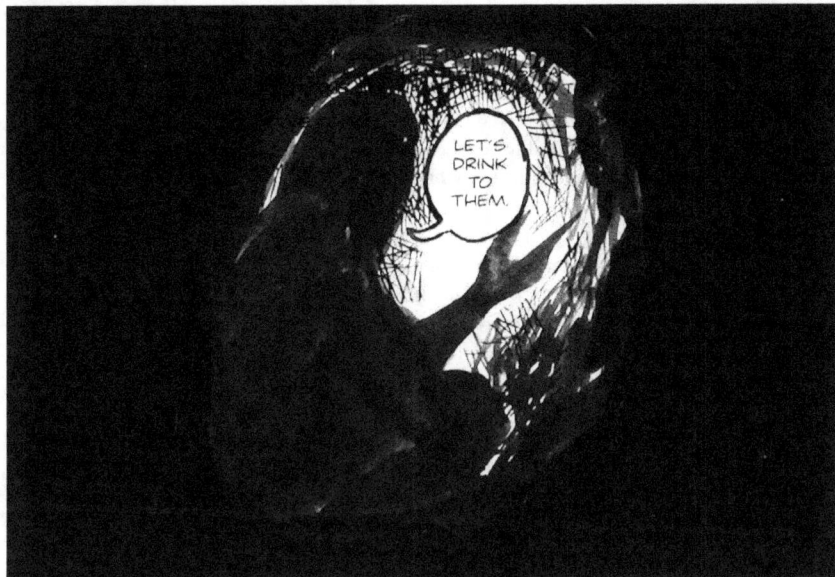

Invitation to the Reader from the Tlatoani to Enter the Graphic Narrative Space in *Zotz* #1. © 2011, Daniel Parada.

the cliffs to their deaths. They did not want to be captured or enslaved. They did not want to live the undignified life and endure the brutality of Castilian rule" (issue 3, 86). The incorporation of this legend in the *Zotz* storyworld does the important work of reminding the reader of the brutal reality that Amerindians faced as a result of Spanish colonialism in the region. This is not, however, central to the storyworld, which reimagines this painful past in order to carve out a space in which Mesoamerican culture is archived in its oral, visual, and textual complexity. In this regard, it is significant to recall Anzaldúa's assertion in *Light in the Dark / Luz en lo oscuro* that "Using the creative process to heal or restructure the images/stories that shape a person's consciousness is a more effective way of healing" (35), which is what Parada's comic series does in its creation of an archival nepantla. As this chapter demonstrates, the Nahua concept of nepantla, as applied to cultural studies by Taylor and Anzaldúa, helps the reader to understand the way in which Parada's alternative Mesoamerican archive decenters colonial historiographical discourse, a useful repository for those seeking to understand this history in decolonial perspective.

Notes

1. *Coloniality at Large* is a foundational text in the adoption of this theoretical frame in the field of Latin/x American studies in which leading scholars discuss the impact and ripple effect of the coloniality of power and knowledge inherent to European colonialism in the Americas,

a concept that has been developed by Aníbal Quijano and adopted by Walter Mignolo in his theory of colonial difference. Mignolo understands the coloniality of power and knowledge as a social hierarchy through which Indigenous subjects and experiences are differentiated and objectified as the colonial "other" based on Euro-dominated, geopolitical assumptions.

2. For a comprehensive look at the demographic devastation at the time of colonial contact, see Daniel T. Reff, "Disease and the Rise of Christianity in the New World," *Plagues, Priests, and Demons*, 122–206.

3. José de Rabasa (*Writing Violence of the Northern Frontier*) is well known for his critique of epistemic violence, arguing that "Spain's colonial project inaugurated a form of modern imperialism that constituted Western civilization as a paradigm to be imposed on the rest of the world. These political corollaries reveal power relations that were first exerted in the sixteenth century but are still in full force today" (95).

4. For a formal analysis of *Zotz*, see Jorge Santos (this volume).

5. Anzaldúa also discusses the process of writing as a feminist act for Chicanas that works to heal trauma, in the chapter of Borderlands/La frontera titled "The Path of Red and Black Ink." In a later chapter ("Towards a New Mestiza Consciousness"), she goes on to argue that the fragmentation that takes place in the borderlands also has a creative impetus, in that the new subject that is created there is made stronger via the process of mestizaje. Taylor also unpacks hybridity, mestizaje, and transculturation in postcolonial context, favoring the term transculturation in her analysis (*The Archive and the Repertoire*, 108).

6. For an overview of the variants of these solar and lunar myths among different Mesoamerican traditions, see Oswaldo Chinchilla Mazariegos, *Art and Myth of the Ancient Maya*, 159–84.

7. See Tedlock's edition of the *Popol Vuh*, 33.

8. See Parada's introduction to issue 2 in which he outlines the parameters of the series (7).

9. Tedlock notes that the text was written between 1554 and 1558 (given events mentioned in the text contemporaneous to its writing) and the text's authors originate from three lineages that once ruled the Quiché kingdom (the Cauecs, the Greathouses, and the Lord Quichés). Moreover, the text that we know today passed through the hands of a Spanish friar, Francisco Ximénez, who transcribed the copy in Quiché and added a Spanish translation (Tedlock, "Introduction," *Popol Vuh*). Today, we have two books written using the Roman alphabet to substitute hieroglyphic books: the Chilam Balam "Jaguar Translator" (Yucatán) and the Popol Vuh "Council Book" (Guatemala).

10. See Mazariegos, *Art and Myth of the Ancient Maya*, 48.

11. Tedlock explains, "In contemporary usage 'the Quiché people' are an ethnic group in Guatemala, consisting of those who speak the particular Maya language that itself has come to be called Quiché; they presently number close to a million and occupy most of the former territory of the kingdom whose development is described in the Popol Vuh. To the west and northwest of them are other Maya peoples, speaking other Maya languages, who extend across the Mexican border into the highlands of Chiapas and down into the Gulf coastal plain of Tabasco. To the east and northeast still other Mayas extend just across the borders of Belize and across the peninsula of Yucatán. These are the peoples, with a total population of more than six million today, whose ancestors developed what has become known to the outside world as Maya civilization" (*Popol Vuh*, 21–22).

12. Several scholars have pointed to the exclusion of oral and nonalphabetic writing systems by early modern European notions of literacy. On Renaissance philosophy and western notions of literacy, for example, see Mignolo, *The Darker Side of the Renaissance*, 29–67; also see Cañizares-Esguerra, "Changing European Interpretations of the Reliability of Indigenous Sources," *How to Write the History of the New World*, 60–129.

13. Mazariegos reminds us that, scholarly studies on the matter show the "Mesoamerican peoples share a unified religion tradition, distinguished by generalized explanations about the origin of the world, the gods, humanity, and social institutions that become manifest in mythical narratives. Maya mythology and religion are best understood within this framework" (*Art and Myth of the Ancient Maya*, 22).

14. Frederick Aldama's body of work, the leading scholar in Latinx comics studies, shows how Latinx creators, characters, and scholars use comics to create an alternative, living, breathing archive. In *Your Brain on Latino Comics*, Aldama unpacks the sordid past of Latinx representation in comics as he outlines the way in which this has changed in more recent comics production. In *Latinx Superheroes in Mainstream Production*, for example, Aldama writes that the book is "[a]bout excavating a living, breathing archive. It's the beginning of an articulation of *how* creators (authors, artists, animators, and directors) use a whole variety of shaping devices to make (and erase) Latinx superheroes in comic book storyworlds" (6). As this chapter demonstrates, *Zotz* is one storyworld, among many, that does this invaluable work.

15. See McCloud, "Time Frames," *Understanding Comics: The Invisible Art*, 94–117.

16. Several other deities are represented in the *Zotz* storyworld. For example, from the Mexica pantheon, there are several references to *Huitzilopochtli*, a primary deity given his role as both sun and war god. In the Mexica myth of their foundation of Tenochtitlán, *Huitzilopochtli* (translated in Nahuatl as Hummingbird of the South) led the first group of Mexica to their new imperial seat in the central valley of Mexico. There are also references in the comic to *Tlaloc*, the god of rain and *Tezcatlipoca*, the trickster god. Tezcatlipoca, also a shape-shifter like Quetzalcóatl, appears in issue 1 and then again in issue 3 as the deity overseeing the boys in the form of a Mexican priest.

17. See Samuel Martí and Gertrude Prokosch Kurath, *Dances of Anáhuac: The Choreography and Music of Precortesian Dances*.

18. Tedlock notes that, "When they [the tlatoani] introduce the first episode of a long cycle of stories about the gods who prepared the sky-earth for human life, they propose that we all drink a toast to the heroes" (29–30). Tedlock points to the appearance of this same trope again when, "Having accounted for three aboveground episodes in the lives of Hunahpu and Xbalanque, the Popol Vuh goes back a generation to tell the story of their twin fathers, One Hunahpu and Seven Hunahpu (at the beginning of Part Three). This is the point at which the authors treat us as if we were in their very presence, introducing One Hunahpu by saying, 'Let's drink to him'" (35).

Works Cited

Aldama, Frederick. *Your Brain on Latino Comics: From Gus Arriola to Los Bros. Hernandez*. Austin: University of Texas Press, 2009.

———. *Latinx Superheroes in Mainstream Comics*. Tucson: University of Arizona Press, 2017.

Anzaldúa, Gloria. *Borderlands / La frontera: The New Mestiza*. 1987. Berkeley, CA: Aunt Lute Books, 1999.

———. *Light in the Dark / Luz en lo oscuro: Rewriting Identity, Spirituality, Reality*, edited by Analouise Keating. Durham, NC: Duke University Press, 2015.

Bassie-Sweet, Karen. *Maya Sacred Geography and the Creator Deities*. Norman: University of Oklahoma Press, 2008.

Batalla, Guillermo Bonfil. Trans. Philip A. Dennis. *México Profundo: Reclaiming a Civilization*. Austin: University of Texas Press, 1996.

Cañizares-Esguerra, Jorge. *How to Write the History of the New World: Histories, Epistemologies, and Identities in the Eighteenth-Century Atlantic World*. Stanford: Stanford University Press, 2001.

Clendinnen, Inga. *Ambivalent Conquests: Maya and Spaniard in Yucatán, 1517–1570*. Cambridge: Cambridge University Press, 1987.

———. *Aztecs, an Interpretation*. Cambridge: Cambridge University Press, 1991.

Hulme, Peter. *Colonial Encounters: Europe and the Native Caribbean 1492–1797*. London: Routledge, 1992.

Kurath, Gertrude Prokosch, and Samuel Martí. *Dances of Anáhuac: The Choreography and Music of Precortesian Dances*. Chicago: Aldine Publishing Company, 1964.

Mazariegos, Oswaldo Chinchilla. *Art and Myth of the Ancient Maya*. New Haven, CT: Yale University Press, 2017.

McCaa, Robert. "Spanish and Nahuatl Views on Smallpox and Demographic Catastrophe in Mexico." *Journal of Interdisciplinary History* 25, no. 3 (Winter 1995): 397–431.

McCloud, Scott. *Understanding Comics: The Invisible Art*. Harper-Perennial, 1993.

Mignolo, Walter. *The Darker Side of the Renaissance: Literacy, Territoriality, and Colonization*. Ann Arbor: University of Michigan Press, 1995.

———. "The Geopolitics of Knowledge." In *Coloniality at Large: Latin America and the Postcolonial Debate*, edited by Mabel Moraña, Enrique Dussel, and Carolos A. Jáuregui. Durham, NC: Duke University Press, 2008.

Moraña, Mabel, Enrique Dussel, and Carolos A. Jáuregui, eds. *Coloniality at Large: Latin America and the Postcolonial Debate*. Durham, NC: Duke University Press, 2008.

Norton, Marcy. *Sacred Gifts, Profane Pleasures: A History of Tobacco and Chocolate in the Atlantic World*. Ithaca, NY: Cornell University Press, 2008.

Parada, Daniel. "Zotz #1." *Zotz: Serpent and Shield*, no. 1, Daniel Parada & Jorge Parada, 2011.

———. "Zotz #2." *Zotz: Serpent and Shield*, no. 2, Daniel Parada & Jorge Parada, 2013.

———. "Zotz #3." *Zotz: Serpent and Shield*, no. 1, Daniel Parada & Jorge Parada, 2016.

Rabasa, José de. *Writing as Violence: The Historiography of Sixteenth-Century New Mexico and Florida and the Legacy of Conquest*. Durham, NC: Duke University Press, 2000.

Reff, Danielt T. *Disease, Depopulation, and Culture Change in Northwestern New Spain, 1518–1764*. Salt Lake City: University of Utah Press, 1991.

———. *Plagues, Priests, Demons: Sacred Narratives and the Rise of Christianity in the Old World and the New*. Cambridge: Cambridge University Press, 2005.

Taylor, Diana. *The Archive and the Repertoire: Performing Memory in the Americas*. Durham, NC: Duke University Press, 2003.

Tedlock, Dennis. *Popol Vuh: The Definite Edition of the Mayan Book of the Dawn of Life and the Glories of Gods and Kings*. New York: Touchstone, 1996.

Critical Impulses in Daniel Parada's *Zotz*: A Case Study in Indigenous Comics

Jorge Santos

Daniel Parada's serialized graphic novel *Zotz: Serpent and Shield* (2011 to the present) begins with a moment of graphic orality. The first issue opens with a timeline of historical events that lead the reader directly into the comic's primary narrative, which follows twin boys Pakal and Kaan as they seek vengeance for the decimation of their tribal village at the hands of local bandits. The greater narrative is a work of historical fiction that imagines a Mesoamerican world that resists Spanish conquest by repelling Cortes and the conquistadores. The timeline is presented as white text on a black background, in the graphically simplest terms: as written text that must be consumed visually. Even Parada's opening pages resemble a historical timeline, with dates preceding key events in the narrative's past that influence its present. Yet Parada also subtly undermines the relatively straightforward manner in which this timeline is presented. Halfway down the page, the reader learns that in the year 5 Lord (C 1521), "the Castilian people were driven out of Tenochtitlan" by the Aztec Triple Alliance, restoring order to the Mesoamerican peoples of the sixteenth century (*Zotz* #1, 1). *Zotz* assumes that readers possess, at a minimum, a cursory knowledge of the history of colonization of Mesoamerica and would recall that Cortes ultimately conquers the Aztec empire in the name of Spain. This turn away from familiar history inverts the reader's knowledge of the way this conflict plays out in favor of the alternate universe in which the events of the comic will unfold. The comic signals this inversion with the white text on a black background, an inversion of the way written marks on paper typically appear. Further, a single unbordered panel of a shadowy narrator at the bottom of the page reveals that the written text is actually spoken exposition; thus, the opening timeline closes on a moment of orality (see fig. 9.1). As the story of Pakal and Kaan begins, this narrator addresses his listener-readers directly: "Let's drink to them," the narrator instructs (2). This simple command invites the reader to participate in the narrative, a gesture typical of the meta-cooperative aspects of graphic narrative storytelling. Additionally, this transition from written history to orality gestures to the way the comic will make use of both oral transmissions (a staple of Indigenous cultural traditions), and graphic (as in written or non-oral) methods of producing history. Jessica Rutherford's chapter in this collection, "Visualizing an Alternate Mesoamerican Archive: Daniel Parada's Comic Series Zotz in Historical Perspective," delineates Parada's use of Mesoamerican myth and history to argue that Zotz occupies a space of "nepantla" with its alternate and historical archive/repertoire. My contribution focuses on *Zotz*'s use of graphic narrative to weave oral and graphic sources of Indigenous culture as interdependent epistemological modes, rather than treating them as distinct, a dichotomy that often reproduces a colonialist binary that links the oral to the primitive. *Zotz* thus activates Christopher B. Teuton's "critical impulse" for reading Indigenous literature, a mode that seeks to collapse the problematic binary that segregates the oral from the graphic in order to forge a critical balance between the two. Using Parada's *Zotz* as a case study, this chapter focuses on the way that graphic narrative can mediate between the oral and the graphic and achieve the balanced "critical impulse" Teuton advocates.

The critical language for this study is drawn from Teuton's *Deep Waters: The Textual Continuum in American Indian Literature* (2010). Teuton argues for the treatment of oral (i.e., sound-based) and graphic (i.e., written) modes of Indigenous culture as interdependent modes rather than as distinct or dichotomized. His work "critiques and decenters the standard definitions of *orality* and *literacy* that provide a structuring binary common to Native American literary studies" (xv).[1] This binary, Teuton contends, reifies colonialist attitudes that cast Native American culture as primitive precisely due to its oral dimensions and traditions, as opposed to the "graphocentrism" of European culture which privileges the long-term accumulation of information via the written word. Paraphrasing the work of Victor Li, Teuton contends that "like the concept of the primitive, oral culture comes into being and remains useful because it is a handy theoretical foil with which the West can define itself" (11). According to Teuton, this produces a sort of counter-reductivism, in which orality grounds claims to literary authenticity—but even this still reifies a troubling binary (10). As a result, even if unintended, written text is privileged as more epistemologically sound in its capacity to produce "truth" (25). Pushing back against these trends, Teuton urges scholars to treat the oral and the graphic as interdependent modes to collapse this problematic binary. Working with Jacques Derrida's deconstruction of logocentrism, Teuton develops a set of literary impulses present in Indigenous literature: the oral impulse, the graphic impulse, and the critical impulse (31–34).[2] For Teuton, the oral impulse "emphasizes a relational and experiential engagement with the world through sound-based forms of communication," while the graphic impulse "expresses the cultural desire for

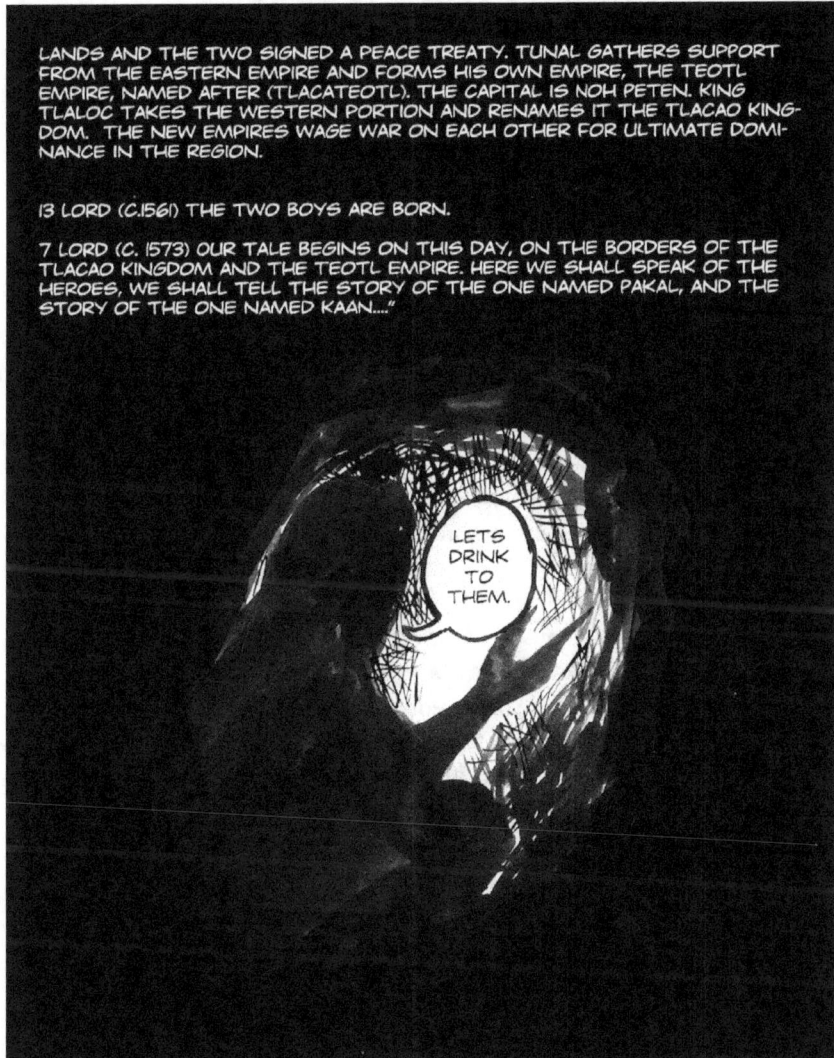

Figure 9.1. *Zotz* #1, p. 4.

the permanent recording of cultural knowledge in formats that will allow for recollection and study" (31). However, the critical impulse mediates the two, bringing them into concert by allowing "for the flow of ideas that may account for tradition as well as innovation, individuality as well as community, memory as well as record" in a reciprocal system (34). Given the interdependent nature of multiple narrative registers of the comics form, graphic narrative seems ideally posed to achieve the balanced dialogism that Teuton urges. In this context, I will demonstrate comic's capacity for the critical impulse as a reading protocol for Daniel Parada's *Zotz*.

The great potential in the union between Indigenous literary tradition and graphic narrative has not gone unnoticed by comics scholars. Scott McCloud opens his foundational study *Understanding Comics: The Invisible Art* (1993) by taking a long view to the development of the medium—a trajectory he begins with a "pre-Columbian picture manuscript," which he then reads sequentially like a comic (10–11). Margaret Noori builds on this insight in her contribution to *Multicultural Comics: From Zap to Blue Beetle* (2010), as her study on the art and comics of the Anishinaabe people provides important links to the proto-comics from which McCloud draws inspiration. As Noori notes, the multivalent medium of graphic narrative form seems ideally suited to meet the needs of the polyvisual and polyvocal nature of Native American art. Noori writes:

> The oral tradition, rather than being romanticized as a signifier of illiteracy or preliteracy, can be recast as an alternate means of narrative transmission [. . .] Furthermore, the layered construction of sound and meaning is perfectly suited to the comic format, where text, line, and color combine to communicate action and relationships. (Noori 58)

Despite this potential, we must acknowledge that the relationship between comics and indigeneity has never been quite so rosy. In the past, the comics industry often proliferated negative or stereotypical images of Native peoples, as the work of Michael Sheyahshe and Chad A. Barbour evinces.[3] Fortunately, many independent comic creators today are more committed to faithful representations of Indigenous peoples and their cultures—comics poised to fulfill Teuton's critical impulse. As Tony Chavarria highlights, "Native art, without the aid of a written language in most instances, developed as a unique visual communication system; symbols float, merge, separate, and repeat, creating unique layers of meaning accessible to individuals, families, clans, and villages, each reading elements within their own understanding, [. . .] it was a natural step that some of these emerging artists would delve into the medium of comics" (Chavarria 48). Sarah Henzi, in her own study of Indigenous comics, also notes how "images speak beyond linguistic, cultural, and generational gaps—an element that is becoming increasingly important given those gaps, caused by shame, lack of education and, more importantly, governmental assimilation policies" (36). And while not precisely the same dynamic as the conflict between orality and the graphic outlined by Teuton, the field of comic studies has mapped the medium's own need to mediate between divergent narrative sources—specifically, between word and image. After all, the comics medium is powered by interdependent registers of narrative information, a juxtaposition that forces the reader to reconcile these disparate registers. Therefore, embedded in the graphic narrative form is precisely the sort of reading practice that might activate Teuton's critical impulse.[4]

For Teuton, the critical impulse can maintain a healthy continuum between oral, or sound-based forms of discourse, with graphic or visual forms of signification—very similar to the oft-contested relationship between word and image in graphic narrative. Similar to the treatment of the oral and the graphic in Indigenous literature, there are a variety of approaches to the relationship between word and image in graphic novel scholarship—with some scholars doubting whether or not textual elements are even essential to the medium while others try to maintain a critical balance. For example, while Thierry Groensteen privileges the image over the textual in his introduction to *The System of Comics* (1999), he nonetheless acknowledges that graphic narrative typically operates via two registers, "the iconic and the linguistic" (Groensteen 128). Like Groensteen, many scholars privilege the image over the text as the primary vehicle through which comics create meaning. However, as Scott McCloud notes, "Words and pictures in combination may not be my definition of comics, but the combination has had tremendous influence on its growth" (McCloud 152). Charles Hatfield further distills the debate by commenting:

> Still, responding to comics often depends on recognizing word and image as two "different" types of sign, whose implications can be played against each other—to gloss, to illustrate, to contradict or complicate or ironize the other. While the word/image distinction may be false or oversimple, learned assumptions about these different codes—written and pictorial—still exert a strong centripetal pull on the reading experience. We continue to distinguish between the function of words and the function of images, despite the fact that comics continually work to destabilize this very distinction. This tension between codes is fundamental to the art form. (Hatfield 133)

Interestingly enough, while these debates are certainly distinct, the manner in which comics scholarship tends to privilege the graphic (or image) over the oral (or textual) closely mirrors the same debate Teuton delineates in *Deep Waters*.[5] Taken this way, Hatfield's explication of the tension between word and image and the manner in which the two interrelate to either supplement or complicate the signification of the other closely resembles Teuton's critical impulse. We might even go as far as to suggest that the oral in Teuton bears the same relationship to the graphic as word does to image in how the medium is typically theorized—by privileging one over the other. Of course, this is a multifaceted debate in comics scholarship, which I will neither attempt to completely recapitulate nor resolve here.[6] For my purposes, it is enough to highlight that despite the privileging of one register over the other, when words and image are both present in graphic narrative storytelling, their relationship is often one of *interdependence*. Therefore, in regard to the scope of the present study, I will generally map "the oral" to the textual and the "graphic" to the image. While in a broader sense, this easy analogy might prove reductive, it does offer a reading protocol through which I can explicate the manner in which the comics medium can potentially enact Teuton's critical impulse.

In this spirit, *Zotz* proves an interesting case study in how the critical impulse can manifest on the comics page. Parada states on his website that his impetus to create *Zotz* was "the lack of Mesoamerican stories in our popular culture," and his meticulously researched historical fiction seeks to fill that gap (www.zotz.com). However, Parada does not limit this animus only to his Mesoamerican cast and setting, but in telling the narrative in a manner that honors their cultural traditions as well. In this regard, *Zotz* functions as an exploration of Mesoamerican culture cut short by colonization as much as an epic adventure of revenge and reckoning. In service of this project, elements of Mesoamerican storytelling and narrative tradition permeate the comic, and Parada makes use of the interdependent nature of word and image in graphic narrative to avoid the pitfalls in the representation of the oral and the graphic feared by Teuton and others. The comic introduces its oral dimensions early and frequently in the comic while slyly destabilizing their typical attributes. Casting the historical timeline that opens *Zotz* as a form of orality signals the importance of spoken forms of knowledge creation in the comic—a motif, Teuton warns, that can often lead to reductive representations of the role of orality in Indigenous culture (10). Responding to the foundational work of Walter Ong and Louis Owens, Teuton writes:

> Echoing Ong's notions of the "oral mind," Owens claims that oral tradition represents a communal, anonymous, pre-historic literature of origin for Native Americans that is determinative of a specific type of oral consciousness. For the Native American writer oral traditions are communal, whereas writing is an individualistic form of communication (1992, 10). When a Native writer writes he or she becomes imbricated in the individualized Western World. That person is no longer a mouthpiece of tribal tradition but a single creator of a story (17).

The implication here, of course, is that adherence to oral traditions belies individuality or personhood in favor of the communal consciousness stereotypically associated with Indigenous tribal life. As a result, orality is often interpreted as a static form of knowledge creation incapable of personal expression, while the written word is dynamic and fluid. However, *Zotz* sidesteps such problematic reductions by committing to an interdependent relationship between the oral and the graphic. McCloud refers to such juxtapositions of word and image as "interdependent combinations"—image/text arrangements "where words and pictures go hand in hand to convey an idea that neither could convey alone" (McCloud 155). Parada makes use of such arrangements regularly in the comic—including the initial pages that follow its fictionalized historical timeline.

Zotz's primary narrative begins with a two-page, full-color sequence of a traditional comic layout followed by an unbordered image filling the entire page—the only color pages in the entire fifty-page first issue (the shortest of the three voluminous issues released thus far). These opening pages depict the bloody carnage of an unspecified battle somewhere in the heart of the Aztec empire (see fig. 9.2). The first page opens with a close shot of frogs devouring flies—flies, it is revealed in the final panel, lured in by a field of corpses. The shots continuously zoom out to the following full-page panel of countless Aztec warriors lying lifeless and destroyed in the foreground of the shot as a crumbled city looms on the horizon line. Unifying the two pages is a scant bit of floating narration, bracketed by quotation marks that signal to the reader that they are being spoken to: "We heard stories of the burning cities, the scattered corpses, the ravaging, the weeping, and the warriors whose blood watered our precious earth. Luckily this was far away . . ." (*Zotz* #1, 4–5). Initially, this arrangement seems to invoke some of the troubling aspects of how orality is figured in Indigenous literary traditions. The use of the first-person plural ("We"), unattributed to a specific narrator, suggests the sort of communal, nonindividualistic tropes Teuton condemns. This feature is potentially heightened by the first page's final panel, a close-up shot of a fallen Aztec warrior, his face frozen in perpetual anguish. The intimacy of the visuals imply individuality, but the floating text, which refers to him as simply one of the many "warriors whose blood watered our precious earth" undercuts this effect, as does the first plural possessive "our." However, the sequence of the panels moves us away from this scene to a broader expanse, implying a distancing from both the contents of the page and the typical manner in which its ideas are transmitted. The distancing effect of this opening sequence is key to unpacking how Parada activates Teuton's critical impulse by inverting the typical roles of both oral and graphic signifiers.

This inversion is made evident by the simultaneous presence of both oral and graphic registers on the page, each of which contextualize and complete the information provided by the other. The distance implied in both the arrangement of the shots (zooming out and away from its subjects) and the relative proximity of the events depicted to their unnamed narrator ("Luckily this was far away") resist the sort of reductive claims to narrative authenticity to which oral tradition is often reduced. After all, the voice we hear (read) does not wield narrative authority over the events depicted. Rather, it draws our attention to a subjective and incomplete knowledge of the event, one more concerned with what the battle portends for the speaker's own corner of this violent new world (so to speak) than with establishing any universal understanding. Visually, the depiction of the broken bodies of the Aztec warriors fills the page and draws our attention to what is missing—the conquistadors. The lack of Spanish soldiers reminds the reader of their elimination from the narrative from the outset and

Figure 9.2a/b. *Zotz* #1, pp. 6–7.

brings one to the stark realization that these Aztecs must have *killed each other*.[7] This detail is essential, as it undercuts the communal character of the floating narration's use of the first-person plural. "We," then, refers not to an overall Aztec consciousness, but a distinct and localized tribal identity "far away" from this carnage. "Luckily," in this case, further implies this distinct identity remains unaligned with either side of the conflict depicted—a truth that will bring its

own dire consequences to Pakal and Kaan later in the narrative when Aztec bandits decimate their village leaving no other survivors.

The distance from which the narration speaks also pushes back against the notion that orality is static, more prone to memorization and uncritical recital than the interpretative nature associated with the graphic. Drawing from the work of Derrida and post-structuralist approaches to orality, Teuton contends that the "immediacy" associated with orality—that it responds to culture while the written word records it—must be deconstructed in order to achieve an interdependent balance between the two forms (Teuton 24). The relationship between the words and the images in this opening sequence work to achieve this balance largely by placing the reader at a critical distance while also inverting the typical functions associated with the oral and the graphic. First, the floating text is in past tense, implying distance not only across space, but across time (of course, in comics these are one and the same). The "stories" alluded to by the narrator, then, amount to little more than hearsay that must be interpreted in regard to what they may portend for Pakal and Kaan's village. Via this inversion, it is the images themselves that attend to the particular by revealing graphically what could only be gestured to orally. The flat color scheme of the comic intensifies this effect. As McCloud outlines in *Understanding Comics*, these sorts of color schemes "objectify their subjects" as "we become more aware of the physical form of objects than in black and white" (189). In the world of *Zotz*, the graphic levels of the text attend to the immediate by giving it form and color, freeing its oral dimensions to explore and interpret the meaning of these images. It is the distance between the opening pages color images and its floating narration that the reader must reconcile. By pulling together these different registers into a critical balance, the reader can close the gap between them in order to imagine the future violence they foreshadow.

Yet Parada manages to use orality in its traditional role of world creation without limiting it to that role. The reader encounters similar gestures that collapse the oral/graphic binary in the opening pages of *Zotz* #2, which opens with a pronunciation guide that coaches readers on how to read the comics potentially unfamiliar languages. The lengthy guide instructs readers how to pronounce these words correctly by having them sound them out. For example, Parada writes:

> The "a" sounds like the letter "o" in the English word *how*. The e sounds like the "e" in the word *get*. The letter "I" sounds like the "ee" in the word *deep*. The "o" sounds like "oa" in the word *goat*. And the "u" sounds like the "oo" in *boo*. Some of the consonants also vary. (*Zotz* #2, 6)

The pronunciation guide closes on example words alongside phonetic spellings the reader may use to practice, with the definitions and linguistic roots of the words in parentheses. While this material may seem ancillary to readers, opening the comic in such fashion does introduce key reading protocols before proceeding into the world of *Zotz*. First, the parentheticals inform readers which language or dialect each word originates from, disrupting any tacit or unconscious assumptions regarding Indigenous linguistic homogeneity. Second, and most important for the purposes of this study, it expects the reader to enter the world of the comic not through its images, but through its *sounds*. In this regard, the reader is expected to cooperate in the building of a comic world via its oral dimensions, not its visual ones. While this may feel like the sort of communal consciousness typically associated with oral traditions, the meta-cooperative aspects of the graphic narrative medium—that elusive phenomenon McCloud famously refers to as "closure"—undercut this effect by having the individual reader participate in the oral building of the *Zotz* storyworld rather than simply receiving it.

Although *Zotz* includes many inversions as the ones outlined above, it does not content itself only with such strategies. After all, to settle for inverting the roles of the oral and the graphic might simply reproduce the same binary, even if its values are reversed. As such, more traditional depictions of oral culture also permeate the comic—but even in these scenes, these traditions are slyly destabilized or undercut. For example, the pages that follow the opening color sequence of its first issue, *Zotz* switches to black and white, as we enter Chan Village, the fictionalized home of Pakal and Kaan "on the border between the Tlacao Kingdom and the Teotl Empire" (*Zotz* #1, 6). After a few, largely silent scenes that employ silent images to build an impression of village life—from hunting and dining to tribal games and customs—orality takes center stage at a traditional scene of a tribal leader reciting a creation myth at a campfire (see fig. 9.3). The switch to a black-and-white color scheme signals to the reader that the world built by orality is more invested in "the ideas behind the art," as McCloud claims, rather than some form of static knowledge creation. In short, if color objectifies, Parada uses black and white to *subjectify*. This scene draws our attention to the ways storytelling shapes the lived experiences of the individual members of the tribe. The tone of the campfire scene further illustrates these subjectifying aspects. While the telling of the creation myth of "The Lady of the Moon" clearly serves a communal function, it is not simply designed to transmit a static mythological lesson as the tale entertains its audience rather than educates. Smaller nuances, such as the older hunter in the top panel requesting a different story, or Pakal and Kaan snickering about its more lurid details, also imply differing relationships to the story by its individual listeners—from reverence, to curiosity, to sophomoric in-jokes. Even the myth itself, which centers on the conflict between the twin gods Xbalanque and Hunahpu, makes it clear that this story should be read more as analogues to the *Zotz*'s twin protagonists rather than as a representation of some form of communal consciousness.

In fact, Pakal and Kaan themselves might represent the fulfillment of the critical impulse more than any particular arrangement of word and image in the comic by embodying these impulses themselves. The comic introduces the boys through a tribal ball game. Through their competition, each is subtly aligned with either the oral or graphic impulses—associations Parada will undercut in *Zotz*'s typical fashion. First there is Pakal, the physically stronger of

Figure 9.3. *Zotz* #1, p. 15.

the pair who mocks his brother for being weaker than him "because you read too much" (*Zotz* #1, 13). This aside seemingly aligns Pakal with the oral, or non-graphic forms of knowledge, a facet reinforced perhaps by the fact that he is the one that is able to commune with a trickster God in the second issue (*Zotz* #2, 99). Yet, by initially aligning Pakal with physicality we associate him more with the visual, or "graphic," elements of the story. For example, the conversation with the trickster god comes after a large-scale battle, the aftermath of which marks Pakal's wounded body. The conversation itself draws our attention to Pakal's own experience rather than some universal tribal lesson, as the the graphic and oral work in commune to both individualize and subjectify Pakal. Conversely, aligning his twin brother Kaan with language establishes that their culture is not exclusively an oral one—a pernicious presumption often produced by the oral/graphic binary. It also makes clear that they did not need Europeans to introduce written knowledge accumulation to their society. They already had it (which is true). Further, while Pakal is communing with the trickster god, Kaan leaves to explore his emerging sexuality with the help of a pair of tribal women and peyote in a visually explicit scene (*Zotz* #2, 94–97). If Parada aligns Kaan with the graphic (so to speak), then we might read this moment as a clever manifestation of the graphic's ability to explore an individual consciousness. However, even these tacit associations are undercut the moment they are introduced, as Kaan, the weaker more studious brother, wins the ball game over his stronger brother. This leads Pakal to complain that he isn't simply a physical specimen: "Hey! Don't try to make me look stupid. I read too. Just not as much as you" (*Zotz* #1, 13). More importantly, both Pakal's conversation with the trickster god and Kaan's sexual encounter follow the boy's success on the battlefield over the dreaded "Black Crocodile Commander"—a battle that prominently calls back to the opening ball game when Pakal realizes that "If I can hit a ball . . . I can hit a lance" (*Zotz* #2, 74). Much like achieving a critical balance between oral and graphic storytelling, Pakal and Kaan may be formidable individually, but can only access their full potential when they acknowledge and balance their respective skillsets. This thematic is heightened by the imagery of Pakal and Kaan post-battle, when they are given matching ceremonial garb by the mercenary tribe for which they fight (see fig. 9.4).

What I have presented here is not intended as a holistic remedy to the ongoing scholarly discussions in Indigenous studies regarding oral or written traditions, or the parallel debates on the unequal relationship between word and image in comic studies. The study of Indigenous literatures and graphic narratives alike are both "New Worlds" in a sense, worlds demanding exploration, navigation, and mapping to build on the work of those who have come before. Therefore, much like *Zotz* itself, I leave this story unresolved until some future date—if in fact it can even be resolved—settling for offering only one potential discursive orientation. And, of course, without the work of the critical traditions I invoke, even this modest contribution would be left unsaid (so to speak). Perhaps, as a wistful Kaan supposes toward the end of *Zotz* #3, "It will never end, nothing ever does. But right now, I see this world is out of balance. We have to fight to restore it" (89). In this sense, perhaps resolution of these debates between the oral and the graphic, or between word and image, shouldn't be our goal. Rather, as Teuton insists, restoring and maintaining *balance* is critical, even if the precise manifestation of this sentiment remains elusive. As scholars, then, we should take our cues from Kaan—"Until we find what these things truly mean, we'll work to this goal" (89).

Figure 9.4. *Zotz* #3, p. 78.

Notes

1. The field of "Native American Literary Studies," as Teuton labels it, is a wide and diverse one, as is the scope of such studies. Many studies focus on the local by theorizing the work of one of the hundreds of tribal traditions present in Indigenous literary studies. There are also hemispheric and globalist approaches to complement these. Reflecting this diversity are the wide range of terms available for referring to these bodies of literature—"Native American, American Indian, Mesoamerican, Indigeneities of the Americas," to name only a few. Even though the focus of this study is on a depiction of a specifically Mesoamerican world, I will nonetheless use the broad term "Indigenous comics" and related permutations when referring to this literature—with the exception of using the preferred terms of particular scholars for using their work. My reasoning for this choice resonates with Chadwick Allen's approach to Indigenous literary theory in *Trans-Indigenous: Methodologies for Global Native Literary Studies* (2012) by trying to reach the global through the local. Allen writes, "Within a context of ongoing (post) colonial relations, shouldn't the objective of a global Indigenous literary studies in English run more along the lines of 'together (yet) distinct?'" (xiii). Like Allen, I do not seek to sacrifice the specific in the name of the universal. However, while my work focuses on the particularities of a specific literary production (*Zotz*), I nonetheless believe that my work here bears broad relevance for the field of Indigenous literary studies.

2. For an overview of Derrida's, as well as other prominent theorists', post-structuralist approaches to logocentrism, see *Deep Waters: The Textual Continuum in American Indian Literature*, chapter 1: "The Oral Impulse, The Graphic Impulse, and the Critical Impulse: Reframing Signification in American Indian Literary Study."

3. For more, see Michael Sheyahshe, Native *Americans in Comics Books: A Critical Study* (2008); Chad A. Barbour, *From Daniel Boone to Captain America: Playing Indian in American Popular Culture*.

4. Now, I am wary of the potential for reductivism in such an approach. After all, individual tribes do not have the same relationship to orality, the graphic, or the coloniality that produced the binary between the two. As Derek Parker Royal warns in his study of Native American detective/noir comics, "When reading multiethnic comics, it is important to note the subtleties and particularities of communal representations and to resist the urge to oversimplify [. . .], the sheer diversity of histories and traditions makes suspect any attempt to standardize our understanding of Native cultures" ("Native Noir").

5. For a lucid and thorough overview of how orality has been approached or positioned in Indigenous literary studies, particularly in regard to oral-literate theory, see Teuton, *Deep Waters: The Textual Continuum in American Indian Literature*, "The Oral Impulse, the Graphic Impulse, and the Critical Impulse: Reframing Signification in American Indian Literary Study."

6. For an excellent overview of this debate, see Barbara Postema, *Narrative Structure in Comics*, chapter 4: "Combining Signs: Image-Text relations."

7. A lone conquistador appears once throughout the nearly three hundred pages of the first three issues, when raiders devastate Kaan and Pakal's village. The conquistador is a member of the raiding party, which is otherwise made up of other Native warriors.

Works Cited

Allen, Chadwick. *Trans-Indigenous: Methodologies for Global Native Literary Studies*. Minneapolis: University of Minnesota Press, 2012.

Barbour, Chad A. *From Daniel Boone to Captain America: Playing Indian in American Popular Culture*. Jackson: University Press of Mississippi, 2016.

Chavarria, Tony. "Indigenous Comics in the United States." *World Literature Today*, May–June 2009, 47–49.

Groensteen, Thierry. *The System of Comics*. Translated by Bart Beaty. Jackson: University Press of Mississippi, 1999.

Henzi, Sarah. "'A Necessary Antidote': Graphic Novels, Comics, and Indigenous Writing." *Canadian Review of Comparative Literature* 43, no. 1 (2016): 23–38.

McCloud, Scott. *Understanding Comics: The Invisible Art*. New York: Harper-Perennial, 1993.

Noori, Margaret. "Native American Narratives from Early Art to Graphic Novels: How We See Stories / Ezhi-g'waabmaananig Aadizookaanag." *Multicultural Comics: From Zap to Blue Beetle*, edited by Frederick Luis Aldama, 55–72. Austin: University of Texas Press, 2010.

Parada, Daniel. "Zotz #1." *Zotz: Serpent and Shield*, no. 1, Daniel Parada & Jorge Parada, 2011.

———. "Zotz #2." *Zotz: Serpent and Shield*, no. 2, Daniel Parada & Jorge Parada, 2013.

———. "Zotz #3." *Zotz: Serpent and Shield*, no. 1, Daniel Parada & Jorge Parada, 2016.

Postema, Barbara. *Narrative Structure in Comics: Making Sense of Fragments*. Rochester: RIT Press, 2013.

Royal, Derek Parker. "Native Noir: Genre and the Politics of Indigenous Representation in Recent American Comics." *ImageTexT: Interdisciplinary Comics Studies* 5, no. 3 (2010). http://www.english.ufl.edu/imagetext/archives/v5_3/royal/.

Sheyahshe, Michael. *Native Americans in Comic Books: A Critical Study*. Jefferson, NC: McFarland, 2008.

Teuton, Christopher B. *Deep Waters: The Textual Continuum in American Indian Literature*. Lincoln: University of Nebraska Press, 2018.

The Battle for Recollection: Maya *Historietas* as Art for Remembering War

Brian Montes

> *Memory is, above all, archival. It relies entirely on the materiality of the trace, the immediacy of the recording, the visibility of the image.*
> —Pierre Nora (1989, 13)

Lasting for more than half a century (1847–1910) Yucatán's Caste War represents what may be considered the pinnacle of Maya resistance throughout Mexico and the Yucatán Peninsula.[1] According to historians Nelson Reed (1964), Terry Rugeley (1996), and Don E. Dumond (1997), rebel Mayas, in their attempt to reclaim appropriated lands, began an aggressive attack on Spanish- and Créole-controlled cities. With the aid of British Honduras, the Maya would nearly deliver the peninsula from foreign rule. Then, for reasons presently contested, rebels ended their insurrection and retreated deep into the dense forests of present-day Quintana Roo, Mexico, establishing as their capital the political and culturally autonomous city of *Noj Kaj Santa Cruz Balam Nah Kampolkolche Ka*. For the next seventy years, the Maya would defend their territory against foreign encroachment.[2] Inspired by the appearance of a cross etched onto the bark of a tree, these rebels would become known throughout the state of Quintana Roo as the last group of independent Mayas (Larsen).[3]

Today, the history of Yucatán's Caste War is written and spoken about by a diverse group of peoples ranging from historians, anthropologists, Mexican officials, and local community leaders, all of whom speak of the conflict in their own idiosyncratic ways. The Caste War of Yucatán is without doubt an important element of contemporary Maya history, culture, and folklore. And yet, it came as a surprise when I was gifted, upon a visit to Quintana Roo's "Maya Zone" in January of 2018, a ten-page *historieta* (comic book) on the famed Indigenous uprising titled *Manuel Antonio Ay: El Primer Mártir de la Guerra de Castas*.[4]

Produced by a collective of local writers and artists working in conjunction with the Museum of the Caste War and the Tihosuco Community Heritage Preservation Project, the issue, published in 2017, was the third in a series of locally developed *historietas* commemorating the Caste War and its leaders.⁵ The first issue of the series, published in 2015 and titled *Un Héroe Por Conocer: Cecilio Chi, El Gran Líder de la Guerra de Castas*, chronicles the role of famed Maya leader Cecilio Chi as a transporter of arms between British Honduras and the Yucatán Peninsula. Returning to his home in Tepich, Cecilio is ultimately betrayed and murdered by associate Anastasio Flores (the causes of his betrayal still debated). The second issue of the series titled *Tihosuco y Jacinto Pat: La Asombrosa Vida del Líder de la Guerra de Castas* and published in 2016 chronicles Maya leader Jacinto Pat's communication with Miguel Barbachano, governor of the state of Yucatán, as they discuss a possible end to the war. Filled with themes of courage and betrayal, the issue also ends with the tragic assassination of its protagonist and his family.⁶

As a scholar of Caste War memories and purveyor of Caste War knowledge, the *historieta* gifted to me that day—along with the previously published *historietas* provided to me on later dates—represented a significant shift in the production and dissemination of information regarding the uprising. Literature published on Yucatán's Caste War, although wide ranging and well researched, has long been criticized by local activists for being monopolized by nonnative scholars and for being presented as a conflict absent of racial antagonism. According to Maya activist Genero Pool Jiménez,

> *Lo primero lo que quiero decir, es que todos los escritores que hay lo hicieron los blancos, como les parecía y convenía a ellos; así se expresan de los Mayas . . . Ellos narran los sucesos ocurridos en forma ofensiva y despectiva, siempre en contra de nosotros . . . todos los libros que ellos hacen, es difícil que lleguen hasta nosotros por sus altos costos . . . Por esa razón, he pensado que los "blancos" no saben la verdad de la historia . . . Por eso, vino a mi pensamiento que nadie entre los "blancos" saben de nuestra historia; la verdad solamente los ancianos que queden en los pueblitos la saben. Por eso dije, necesito escribir la historia de la lucha realizada.*
>
> [The first thing that I want to say is that everything that has been written has been written by the Whites, how they perceive the war and its convenience towards them, that is how it has been expressed to me by the Maya . . . They speak of the war in ways offensive and disrespectful, always in opposition to us . . . All the books that they write are difficult for us to obtain because of their high costs . . . For that reason, I believe that the Whites do not know the truth about our history . . . for that reason; it has occurred to me that nobody White knows our history. The truth is that only the elders that continue to live in the villages know the truth. For that reason, we need to write the history of our real battle.] (9–15)

Front cover of issue #3 featuring title and cover art (artist unknown).

While it can be argued that research published by nonnative scholars on the Caste War has provided significant contributions to our understanding of the conflict, it remains today the opinion of many who identify as Maya throughout the state of Quintana Roo that scholarship published on the Caste War has routinely omitted the voices of those impacted most by the rebellion.[7] Keenly aware of the power that history and memory hold in strengthening the cultural convictions of society (Nora 285), the Maya of Quintana Roo's "Maya Zone" are, as a

Back cover of third issue featuring a photo of individuals who contributed to the development of the series as well as a feedforward to the series upcoming issue "Guerra de Castas."

result of feeling silenced by those considered experts in the field of Maya Studies, attempting to assert their own observations of history in order to promote a process of self-representation. This has included rechristening Columbus Day the Day of Indigenous Resistance, utilizing a distinct form of time known by locals as *la hora rebelde* (rebel time), and asserting, through innovative and

Maya *Historietas* as Art for Remembering War   201

Rendering of Manuel Antonio Ay by Maya artist Marcelo Jimenez. Original (acrylic on canvas (50x70)) located in room 1 of the Museum Maya Santa Cruz Xbaalanaj in Felipe Carrillo Puerto, Quintana Room Mexico.

culturally inspired forms of music and art, their own often ignored accounts of history, culture, and society.

A comic series developed by Mayas, written in Maya, and drawn by contemporary Mayas thus represented the possibility of historiographical revision in a very popular literary medium (*historietas*) by which contemporary Mayas could emphasize (as writers, as artists, and as readers) their own insight and understanding of the Caste War uprising. Hence, my intellectual intrigue when gifted the third issue of the series. Could locally developed comics on the Caste War be used to address the void of native subjectivity? Could local ethnohistory be represented in the inimitable medium of comic book storytelling? The answer, upon my analysis of the third issue, is yes.

The First Martyr

Printed on 8 × 10 glossy paper and totaling ten pages in length, the third issue of the series, published in 2017, is fashioned in typical comic book style with classic comic book characteristics. The issue is presented with texts and images formed into panels and divided by gutters that allow the panels to be placed into a sequence.[8] Each panel is also given a narrator or storyteller box while dialogue between characters are found in word balloons placed in relation to the speaker.[9] The protagonist of the story is Manuel Antonio Ay, chief of the village of Chichimila, with historical figures Cecilio Chi and Jacinto Pat, characters highlighted in the first two issues of the series, making reoccurring appearances. These three individuals, Jacinto Pat, Cecilio Chi, and Manuel Antonio Ay, are the primary protagonists of the Caste War with Manuel's assassination serving as an inspiration for the insurgency moving forward. This is the primary purpose of the third issue, to detail Manuel's life journey from a peasant worker to Maya leader who, with the aid of Jacinto Pat and Cecilio Chi, begins to organize the rebellion against the ruling Spanish aristocracy. Unable to attend one of the clandestine meetings with Jacinto and Cecilio, Manuel is instead provided with a letter detailing their plans for the rebellion. In a rather tragic turn of events, however, the letter is intercepted by Yucatec soldiers and as a result, Manuel is captured and assassinated.

Addressing the multimodality of this issue, I focus my analysis of the *historieta* on three individual frames, the first of which opens the issue, a second frame located midway throughout the story, and the last and concluding frame of the issue. Aside from the cover of the *historieta*, which itself induces a sense of cultural nostalgia (a drawing of two men dressed in traditional white shirt with embossed sleeves and white pants in the process of shaking hands), the opening frame of the issue is the most influential.

Presented as the largest frame of the issue, the opening panel immediately sets the tone for what is presented in terms of the textual, linguistic, spatial, and visual modes used to compose the comic's message by presenting the reader with an image of three brown-skinned men (noting here that they are neither red nor white skinned), working in an open field while speaking to one another in Maya. One of the men, understood as the main protagonist Antonio, is centered and bare chested. The three men presented in the image are not pre-Columbian hyperaggressive warriors dressed in ornate feathers but rather peasant farmers, two of whom are dressed in white shirts and pants, kneeling and working the land.[10] This is a very normal and subdued image given that the lifestyle of most Maya men in Quintana Roo's Maya Zone today is that of agriculturalist. It is not until we read the narration that the historical and cultural framework for which the rest of the story is told becomes clear.

The opening panel begins with a text box that reads, "*Ichil Tresientos jaabo'obe' le Maaya'obo' jach beetaab óolaj ti'ob tumen le ts'uulo'obo!*" [*for three hundred years the Mayas were mistreated by the Spanish!*]. The narrative of abuse presented by the opening sentence of the issue is both intellectually and culturally significant. The introduction of the Spanish or *ts'uulo'ob* (foreigners) as the perpetuators of abuse against the Maya sets the tone for the racial politics understood throughout Quintana Roo's Maya Zone today. The message is made clear; this is a story about racial oppression that challenges the argument presented by some scholars today that Yucatán's Caste War was not a race war but rather a class conflict absent of any racial antagonism. In Mexico there are 17 million Indigenous people, with twenty-eight distinct languages. The

Maya *Historietas* as Art for Remembering War 203

The frame above depicts the three protagonists of the issue discussing their lives as workers. As the two men in the forefront discuss the pains of having to work, the man in the background is warning them to stay quiet in fear of what happens when workers are found talking to one another.

argument of *mestizaje* or *mestizo* nationalism popularized by Mexican intellectual Jose Vasconcelos has been used to perpetuate the myth of Mexico as a raceless society. Reflecting upon the memory of their own racialized experience at the hands of the Spanish, the opening panel, however, makes it clear that the exploitation of the Maya did not exist solely on class distinctions but through the perpetuation of racial ideologies. With regard to the historiography of the Caste War, this one frame questions the rhetoric of the uprising as a conflict absent of race by making clear who the dominant and subordinate racial group were.

The narrative of abuse continues as the story unfolds in the subsequent pages. Soon after the issues initial frame, after which plans of revolt are discussed between Manuel, Jacinto, and Cecilio, we the readers are presented with a relatively large frame depicting all three men facing the audience. That the characters are drawn facing the reader is illustration of the panel's encoded message and attempt to break the fourth wall. The opening bubble of the panel reads "*to'one jach yaabo'on*" which translates into "we are more." The significance of this image is that, when offered along with the text, it presents the protagonists as members of a larger community, declaring that although the three of them are located within the parameters of the frame, there are others who exist outside the frames of the panel who similarly support their cause. This includes unseen Caste War combatants who exist within the imaginary of the gutters of the issue as well as, I dare suggest, the readers themselves. That others exist outside the parameters of the frame is culturally significant for those who can read the text in Maya. Yucatec Maya is not a language commonly spoken by persons born outside of the peninsula.[11] Being able to read the issue in its native dialogue infers a decoded message that those who are able to read in Maya, the majority of whom are native born, are also a part of the rebellion.[12]

In the above frame, the three protagonist of the issue all appear to be breaking the fourth wall looking outside of the frame and speaking directly to the reader.

Maya *Historietas* as Art for Remembering War 205

A call to defend the Maya pueblo, as is written in the bubbles of this frame, functions as a direct message to contemporary Maya as well.

To quote Paul Allatson in his summary of Martin Baker's *Comics: Ideology, Power and the Critics* (1989), the comic's meaning is not determined by its formal qualities alone, but also by the "kind of relationship into which the reader is invited" (23).

The last frame, after Manuel is captured and murdered by Yucateco forces, depicts an image of men willing and ready to defend the memory and honor of Manuel Antonio Ay. One of the unidentified men in the frame issues a powerful call in defense of his community, "*Mix táan ak kaa cháaik u pe'ech'el ak kuxtal*" (we will no longer allow that they step on our lives). That these are the words used to conclude the issue is again significant when juxtaposed with the issue's opening sentence. The Maya, as we are told early in the opening panel have long been mistreated. When one considers the multiple socioeconomic issues that continue to plague Mayas today, the call to defend community is not just a historical call but, when read by the readers, a call in defense of the discriminatory experiences lived by contemporary Maya.[13] Paul Levitz, author of *The Power of Comics: History, Form and Culture*, writes, "The interpretation of an image is also likely to be affected by the reality, the individual experience, of each reader"

(163). Although the panels presented in the issue highlight moments from the past, the reader's personal experiences provide what Scott McCloud terms closure, the ability to create a larger whole from fragments. The whole in this sense is not that the Maya rebelled, which is the story presented within the issue, but rather, when read in direct relationship to the reader's lived experiences, serves as a reminder to the fact that life for the Maya has always demanded some form of sacrifice. That the issue is titled *The First Martyr* serves as a blunt reminder that there were and are direct consequences to being Maya.

Memory as Art

Reflecting on Art Spiegelman's iconic *Maus*, Ana Merino once said that testimonials presented in the format of comics and/or graphic novels serve as a type of "history from below," providing counternarratives that subvert the traditional gatekeepers of history (5). As the first and only locally produced retelling of the Caste War in comic form, the *historietas* developed by the Caste War museum in conjunction with the Tihosuco Heritage Preservation Project function in this vein, providing a venue for native storytelling woven from the experience of the Indigenous where issues of representation, self-determination, historical memory, and cultural affirmation are documented and highlighted.[14]

Utilizing a theoretical framework of history and memory developed by Maurice Halbwachs and Pierre Nora, the series of *historietas* on the Caste War are to be viewed not simply as comics, but as a form of *aide-mémoire*, a thought-provoking and intimate cultural artifact through which history is reconceptualized and where the memory of those previously mischaracterized or left in anonymity are no longer rendered invisible.[15] By placing greater emphasis on culturally significant events and persons rather than generalized rhetoric, comics told from the perspective of those historically marginalized like David A. Robertson's *Sugar Falls: A Residential School Story* (2012), *Dreams of Looking Up: How One Family Discovers the Key to Their People's Strength* by the Mille Lacs Band of Ojivwe or Daniel Parada's *Zotz: Serpent and Shield* (see chapters by Jessica Rutherford and Jorge Santos in this book) serve as the visualization of historical memory through a form of multimodal learning through which social, political, and cultural messages are made meaningful through literary and artistic form.

While not diametrically opposed to history writ large, the three issues published thus far provide an account of the past that has relevance and meaning to how contemporary Mayas throughout Quintana Roo's Maya Zone experience the present. In the case of the third issue of the series, the question of race is (re)centered as a driving source of the conflict challenging and further complicating Caste War historiography. Representing what David Middleton terms conversational remembering, the *historietas* developed, in making "use of the past as a resource to engage the interlocutors" (247), function as didactic mediums by which history and memory come together in search for place in the face of historical and academic erasure.[16]

Entering the museum that day I was handed what appeared to be a ten-page comic, one on the legacy of Manuel Antonio Ay and his role in Yucatán's Caste War. What was given to me, however, was a memorandum, one that serves as a tool for remembering a past which the contributors to the series, and the Maya of Quintana Roo, have decided should never be forgotten.

Notes

1. This chapter is dedicated to the memory of all those to which the museum of the Caste War was built to honor.

2. The official date for the pacification of rebel Mayas is 1937 when, after more than seventy-five years of armed conflict, Mexican president Lazaro Cardenas agrees to peace with rebel Mayas.

3. There are over twenty thousand Maya speakers in the Mexican state of Quintana Roo with over 90 percent who claim an ethnic Maya identity (INEGI. *Principales resultados del Censo de Población y Vivienda 2010. Quintana Roo*).

4. Translation of the title is Manuel Antonio Ay: The First Martyr of the Caste War.

5. Directed by Richard M. Leventhal, PhD, Carlos Chan Espinosa, and Filiberto Chan Balam, the Tihosuco Community Heritage Preservation Project focuses on several projects regarding the Caste War of Yucatán and its ties to local heritage and identity. Projects include the preservation of language, collection of historical photographs, documentation of oral histories, as well as the gradual development of a sustainable tourism program run by community members.

6. To date there have been three issues published in the series, all of which were released on the anniversary of the Caste War. Issue #1 is titled A Hero to Know: Cecilio Chi, The Grand Leader of the Caste War. Issue #2 is titled Tihosuco and Jacinto Pat: The Amazing Life of a Caste War Leader.

7. Warning against the dangers of privileging majoritarian sources of information over non-majoritarian ones, anthropologists Victoria Bricker once wrote with regard to Caste War historiography, "I believe that the historical synthesis of white historians are biased because they are based almost exclusively on Spanish sources . . . The history of the Caste War of Yucatán needs to be rewritten with more attention paid the Maya version of the conflict" (257).

8. In the essay "More than Words: Comics as a Means of Teaching Multiple Literacies," Dale Jacobs writes, "as texts, comics provide a complex environment for the negotiation of meaning, beginning with the layout of the page itself. The comics page is separated into multiple panels, divided from each other by gutters, physical or conceptual spaces that through which connections are made and meaning are negotiated; readers must fill in the blanks within these gutters and make connections between panels. Images of people, objects, animals, and settings, word balloons, lettering, sound effects, and gutters all come together to form page layouts that work to create meaning in distinctive ways and in multiple realms of meaning making" (21).

9. The presence of a narrator and in-panel text provides the reader several perspectives from which to read the panels. First, the presence of a narrator provides the reader with what Michel Foucault labels the "author-function" (Bouchard 113), the presence and function of

the author's voice. As the reader, the narrator's voice stands all-pervading, overshadowing the events of the box, and providing the context of the story. Conversely it is the in-panel text that provides depth to the story and to the characters.

10. That comics are used as a format to dismantle historical stereotypes is not coincidence. Derek Parker Royal writes that "because of its foundational reliance on character iconography, comics are well suited to dismantle those very assumptions that problematize ethnic representation." (9).

11. According to the INEGI (the Mexican institution in charge of social and geographical statistics), as of 2015 there were 859,607 fluent Mayan speakers in Mexico (approximately 12 percent of the total population) making it the second most popular native language just after the Nahuatl (the Aztec language). Maya, however, is predominantly spoken in rural areas, with Spanish serving as the *de facto* language for most Mexicans of Maya heritage.

12. Addressing the communicative aspects presented by comics, Paul Levitz writes, "In any act of communication, the meaning (the decoded message) ultimately resides with the receivers . . . the receiver has cognitive reaction (knowing) and effective reactions (feelings) to the signs that are communicated by the compositional elements within panels" (12).

13. While diverse from place to place, native people throughout Mexico continue to struggle with issues ranging from productive rights, education rights, tourism, displacement, voting fraud, and political underrepresentation.

14. Distinguishing the issue from other forms of Caste War literature is the fact that the issue is written in Maya. Language preservation and literacy in Maya is one of the focuses for cultural activist participating in broad and diverse movements of cultural reaffirmation.

15. Based on the analysis of Pierre Nora and Maurice Halbwach, memories, under the auspices of collective memory, is invoked as a counterweight to history as it attempts to reshape, revise, and rewrite dominant narratives. Studies written in this vein tend to argue for the need to preserve or salvage the memories of individuals or small communities as antidotes to the narrative of dominate groups.

16. Although developed in conjunction with the Penn State Cultural Heritage Center, the autonomy provided by the framework of their working relationship allows the developers to engage in forms of textual and artistic expression free from the forms of social gatekeeping typically associated with corporately structured entities the likes of mainstream publishing companies and/or peer-reviewed scholarship.

Works Cited

Allatson, Paul. "Ilan Stavan's Latino USA: A Cartoon History (of Cosmopolitan Intellectual)." *Chasqui* 35, no. 2 (2006): 21–41.

Bouchard, Donald F. *Language, Counter-memory, Practice: Selected Essays and Interviews by Michel Foucault*. Ithaca, NY: Cornell University Press, 1980.

Bricker, Victoria. "The Caste War of Yucatán: The History of a Myth and the Myth of History." In *Anthropology and History in Yucatán*, edited by Grant Jones. Austin: University of Texas Press, 1977.

Chavarria, Tony. "Indigenous Comics in the United States." *World Literature Today* 83, no. 3 (2009): 47–49.

Dumond, Don E. *The Machete and the Cross: Campesino Rebellion in Yucatán*. Lincoln: University of Nebraska Press, 1997.

Halbwachs, Maurice. *On Collective Memory*. Chicago: University of Chicago Press, 1992.

Jacobs, Dale. "More Than Words: Comics as a Means of Teaching Multiple Literacies." *English Journal* 96, no. 3 (2007): 19–25.

Jiménez, Genero Pool. *Historia Oral de la Guerra de Castas 1847: Según los Viejos Descendientes Maya*. Mérida: Universidad Autónoma de Yucatán, 1997.

Larsen, Helga. "Trip from Chichen-Itza to Xcacal, Q.R., Mexico." *Ethos* 1, no. 2 (1965): 5–41. Print.

Levitz, Paul. *The Power of Comics: History, Form and Culture*. New York: Continuum International Publishing, 2009.

McCloud, Scott. *Understanding Comics: The Invisible Art*. New York. William Morrow, 1993.

Mereno, Ana. "Memory in Comics: Testimonial, Autobiographical and Historical Space in MAUS." *Transatlantica* [Online], 1 (2010).

Middleton, David. "The Social Organization of Conversational Remembering: Experience as Individual and Collective Concern." *Mind, Culture, and Activity* 4, no. 2 (1997): 71–85. Print.

Montejo, Victor. "The Multiplicity of Mayan Voices: Mayan Leadership and the Politics of Self-Representation." *Indigenous Movements, Self-Representation, and the State in Latin America*, edited by Kay Warren and Jean Jackson. Austin: University of Texas Press, 2002.

Nora, Pierre. "Between Memory and History: Les Lieux De Memoire." *Representation* 26 (1989): 7–24. Print.

Reed, Nelson. *The Caste War of Yucatán*. Stanford: Stanford University Press, 1964.

Ruegely, Terry. *Yucatán's Maya Peasantry and the Origins of the Caste War*. Austin: University of Texas Press, 1996.

Sheyahshe, Michael. Native *Americans in Comics: A Critical Study*. Jefferson, NC: McFarland, 2008.

Turey El Taíno and *La Borinqueña*: Puerto Rican Nationalist and Ethnic Resistance in Puerto Rican Comics Dealing with Taíno Cultural Heritage

Enrique García

When I began my career at Middlebury College in 2008, I attended a presentation by a Puerto Rican poet from New York City. As he addressed the Latinx students in attendance, I was surprised that he self-identified as a member of the Taíno tribes of Boríkén. Since I was raised on the island, the official discourse taught to me in school there was more akin to the Latin American concept of "mestizaje," as opposed to more blatantly racist Eurocentric ideas that excluded Native American cultures from the American identity. Thus, I had learned that I have biological connections to the Taínos (mixed with European and African genes), that these tribes are currently extinct, and that we, Puerto Ricans, had adopted aspects of their culture that remain embedded in our contemporary society. This is not what the Puerto Rican poet was saying in his lecture, however, as he was arguing that he was a Taíno and in the process, he was simultaneously defying both Hispanic and Anglophone colonialism. This particular event made me more self-aware of how Taíno culture is perceived in both the island and the diaspora, especially because I had grown up with the adventures of Turey El Taíno, one of the most relevant comic book characters published in Puerto Rico. In this chapter, I will explore the controversies surrounding our Taíno heritage and Puerto Rican ethnic and nationalist identity by analyzing how the comic book *Turey El Taíno* fits within the ICP's (Instituto de Cultura Puertorriqueña) didactic goals and how similar or different the series' portrayal of the Taínos as a symbol of resistance against Spanish and United States imperialism is in comparison to other recent comic book portrayals of this Indigenous heritage (such as Edgardo Miranda-Rodríguez's *La Borinqueña*) after the apocalyptic arrival of Hurricane María in 2017.

Taíno Culture, Identity, and Puerto Rican Nationalism

After Puerto Rico was devastated by Hurricane María in 2017, one of the biggest points of contention and disappointment on the island was the lack of support by the United States government under the presidency of Donald Trump. The "diaspora" Puerto Rican communities mobilized to help, and even some media outlets and TV shows like *The Simpsons* criticized the president, whose actions were very dangerous and whose delay in signing the federal bills to help with the island's reconstruction arguably claimed hundreds of additional lives. In March 2018, the US publisher Lions Forge Comic released a graphic novel titled *Puerto Rico Strong*, which collected comic book vignettes about the Puerto Rican struggle after the natural disaster, with the goal of raising funds for the victims of the hurricane (and in a way also victims of Trump's irresponsible behavior). Many of the short segments were created by young Puerto Rican artists from the diaspora who wanted to help in the reconstruction of their ancestral home. As I read through the different segments of this collection, I was intrigued by the use of Taíno references by several of the artists, especially because I thought the topics would deal with more contemporary themes. In the various introductions provided by the editors, they mention that "the stories range from intimate family traditions to uncovered histories" (6) and "what's sad is that I didn't learn about Puerto Rico or its history in school (in the United States)" (7). These statements show that the book intended to provide US audiences with more cultural knowledge about how the island had suffered through both Spanish and United States colonialism and imperialism before the hurricane, with the Taíno culture presented as the foundational stone of Puerto Rican identity and the first victim of Eurocentric ideology (7).[1]

The story "Areytos,"[2] included in the collection, is about the cacique (chieftain) Agüeybaná II and how he defied Spanish colonialism. Even though the story has a nihilistic ending as the cacique's army is wiped out by the European invaders, the last page includes the statement that scientific studies have determined that over 60 percent of Puerto Ricans have "Taíno blood" and the final image shows Agüeybaná's statue located in the city of Ponce with an additional drawing of a Puerto Rico national flag. This is an obvious attempt at establishing a nationalist link to the Indigenous tribes but also in sharing the suffering between the apocalyptic moment of the Spanish conquest with the nihilistic feelings of the Puerto Rican communities after the Hurricane María disaster (50). In "A Taíno's Tale,"[3] a teacher in an elementary Puerto Rican school[4] teaches the students about how "awesome" the Taínos were and how interesting their gods, heroes, and customs were. This particular story is important in legitimizing the Taíno culture as a source of identity within the island's education system and a way of diverging from Eurocentric Christian creation myths that are usually fed to children by the Hispanophile and Anglocentric traditions. In addition, the stories "Taíno Online"[5] and "Knowledge of Self"[6] feature young Cubans and Puerto Ricans respectively who realize how important the Taíno legacy is to their Caribbean identity. "Self" is provocative in featuring a Latinx character who complains about the American education system's erasure of his connections to the Taíno by not including Native American cultures in the curriculum. It is the "Boricua" Latinx who educates him about his heritage, his own knowledge having been acquired after a visit to one of the Taíno museum villages run by the Puerto Rican government. At the end of the story, it is hinted that the museum guide told the young Puerto Rican visitor that Taínos still lived in the mountains, which points to the main debate about Taínos and Puerto Rican identity, specifically the issue of whether the Taíno people are extinct or not (147). An important element in these stories is the positive portrayal of the Puerto Rican government in institutionalizing the Taíno culture as part of the Puerto Rican identity with the role of the teacher in "A Taíno's Tale" and the ceremonial park that the Latinx youth visited in "Knowledge of Self."

It is difficult to summarize in a few pages the evolution of the role of the Taíno heritage in Puerto Rican culture and nationalism, but it is nevertheless important to elaborate a few crucial points before directly exploring comic books such as *Turey El Taíno* and others. First, according to Puerto Rican history scholar Ricardo Alegría, some of the oldest literary/European narratives from the region that incorporate Taíno culture are the fifteenth- and sixteenth-century colonial writings of Catholic priests such as Ramón Pané and Bartolomé de las Casas.[7] The Taínos did not have a formal writing system, so our modern-day access to their legacies is filtered through the conquerors' lenses. However, according to scholar Mercedes López-Baralt, Spanish authors, such as Pané, interviewed the local tribes in the process of transcribing their legends into European languages. Basing her arguments on intertextual and Bakhtinian theory, López-Baralt observes the presence of a polyphony of voices and Indigenous authorship embedded in these colonial narratives seen as the beginnings of the "New World" consciousness (16).

When modern Puerto Rican nationalism began to rise in the nineteenth century, it followed a pattern set by other Latin American countries where the ruling "criollo" colonial aristocracy and bourgeoisie used the exploitation of Indigenous and Afro-Latino citizens as a cultural weapon against the imperial authorities.[8] There was one important difference, however: at the time, the Puerto Rican Indigenous populations had supposedly disappeared, as opposed to other Latin American countries (such as Mexico, Peru, and others) where the Native American groups still had a more tangible presence. In his article "Los límites de la narrativa indianista en Puerto Rico: Tapia, Betances y Marqués," Puerto Rican literature scholar Ramón Luis Acevedo states that the Taíno, even though they are part of our heritage, ceased to exist during the first century of the conquest. Puerto Rican identity was formed from the end of the eighteenth

Puerto Rico Strong "A Taíno's Tale." Puerto Rican teacher inspires children to be proud of their Taíno heritage.

century on, as it began to be distinguished from the Taíno, African, and Spanish legacies (93). Acevedo also states that the Taínos were not Puerto Ricans because Puerto Ricanness is not based on geography but is historically and culturally defined (93). He believes that Puerto Ricans are actually more African than Taíno and assumes that racism may play a role in some Puerto Ricans' preferring to embrace Taíno identity (94). In his article, he further explains how local nationalist writers from the nineteenth century used the "idea" of the Taíno to write novels against Spanish colonialism but their representations were affected by the criollo writers' individual realities. For example, Acevedo explains in detail how Alejandro Tapia wrote *La palma del Cacique* while living in exile in Spain. The novel criticizes the Spanish conquest and genocide of the Taínos because that fit the nineteenth-century nationalist goals, but it is biased and Eurocentric, as the text blames the Indigenous people for their own destruction (98). Acevedo adds that another Puerto Rican nationalist hero, Ramón Emeterio Betances, wrote a small novel titled *The Two Indians* while exiled in Paris. Because French culture at the time was very hostile to Spanish hegemony and masculinity, Betances was able to make his novel more subversive against Spain than Tapia did his by changing the gender paradigm from a Spanish male protagonist and his Taína lover to the exact opposite, a Spanish female character and her Taíno lover (100–101).[9]

After reading Ramón Luis Acevedo's article, I reread both Tapia's and Betances's novels to confirm his thesis and that made me rethink the role of Taíno subjects in Puerto Rican nationalist ideology. The Taínos are typically portrayed as a group that became extinct in early colonial times, but remained a part of our national culture and consciousness. However, if they are truly extinct, then our cultural contact with them has occurred through Spanish conquerors, white criollo elites, and contemporary Puerto Rican authors.

Puerto Rico Strong "Knowledge of Self." Latinx Boricua youth is concerned about the erasure of Taíno identity in the United States curriculum after visiting ceremonial park in Puerto Rico.

Our access to them is part of an intertextual and postmodern pastiche that forms Puerto Rican identity, yet it is difficult to narrow down a pure Taíno biological identity from that "mestizaje" which is certainly problematic today. In my most recent trip to Puerto Rico in 2018, I found fascinating that for being considered officially extinct, the Taínos are still very present in local authors' attempts to provide a Taíno point of view to the Puerto Rican youth. Examples that I found in the local bookstore were Miriam Ramírez's *El ultimo taíno* (about a contemporary Puerto Rican boy finding and meeting a frozen Taíno boy from ancient times) and Jose Muratti-Toro's short novel *La furia de Juracán* (a precolonial tale about Taíno characters surviving a hurricane). The main question I began to formulate was: what was the official discourse of the ICP about the Taínos? This institution is very influential in the perception we have about the Taínos' role in Puerto Rican nationalist ideology. Are they also able to influence the Taíno representations in comic books such as *Turey El Taíno* and others?

The ICP publishes its own didactic comic titled *ICePé.cómic*, in which a group of kids and their grandfather learn about different aspects of Puerto Rican history and culture. In 2002, an issue dedicated to "Nuestra herencia taína" (Our Taíno Heritage) features the children protagonists Inés, Pepe, and

Ceci on a visit to the "Centro Ceremonial Indígena de Caguana" in the town of Utuado. In the first few pages of the story, the children learn educational tidbits from the local tour guide and from famous Puerto Rican historian Ricardo Alegría, who played an important role in the inclusion of the Taínos in Puerto Rican popular culture.[10] When the children return to their grandfather's house, Inés is able to open a time travel gateway to the past (Aguado 5). The kids meet the Taínos and become friends with a Taína named Baguana, who looks exactly like Inés because they are supposedly "spiritual twins." This is a charming didactic story, but it carefully incorporates the ICP's discourse about Taíno heritage. In the last segment of the story, the children and their grandfather list the important Taíno contributions to the Puerto Rican culture and the grandfather proclaims that their heritage has not disappeared (12–13). He then explains that contemporary Puerto Ricans are biologically connected to the Taínos, while pointing at the headline of a Puerto Rican newspaper that reads "Sangre taína fluye en las venas de Puerto Rico [Taíno Blood Still Flows through Puerto Rico's Veins]." The second important legacy the characters bring up are Taíno objects used to this day; for example, the "hamaca" (hammock) and musical instruments such as maracas and güiros. The last cultural element they mention are the names of towns, rivers, lakes, and fruit, and the story ends with the grandfather explaining that the Taínos are still in our Puerto Rican blood and soul. The story thus establishes several continuities between the Taínos and contemporary Puerto Ricans: biological, material, linguistic, and geographic.

While I can appreciate the didactic goals of the comic book, I find bizarre the racial connections that the writer establishes at several points in the story. One example is Ricardo Alegría's claim that Inés, unlike the other kids, looks like a Taína (2). In the story, this is presented as a heart-warming scene, in which the famous scholar is using the girl as an example of how we are still biologically connected to the Taínos. However, in this day and age it looks more like a racialization of the girl's body by a white man, who is trying to mark her as a person of color in relation to the other kids, a very problematic position. Later in the story, Inés's grandfather agrees with the racialization of his granddaughter but then brings the tired "mestizaje" trope and explains how she is different to the Taínos because Puerto Ricans are formed by the interaction of three distinct cultures (4). It seems the point of the scene is to highlight her racial connection to the Taínos but without allowing her to fully embrace that particular identity because she should not forget her Spanish and Black heritage.

The strange thing about this story is that Inés's biological connection is what in fact opens the time portal to the past. Somehow mystically, the Taína Baguana is able to communicate with the children because she was able to connect with Inés (through race, it seems) but also through the river and geography of the island that they share in their different timelines. The latter is important

ICePé.cómic. On a visit to the "Centro Ceremonial Indígena de Caguana," Inés is racially defined as Taína by scholar Ricardo Alegría.

because, as mentioned above, scholar Ramón Luis Acevedo had ignored the geographical connection of Puerto Rican nationalism to the Taínos, as he established that modern nationalist ideology was formed after that ethnic group had become extinct in early colonial times. This ICP comic portrays Taínos and Puerto Ricans as different because of their historical placement (which is why they need to time travel in order to meet). However, at the end of the story, it is revealed that one of the Taíno bones found in the present is holding a Puerto Rican flag pin given to the Taínos by Pepe, one of the time-traveling children. This scene is similar to the one in *Puerto Rico Strong* featuring the Agüeybaná statue drawn with a Puerto Rican flag. With this imagery and fictionalized contact with precolonial Indigenous tribes, the Taínos are absorbed as an integral part of Puerto Rican nationalism. This complex relationship between real or imaginary/fictional Taínos and contemporary Puerto Rican identity as conceptualized in artistic works and sanctioned by academic and government nationalist discourse is what prompted me to revisit the series *Turey El Taíno*. This series was a self-published Puerto Rican comic book sponsored by both private enterprises and public entities such as the ICP and other Puerto Rican government institutions. Even though the series had didactic goals, its representation of Taíno culture is in the form of a postmodern pastiche, as I will explain in the following section.

ICePé.cómic. Problematic representation of Inés as Taína.

Turey El Taíno's Postmodern Resistance

Turey El Taíno is probably the most recognizable Puerto Rican comic book of all time. It takes place on the island of Borikén (original Taíno designation of the island) shortly before the arrival of the Spanish conquerors (although there are glimpses/premonitions of them in three of the issues). The main character is Turey, a Taíno of short stature, who is clumsy but tries hard to fit in the role of a Taíno warrior. The series lasted thirty-six issues (the longest series published in the island) and ran from October 1989 to June 1995.[11] Starting on October 29, 1989, the series was also published as a newspaper strip in the now-defunct *El Mundo* newspaper. It was later (in 1991) moved to *El Nuevo Día*, the most prominent Puerto Rican newspaper, where it ran for over fifteen years. It would not surprise me if Puerto Ricans are more familiar with the newspaper strip than the comic books, since the latter were more difficult to find until they were finally collected by the ICP in 2006. Ricardo Álvarez-Rivón was the main artist/

writer of the comic book, although he had several guest artists who later created their own comic books. His wife, Magali Meléndez, was the main editor of the comic and an integral part of its creation and publishing. The series was self-published through their company Editorial Manos. According to one of the couple's interviews with scholar Luis Lacourt, they began to publish 10,000 copies per issue, which were distributed in comic book stores, magazine stands, and pharmacies around the island.[12] The series struggled to sell at the beginning of its run and sometimes the publishers would get 6,000 of the 10,000 printed copies returned. This made them reduce the print run to 7,000 copies per issue as they wanted to minimize their losses.

One thing that saved the series was the local support offered by both private enterprises and the government. The Puerto Rican government's energy company (Autoridad de Energía Eléctrica) and later the Department of Education participated with different types of sponsorship. In addition, Turey became the local mascot for private companies such as Keebler and his trading cards and minicomics were part of Wendy's Kids' Meals. When perusing copies of the original print run, one can observe various important elements related to the series, such as sponsorship, letters, and important documentation that Álvarez-Rivón shared with the audience. For example, at the beginning of the series, most of the ads included in the comic were from private companies like Wrangler, Keebler, and others. As the series and its protagonist began gaining more visibility, academic, corporate, and government support increased. The largest local comic book stores in the Metropolitan area also added their sponsorship.

I had previously read half of the series' thirty-six issues because I had bought some printed copies during *Turey*'s initial run, and I was able to purchase some additional unsold copies in the ICP building in the mid-2000s. Since I had not read the complete series, I was reluctant to write about it, but I found out that a beautiful set of two hardcover volumes collecting the entire series was published by Puerto Rico's Education Department in 2006. After reading the whole series, I was able to assess how this graphic narrative works in its representation of the Taínos, and evaluate its importance within Puerto Rican popular culture. I immediately noticed some similarities with comics from other Latin American countries. Indeed, in an interview, Álvarez-Rivón stated that when he was creating his Taíno character, he was reading comic books such as *Condorito* and *Mafalda* that have become national icons in Chile and Argentina. He wanted to create a character that would become "the" Puerto Rican icon and chose a Taíno warrior in precolonial times as a subject. The author did not want to create a superhero in the vein of Superman, who solves problems by the use of force. He wanted a more comedic and subtle character that was not perfect or powerful and who did not win all the time.[13] This is important to point out, as it defies the imperial ideology typically embedded in the superhero genre that has a stronghold in the comic industry from the United States.

Turey El Taíno. Ricardo Álvarez-Rivón's representation of Taínos reflecting contemporary issues of Puerto Rican masculinity.

Turey El Taíno. Ricardo Álvarez-Rivón's parody of the conventions of the superhero muscular body.

One important biographical detail about Álvarez-Rivón is that he has three Caribbean cultural identities. He was born in Cuba but his family fled the island for the United States in 1959 (when he was nine), after his father began to disagree with some of the Revolutionary government's political decisions. In an interview, the author explains that he spent four years living in Florida, which had a very different ethnic make-up back then.[14] This was the first time he experienced racism and was positioned in the role of an "other." His family then moved to Puerto Rico, which has been his home since. As a consequence, Álvarez-Rivón has his original Cuban heritage, his brief traumatic experience as a Cuban immigrant in the United States, and a second life as a Puerto Rican. Puerto Ricans tend to assume that Cuban Americans always love the United States due to their differences with the Cuban revolution, but Álvarez-Rivón seems not to have a nostalgic vision of this country and its mostly propagandistic superheroes either. By situating the plot of his comic in the Taíno precolonial era, he is able to create an adventure narrative targeting Puerto Rican children through a comic that does not conform to US superhero genre conventions.

Turey El Taíno is also similar to France's *Asterix*, where the main characters are Gauls (and exist before the modern French state) but behave in a way that would be understandable to young contemporary French children. In a similar manner, Álvarez-Rivón's characters speak Spanish, use Puerto Rican slang, and have recognizable Puerto Rican mannerisms and behavior. While Turey's comic book tries to recreate Taíno adventures based on the few facts that were actually recorded about this Indigenous society, the story lines are also very recognizable to modern Puerto Rican audiences as they function simultaneously as parodies of the twentieth century. The first (and my favorite) story line covers the first three issues and is the longest one in the series. Throughout this story, Álvarez-Rivón presents us with a portrait of Taíno society from a contemporary point of view where he exposes the contemporary Puerto Rican reader to Taíno vocabulary (explained in a glossary at the end of each issue), mysticism, and a confrontation with traditional social order and customs. The antagonists in the story are the Caribes, an enemy tribe from the neighboring islands. The comic portrays them as savage cannibals, a concept promoted by the Spanish conquerors and still a controversial and problematic idea embedded in Puerto Rican popular culture and education. However, the first story line ends with Turey befriending a Caribe tribesman, an interesting ending that provides a message about how the readers have to be open to other cultures even if we find them threatening.

Álvarez-Rivón does not have too much material about the Taínos and, as the series progresses, he has to dive into the "postmodern well" to acquire intertextual genres and references that would sustain the interest of a modern audience. Some examples include a parody of modern medicine in which a Caribe shaman wants to sell a flu medicine to other Native American tribes and wants to use Turey as a test subject (issue 10); a story exploring Turey's wife Yaya's problems with her weight as if she were a modern Puerto Rican woman (issue 13); a plot where Turey dresses as a superhero (similar to Batman) and fights a vampire (issue 14); a bizarre satire of modern religious fundamentalism but with a strange Native American sect (issue 15); a free adaptation of Mark Twain's *The Prince and the Pauper* where Turey impersonates a cacique from another tribe (issues 16 and 17); a sci-fi adventure in which he meets aliens (issue 25); a brush with pirates in a time-travel story (issue 28); and a sort of "professional wrestling" tale during the Taíno era (issue 29).

To me, the most interesting issue is number 30, where the action takes place in modern Puerto Rico and the Taínos supposedly no longer exist. In this story, the protagonist is Narciso, a Puerto Rican man of short stature (similar to Turey in size), who is an unemployed actor living in the capital, contemporary San Juan. Because he is short, Narciso cannot obtain any good acting roles, just as Turey was unable to find his warrior role in his society because he did not fit the Taínos' expectations (which ironically should be defined more as Anglophone

Turey El Taíno. Ricardo Álvarez-Rivón's postmodern depiction of Taíno life that incorporates lucha libre and vampires.

superhero expectations). Narciso is out of money and his landlord wants to throw him out of his apartment. His agent suggests that he try out for a *Turey El Taíno* play to be performed to an audience of children. He is disgusted by the opportunity of portraying a comic book character but he finally decides to go to the audition. As he returns home, his Turey costume gets stuck onto his body and he cannot get inside his apartment because his landlord is waiting for him at the door. He wanders around still dressed as Turey and suddenly sees a thief assaulting an innocent victim. He decides to interfere and then goes on a hero spree (saving and helping other people) because he is inspired by the costume. His life as a modern Puerto Rican was dull and mediocre but as soon as he embodies Turey, he becomes a better person, more courageous, and finally even finds love. This story appears to be just a playful digression from the main story line of the comic, yet it is important because it features a contemporary Puerto Rican who gets to embody "Taínoness" and as a consequence improve his life by being able to perceive himself outside of the traditional Hispanic/Latin/Anglophone conventions. Under his previous life, Narciso was a loser with no prospects but by performing the character of Turey (with whom he shares physical attributes), he is able to find the courage to act beyond his own immediate interests and finally successfully capitalize on his acting talent. This particular issue has a similar approach to the ICP comic book series (*ICePé.cómic*), which brings the Taíno culture into our modern Puerto Rican reality but the Taínos themselves remain in the past.

Because *Turey El Taíno* is set prior to the Spanish conquest of the Caribbean, the story does not have an antagonistic political approach that could be interpreted as revolutionary in terms of establishing a clash between conqueror vs. oppressed as was common in the nineteenth century. The Spanish ships are seen at the end of issue 10, and in issue 28, Turey time-travels in the Caribbean

Turey El Taíno. Ricardo Álvarez-Rivón's cover art blends Taíno life with twentieth-century Puerto Rico.

Sea and helps a Taína woman escape the grasp of evil European pirates. Western European culture is thus portrayed as destructive in the few moments it appears in the series. Still, by setting the action before the conquest, Álvarez-Rivón is mostly able to avoid the controversial depiction of the Spanish legacy that is considered the base of the modern industrialized Caribbean civilization. As a consequence, Puerto Rican readers can, for the most part, avoid the political internal conflict of having to choose between a Hispanic culture associated with both imperialism and civilization and the Taínos who were victims of the

Turey El Taíno. In this sequence, Narciso gets empowered by donning Turey's costume.

conquest. They just have to imagine their modern collective experience in a postmodern embodiment of a utopian Taíno past that allows them to escape briefly from the failures of nationalist ideology and the colonial infrastructure. However, after the protests in Vieques in 1999 and the aftermath of Hurricane María, a more antagonistic approach was needed. As a consequence, more recent Puerto Rican comic books have focused more on the clashes between the Taínos and European imperialism. An example of this is *La Borinqueña*, which is probably the highest-profile Boricua comic produced by a Latinx Puerto Rican artist in the late 2010s and with certainly the most provocative political use of the Taíno as foundational figures of ideological resistance.

La Borinqueña and the Power of Taíno Identity

Edgardo Miranda-Rodriguez's *La Borinqueña* is arguably the most hyped Puerto Rican comic book since *Turey El Taíno.* When its first issue came out in 2016, the Puerto Rican and Latino media loved the idea of a new Puerto Rican superheroine following a pattern where the American press constantly celebrates how the superhero genre is becoming more inclusive of non-WASP[15] superheroes. This particular comic book features Marisol, a female Afro-Puerto Rican Latinx protagonist, who obtains her powers and costumes from the Taíno deity Atabex and, as described by scholar Ivonne García, is an intersectional character in terms of race, gender, and ethnicity. The series currently consists of only two issues, which can be bought online on Miranda-Rodríguez's website SomosArte.com. *La Borinqueña* is more difficult to acquire and more expensive than the *Turey* comic books were, because each issue costs $19.99 due to higher production values. Miranda's art is very dynamic, beautiful, and professional, and the quality of the stock paper is as glossy as any Marvel and DC comic book. Although Miranda-Rodriguez presents a heroine with a multicultural identity that fits what the ICP defines as Puerto Rican, many of those who now identify as Taíno will like how he positions Taíno culture as the foundation of the island, and thus decentralizes the Spanish heritage from its position of power. However, before addressing the *La Borinqueña* comic, I would like to discuss some of the controversies about the new conceptualization of Taíno identity reflected in the work of other Boricua Latinx authors.

As I investigated why some Puerto Rican Latinx authors wanted to resurrect Taíno identity from the mestizaje pastiche that is officially taught in Puerto Rican schools, a few particular readings made me understand better their position. First is the idea of "cultural mestizaje," which has been questioned recently by Latin American scholars. In her doctoral dissertation, scholar Sherina Feliciano-Santos writes about how the Puerto Rican mestizaje of three races (African, Taíno, and Spanish) reflects an unbalanced distribution of power, desirability, and inhabitability in Puerto Rican nationalism:

> The national trope of the racial triad is understood to apply to all Puerto Ricans both in terms of genetic and cultural ancestry, delineating an ideological ranking of desirability and inhabitability (affecting acceptable ancestry claims) for each root. This ideological ranking privileged Spanish ancestry as desirable and appreciatively inhabitable; African ancestry was considered undesirable and inhabitable, while Taíno ancestry was desirable and uninhabitable. Ultimately, though the racial blending myth was supposed to espouse racial equality as an essence contained within the ancestry of each Puerto Rican, in effect it delineated a hierarchy of racialized heritages with different levels of desirability and inhabitability. (73)

The dominance of Eurocentric values in the Puerto Rican mestizaje has been criticized recently by many scholars who then see the recent Taíno movements as a way of rejecting both US and Spanish colonialisms. For example, scholar Yolanda Martínez-San Miguel writes, when discussing the neo-Taíno movements, that "what could be seen as a useless anachronistic reinvention of a 'Boricua coquí' can also be conceived as a productive example of Spivak's 'strategic essentialism' with the possibility of a powerful political agenda" (n.pag.). However, she also warns that conflating indigeneity with nationalism and producing a notion of identity grounded on racial purity is already unimaginable in the context of Caribbean postcolonialities (n.pag.).

One of the most interesting books published about the reclamation of Taíno identity is Indigenous scholar Tony Castanha's *The Myth of Indigenous Caribbean Extinction*. Castanha is of Puerto Rican descent and was raised in Hawaii after his mother's family moved there. He is a fierce defender of Taíno identity and in his preface he explains how, when he returned to visit Yauco, his mother's hometown in Puerto Rico, he found a local children's textbook that explained Taíno culture. He writes that the book was accurate enough until the ending, which proclaims the Taínos perished at the hands of Spanish men while "behind the Spaniard stands a somber and attractive Native woman, still very much alive, presumably to be assimilated into the Spanish patriarchic realm" (xiii). This sounds very similar to Alejandro Tapia's novel I mentioned earlier, in which the Taíno man dies and the Taína woman elopes with the Spanish conqueror. Castanha explains that his book explores "native continuity" and he disagrees with Ricardo Alegría's statement that Taínos have disappeared and that we practically only inherit culture and biology from them. Castanha writes:

> To him, a viable Indigenous presence ceased to exist at this time. I dispute this. Although Native continuity does refer to the physical and genetic survival of the Indigenous population, it most importantly concerns cultural survival and continuity, or how *all peoples* over time have had to adjust in various ways to their particular circumstances and environments, or face possible extinctions. (6)

I think Castanha would have disagreed with the racial heritage classification presented in the *ICePé.comic* discussed earlier, where Inés is the character biologically connected to the Taínos. Castanha mentions that his study "does not rely on divisive Darwinian biological notions of "racial purity [and] blood quantum measurements" (6). He mentions that this is a racist colonial technique where miscegenation is used as a way to perceive the Indigenous people as less real and as a remnant of the past (6). He envisions mestizaje more along the lines of Peruvian writer José Arguedas, where "mestizaje is not about the concept of race but cultural continuity" (9). Castanha also resents Puerto Rican anthropologist Jorge Duany's assumptions that "the African presence has been debased by the cultural nationalist ideology and discourse" because Jíbaro/Boricuas acknowledge African contributions (15).

Edgardo Miranda-Rodríguez's comic book *La Borinqueña* attempts to establish this important nationalist continuity to the Taínos while not necessarily framing the characters within a Taíno identity. In her book chapter, "Diasporic Intersectionality," scholar Ivonne García explores the intersectional characters of Roberto Clemente (from the graphic novel *21*) and Marisol (*La Borinqueña*) and how both are created by diasporic Boricua comic book creators. García states that these two works deploy "diasporic intersectionality" that not only acknowledges but privileges the Puerto Rican migrant experience. She also adds that both creators, "Instead of reifying masculinity, whiteness, and upper class culture, . . . rely on . . . intersectional identities . . ." (72). García acknowledges that the theories of intersectionality are still debated and difficult to define as the term evolves. However, she understands it as the deployment of simultaneous identities to represent the experience of marginalized subjects, as a foundational characteristic of diasporic subjectivity in the Puerto Rican context (73–74).

In *La Borinqueña*, it is clear that Edgardo Miranda follows the holy trilogy of Puerto Rican nationalism (Spanish, Taíno, and African), but he also adds Anglo culture (La Borinqueña is bilingual) and asserts the character's Black identity as desirable by making her a scientist (like *Black Panther*'s Shiri). Still, the most important aspect of Marisol's Puerto Rican identity is that precisely the Taíno heritage is its foundational element. I was very moved when I saw this construction of Puerto Rican identity in the comic book, because when Marisol encounters the Taíno deity Atabex in the Puerto Rican cave, it is obvious that the island as a geographical entity is what empowers her and not the colonial culture that arguably has dominated Puerto Rico for over four hundred years. As a consequence, Miranda-Rodríguez's Puerto Rican nationalism is not just about a collection of beings that populate the island and share geography and culture. His nationalism is ideological and inclusive of the oppressed living beings that are victims of foreign imperialism, which includes two brands of anti-imperialism in the two-page montage that covers La Borinqueña's mystical vision provided by Atabex: one side of the spread presents imagery of resistance to the Spanish colonization process that includes the Taínos, nationalist figures such as Mariana Bracetti, and the nationalist revolt "The grito de Lares," and the second side opposes modern United States hegemony including the struggles of the LGBTQ communities, the Ponce Massacre, and the plight of the Puerto Rican soldier in twentieth-century warfare. La Borinqueña is empowered by the island (Borikén or Puerto Rico) to protect its people, but this power is built on the foundation of Taíno culture, and does not stem from the two oppressive Eurocentric traditions. In the first issue, the transcendental scenes are the ones in which La Borinqueña fulfills her destiny and power and interacts with Atabex (the mother of Borikén) and Yúcahu (spirit of the sea and mountains). That is precisely when she encounters her "disappeared" Taíno-self.[16] Scholar Ivonne García offers a similar interpretation:

> In having this Indigenous "mother goddess" provide Marisol with a panoramic view of Puerto Rican struggle and suffering, also through different but related geographical locations, Miranda-Rodríguez implies that conflict and strife have been and still are a part of the Puerto Rican identity. Invested with the powers of Indigenous spirituality and transformed from a nerdy, bespectacled college student into a magical suit-clad superhero, Marisol, now La Borinqueña, goes on to save the day. (79)

Of course, after the Hurricane María disaster, nothing was the same and that is reflected in the recent *La Borinqueña* comic books. Before releasing the second issue, Miranda-Rodríguez made a deal with DC Comics to publish *Ricanstruction*,[17] a paperback anthology in which artists could use DC characters to team up with La Borinqueña and therefore raise some financial support for the island. In the story "Today, Yesterday, and Tomorrow," written

La Borinqueña. La Borinqueña's mystical vision provided by Atabex.

by Will Rosado,[18] Supergirl and La Borinqueña team up to help the mayor of Loiza and some people trapped in their cars after the devastation of the hurricane. While cleaning up the debris, La Borinqueña finds a broken cemí[19] and when she touches it, she is able to embody the historical character of female cacique leader Yuisa, who is also dealing with a hurricane disaster, but in colonial times. It is important to note that in Rosado's story, Black characters and Spanish colonizers are also helping, thus providing a united front consisting of the three ethnic groups in Puerto Rico. La Borinqueña wakes up from the mystical experience and thanks Supergirl for helping (thus addressing indirectly the US audience). She also admires the Taíno chieftain's leadership and thanks Yuisa for "showing me your compassion for our people and the strength to lead

La Borinqueña #2. La Borinqueña has mystical contact with legendary Taíno cacique Mabodamaca.

them through tough times. You inspire me to continue to do whatever it takes to make things right on the island and I will do everything in my power to always protect the people of Puerto Rico" (Rosado, 72).

After *Ricanstruction*, the second issue of *La Borinqueña* addressed Hurricane María's devastation and the corruption of American corporations. Miranda-Rodríguez created Dulcinea, a fictional corporation that represents everything evil in the colonization and exploitation of Borinquen / Puerto Rico. The plot of the issue ends with a cliffhanger where La Borinqueña is trapped in the Puerto Rican star amulet she possesses and is held captive by the evil corporation. Dulcinea is taking advantage of the reconstruction of Puerto Rico to make money and wants to dispose of La Borinqueña, who not only fights the corporations in her superhero form but also, as Marisol, supports and protects

Ricanstruction. In Will Rosado's "Today, Yesterday, and Tomorrow," La Borinqueña meets legendary cacica Yuisa and shares her pain.

the University of Puerto Rico students who are protesting the actions of the government and the US corporations. In an emotional scene, La Borinqueña touches the statue of Cara del índio in Isabela, which allows her to communicate with cacique Mabodamaca and to embody his destruction at the hands of the Spanish. At the end of the experience, the superheroine is inspired and says to the cacique, "Cacique Mabodamaca . . . Thank you for your strength and for your sacrifice. I am beginning to understand now that everything here is connected. History, Nature, Spirituality . . . All of it. When I begin to understand it all, then I know I can make a change" (n.pag.).

It is important to point out that Miranda-Rodríguez portrays Puerto Rican culture as racially and ethnically mixed but positions the Taíno heritage at the center of the model, downplays Christian elements in the nationalist mysticism associated with European imperialism, and vilifies capitalist corporations. He gives us a heroine that is racially Black, and there is even a scene in issue 2 where her Afro-Caribbean heritage is asserted when the Black Afro-Caribbean man she saves in New York sees her as Yemayá (the Yoruba Orisha / Goddess).[20] However, she is also able to communicate with the Taínos because she shares with them a political ideology of resistance as well as the cultural elements associated with the traditional cultural nationalism that embodies a shared racial, cultural, and geographical experience. Ironically, the author achieves this message through the superhero genre, a type of narrative normally associated with American exceptionalism. As a diaspora comic book creator he is able to integrate the American lore into the resistance ethnic nationalist ideology, and the two clash to produce a wonderful contrast in a work that hopefully will be able to maintain its economic independence and subversive streak.

As I was growing up in Puerto Rico, I thought the Taínos were extinct because I was embracing national ideas that, although well intentioned in the mid-twentieth century, have now become outdated as perceptions of race, gender, and identity are changing. One of the articles that more recently made me understand the quest for a Taíno identity was scholar J. Klor de Alva's article "Aztlán, Borinquen and Hispanic Nationalism in the United States," in which the writer explores how similar the utopian Indigenous aspects of Aztlán and Borinquen are for Latinx Mexicans and Puerto Ricans respectively. Even though their goals may not be achievable (or may seem too far-fetched and utopian to some), they are actually good for uniting the Latinx communities (158). The difference, according to Klor de Alva, is that Puerto Ricans (inside and outside the island) share American citizenship, so their geographical and political relationship is more intense and interactive in comparison to the Chicanos' relationship to Mexico (154). Klor de Alva further suggests that these Latinx Boricuas could play a role in the ideological development of Puerto Rico:

> The shift from a deployment—for purposes of political organization—of romantic, naïve symbolic forms, to a reliance on a very real fervor for independence gave Puerto Rican cultural nationalists a continuous public forum. Whether this forum can ultimately become an effective one for political organizing in the U.S. depends on the fate of Puerto Rico, and the extent to which the interest in the island's independence can be transformed, through a class-based cultural nationalism, into an interest in pro-independentism electoral politics. (159)

The reason why both *Turey El Taíno* and *La Borinqueña* are important comic book narratives is that, even though one is from the island and the other one is from the US mainland, both position the Taíno heritage at the center, as a foundational element of Puerto Rican identity. *Turey* avoids anti-Spanish sentiment for the most part, so it is not typically perceived as a political comic. However, by recreating modern Puerto Rican society through a Taíno performance, it allows Puerto Ricans to embody a part of their culture that the schools teach is there in their biological DNA and culture, but which they cannot access as an ethnic identity. The comic book is an important step in allowing Puerto Rican readers to begin reconceptualizing themselves inside the mestizaje that is biased mostly toward Eurocentrism. Still, *Turey El Taíno* follows the well-intentioned ICP institutional approach that tries to bring the Taínos to the present to be absorbed into a modern Puerto Rican nationalism that has not always worked. *La Borinqueña* provides a more aggressive struggle and decolonizing narrative. While Miranda-Rodríguez offers a more Latinx antagonistic view against the two empires and positions the Taínos as founding fathers, he still believes in the cultural and geographical connections with the Taínos that the ICP promotes in their comic about the Taíno heritage. However, the main difference is that he does not want to bring the Taínos to us (like Álvarez-Rivón's *Turey* does); he wants to bring us to the Taínos. This is why La Borinqueña's source of power comes from the cemís and Taíno goddesses and not from the European traditions. The comic thus signals that we are part of a mixed culture, but we can exist outside of Eurocentrism and the modern Western politics that have given us so much pain and a world where the actions of President Donald Trump are made possible.

Notes

1. Editor Neil Schwartz writes: "I also have learned more about Puerto Rico than I have ever known, and I find that to be both wonderful and sad. Wonderful because of the amazing culture that began with the Taíno and has continued to thrive, despite what they've been through" (*Puerto Rico Strong*, 7).

2. Vita Ayala and Jamie Jones, "Areytos," *Puerto Rico Strong* (Lion Forge, 2018), 41–50.

3. Alejandro Rosado and Shariff Musallam, "A Taíno's Tale," *Puerto Rico Strong* (Lion Forge, 2018), 80–85.

4. I assume it is a Puerto Rican school because there is a Puerto Rican flag in front of the building.

5. Joanette Gil, "Taíno Online," *Puerto Rico Strong* (Lion Forge, 2018), 140–42.

6. Javier Cruz Winnick, "Knowledge of Self," *Puerto Rico Strong* (Lion Forge, 2018), 143–47.

7. For more insight about the history of the Taínos, read Ricardo Alegría's "The Study of Aboriginal Peoples: Multiple Ways of Knowing."

8. Scholar L. Atono Cutler writes: "The 19th century saw the development of nationalistic sentiments, primarily among the criollo class of the island. One expression of these tendencies took the form of what is referred to in Latin America as the Indigenismo movement, or the nationalistic appropriation of Indian imagery and incorporation of this imagery as a symbol of national identity. Indians came to be viewed as the first Puerto Ricans that resisted the Spanish empire or as victims of the abuses and brutality of colonization. Most intellectuals of this era agreed on the "extinction" of the Indians in the early colonial period, but they also concluded that the bulk of the Puerto Rican rural populations (i.e., not the whole population of the island) result from biological and cultural mixing of Indians, Spanish, and Africans" (n.pag.).

9. It is important to note that by this time the Taínos had already become nationalist metaphors of a subaltern identity used by the Puerto Rican bourgeoisie for revolutionary purposes.

10. Scholar L. Atono Cuter writes that Alegría played a very important role because he used the "three races/culture" idea as the basis of Puerto Rican identity which he was able to institutionalize through the government and the Instituto de Cultura Puertorriqueña (ICP). Cuter adds that while this hybrid mode was key in creating a more homogenous identity on paper, "it is also based on a fallacy of racial, cultural, and class equality" (n.pag.). This approach shifted Puerto Rican nationalism from an ideological and political concept to a cultural model. Some of these criticisms are evident in the ICP comic's presentation of Taíno heritage.

11. Luis J. Lacourt, "Turey El Taíno, para siempre: parte 1 de 2."
12. Luis J. Lacourt, "Turey El Taíno, para siempre: parte 1 de 2."
13. Luis J. Lacourt, "Turey El Taíno, para siempre: parte 1 de 2."
14. Luis J. Lacourt, "Turey El Taíno, para siempre: parte 1 de 2."
15. White Anglo-Saxon Protestant.
16. *La Borinqueña*, issue 1.
17. I will discuss more about Borinqueña and her crossover with DC Comics in my upcoming book about Puerto Rico and the superhero genre.
18. Will Rosado, "Today, Yesterday, and Tomorrow," *Ricanstruction*, 68–73.
19. A cemí is a small sacred icon that used to be sculpted by the Taínos.
20. This scene is important for the author to avoid accusations of being too nostalgic about Taíno culture and ignoring Blackness.

Works Cited

Acevedo, Ramón Luis. "Los límites de la narrativa indianista en Puerto Rico: Tapia, Betances y Marqués." *Revista de estudios hispánicos* 25, no. 1–2 (1998): 93–112.

Aguado Charneco, Antonio, and Hector Virella. "Nuestra Herencia Taína." *ICePé.cómic*. Instituto de Cultura Puertorriqueña. Issue 2 (2002); 2nd ed. (2008).

Alegría, Ricardo. "The Study of Aboriginal Peoples: Multiple Ways of Knowing." In *The Indigenous People of the Caribbean*, edited by Samuel Wilson, 9–19. University Press of Florida, 1997.

Álvarez-Rivón, Ricardo. *Turey El Taíno*. Tomo 1, Programa de Servicios Bibliotecarios y de Información, 2006.

———, *Turey El Taíno*. Tomo 2, Programa de Servicios Bibliotecarios y de Información, 2006.

Betances, Ramón Emeterio. *Los dos índios*. Trans. José Emilio González. Congreso Nacional Hostosiano, 1998.

Castanha, Tony. *The Myth of Indigenous Caribbean Extinction: Continuity and Reclamation in Borikén (Puerto Rico)*. Palgrave McMillan, 2011.

Cuter, L. Atono. "Indigenous Revival, Indigeneity, and Borikén." *Centro: Journal for the Center of Puerto Rican Studies* 27, no. 1 (Spring 2015): 207–47.

Feliciano-Santos, Sherina. "An Inconceivable Indigeneity: The Historical, Cultural, and Interactional Dimensions of Puerto Rican Taíno Activism." Unpublished dissertation, University of Michigan, 2011.

García, Ivonne. "Diasporic Intersectionality: Colonial History and Puerto Rican Hero Narratives in *21: The Story of Roberto Clemente* and *La Borinqueña*." *The Routledge Companion to Gender, Sex and Latin American Culture*, edited by Frederick Luis Aldama, 71–82. Routledge, 2018.

Klor de Alva, J. Jorge. "Aztlán, Borinquen and Hispanic Nationalism in the United States." *Aztlán: Essays on the Chicano Homeland*. Academia/El Norte Publications, 1989, pp. 135–71.

Lacourt, Luis J. "Turey El Taíno, para siempre: parte 1 de 2." https://web.archive.org/web/20111110072658/http://www.f3comics.com/?p=1097.

López-Baralt, Mercedes. *El mito taíno: Raíz y proyecciones en la amazonía continental*. Huracán, 1976, 3rd ed., 1999.

Lopez, Marco et al., eds. *Puerto Rico Strong*. Lion Forge, 2018.

Martínez-San Miguel, Yolanda. "Taíno Warriors?: Strategies for Recovering Indigenous Voices in Colonial and Contemporary Hispanic Caribbean Discourses." *Centro: Journal for the Center of Puerto Rican Studies* 23, no. 1 (Spring 2011): 196–215.

Miranda-Rodríguez, David. *La Borinqueña*. Issue 1. Somos Arte, 2016.

———. *La Borinqueña*. Issue 2. Somos Arte, 2018.
Miranda-Rodríguez, David, ed. *Ricanstruction: Reminiscing & Rebuilding Puerto Rico*. Somos Arte, 2018.
Muratti-Toro, José E. *La furia de Juracán*. Editorial 360, 2017.
Ramírez, Miriam. *El último taíno*. Self-published, 2018.
Tapia y Rivera, Alejandro. *La palma del cacique*. Puerto Rico eBooks, 2015.

PART III
DECOLONIAL IMAGINARIES
TERRA NORTH

Securing Stones in the Sky: Word-Drawn Recreations of Oral Trickster Tales

Jordan Clapper

> *So you see, we got to keep our language. God liked us so much, he let us walk away from the tower with our words. So we walked across the water, and God raised stones we could step on. We walked and kept walking. The stones eventually led us to land. We stepped onto the shore and kept walking.*
> —Grandmother

My grandmother told me this story at her kitchen table in her home on White Eagle in Oklahoma. She did so that I might pass it to my son. If there's a planet left in my son's future, he may tell his children, for narratives, one might well argue, not only *are* transferable, but *must* be transferable for them to function as narratives. As James Phelan puts it, narrative "is telling a particular story to a particular audience in a particular situation for, presumably, a particular purpose" (Phelan 4). For many Indigenous tribes of North America, this transferability has traditionally taken the form of orality. But orality has certain limitations.[1] Historically, oral narratives are embodied by a storyteller, but access to a physical storyteller is not always possible for those interested in engaging with Indigenous stories. Comics are one way to help bridge this transferability gap, allowing listeners to experience traditional stories through the dual representations of visual art and text.

Natives have had a limited role when it comes to comics, usually "appearing as sidekicks, the easily disposable, and the preternaturally ecological" (Aldama 2010). This kind of appropriation, "removing Indianness—or better fragments of it—from context," as Richard C. King views it, casts Natives as "alien forms, according to Eurocentric ideals, fears, and preoccupations" (215). These images have a weighty tradition in the United States and Canada, like other racial stereotypes in the comics tradition; they are "positioned against mythical images of America's physical, moral, and intellectual superiority" (Pewewardy). Western artists and writers have frequently appropriated and colonized Indigenous characters, images, and identities; the kachina-themed Hopi villains in Buzz Dixon's *NFL Superpro* or the Indigenous-powered superheroes like Black Crow are examples. As Michael Sheyahshe puts it, "stories reflecting the noble savage theme became extremely popular" (9) as the popularity of comics grew. In this way, indigeneity has served as a commodifiable substance that can be molded into whatever the artist, writer, or culture needs it to be.

How, then, do Indigenous peoples use comics to tell their stories? Is indigeneity drowned in the comics medium, or can indigeneity be made a driving force of narratives in this form? While historically, comics have not been kind to Indigenous characters, over time, new images of ethnic characters have become "a strange mix of cultural hybridity" (Pewewardy) that enables Indigenous comics to "rid themselves of the shackles of misrepresentation" (Sheyahshe 11). And resistance is evident. Tony Chavarria has shown how Indigenous artists represent their traditions "as a foundation mixed with outside influences to comment on their world and lifeways" (49), texturing their art and "smash[ing] superficial boundaries to become anthropological texts, social commentary, commercial enterprise, and, ultimately, fine art" (48). Sarah Henzi has illustrated the ways that Indigenous writing and revisioning have textured the comics scene, while Jessica Langston has examined similarities between oral storytelling and graphic form: their use in educating further generations, their fluid treatment of time, their adaptability across "socio-historical contexts and audiences," and their interactivity between "teller and audience, or between the images and reader" (116). Among this variety of Indigenous comics, one subgenre that has not received much scholarly or creative attention is the Indigenous narrative that uses comics to relate tribe-specific cultural stories and traditions. These texts rest at the intersection of Indigenous tradition and contemporary comic form, making use of a modern medium to relate formative, world-building narratives—like my grandmother's story—from specific tribes. The collection of graphic trickster tales that forms the focus of my discussion illustrates the striking potential of comics to transfer Indigenous narratives through visual and verbal projections of orality, representing voice, character, and Native worldviews to further texture this medium.

Trickster: Native American Tales, A Graphic Collection (2010)[2] brings together Indigenous storytellers with non-Indigenous artists to relate their trickster stories from specific tribes. But its storytelling agency is clearly secured in the hands of the storytellers and their tribes through various visual and textual techniques. In these tales, visual strategies serve and even enhance the strategies of oral narrative.

The comics in *Trickster* keep orality, and thus indigeneity, as their defining force through various textual means. Above, we have the first panel of "Rabbit's Choctaw Tail Tale." On the surface, the art certainly seems western. Pat Lewis's

Opening panel of "Rabbit's Choctaw Tail Tale."

cartoony style, complete with overly expressive faces, oversized, dark eyebrows, simplistic features and colors, and three-fingered hands carries features of western cartoons at large. The images complement the story that follows, the tale of how Rabbit, a trickster figure, lost his long tail due to his arrogance and his talkative nature. In this first panel, indigeneity signals itself as the central storytelling force of this tale. The second word of the title, Choctaw, speaks to a specific culture, that of the storyteller, Tim Tingle, listed in the contributors' section as "an Oklahoma Choctaw and touring storyteller and writer" (Dembicki 231). While the storytelling credits are a paratextual feature, here they signal indigeneity by showing the connection between the narrative power of the words, inspired by the oral tradition, and the storyteller's connection to a stated cultural group.[3] The credits recognize the interdependent narrative and artistic features of the story: the words are by Tim Tingle; the pictures are by Pat Lewis. This attribution is shared by other comics in the collection. Often, authentication follows levels of "historical continuity" that require "adjudication at state, federal, and global levels," as Stephanie Nohelani, Andrea Smith,[4] and Michelle H. Raheja theorize (111). The spectrum of cultural identities is defined by federal standards, such as blood quantum, that are aimed at Indigenous erasure over time. In comics like those in *Trickster*, indigeneity is perpetuated through the visual and textual representation of identity through cultural stories. The collection signals that the orality is the driving force behind the narrative, and their oral provenance is expressed in various visible and textual techniques that relate back to the many voices that the orator must adopt to tell their tale.

In this way, the narration that pervades the frames recasts the western art to serve Indigenous stories. The opening sentence—"Way and way long ago, in the woods of Choctaw Country, lived Rabbit" (Tingle 79)—signifies the oral tradition working in concert with the western artist's images. This tale is not just a tale of *a* rabbit that loses its tail; it is a tale of Rabbit, a trickster figure and worthy of his own capitalized identity, inspired by a specific cultural tradition. Rabbit is not a western figure simply because he is drawn by a western artist; he is an Indigenous figure that has been brought into a contemporary art form. As Kai Mikkonen puts it, "The viewing of images in comics is also obviously indirect to the extent that pictures interact with the words that surround them, are superimposed on them, or are placed within their space, and thus what is seen in the images becomes filtered and interpreted by words and verbal statements" (75). The non-western orality shapes the interpretation of the western art, necessitating a shift away from the purely western view of the art to an interpretation that must first filter through the words. The art styles and narrations in *Trickster* converge to showcase indigeneity in a postcolonial world. This type of collaborative comic, forged by Indigenous storytellers and western artists, thus constitutes a hybrid form that reframes seemingly western traditions of comics storytelling to embrace indigeneity and relate a tale that is accessible to Indigenous and western readers alike.

In traditional Indigenous tales, the orator takes on a number of personas, characters, spirits, and voices. Comics adapt these roles in different ways. The tale "Coyote and the Pebbles" offers a vivid example of how comics can represent the many voices typical to Indigenous narrative in distinct ways. A trickster tale told by Dayton Edmonds, a Caddo storyteller and minister, with art by Micah Farritor, "Coyote" explains the origin of the stars while imparting the wisdom of accepting what we cannot change. This trickster tale does the dual work of explaining one aspect of a culture's world and delivering a moral that grounds the cosmic mess-up of the eponymous Coyote. The voices fall into three distinct categories. The most powerful voice is that of the narrator, which I refer to as the "orator" here to emphasize the orality behind the narrative. The orator delivers the context in the form of narration boxes, rectangular text bubbles that give larger meaning and explain the storyworld to both insiders and outsiders of the tale. Visual narratives must split up this world-building force. Within visual media, narration "relates intimately to the effort to distinguish telling from showing or presenting from representing" (Herman et al. 342). The narration stems from the orator relating details from a heterodiegetic position, only existing as it relates to the temporally distant path it has traveled to be related by the orator through the narration. The other voices are embodied in the characters—the individual agents that are subject to the world-building force of the narration and the narrative as a whole—and the moral agent, the entity within the narrative that delivers guidance for both the characters and the listeners. Here, it is represented by the Great Mystery, a higher order character. In practice, these voices overlap depending on the story. For "Coyote and the Pebbles," however, these roles are distinct and are represented in different ways, both textually and visually.

The orality in "Coyote and the Pebbles" is first enacted by text boxes, which channel the cultural focalization to frame the story as an Indigenous one. The story opens with images of the landscape of the night and the creatures that inhabit it. The narrative boxes frame the story: "When the Mother Earth was extremely young, things were not as they are now. Just as things are not now as they will be, for growth and change are constant. One night, the night creatures gathered and called to the Great Mystery, the mystery that dwells within us and around us" (Edmonds 5). The art doesn't immediately signal a specific type of experience, but the narrative boxes provide context as to the time and place of the narrative: a nighttime version of Earth not long after its creation. The visual art, contained by the narrative time frame, cannot depict the relation to the present of the listener. The textual narration does the work of relating this temporally distant narrative to the point of view of a present-day listener.

The orator accomplishes this relation within a single instance in the narration: "Coyote, a day-and-night creature, was a little late for the meeting. Some say he was running on Indian time" (Edmonds 8). The orator puts a textual flourish into the story that could not have been possible if the story had not traveled through colonial times in order to be delivered. This referential humor, in line with other uses of humor within trickster tales, uses the language of the colonizer to refer to the culturally intended audience: Natives. "Indian" is still used as the pejorative and legal terminology for the colonized Indigenous population in the United States. The colonizing power is diminished by activating an insider joke by referring to "Indian time," the term used to refer to the lateness Natives see themselves experiencing when adhering to the western idea of punctuality. Things get done when they're done. This is an informed stance, one that bolsters the orator's reliability, something that Derek Parker Royal comments on in examining (and appreciating) Native noir comics: "our appreciation and enjoyment of a comic becomes dependent on its author's representational reliability and resistance to objectification." Filtered through an orator that has experienced the colonial lineage, this joke is an instance where, as Jessica Langston hopes, "these texts are adopting *and* adapting the colonizer's tradition for their own purposes" (122). "Coyote" sits squarely within this Indigenous "tradition," of self-referential comedy that both highlights and trivializes, but also recognizes colonial trauma. It centers the comedy around Coyote, as well as putting the orator within this lineage of Indigenous storytellers, part of the "some say." This kind of "insiderness" is not immediately evident in the art and requires the orator to make a connection to a larger body of knowledge. As Scott McCloud puts it, "Pictures are received information. They need no formal education to 'get the message.' The message is instantaneous. Writing is perceived information. It takes time and specialized knowledge to decode the abstract symbols of language" (McCloud *Understanding* 49). The narration is able to refer back to the larger narrative power and structure of the orator and the larger community that could construct a joke around the concept of Indian time.

The narration maintains a consistent presence throughout the story by interpreting the actions and images that we are presented with, which equally maintains the explicit presence of the orator. Some of the clarifications are minor and confirm what the reader can observe themselves, such as explaining that Coyote approaches a lake to collect the pebbles and that he then drops them into his shirt (Edmonds 11), but some of the explanations relate specifically to the abilities of the characters and to the larger cultural usage of these characters. On the first page of the comic, the characters pictured are Owl, Deer, Raccoon, Rabbit, and Fox, with subsequent pages introducing more characters. These characters are all depicted as animals, with nothing notably spectacular about their appearances. On the first panel of the second page, we see Rabbit at one corner of the panel, but on the opposite side, we see a man in a shirt with a frog printed on the front. We're initially introduced to all of the characters as animals, so the presence of a human is surprising. The second panel has Fox speaking, "Frog is right. The day creatures have the sun . . ." This is Frog, not just some human. Reading top to bottom, Fox's dialogue is privileged first, so at the bottom of the page, the narration box that comes in serves as a transition to the third panel: "Fox then changes into a woman" (6), the first gendering of a character in the narrative. Fox is now depicted as a human female: her hair is orange and white; her fur is now depicted as clothing; and we see the remnants of her tail. The narration establishes the shape-shifting abilities of these creatures by explaining their ability to "change," which distinguishes them as nonhuman, despite their human forms, and speaks to their importance and power.

When Coyote and Raven meet to discuss Coyote's tardiness, the seven panels that show their interaction are guided by the narrative boxes that make use of ellipses to texture the panel transitions and temporality of the individual panels. We have three panels of them speaking in their animal forms. Coyote transforms from an animal with an accompanying text box that reads, "Coyote turns to his human form . . ." (8). Crow lands by the sixth panel, then changing "into her human form . . ." (9). These transformations and their descriptions are always accompanied by ellipses, suggesting that they are always descriptions in progress. We aren't necessarily made privy to these details after the fact but as they are occurring, again giving the story a certain presentness. The transformations become more rapid, some creatures like Fox changing back and forth from animal to human to animal with the span of only three panels (16–17), but the orator does not continually address them. The narration builds what could be considered fantastic elements as purely mundane, just facts within the given cultural worldview.

The ellipses in the narration are also a textual-visual indicator that the orator is withholding information from the reader. When the narration states,

Coyote transforms.

"Coyote turns to his human form . . ." (Edmonds 8), or "As Raven changes into her human form . . ." (9), the narration box is not there simply for the sake of clarification, nor a stylistic exclusion of an artistic detail. The box indicates a moment of representative exclusion and slow-down. It would not be difficult for the artist, in theory, to represent states of transformation, remnants of which we see in Fox's transitory tail. In Proudstar's *Tribal Force*, characters like Little Big Horn undergo transformations, and in Elizabeth LaPensée's *Deer Woman: An Anthology*, numerous women transform into a revisioning of the mythical Deer Woman, many of which show transition images. The ellipses in "Coyote" signal a narrative compromise between the orator and the artist. The ellipses slow down the transition between the center panel and the bottom panel. Coyote and Raven are in their animal forms, and then Coyote is not. The reader is left to dwell on that bit of narration. There is no puff of smoke or any other such stylistic representation to indicate that the transformation is quick, nor are there transitory visual indicators to suggest that the process is slow. It is a moment of temporal uncertainty. Those within the culture may have a greater understanding as to how these transformations occur, but outsiders probably would not. The orator creates this moment as a way to signal that there is something we don't know, that we do not get to know, by relegating the transformations to the gutter, "an absent space that is part of the story . . . where the reader fills in the blank between pictured moments, participating imaginatively in the creation of the story" (Chute 23). In this way, the orator becomes not only a contextualizer, interpreting the actions and locations for the listener/reader, but also a cultural knowledge-keeper, one that speaks to two implied readers. You may not laugh at "Indian time" because you simply won't get it if you aren't part of the in-crowd; you may grapple with these temporally slow moments because how these transformations work may not have a suitable correlative in your mind.

In other ways, the ellipses, while still maintaining narrative control, turn the reader's eye to the art, creating a symphonic effect between these different types of storytelling. As Coyote is searching for a place in the sky to secure his stones and paint his portrait, the orator sets the panel, "Coyote looked and ran to the left, then to the right . . . left again, then right, faster and faster, looking for a place to draw his portrait" (Edmonds 13). This occurs in a single panel. The art simply depicts Coyote, in human form, holding onto a tree with one hand. He looks to be mid-step, but the art does not intrinsically suggest panic. The narration fills in these gaps, doing the narrative work of slowing down the panel by making the reader linger, the ellipses creating those gaps, while also speeding up the action contained within the single panel. According to the narration, Coyote performs five specific actions: looking and then running at least four directions, but even then, the narration suggests there could be even more we aren't seeing.

It interprets the art for us while allowing us the cognitive space to imagine what actions aren't being explicitly depicted. Examining the ways in which narrative space is depicted, Marie-Laure Ryan recognizes that "many stories cannot be followed without mentally simulating the movements of characters, whether physical or mental, through the storyworld" (*Narrative Space*). In a medium where some of the interpretation has been done for the reader, the orator is an integral part of the depiction of specific movement in frames where that movement may not be easily parsed from the image.

On the final page of the comic, the ellipses turn us to the art again, each panel making use of present tense to reference the implied readers' present time.

Coyote is set atop the first frame and howling at the sky. The narration beckons us to both recognize Coyote's plight and to look past it, to appreciate the action and the art that depicts his mistake. The ellipses leading out of the first panel are continued into the second panel. Coyote is focused in the frame, but narratively, the reader is guided to the pebbles in the sky, to take in the whole of the narrative picture present. Hillary Chute sees comics as resisting a "linear reading in the same way prose" compels us to do so, a "[comic's] 'all-at-onceness,' or its 'symphonic effect'" (25). We linger in the art, guided by the ellipses, and stay in that moment. The last panel sees the ellipses pull double-duty in keeping us lingering in time and in space. The narration does the interpretive work by bringing the story into a present worldview. Until this last page, the story is narrated in the past tense; here, it is in the present. The stones didn't "become" or face any further interpretation. We *call* them stars. They are at once the objects that Coyote and the night creatures placed there *and* the present-day celestial bodies that we can observe and experience for ourselves.

Word-Drawn Recreations of Oral Trickster Tales 245

Coyote rushes to find space to draw his starry portrait.

The methods by which the orality is invoked in the comic correspond to their role in the story. These forms of delivery are represented aesthetically and confer certain expectations about the speaker. Characters' speech bubbles are smooth, unfettered by texture or variation. They are perfectly round, and each one leads to a mouth, to signify the owner of that speech. The speech bubble is the correlative to the quotation mark: unfettered, direct discourse that corresponds to a particular character. In "Coyote," the owner of a speech bubble is never in question. No speech bubbles go off the frame, locking them in the temporality of that frame. Their smoothness signals that a reader does not need to focus on the technique, the use of the speech bubble (similar to how we might ignore quotation marks). The narration boxes are far more rigid, consisting of rectangular boxes with no special fonts. This style corresponds to their function. The orator is temporally situated from the position of the story as it is told, filtered through the perspective of a speaker looking back through time and telling the story from an implied present, far forward but still in the world of the narrative. Their set style confers a certain kind of signposting. We're meant to pay special attention to them and treat their descriptions as objective. The orator is the only voice that does not directly interact with the rest of the voices in the narrative. The narrative boxes' presence changes the focus of the reader, and when the orator is not present, our focus shifts back to the characters or the Great Mystery.

The Great Mystery is distinguished from the other characters in the story in the form of a great, booming voice that confers knowledge onto both the characters and the listeners/readers of the tale. The Great Mystery provides the greatest visual variation of the voices in "Coyote." It alone speaks in jagged, enlarged speech bubbles with no guiding line. The font is the same as those in other speech bubbles and the narration boxes, but the font is bolded, giving visible weight to the words being spoken. When the night creatures call on the Great Mystery, it responds, "What is it that you need?" (Edmonds 5). It conveys knowledge to both characters and listeners. The characters lack the knowledge to change the world, to put light in the night sky, so the Great Mystery provides

Stones in the sky.

that knowledge. The bolded words are ones to stop and listen to rather than argue with; there is little to interpret, as the wisdom dispensed is more or less unquestionable to the characters and the implied reader. Its jagged edges distinguish it as more than a mere speech bubble; its words are not purely meant for character-to-character interaction. The knowledge it contains cannot be visibly represented in something as plain-spoken as speech, but looks as though it is pushing against the rounded edges of the normal speech bubble. The characters speak to each other with smoothness, and we are but voyeurs to their conversations; the Great Mystery speaks to both the reader and the characters, and we are meant to listen.

The Great Mystery instructs the night creatures.

The Great Mystery's oral wisdom is unbound from the typical contained temporality of the comic frame by bleeding into the gutter. The Great Mystery explains, after hearing their call for light.

These lines are some of the first that vary from the walled-off chronology of the panels. Any block or bubble of text corresponds to some measure of temporality in the panel where it is used. Each panel represents a specific chunk of story time, so each use of text correlates to the temporality contained in that box. For example, in the panel where Coyote turns into his human form (8), the narrative box explains the act of transformation leading up to the panel, Raven speaks, and Coyote speaks. This is the measure of time contained in the panel: the aftermath of the transformation and the space of two lines of dialogue between Raven and Coyote. Once we change panels (and subsequently pages), we move forward in the narrative to the next chunk of time, where Coyote is despondent and says, "They think only of themselves!" (9). The first two instances of the Great Mystery speaking vaguely correspond to the story time in the panels. "What is it you need?" (5) relates to the question spoken in the previous panel, hovering above a great waterfall but still contained in the panel, and the first set of instructions, those of going to the bodies of water to retrieve stones (7), is also contained in a panel. Both of these sit above panels of scenery, suggesting a certain timelessness to their employment. McCloud points out that words "have been telling stories clearly for millennia. They've done just fine without pictures," so in comics, they need to flow with the images, to "work together seamlessly enough that readers barely notice when switching from one to another" (McCloud *Making Comics* 31). These bubbles function as a form of dialogue, characterized by the scenery, but no characters are in the panels for these first two bubbles, suggesting that they are situated in the temporality of that panel.

The next two bubbles break with the formatting of the rest of the comic in one significant way: they exist in the gutter. "Gather for me . . ." and "I want you to . . ." (7) exist in a liminal position on the page. By their positioning in the gutter, they are unbounded from a strict narrative representation of time in the comic. The third bubble hovers between a panel of the night creatures gathering stones, as per instruction, and a panel of a few of the night creatures carrying those stones, jagged like shimmering stars, up a mountain. The Great Mystery is likely not speaking in the moment contained in the panel. The next bubble follows a similar fashion, overlapping the panels and gutter between the previous panel and the final panel, the characters reaching high, with human hands, to put the stones in the sky. The Great Mystery is visibly able to pass through and speak to different times, suggesting that we are to pay attention to these words in our own experienced time to hear the lesson: this is how we came to have our stars, and we should learn something from Coyote's mistake. This expression of myth, which relates to a certain culture's experience with meaning and the world, as Paula Gunn Allen points out, connects readers past and present. As she puts it, "the mythic dimension of experience—the psychospiritual ordering of nonordinary knowledge—is an experience that all peoples, past, present, and to come, have in common" (Allen 104), this experience related through the comic to present readers.

The only one who never hears the Great Mystery's words is excluded from the narrative purview of the great speaker: Coyote. The proximity of the written word to the characters or scenes being described is essential to their interactivity with one another. Coyote never hears the wisdom of the Great Mystery, which generates a sense of empathy for Coyote's uninformed position. In the beginning, he is late to the meeting and does not hear the instructions, rather receiving the information through his interaction with Raven. Coyote is a trickster: his engagement with the world is inherently flawed, both from his devil-may-care attitude and his very mythos, the fact that his archetype is meant to be a great disrupter to the universe. We initially see that he is positioned as an outsider, "a day-and-night creature" (Edmonds 8), which is reinforced narratively by his always being outside certain types of knowledge and being pushed away by the "true" night creatures that seek wisdom from the Great Mystery.

He essentially receives the same information secondhand, but his bravado is on full display: "I am the greatest artist in the world! Therefore, my drawing will be the largest and the best!" (9). His laziness causes the sky to become filled with the other creatures' portraits, until there is only one space left. He rushes, and "Keeping his eyes on where he wanted to be," which is a hint to the moral of the story, "and forgetting to watch where his feet were going . . . Coyote tripped, fell, and spilled his pebbles from his pouch, hat, and shirt" (13–14); the subsequent explosion destroys all of their portraits and leaves the sky as we see it now. Coyote is blamed and chastised for the destruction, and the creatures call on the Great Mystery once more. "What is going on?" (15), asks the Great Mystery. As the night creatures explain Coyote's error, he begins to retreat, hiding behind a rock. When the Great Mystery speaks again and tells them to sit, Coyote runs, separated from the other characters and the Great Mystery's speech bubble in the panel by a rocky cliff. Coyote has removed himself from the proximity of the other night creatures and thus subsequently misses the Great Mystery's further counsel. Coyote tends to be visibly separated from the Great Mystery's speech bubbles either by physical landmarks, like the cliff, or by gutters between panels. Here, the reader can see that Coyote is not privy to the Great Mystery's knowledge. This lack of access to the Great Mystery's knowledge is displayed visually and aids in showing the tragic nature of Coyote's archetype: cosmic clumsiness and never being in the right place at the right time. His lateness preempts his lack of proximity to the Great Mystery's teachings, and his fear and shame causes him to run away and miss the moral of the tale:

> The order of creation is already in place. Because the order of creation is already happening. We cannot change what has happened. We cannot go back to last month, last week, or even five minutes ago. Healing can happen. By looking at yesterday and its consequences, one can change tomorrow. (Edmonds 16–17)

The Great Mystery's words seem to reference a contemporary grappling with colonialism. Native peoples cannot change the history of colonization, but understanding that history can have ramifications on the future. Coyote's ignorance, the dissociation reinforced by the images, offers the implied reader an opportunity to connect with both the veiled lesson challenging colonialism and with Coyote's status as an outsider.

Coyote flees from the night creatures.

Is there a guiding force in comics that draws together all of the forms of representation on the page that puts the orator at its center? In comics, the mega-narrator is the entity that controls both the images and the text that come together in panels to relate a narrative. The storyteller in comics like "Coyote" functions in a similar manner, but the storyteller's roles have been divided into these different voices. But does this storyteller have control of the images? Why not simply use the term mega-narrator? For Kai Mikkonen, mega-narrator is related, in part, to the implied author:

> The two options of an extended mega-narrator or an implied author may or may not be accompanied by a (re)conceptualisation of the issue of narrative agency in comics through a new theoretical term . . . In comics storytelling, a similar "graphic composition device" or "comics composition device" could be envisioned. Concomitantly, a narrator in comics would then only refer to narrators as characters, or narrative voices when they can be distinguished from the author(s), i.e. cases when a narrative comic represents in some sense the act of narration itself, such as shows the narrator telling a story, while the overall narration is conceived in terms of an impersonal activity (narration) or "device." (135)

The mega-narrator is the entity that responds to the narrative situation present on the page. In many comics, *who* is responsible for the images we are given is not always clear. The art is, in part, a device either wielded by or responded to by the mega-narrator. Viewing the art as a "device" rather than its own narrator-based entity allows us to take up and examine the elements that a mega-narrator would have more control over, that is in the representation and interpretation of the elements on the page and mediating them to the reader. Each time an oral story is retold, it is authored anew; the author marks their place in the lineage that produced the narrative. Rather than a mega-narrator, a "mega-orator" puts emphasis on the orality of the text without needing to be constrained by the art.

"Coyote" and its orality contributes to the larger comics tradition, one with Indigenous input and grounding. Scott McCloud, a comics artist and theorist, helps us understand the complicated and culturally complex path that comics have taken to get to where they are today. He argues for the inclusion of the Bayeux Tapestry to Egyptian pictorial stories (hieroglyphics excluded) to complicate the notion of a purely western comics history. McCloud applies his definition of comics, "juxtaposed pictorial and other images in deliberate sequence, intended to convey information and/or to produce an aesthetic response in the viewer" (*Understanding* 9), to help explore the broader range of what constitutes a history of comics. McCloud's definition is open-ended, leaving open non-western modes of storytelling. For example, McCloud presents the story of Eight-deer Tiger's-claw, a Mixtec ruler, which was chronicled in a painted depiction and "'discovered' by Cortés around 1519" (10). McCloud, by including the Mixtec story, positions indigeneity directly within the comics tradition without suggesting that textual accompaniments, which would exclude a great number of Native languages and stories from the tradition, are the make-or-break component of comics. Jessica Langston examines the ways in which comics, the graphic novel in particular, are "key contemporary complement[s] to orature—not intended to replace the oral tradition, but rather to supplement and support it" (114). She connects comics to the earlier tradition of wampum belts, in particular Haudenosaunee wampum and Haida carvings. These practices, like comics, represent a physical, storable medium for stories. She also outlines four similarities between oral storytelling and comics: the lineage of knowledge and its transferability, the fluidity of time, the adaptability across various social and historical fields, and collaboration "between the teller and the audience, or between the images and the reader" (116). Consider the story poles of Joe Hillaire, orated by his daughter, Pauline Hillaire, in *A Totem Pole History: The Work of Lummi Carver Joe Hillaire*. The pole, like the image in a comic or wampum, is a part of the storytelling tradition, but the orator must relate the tale to the audience; the image and the oral work in conjunction to a larger tradition of storytelling.

The presence of an Indigenous storyteller in the storytelling process in a comic is not just crucial: it is a requirement, as they are the one to inform the art, the mega-narration, and the connection to indigeneity. Equally, the variations in storytelling show a flexibility and a conversation, a form of "evoking" described in Marie-Laure Ryan's examination of *Alice in Wonderland*: "the verbal and the visual version blend in the mind of the reader-spectator into one powerful image, each version filling in the gaps of the other" (139). In a comic retelling of an Indigenous tale, the narrative is expressed through both the textual and the visual to create a hybrid experience. This adaptability extends to contextual situations that can include the time of the telling and the audience, should they be Indigenous or western, or both, the range of representation allowing for several kinds of audiences. McCloud's examples show the ways that narrative has been transferred to a visual-textual medium, and "Coyote" is another extension of this transferability and visual orality. Indigenous storytellers have played an active role in the development of comics and in their contemporary trajectory, as comics "are historically one of the original formats of Native narrative" (Noori 59). The "implied author" of the comics tradition is not some white man sitting at a desk pumping out superhero comics; it is a lineage.

The last textual piece we are given in "Coyote and the Pebbles" is a uniquely stylized text box. The words contained within, "The End," are hollow and empty: the image of the nightscape mountain is visible in the words and the narration box, unlike any other text box in the rest of the comic. Sheyahshe points out why we study Native characters and, by extension, Native people that compose comics: "We are investigating not only *just* comic books or *just* the Indian characters in them, but also the understated meaning of the negotiated relationship of these two elements to each other" (190). Indigenous comics that relate traditional tales have a connection across time, describing the past, the present, and what will happen. No story that can be retold in such a manner truly has an end, because it describes a world always in process, the order of creation "already happening" (Edmonds 16). As long as it can be read, can be heard through the many voices of our many orators, like Indigenous peoples and indigeneity itself, comics like "Coyote" show a continued resistance to colonial endeavors in the comics tradition and what Indigenous inclusion and orality generates in that sphere.

Notes

1. Orality has a history of being cast as a form of backwardness, of negativity, of non-western primitivity. Margaret Noori, in examining how oral stories are brought to the visual tradition, reverses this stereotype, stating, "The oral tradition, rather than being romanticized as a signifier of illiteracy or preliteracy, can be recast as an alternative means of narrative transmission" (58).

2. The collection is distinctive in that it uses non-Indigenous artists to illustrate these tales. Like the medium of comics itself, this could be seen as problematic. Dembicki addresses this issue in an interview, where he explains that he had to find a way to make storytellers "feel comfortable with the process ... they weren't familiar with how we'd be able to translate these stories into a comic form" (Hansen). The storytellers were given the choice of what artists they would like to represent their tales from a list Dembicki put together.

3. It is not necessarily the person's indigeneity that makes a story inherently Indigenous but the larger connection that a person has to the story's position within a cultural framework that uses the story to explain a world(view) both within the story and for the culture in general.

4. It is worth noting that Andrea Smith's indigeneity has been proven flimsy or nonexistent, and though her response to the ordeal has been problematic, her work on indigeneity is nevertheless important and formative.

Works Cited

Aldama, Frederick Luis, ed. *Multicultural Comics: From Zap to Blue Beetle*. Austin: University of Texas Press, 2010.

Allen, Paula Gunn. *The Sacred Hoop: Recovering the Feminine in American Indian Traditions*. Boston: Beacon Press, 1992.

Chavarria, Tony. "Indigenous Comics in the United States." *World Literature Today* 83, no. 3 (2009): 47–49.

Chute, Hillary. *Why Comics?: From Underground to Everywhere*. New York: HarperCollins, 2017.

Dembicki, Matt. *Native American Folk Tales Take a Graphic Turn*. June 6, 2010. Audio.

———. *Trickster: Native American Tales: A Graphic Collection*. Golden, CO: Fulcrum Books, 2010.

Edmonds, Dayton. "Coyote and the Pebbles." *Trickster: Native American Tales: A Graphic Anthology*. Golden: Fulcrum Books, 2010. 5–18.

Henzi, Sarah. "'A Necessary Antidote': Graphic Novels, Comics, and Indigenous Writing." *Canadian Review of Comparative Literature* 43, no. 1 (2016): 23–38.

Herman, David, Manfred Jahn, and Marie-Laure Ryan, eds. *Routledge Encyclopedia of Narrative Theory*. New York: Routledge, 2005.

Hillaire, Pauline R. *A Totem Pole History: The Work of Lummi Carver Joe Hillaire*, edited by Gregory P. Fields. Lincoln: University of Nebraska Press, 2013.

King, Richard C. "Alter/Native Heroes: Native Americans, Comic Books, and the Struggle for Self-Definition." *Cultural Studies—Critical Methodologies* 9, no. 2 (2009): 214–23.

Langston, Jessica. "'Once Upon a Time This Was a True Story': Indigenous Peoples Graphic Novels and Orature." *The Canadian Alternative: Cartoonists, Comics, and Graphic Novels*, edited by Dominick Grace and Eric R. Hoffman, 113–26. Jackson: University Press of Mississippi, 2018.

LaPensée, Elizabeth, and Weshoyot Alvitre, eds. *Deer Woman: An Anthology*. Albuquerque, NM: Native Realities Publishing, 2017.

McCloud, Scott. *Making Comics: Storytelling Secrets of Comics, Manga and Graphic Novels*. New York: Harper, 2006.

———. *Understanding Comics: The Invisible Art*. New York: HarperCollins, 1993.

Noori, Margaret. "Native American Narratives from Early Art to Graphic Novels: How We See Stories / Ezhi-g'waabamaanaanig Aadizookaanag." *Multicultural Comics: From Zap to Blue Beetle*, edited by Frederick Aldama, 55–72. Austin: University of Texas Press, 2010. Web. November 14, 2018.

Pewewardy, Cornel. "From Subhuman to Superhuman: Images of First Nations Peoples in Comic Books." *SIMILE* 2.2 (2002): n.pag. Web. December 3, 2018.

Phelan, James. *Narrative as Rhetoric: Technique, Audiences, Ethics, Ideology*. Columbus: The Ohio State University Press, 1996. Theory and Interpretation of Narrative Series.

Proudstar, Jon. *Tribal Force*. Mystic Comics, 1996. Tribal Force.

Ryan, Marie-Laure. "Introduction and Overview." *Narrating Space, Spatializing Narrative: Where Narrative Theory and Geography Meet*. Columbus: The Ohio State University Press, 2016.

———. "Still Pictures." *Narrative across Media: The Languages of Storytelling*, edited by Marie-Laure Ryan, 139–44. Lincoln: University of Nebraska Press, 2004.

Teves, Stephanie Nohelani, Andrea Smith, and Michelle H. Raheja. "Introduction: Indigeneity." *Native Studies Keywords*. Tucson: University of Arizona Press, 2015. 109–18.

Tingle, Tim, and Pat Lewis. "Rabbit's Choctaw Tail Tale." *Trickster: Native American Tales: A Graphic Collection*. Golden, CO: Fulcrum Books, 2010. 79–88.

Super Indians and the Indigenous Comics Renaissance

James J. Donahue

Metropolis, Gotham City, Wakanda, Atlantis, Themyscira, Vegas Valley Paiute Reservation, Leaning Oak Reservation. These fictional locations are synonymous with the heroes that defend them: Superman, Batman, Black Panther, Aquaman, Wonder Woman, Captain Paiute, Super Indian.

    The latter two superheroes are not household names whose presence in a blockbuster movie guarantee commercial success. (At least not yet.) Rather, they are but two of the relatively new Native-created superheroes whose current series are both participating in as well as critiquing the superhero tradition in mainstream American comics. Possessing powers that manifested after accidents, secret identities that help protect their loved ones from being targeted, colorful spandex costumes, and an unshakeable moral code insisting that the innocent must be protected from those who would do them harm, Captain Paiute and Super Indian are in one respect Native versions of traditional Marvel- and DC-style comic book superheroes.[1] However, unlike their mainstream world-beater counterparts, Captain Paiute and Super Indian are not engaged in defending the planet from intergalactic threats like Doomsday, Darkseid, or Ares, or even human antagonists like Lex Luthor and the Joker, whose efforts are directed toward world domination or destructive chaos. Rather, these Native-created superheroes focus their attention on their immediate communities: reservations and the problems faced by contemporary tribal communities. With their ongoing hero series, Native creators Theo Tso (Las Vegas Paiute) and Arigon Starr (Kickapoo) are using the genre of the "superhero comic" to productively engage in tribal politics, raising awareness about just a few of the social and political injustices faced by contemporary Native peoples and their reservation communities. Additionally, these artists are also at the forefront of an Indigenous comics renaissance, joining numerous other Indigenous authors in exploring the rich diversity of content, style, and political importance of comic art.[2]

In his article "The Definition of the Superhero," Peter Coogan outlines the various criteria that define the figure of the comic book superhero. Building off of Judge Learned Hand's 1952 copyright ruling (that found "that Wonder Man copied and infringed upon Superman") and noting that both Wonder Man and Superman were "'champion[s] of the oppressed' who combat 'evil and injustice,'" Coogan identifies "[t]he mission convention" as "essential to the superhero genre." Put simply, "someone who does not act selflessly to aid others in times of need is not heroic and therefore not a hero" (77). However, selfless acts of heroism are not enough to identify a character as a "superhero" in the comics tradition (even if Arigon Starr will challenge this idea in her works, as we will see below). Additionally, traditional comic book superheroes must possess some kind of power, given that "[s]uperpowers are the most identifiable elements of the superhero genre" (78). And though it should go without saying, use of these powers must be limited to selfless acts of heroism; the Flash does not participate in track meets. Nor, of course, could Barry Allen do so without sacrificing his "secret identity," the final piece of the "three elements—mission, powers, and identity, or MPI—[that] establish the core of the genre" (82). As we will see below, both Captain Paiute and Super Indian possess the MPI matrix that recognizably identifies the comic book superhero.

Comic book superheroes also often employ a costume, which serves multiple purposes. Most importantly, it separates the heroic identity from the secret identity, allowing the two to remain individual personae (perhaps most famously in the split between the charming and self-confident Superman vs. the bumbling and socially inept Clark Kent). As Coogen notes, "the identity element comprises the codename and the costume, with the secret identity being a customary counterpart to the codename" (78). By noting it as a codename, Coogan is suggesting that the "secret identity" is the "true identity," while the superhero identity is a role, or a performance. We see this in the way that multiple individuals can assume the mantle of a superhero identity—and all wear similar versions of the costume—such as when John Stewart replaced Guy Gardner as Hal Jordan's backup in the Green Lantern Corps, or the way Peter Parker, Miles Morales, and Miguel O'Hara all simultaneously operate as Spider-Man in different narrative arcs. The costume, along with the codename, also does more than simply name the superhero; for Superman, "his codename expresses his character," where for Batman, "his codename embodies his biography." Similarly, Superman's bright use of primary colors not only marks him visually but also suggests his straightforward moral code, whereas Batman's dark costume—useful for prowling the city at night—reminds readers of his questionable moral character, not being above extreme acts of violence and even torture to achieve his ends. Superheroes also tend to—but need not always—possess some sort of emblem on their costume that operates as visual shorthand: Superman's "S" or Batman's bat chest piece have become common symbols in American popular culture, and serve as "iconic representations of the superhero identity" (79).³ Often, but again not always, these costumes employ some sort of mask, protecting the superhero's secret identity (and thus in theory if not in practice protecting the hero's loved ones from becoming targets for revenge). Clark Kent's glasses serve the same purpose, if in a reverse fashion, and some heroes like Wonder Woman wear no mask at all.

Of course, as with all literary genres, these distinctions are fluid by nature, and can be present to greater or lesser degrees without the risk of a character losing his/her superhero status. For instance, the Fantastic Four may have used codenames, but their nonheroic identities were never kept secret from the public. Luke Cage may have briefly gone by the moniker Power Man, but even early on that nickname was secondary to his given name. And the Black Panther is always the King of Wakanda. Similarly, there are various narrative conventions that are employed by superhero comic book story arcs, such as the articulation of an origin story for the superhero's powers (which often is also directly tied to the character's motivations for hero work), as well as continuity within the shared universe populated by other superheroes. As we will see below, both Super Indian and Captain Paiute possess origin stories that explain their powers and clearly tie their missions to local reservation politics. However, neither hero exists in the same "universe" as other superheroes; in fact, one of their functions is to remind readers that mainstream superheroes have never been concerned with reservation populations or their specific needs. This lack of connection to a larger narrative universe, however, should not be read as a deficiency. Not only is such a larger "universe" not possible with relatively new books from independent presses, but such participation would also work counter to the political aims of the two series. Where the various superheroes in the ever-expanding "Marvel Cinematic Universe" are largely engaged in international and even intergalactic warfare, protecting the United States specifically and planet Earth more generally from villains bent on domination, Captain Paiute and Super Indian are hyper-focused on protecting their immediate reservation communities from real-world threats.⁴

As *Captain Paiute* and *Super Indian* demonstrate, Native populations continue to face a variety of threats—physical threats, political threats, and the ever-increasing pressure to abandon their cultural heritage and assimilate into Euro-American culture—and the Native superheroes are used to confront such threats directly. Employing the "MPI matrix" that Coogan articulates, Native comic artists are constructing superheroes that draw from mainstream superhero comics in order to attend to the continued threats to Native peoples living in reservation communities. Additionally, Native-created heroes like Super Indian and Captain Paiute counter what Chris Gavalan has identified as the "superhero's imperial roots." For Gavalan, the "imperial superhero" is a manifestation of an "empire's claim as a rightfully dominating power over global possessions," and as such "[c]ontemporary superhero comics remain haunted by that imperial past" (34). For obvious reasons, Native superheroes break that mold, particularly by resisting the efforts of imperialization/colonization still engaged by the United States and Canada against tribal populations. Native superheroes similarly do not fall into Gavaler's identification of "the wellborn superhero," characterized as "millionaire playboy by day, crime-fighting do-gooder by night" (49)—think of Batman or the Green Arrow—particularly because these superheroes are reservation-born, and live lives "by day" facing all the socioeconomic issues involved in reservation life (which for many includes poverty). In this regard, Native superheroes can be read as charting out a new trajectory for superhero comics more generally, while still employing the foundational traits of the genre. In short, Native superheroes are not just traditional superheroes played by Native actors; rather, they are re-imaginations of the figure of the superhero, constructed to explicitly combat threats that mainstream superheroes have ignored.

Captain Paiute

Employing a visual aesthetic (especially in the cover art) and narrative form reminiscent of Bronze Age comic storytelling (roughly 1970–1985), Theo Tso's *Captain Paiute* follows the adventures of Luther Pah, mild-mannered tribal hydrologist by profession who, chosen by the Paiute water spirit Pah, was granted control over water (employing everything from mist to ice darts, or hardening his skin and giving him super strength, depending on the situation). Engaging contemporary politics immediately with this series, the first page[5] of issue #1 shows Captain Paiute in his costume proudly standing in front of the residents of the Vegas Valley Paiute Reservation (a barely fictionalized version of the Las Vegas Indian Colony reservation), many of whom are holding signs opposing some of the most devastating political pressures currently facing Native reservations: one sign reads "#NoDAPL" (referring to the Dakota Access Pipe Line), another reads "OIL = DEATH" (referencing the various times Indigenous populations have been relocated when their lands were discovered to sit atop oil reserves), and the final sign proclaims "IDLE NO MORE!" (referring to the grassroots protest movement started in 2012 in Canada originally founded to oppose Bill C-45[6]). This opening page is not situated in the story that follows, but rather serves as a visual introduction to the superhero and his mission.

With the first page of the first full issue of the series, Theo Tso boldly presents the reader with a visual rendition of Captain Paiute's "MPI Index"—mission, powers, and identity—as a means of introducing the narrative that follows. Standing in the foreground we have Captain Paiute himself, dressed in a blue spandex suit and mask with red loin cloth and yellow belt, wearing the primary colors that have adorned many mainstream superheroes. Chest out, eyes fixed

Captain Paiute: Protecting the Reservation.

determinedly ahead, Captain Paiute is clearly protecting the reservation inhabitants who are actively protesting some of the various abuses currently being borne by Indigenous populations in North America; as such, Captain Paiute's mission is identified as both protector of his reservation community as well as symbol for the protection of Native rights more broadly. And in a text box at the bottom of the page, Captain Paiute is identified as Luther Pah, whose given name alludes to the water spirit who granted him his powers. Captain Paiute's MPI Index thus serves to identify him as a superhero with strong ties to his reservation community and tribal heritage. And given the loosely fictionalized version of the Vegas Valley Paiute Indians—and especially the real-life concerns they are protesting on the opening page—*Captain Paiute* is also meant to serve as a call to arms for contemporary Indigenous communities standing against myriad real-world problems.

In addition to the MPI Index that clearly identifies him as a superhero, in this first issue the reader is introduced to Captain Paiute's "origin story," an explanation of how he acquired his powers and identified his mission. With most comic book superheroes, the powers are acquired first, and the mission is identified later, such as when Peter Parker draws his powers after being bitten by a radioactive spider; Parker first uses those powers for financial gain (as a professional fighter) before the murder of his uncle Ben—murdered at the hands of a criminal Parker chose not to stop—directed him to a life of heroism. In the case of *Captain Paiute*, Luther Pah understands immediately Spider-Man's dictum that "with great power comes great responsibility"; in fact, such an understanding is one reason why he was chosen. Drawing his power from the water spirit, Captain Paiute must from time to time replenish those powers by immersing himself into water. In one such trip, we are presented with a flashback explaining his origin: after accidentally falling through a crevice while hiking, Luther Pah nearly died of hypothermia before the water spirit manifested to choose Luther as his champion, telling him that "Water is life. You are the chosen one. Defender of the land. Protector of the people." After accidentally spilling sulfuric acid on himself and instinctively flushing it out with the water stored in his body, Pah then began experimenting with his powers and stopping local crime before formally adopting the mantle of Captain Paiute. The short issue #0 that first introduced Captain Paiute has a slightly more detailed version of the origin story: we learn that Pah was the sole survivor of a car crash that took his parents' lives (ominously noting that "someone had plans for me after all . . ."), and that he is only the most recent hero chosen by the water spirit Pah to serve as protector of the Paiute. Explained in the context of the history of the Paiute's oppression at the hands of European colonizers—their forced removal from tribal lands onto reservations and the various abuses of children at boarding schools, including the use of water to violently try to scrub the color off of the skins of Native children—Captain Paiute's origin story is directly tied to his tribal history and traditional beliefs.

Captain Paiute's first enemy is not an otherworldly foe, or even a villain from outside the reservation. Rather, his first enemy is Waylon Williams, former resident of the reservation before his family was kicked off for undisclosed "dark and terrible things. Things no one should speak of." Embodying the common trope of the "evil former friend" long employed by comics writers,[7] Waylon returns to the reservation in the guise of a ground radar specialist in order to gain access to the tribal cemetery. Somehow drawing his powers from his buried ancestors, Waylon—who adopts the name Bad Medicine, whose powers include draining people of their souls and using them to power energy blasts—immediately attacks the reservation residents out of rage for having been (rightfully) banished from the community. While Captain Paiute is off recovering his powers (and giving the reader a chance to read his origin story), Bad Medicine continues to torment the reservation by spreading his "bad medicine" to unleash the residents' rage upon one another. One example of this violence has a tribal police officer about to beat a Black Lives Matter protester while yelling "love it or leave it, Libturd!" alluding to non-tribal-based political activism and situating the comic squarely in support of all contemporary civil rights movements.

My copy of the first issue of *Captain Paiute* (which I ordered from the author directly from his War Paint Studios[8]) came with a short comic insert titled "Why an Indigenous Superhero is Needed?" A reservation resident asks the tribal council to weigh in on the need for Captain Paiute, and asks if he poses a threat, especially if "the government gets wind of him and sends in the military," a not too unreasonable fear given the US government's historically abusive treatment of Native peoples. The council replies that Captain Paiute is necessary to protect the people and their "sacred traditions," adding that murder, rape, and suicide rates have risen across the country among reservation populations. The first council member ends by noting that no other superheroes "have stepped foot on a reservation before," reminding the reader of the large oversight by the mainstream comics industry. Before adjourning the meeting, however, another council member points out that, should the army come, "it wouldn't be the first time that the government has sent soldiers to our reservations [. . .] nor will it be the last time." Read in the context of the story this insert accompanied, Tso suggests that the various problems faced by the Native American and First Nations reservation communities—problems brought to them by the US and Canadian governments, often with the support of military force—are an ongoing concern for Indigenous populations. As such, superheroes like Captain Paiute are needed, as defenders in fictional narratives as well as sources of inspiration for the current generation of Indigenous activists who will stand up for their lands and their rights, as represented on the first page of the comic.

Super Indians and the Indigenous Comics Renaissance 261

Captain Paiute: Black Lives Matter.

Super Indian

Consciously—and even at times satirically—playing with the traditional aspects of the mainstream superhero, Arigon Starr's *Super Indian*[9] also provides a pointed articulation of the various problems inherent in contemporary reservation life. Set on the fictional Leaning Oak Reservation, *Super Indian* follows the heroic acts of Hubert Logan, janitor at the reservation bingo hall, as well as his heroic exploits as Super Indian. Starr's focus on the reservation community is evident from the first pages, which present a cast of characters, including the heroes—Logan / Super Indian, his sidekick General Bear / Mega Bear (who possesses no powers, but does employ a secret identity), and Logan's talking dog Diogi—the villains for the volume ("The Circle of Evil"), and twenty of the Leaning Oak residents (including Logan's family), many of whom appear briefly in minor roles. In short, while Hubert Logan / Super Indian is the eponymous hero, the series' true focus is the Leaning Oak Reservation as a whole and the lives that Logan protects.

Super Indian's characterization as a superhero falls squarely into Coogan's "MPI matrix," possessing a clearly defined mission, explicit powers, and a heroic identity separate from his given name. And like many comic book superheroes, all three are intertwined. Although Super Indian's origin story has not (yet) been narrated in detail, we learn from his character biography that he gained his powers after eating "commodity cheese tainted with 'Rezium,' an experimental element developed by Government Research Scientist Dr. Eaton Crowe to solve world hunger and win the Nobel Prize." We see Starr's pointed sarcasm both in the name of the element—"Rezium," suggesting this element was only included in food sent to reservations—as well as the doctor's name: "eating crow" is an expression used to suggest humiliation after having been proven wrong. That said, Dr. Crowe also won a Nobel Prize, reminding the readers of the long history of white academics flourishing while using Native peoples as experimental (and at times unknowing) test subjects. While Dr. Crowe is a Nobel Prize winner, Hubert Logan remains a janitor. However, the tainted cheese did provide Logan with his powers, and can be read as an accident not unlike those that granted powers to such mainstream superheroes as Daredevil and the Incredible Hulk. Although the full extent of his powers is still unknown, Super Indian has employed a "supersonic punch" in addition to super hearing, super strength, and the power of flight. Additionally, Logan consumed this cheese at a birthday party for the "local bully" Derek Thunder, who, possessing a different set of powers, would grow up to become the villain controlling Technoskin, a giant robot who attempts to turn the population of Leaning Oak into zombies by stripping them of their reservation accoutrements: "Gone are the ribbon shirts. The reservation mullets. [. . .] Conformity *good*. Native culture *bad*." As with *Captain Paiute*, one of the *Super Indian*'s first villains is a former but now disgraced member of the reservation community.

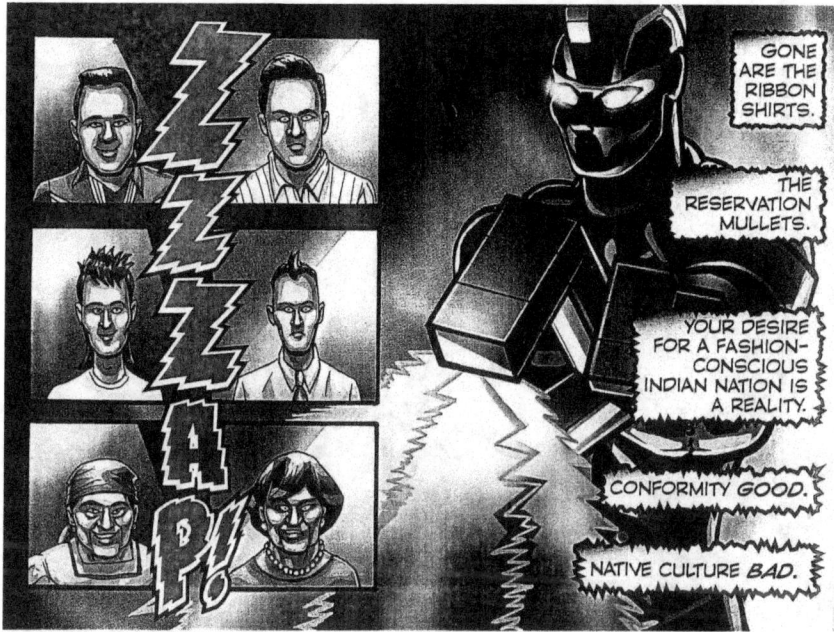

Super Indian: Under Glass.

And here we see Super Indian's mission: protection of the reservation community and his tribe's way of life. In addition to protecting the community from internal threats like Derek Thunder and his efforts at impressing into service an "ambiguously brown army" to serve as cannon fodder for his evil plans, Super Indian also protects the reservation from outside threats, many of which are thinly veiled constructions referencing the ongoing acts of colonization faced by tribal communities. For instance, Super Indian's very first antagonist is "The Anthro," "noted German Anthropologist Professor Karl Von Kelheim," who after discovering magic crystals on the Leaning Oak Reservation grew to a giant and terrorized the reservation. Like many anthropologists in the past have done with Native peoples, Dr. Kelheim literally put Super Indian under glass, trapping him under a giant specimen jar, while attempting to transform local resident Tillie Thunder into his "giant Native bride." Such treatment of Super Indian recalls the case of Ishi, known popularly as "the last Yahi" or "the last wild Indian," who lived the remaining years of his life in the Museum of Anthropology at the University of California, Berkeley, where he was studied by the renowned anthropologist Alfred L. Kroeber. Gerald Vizenor, who has written extensively about Ishi, notes in "Mr. Ishi of California" that Ishi was "captured," "then sustained as cultural property" while "humanely secured in a museum at a time when Natives were denied human and civil rights" (239).[10] Arigon Starr calls to mind not only Ishi and his literal existence "under glass" but all Native peoples who have watched as their cultural traditions have been

Super Indian: Technoskin.

cheaply adopted by white anthropologists in the name of academic enrichment at the expense of actual Native peoples and their immediate concerns.[11]

Comics historians may read another layer into this representation, however, recalling *Superman* #342, "Hero Under Glass!" where Superman is similarly trapped under glass. Although the story lines are vastly different, the visual of both heroes under glass helps to draw the parallels between Superman, iconic champion of Metropolis, and Super Indian, devoted protector of the Leaning Oak Reservation. Like his near-namesake, Super Indian sports a giant red S on his bright blue costume, which is additionally adorned with a belt buckle reading "NDN," common typographic shorthand for "Indian." The clear visual allusion to the Man of Steel connects Super Indian's mission with Superman's— both are self-selected protectors of a people and their way of life—while the belt buckle signals to the reader that Super Indian's mission is focused exclusively on the Native people who previously have not had such a champion. Instead of the lofty and abstract goals of "truth, justice, and the American way," Super Indian's efforts are directed to his reservation and their specific needs. For instance, in "The Curse of Blud Kwan'tum" (which takes up most of vol. 2), Super Indian saves the reservation from Blud Kwan'tum, descendant of a sixteenth-century Spanish nobleman who came to the New World to "tame the savages" and who now blames "the Indios" for his lack of personal and professional success, including being passed over in his job at the Bureau of Indian Affairs by a Hopi administrator. After stealing a cache of gold from a traditional grave, Blud Kwan'tum is cursed, changed to a vampire who must consume the blood of full-blooded Natives until he, too, becomes a "full-blood," thus transforming into that which he hates most. Allowing himself to be bitten, Super Indian defeats Blud Kwan'tum by poisoning him with blood tainted by Rezium.

Alluding to the "blood quantum" laws that the governments of the United States and Canada at one time employed to determine legal status of Indigenous peoples and their tribal rolls, Blud Kwan'tum represents yet another means of the European theft of Native culture (for a useful parallel, think of Lieutenant Dunbar from *Dances with Wolves*, the white savior who symbolically becomes a Native champion). Despite the use of such policies to determine federal recognition and inclusion on sanctioned tribal roles, many Native peoples find "blood quantum" regulations to be another arm of settler colonialism. As Eva Marie Garroutte has written in her study *Real Indians: Identity and the Survival of Native America*, many of those "who object to legal standards of identity ignore the ways that these may affect tribal blood quanta," complaining that "legal mechanisms for establishing connections to tribal communities are culturally foreign" (35). Rather than focusing on genetic parentage and DNA, many Native peoples hold that "[a]n individual's cultural characteristics may actually take precedence over anything else in the determinations of tribal belonging" (76); in fact, as Garroutte notes, "[i]n some cases, whole communities have collectively embraced particular individuals, even though they are not relatives by either law or blood, if they demonstrate cultural competence" (77). In short, "blood quantum" laws are a foreign imposition on Indigenous understandings of individual and communal identity. In light of this, readers are encouraged to recognize in the character of Blud Kwan'tum a continuation of the settler colonial impulse to bodily regulate—down to the individual level—Native peoples, as well as use Native peoples as tools for the development of colonial desires. Blud Kwan'tum's immediate goal was to use the residents of Leaning Oak to fuel his cure, only to be defeated by another "cure" that was proffered to those same residents as a solution to hunger and malnutrition. Super Indian may thus serve metaphorically as a hero for Native peoples generally, but his heroism is in service of his immediate community and its cultural values. In this way, Super Indian is very unlike Superman, who will often divert his attention away from Metropolis to take on the seemingly loftier goal of protecting people from national, international, or intergalactic enemies. For Super Indian—and for Native superheroes more generally—the loftiest goal is the protection of one's immediate community.

Arigon Starr, like Theo Tso, thus uses her series to provide a new spin on the traditional figure of the superhero, focusing the acts of heroism on a smaller scale while simultaneously addressing the persistent threats to contemporary Native peoples. In contrast to the Marvel and DC superheroes whose villains are, increasingly, interplanetary threats that bear little to no resemblance to the social ills faced by contemporary American society, Super Indian exists to combat the persistence of colonial efforts that work to decimate Native culture and imprison—or erase—Native peoples. Starr's efforts to support actual Native peoples is further marked by her inclusion of biographical sketches of "Real Super Indians," bringing to her readers' attention the accomplishments of actual Native people in a variety of professions. With biographies of famed New York City Ballet prima ballerina Maria Tallchief; Jim Thorpe, often referred to as "the greatest athlete of the 20th century"; media icon Will Rogers; Susan LaFlesche Picotte, "the first female Native American doctor in the United States"; and Moses Yellowhorse, MLB's first full-blooded Native pitcher; Starr is using her series to promote the efforts of what we might call "everyday heroes," historical figures whose lives can serve to inspire her readership, particularly her young Native readers. For all that myth-like figures such as Super Indian make for engaging storytelling and inspire readers to greatness, it's the heroics of real people that actually improve the world. One can fantasize about becoming a superhero, but one can actually work toward becoming a leader in one's community.

While there is an exciting series of developments in Native-authored comic narratives taking place today, I do not wish to suggest that the development of Native American superheroes is a new phenomenon. For instance, Jay Odjick's (Anishinabe) *Kagagi: The Raven* uses the genre of the superhero comic to retell the story of the windigo, a man-eating creature popular in traditional Anishinabe stories. Forged in battle against the windigo and its forces of destruction, "one young Anishinabe warrior [named Wisakedjak[12]] who had lost all to the best would lead them" to victory. This hero survives from the times before European conquest to the modern day, eventually passing on his mantle—and his powers—to an unsuspecting high school student who, much like Peter Parker, is bullied by the star athlete in his class and mocked as a nerd. A chance encounter with a minion of the windigo revealed to young Matt his heroic nature, in part by means of the MPI index noted above: the windigo's minion calls him by the name Kagagi, and the attacks against him draw out both Matt's previously unknown powers as well as his superhero costume, a black suit with wing-like straps on the arm bands, befitting a hero whose namesake is a raven. By the end of the book, Matt and "Jack" have temporarily defeated the forces of the windigo while noting that the danger has only been kept at bay temporarily. The book ends with the two heroes supporting each other, with the elder promising to answer all of Matt's questions about his powers and their history. Although this book is little more than an origin story, one important point the reader is left with is the fact that Kagagi's purpose in the present—like Wisakedjak's purpose in the past—is to protect his tribal community from an evil force bent on that community's destruction. The windigo notes as much when he introduces himself to Kagagi by noting that he is "the darkness that resides in the blackest nightmares of all the Anishinabe." Although only the one volume of the book has been released, Kagagi was later adapted as an animated television show of the same name that aired in Canada on APTN Kids (which provides Indigenous-created children's programming) in 2014 (https://aptn.ca/kagagi/), thus taking new life beyond the pages of the comic while also providing more representation for Indigenous superheroes across multiple media platforms.

In another, much more poignant example, originally published in 1996, *Tribal Force* has recently been re-released (with some minor alterations) by the Native Realities Press. Written by Jon Proudstar (Yaqui), the comic focuses on the young Nita, a survivor of child molestation who summons the superhero Thunder Eagle through her own comic artwork. Bearing a symbol on his chest alluding to the Ghost Dance—"a tribute to the countless murdered souls from which he draws his immense power"—Thunder Eagle bears a name, a mission, and an array of powers that clearly provides the necessary "MPI matrix" possessed by other comic book superheroes. However, as the narrator tells us early on: "Just to be clear, this isn't a story about heroes. It's a story about monsters." Following these words, the reader is brought to Nita's home, where an unidentified male authority figure commands the young girl to first take off her jacket, and then remove her pants "nice and slow," suggesting his intention of sexual abuse. Inspired by the hero she has been drawing, Nita stands up to this man,

Tribal Force: Reservation Violence.

demanding that he stop touching her, or this hero will "make war on you." In response, the man assaults Nita, who lies on the ground, bleeding, whispering for Thunder Eagle's help.

This depressing story illustrates yet another problem that reservation populations face: the abuse of those least able to protect themselves (particularly children). In an author's statement following the narrative, Proudstar notes that "[f]or the past twenty-five years, I have worked with Survivors of Child Molestation and Violent Youth Offenders," and that his comic book comes out of his need to present this issue to his readers. More than just a graphic illustration of contemporary social ills, however, this book is also an explicit call to action: "I know this is only a comic book but I hope somewhere, someone reads this and is motivated to make a change or speak out. [. . .] The responsibility of exposing these horrible acts to the light of day has been left to us." With his comic series (he suggests in his author's note that there will be more issues in the future), Proudstar makes explicit what Tso and Starr imply: Native comics are more than just engaging entertainment; the books address real issues, faced by real people, and that call for real solutions. We cannot, in other words, just be readers; we have an obligation to act. In an interview for *High Country News*, Proudstar notes that "[a] lot of kids misinterpret what a warrior is. It has nothing to do with war. A warrior takes care of his village, makes sure the old ones are taken care of, and that the children are safe." This message is reinforced by the cover to *Tribal Force* #1, which pictures Thunder Eagle holding a hatchet, ready to protect a scared young girl (presumably Nita), who lies at his feet, clutching a doll. And as noted in the title, Thunder Eagle is a manifestation of a "*tribal* force," a protector of communities often ignored by law enforcement agencies as well as mainstream superheroes.

Taking part in the larger renaissance of comic art engaged by Indigenous creators across North America—addressing a wide variety of subject matter and aesthetic styles—Native-authored superhero comics also function as a direct political appeal to their audiences. Presenting a variety of social, political, and physical assaults on tribal communities—particularly those living on reservations—these superhero comics address the historical legacy of colonialism and its various contemporary manifestations. Similarly, these comics all remind the reader that the villains are not intergalactic forces or unrealistic super villains; rather, they are the political issues that Captain Paiute faces down, the nefarious individuals Super Indian confronts, or the "monsters" that children like Nita need protection from. As socially conscious as they are entertaining, as much activist stances as artistic creations, Native American superhero comics reimagine the traditional figure of the mainstream comic book superhero as a figure of Native resistance and political action in the face of the real dangers faced by Indigenous people in North America.

Tribal Force: Thunder Eagle.

Notes

1. As Chris Gavaler has pointed out, technically only Marvel and DC employ "superheroes," as they "have maintained a jointly owned registered trademark on the word 'superhero' since 1979" (2). He also notes that "the history of the superhero is largely a history of DC and Marvel" (3). Native creators are working outside of these larger publishing houses through smaller publishers. However, the recently founded Native Realities Press (https://www.nativerealities.com/) is publishing works from Native comics artists, including reprinting Jon Proudstar's 1996 comic *Tribal Force*, which I will discuss briefly at the end of this chapter.

2. Although space prohibits a fuller discussion of Native-authored superheroes in comics, I would like to draw attention to Daniel H. Wilson's work on the Earth 2 series for DC comics. A Cherokee science fiction writer perhaps most famous for his novels *Robopocalypse* and *Robogenesis*, Wilson also authored some of the titles in the "World's End," "Society," and "Future's End" series. However, none of these series focus on Native American heroes, even if parts of the series can be loosely read as representations of traditional Cherokee beliefs.

3. In some of the early advertising for the 2017 superhero movie *Justice League*, DC employed logos to stand in for the characters themselves: Superman, Batman, Wonder Woman, the Flash, Aquaman, and Cyborg.

4. Marvel's 2018 film *Black Panther* stands out as a counterexample that proves the larger point. Although tied into the larger Marvel Cinematic Universe, Black Panther's primary concern is the protection of his nation Wakanda, but not from any direct international or intergalactic threat (even if he was included as a hero in the following Avengers movie, *Infinity War*, fighting the alien threat Thanos). There is a case to be made that the nonwhite superheroes—Luke Cage as well as Black Panther—in the MCU are more focused on local community than their white counterparts. However, I do not have the space here to flesh out such an analysis.

5. To keep from littering this article with "(n.p.)," I will note here that none of the comics under discussion have page numbers.

6. An omnibus bill that covered a variety of topics, including an overhaul of the Navigable Waters Protection Act of 1882. First Nations, Métis, and Inuit peoples opposed this bill (which, sadly, was passed) in an effort to protect their treaty rights in general and preserve their waterways specifically. Since 2012, the movement has grown to encompass numerous concerns related to Indigenous rights throughout Canada.

7. Paradigmatic examples include such pairs as Professor X and Magneto as well as Wolverine and Sabertooth from the *X-Men* series, Batman and Two-Face, and some versions of Superman and Lex Luthor.

8. Another issue I would like to raise, though space prohibits a fuller discussion, is that many Native comics artists are working as independent creators or with small press distribution. On the one hand, this likely allows the creators much more control over the creation; on the other hand, the lack of a national distribution machine (such as enjoyed by Marvel and DC) severely limits the readership of these works. Small press/independent creations are also likely to go out of print more quickly. Ideally, bringing attention to these creators will help to increase their visibility as well as the potential reach of their work.

9. Although I will only be working with the print volumes, readers can also follow *Super Indian* online at http://www.arigonstarr.com/, where Starr also publishes new stories before they come out in print. The Internet offers wonderful possibilities for Native creators to share their work with a large and diverse audience.

10. The interested reader is also directed to Vizenor's essay "Ishi Bares His Chest: Tribal Simulations and Survivance" in the collection *Partial Recall: Photographs of Native North*

Americans. Photographs of Native peoples by non-Natives provides another fruitful area of study for the phenomenon of Native peoples "under glass" in terms of the camera lens.

11. Anthropologists have long been a popular target for Native writers, as figures who aptly represent a variety of interests—personal, professional, colonial—that have kept Native peoples oppressed in North America. One of the most biting critiques of the anthropological study of Native peoples was penned by Vine Deloria Jr., who wrote in *Custer Died for Your Sins: An Indian Manifesto* that "[b]ehind each policy and program with which Indians are plagued, if traced completely back to its origin, stands the anthropologist" (81).

12. Wisakedjak is the name of a traditional trickster figure in Anishinabe legend. He is often known in English as Whiskeyjack, which is also the common name for the Grey Jay, a bird Indigenous to the boreal forests of North America.

Works Cited

Coogan, Peter. "The Definition of the Superhero." *A Comics Studies Reader*, edited by by Jeet Heer and Kent Worcester, 77–93. Jackson: University Press of Mississippi, 2009.

Deloria, Jr., Vine. *Custer Died for Your Sins: An Indian Manifesto*. Norman: University of Oklahoma Press, 1988.

Gavaler, Chris. *Superhero Comics*. London: Bloomsbury, 2018.

Garroutte, Eva Marie. *Real Indians: Identity and the Survival of Native America*. Berkeley: University of California Press, 2003.

Odjick, Jay, et al. *Kagagi: The Raven*. Coquitlam, BC: Arcana Comics, 2010.

Proudstar, Jon. "The first comic book with an all-Native American superhero team returns." Interview with Bryn Bailer. *High Country News*. Posted February 17, 2014. Web. Accessed July 6, 2018.

Proudstar, Jon, et al. *Tribal Force*. Issue #1. Albuquerque, NM: Native Realities, 2017.

Starr, Arigon, et al. *Super Indian*. Vol. 1. West Hollywood, CA: Wacky Productions Unlimited, 2012.

———. *Super Indian*. Vol. 2. West Hollywood, CA: Wacky Productions Unlimited, 2015.

Tso, Theo, et al. *Captain Paiute*. Vol. 0. Albuquerque, NM: Native Realities, 2015.

———. *Captain Paiute*. Vol 1. Albuquerque, NM: Native Realities, 2017.

Vizenor, Gerald. "Ishi Bares His Chest: Tribal Simulations and Survivance." *Partial Recall: Photographs of Native North Americans*, edited by Lucy R. Lippard, 64–71. New York: New Press, 1992.

———. "Mr. Ishi of California." Native *Liberty: Natural Reason and Cultural Survivance*. Lincoln: University of Nebraska Press, 2009. 239–55.

Seeing Histories, Building Futurities: Multimodal Decolonization and Conciliation in Indigenous Comics from Canada

Mike Borkent

In North American comics, depictions of Indigenous peoples are typically developed by non-Indigenous creators, too often in ways that draw wholly or in part on negative stereotypes and caricatures (see C. King; Sheyahshe). Even more nuanced and intentionally allied depictions still run the risk of inadvertently misrepresenting or distorting Indigenous figures and events through a lack of awareness and experience necessary to inform rich multimodal representations of particular cultures. A recent example from Canadian literature is Chester Brown's (Anglo-Canadian) bestselling, heavily researched biography of the revolutionary Métis leader Louis Riel. The comic celebrates Riel's denial of colonial nationalist discourse (Lesk) but imposes boundaries "upon Riel regardless of his cultural values or beliefs" (Gray 178), including erasing the significant contributions of women upheld in Métis histories of the same events (Cutrara). Self-awareness and research on the part of non-Indigenous creators is increasingly common, and serves to develop more diverse stories and nurture a politics of learning and respect. Nonetheless, comics still require greater diversity of creators from varied traditions to nuance the fraught spaces of representation. Thomas King (Greek-Cherokee) famously argued that "[t]he truth about stories is that that's all we are" (2, and throughout): who better to tell their stories, to enrich and contest perspectives, than those who know them intimately?

Such a question reflects a decades-old challenge against cultural appropriation in Canadian literature. Daniel David Moses (Delaware-Tuscarora) and Lenore Keeshig [-Tobias] (Ojibway) presented it succinctly through their 1989 seminar: "Whose Story is it Anyway?" and Keeshig's more emphatically titled editorial, "Stop stealing Native stories."[1] Such actions and works, along with that done by other Indigenous activists, critics, and allies, transformed the Canadian literary scene by raising awareness of the common appropriation of stories, identities, and voices, and by encouraging publication opportunities for Indigenous counternarratives (see Fee; Godard).

Today, the fruits of this activism are plentiful in Canadian literatures. They are also emerging in Canadian alternative comics through works from publishers like HighWater Press and Arsenal Pulp Press, and organizations including the Healthy Aboriginal Network (which produces Indigenous wellness comics, including Steven Keewatin Sanderson's (Cree-Scottish) *Darkness Calls*). Writers like Louise Flaherty (Inuit), Drew Hayden Taylor (Ojibway), Jennifer Storm (Ojibway), Katherena Vermette (Métis), and Brian Wright-McLeod (Dakota-Anishnabe), along with others like the creators discussed below, are creating and collecting a wide variety of stories, Indigenizing the comics medium in Canada. More broadly across Turtle Island (North America), other projects, such as Kickstarter funded initiatives like Native Realities and Alternative History Comics (which put out the award-winning *Moonshot* anthologies, as well as other groundbreaking works: see Anderson and Carnes, this volume), are also publishing Indigenous comics, or as C. Richard King wittily calls them, "alter/native comics" (throughout). (Note that while it may at times be necessary to take a wider perspective on writings from Turtle Island to reflect Indigenous sovereignty across imposed state borders, or international anthologies, I maintain a state-delimited approach here because of the different histories of colonization and the Canadian focus of the comics I analyze.) It comes as no surprise that Indigenous perspectives are entering comics primarily from these alternative publishing positions, rather than the mainstream comics industry, which has typically reinforced the "imperial imaginary" (215). As Charles Hatfield argues, "much of the creative promise of [...] comic art rests in the undercapitalized and therefore fragile microcosm of alternative comics. [...] From alternative comics has come a dramatic influx of work that challenges both the formal and cultural boundaries of comic art" (31). Alternative comics challenge representational assumptions, and Indigenous writers have embraced them to, among other topics, transform colonial representations of Indigeneity in Canada.

Moreover, the multimodality of these works is productively seen in light of Métis artist and scholar David Garneau's reflections on conciliation, as something distinct from reconciliation between Indigenous and settler peoples. Rather than reinforcing the underlying logic of assimilation at work in the reconciliation discourse, conciliation asserts the necessary and ongoing respectful process of navigating differences that the Western ethos cannot assimilate. While recognition can still lead to assimilation, respect requires a fundamentally different epistemic position that denies homogeneity (Coleman), which makes space for the dynamic process of conciliation. In this chapter I will examine the differences in comics between modalities, and how the process of navigating what is shown and withheld, enacts Indigenous sovereignty in dialogue with non-Indigenous interests, which in turn models conciliatory processes. C. Richard King rightly notes that since comics offer Indigenous creators the space to "reimagine themselves, defining themselves in their own terms, while determining acceptable modes of address and the means of circulation, they afford them important occasions to assert representational or visual sovereignty" (222). King's conclusion aligns well with Garneau's work on conciliation and artistic display practices. As I show, comics present a particularly significant contribution to the storytelling practices of Indigenous creators through their capacity as a mediated form of what Garneau describes as "Aboriginal sovereign display territories," which support a dual insider/outsider readership through guidance from Knowledge Keepers.

Guided engagement with Indigenous perspectives on place, culture, and healing is crucial for a conciliation process that emphasizes the well-being of all, rather than maintaining colonial practices of Indigenous erasure. Canadian colonial history is replete with practices that sought to dispossess Indigenous peoples of their territories and to assimilate them into the settler populace (for a brief overview, see Woolford 82–85; see also Daschuk).[2] This history focused on systematically rupturing kinship relations between families, cultural communities, and their lands that were often maintained through stories (Justice 78–88). Following contact with Europeans, there were instances of reciprocity between settler and Indigenous peoples (including alliances in wars and trade and support for settlers learning to live through the winters), but there were also negative impacts for Indigenous communities from the beginning. These included successive epidemics that decimated Indigenous communities, perhaps supporting the false notion of *terra nullius*, of an empty landscape awaiting expropriation, and the notion of the "dying Indians," who settlers conceived as inferior. While the British *Royal Proclamation of 1763* recognized Indigenous territory rights prior to settlement, including the requirement that lands be bought or ceded through treaties in exchange for goods or services from the state, treaties were made and often broken (or in British Columbia, rarely established in the first place). Treaties and reserve regulations divided Indigenous peoples from each other and from the territories that provisioned hunting grounds, sacred sites, and other social and cultural necessities.

Shortly after the *Indian Act of 1876* officially rendered Indigenous peoples wards of the state, thereby legislating the colonial belief in Indigenous inferiority and state paternalism, a new wave of more overt assimilationist policies were enacted through the residential school system. As it was summarized in the 2008 "Statement of Apology" to the survivors of the schools from the prime minister of Canada,

> Two primary objectives of the residential school system were to remove and isolate children from the influence of their homes, families, traditions and cultures, and to

assimilate them into the dominant culture. These objectives were based on the assumption Aboriginal cultures and spiritual beliefs were inferior and unequal. Indeed, some sought, as it was infamously said, "to kill the Indian in the child." (Harper n.p.)

Children were taken from their families and "educated" by missionaries on Western ways. They were forbidden to speak their Indigenous languages or engage in cultural practices. Many died of malnutrition and disease, and many were sexually, physically, and psychologically abused (see Miller; Milloy). Many of these children returned traumatized to their communities, and went on to have their own children taken in turn to the residential schools. Even after the schools were shut down for their unconscionable conditions, the state continued to remove Indigenous children from their homes, placing them in the child welfare system instead. Today, this latter period is commonly called the "60s Scoop" (see Fournier and Crey). These successive cycles of separation, trauma, and cultural erasure reflect a disturbing, ongoing politics of ethnocide against Indigenous peoples (see Daschuk; Palmater, "Genocide").

While Indigenous communities have been extremely resilient in the face of this long history of attempted ethnocide, it has come at great cost, including interlinked issues surrounding poverty, mental health, and substance abuse (Palmater, "Stretched"). *The Royal Commission on Aboriginal Peoples* published a 1996 analysis of colonial impacts on Indigenous communities, and *The Truth and Reconciliation Commission of Canada* published a 2015 analysis of the residential school system. Both commissions offered many recommendations for how the state could support the healing and renewed autonomy of Indigenous communities. Shamefully, most of these recommendations, from both commissions, remain unimplemented (see CBC Radio). However, the growing understanding of Indigenous and colonial history in Canadian society provides some hope that Canada may be moving toward a future grounded in conciliation.

Storytelling, including the documentary work of those national commissions of Indigenous colonial experiences, plays a crucial role in Indigenous resilience and in developing this conciliatory future. Cherokee scholar Daniel Heath Justice writes of Indigenous literatures that "imagination has always been vital to resisting, countering, and undoing the ravages of colonialism, especially given how relentless the attacks on our kinship networks and connections have been" (86). Indigenous representational sovereignty sustains these imaginative patterns of resistance by reinforcing kinship networks (between peoples, lands, and creatures) and other culturally specific values. Comics, with their multimodal capacity to develop immersive and visually complex re-presentations of history while modeling cultural reclamation and decolonial healing, provide another alternative space of resistance and reformulation to add to the imaginative work of Indigenous literatures Justice describes. In what follows, I analyze several examples to argue that comics provide a unique space for Indigenous creators to visualize the traumas of Canadian colonial history, to offer paths to decolonial healing through cultural reclamation, and to model conciliation between Indigenous and non-Indigenous peoples into the future.

Access and Sovereignty

One particularly significant aspect of the Indigenous comics discussed here is the use of the medium as a tool to unsettle perspectives on Canada's colonial history and its connection to contemporary society. Sarah Henzi borrows and expands on Kwakwaka'wakw historian Gord Hill's notion that such comics offer a "necessary antidote" to the historical misrepresentation of Indigenous experiences in Canadian dominant culture. She adds, "For Hill, the strength of the comic book is how it uses minimal text with graphic art to tell the story, making it more accessible not only for youth, but for those who may not want to, or cannot, read at length about this history of colonialism" (25). Henzi discusses important nonfiction comics by Hill, David Alexander Robertson, and Richard Van Camp, who use the medium to present accessible stories about Indigenous histories and relationships. Such works, as well as their fictional counterparts (some discussed below), employ the accessibility of the medium to promote the transmission of a clear counter-discourse that revisualizes and decolonizes received concepts about Canadian and Indigenous experiences and cultures, establishing new values and perspectives. As I show, these patterns of revisualization, through strategic spatial and structural cues and visual anchors and metaphors, are crucial to expressing and promoting a decolonial and conciliatory project through accessible yet revolutionary forms.[3]

The multimodality of comics presents opportunities to adjust, fragment, and orchestrate information strategically and to draw upon multiple literacies for comprehension (El Refaie). Such multimodal manipulations encourage readers to engage in making inferences about how various cues connect to build viewpoints and interpretations (Borkent), as the reader works to resolve what Charles Hatfield calls the "tensions" between different modalities, their presentation, and the cumulative impacts of these strategies on the reading experience (see esp. ch. 2). This process of navigating and building comprehension encourages a level of readerly awareness of the patterns of storytelling and how we actively participate in building interpretations of the story slowly, incrementally, recursively, and dialogically (Chute). Because of this combination of awareness and engagement, Jessica Langston argues that the graphic narrative form is particularly well suited to reflecting a mediated version of traditional Indigenous orature which also employs multimodal, accessible, and interactive storytelling practices.

These parallels between comics and orature may make comics particularly appealing to creators interested in practices of cultural reclamation, especially those who retell traditional stories. A notable and innovative example of such an approach is Michael Nicole Yahgulanaas's popular development of a style of comic book art he calls "Haida manga," through which he melds traditional Haida painting and carving practices and epistemologies (seen in building panels, totem poles, and bentwood boxes) with comics conventions, in order to tell his Haida story (Spiers). Yahgulanaas's use of Haida art practices presents a fundamentally different perspective on the materialization of place and time relative to Western comics tradition (Harrison). In a comic entitled "The Gutter" (reprinted in Harrison 51), Yahgulanaas connects the typically white spaces of the spaces between panels (the gutter) to the colonial idea of *terra nullius*, "so beloved by colonizers because *empty land* means *my land*." Harrison comments, "the conventional gutter is, then, to Yahgulanaas, a picture of European self-granted permission to imagine into space defined as empty whatever it wanted, and to imagine out of that space whatever it wanted to as well" (58). Harrison suggests that by replacing the traditional Western layout with a darkly painted Haida bentwood box design, Yahgulanaas reformulates how the medium reflects culturally specific discourse communities and places, rather than a colonial blank slate. Thus, Yahgulanaas develops a conspicuously Haida discursive, political, and historical intervention into received dominant practices of comic book storytelling. Yahgulanaas's reworking of the medium also illustrates that comics conventions can be adapted while remaining quite accessible to readers.

While generally employed for their accessibility, comics conventions can also be manipulated to purposefully interrupt reader assumptions to build a different understanding of community and communication. For instance, viewer comprehension of the comics-inspired paintings by Métis artist David Garneau (see fig. 14.1) is informed by readerly expectations of panels reflecting moments in event sequences and speech balloons locating and expressing discrete voices. As the title tells us, the painting depicts the *Aboriginal Curatorial Collective Meeting*, which is visualized through the comics conventions of panels and empty speech balloons arranged upon a canvas. As Garneau discusses in "Imaginary Spaces of Conciliation and Reconciliation,"[4] this painting is a visual "mnemonic device" (21) that "is an attempt to picture my memory of an event without violating the privacy of those who were there" (21). He continues, "I hope viewers will read argument, agreement, frostiness, overlapping dialogue, shared and evolving ideas, and innumerable other things into these shapes and thereby get a sense of the scene. I also imagine that many will feel frustrated that their comprehension is restricted" (21). The painting reveals the event's interactive multimodal discourse through the placement, layering, and shape of the empty speech balloons (on "balloonics," see Forceville et al.). Concurrently, the painting reflects a specific politics of voice and representation that includes revoking the viewer's access. Here, Garneau is "refusing to be a Native informant" (23) by building "irreconcilable spaces of Aboriginality" (25) in which he "visualize[s] Indigenous

Figure 14.1. David Garneau's painting *Aboriginal Curatorial Collective Meeting*. 2012. Oil on canvas, 5'x4'.

intellectual spaces that exist apart from a non-Indigenous gaze and interlocution. The idea is to signal to non-Indigenous spectators the fact that intellectual activity is occurring without their knowledge" (25). Garneau has adapted a Western discursive tradition to reflect Indigenous spaces of thought, while heightening the insider-outsider dynamic for those who had not witnessed the meeting. Thus, the painting evokes Indigenous resistance to cultural appropriation. It highlights that Indigenous creations are not required to be accessible to all. Further, this inaccessibility contributes to the meaning of a text through the elicitation of spaces apart, of recognizing Indigenous sovereignty within practices of representation. As such, inaccessibility can educate the reader to recognize and support varieties of Indigenous nationalist autonomies, which can encourage a necessary shift from recognition of, to respect for, differences.

The differences between readers' backgrounds, experiences, biases, and interests means that accessibility is not a fixed property of a work, but a spectrum of engagement and response, and will vary within and between Indigenous and non-Indigenous readerships. Thus, representations of residential schools or other colonial institutions and practices discussed below will mean very different things to Indigenous readers (with varying degrees of exposure to the systems and their aftereffects) and non-Indigenous readers (who have varying degrees of knowledge of and association with the people, institutions, and cultures that developed and worked in the systems). Thus, there are a wide range of insider and outsider positions in relation to Indigenous comics. While they generally promote accessibility through the use of English and relatively clear pictorial depictions, this access is complicated in various ways depending on the readership.

In the following graphic novels, there are two general audiences which the texts might inform in fundamentally different ways. Like the double voice seen in children's literature (engaging both parent and child readers), I would suggest that the following comics develop varied layers of access and intentional education for Indigenous and non-Indigenous readers. These differences of access also align with modalities, such as through the integration of some Cree kinship terms into a predominantly English-language comic, or through depictions of or allusions to culturally significant practices or objects that have varying degrees of understanding based on backgrounds. Garneau theorizes a means of navigating and engaging these variable responses through the concept of "Aboriginal sovereign display territories" (29), which are created through controlled presentation and interaction. In such display territories, non-Indigenous viewers come as guests, and the Indigenous creator guides their experience as a Knowledge Keeper who shares their stories and contextualizes the artistic expression (29). He describes such an experience with the Denesuline/Saulteaux artist Alex Janvier giving an exhibition tour: "until he explained [his artworks], until he talked them into life, they remained oblique hints. It was the combination of visual art, embodied knowledge, and a gathering of engaged participants that made the experience significant, that made it exceed the colonial container" (29). I would argue that comics present a mediated space that aligns well with many of the dynamics of display territories, as a particularly productive form of multimodal guidance and engaged readerly participation. While mediated communication can never be fully responsive to an individual reader's reactions, its fragmented and contemplative qualities induced through multimodal interactions promote a more self-reflexive and nuanced response when read carefully (Chute). Moreover, as conciliatory spaces, display territories actively work to show "how Indigenous people have changed and adapted within contact" (Garneau 29) and "function as a cultural lab where artists would struggle creatively with the contemporary world as well as with traditional forms" (29). Similarly, the creators of the graphic novels I discuss adapt the medium to express Indigenous experiences and concepts, and strategically guide readers through them. As such, display territories cleverly give visitor/readers "a sense of the real without violating it" (29). Such representation gives a sense of truths, without tokenizing Indigenous experiences and artworks as illusions of "authenticity." At the same time, "[s]haring in a discourse about histories, responsibility, and transformation among artworks and with other human beings is a corrective to the colonial desire for settlement" (31), which supports the ongoing process of conciliation by learning about our differences through the mediating role of sovereign display territories, which can affirm a politics grounded in respect and care.

The two works I discuss enact the goals of Aboriginal sovereign display territories and establish a conciliatory dynamic between Knowledge Keeper authors and visitor-readers. The multimodality of the medium helps immerse all readers in a complex storyworld, drawing them into a participatory relation to the material by strategically exploiting the properties of the medium to direct readers to experience and learn from Indigenous stories. For Indigenous readers of these graphic novels, the works strongly encourage healing through cultural reclamation. For non-Indigenous readers, the stories teach the cruel histories that have informed Indigenous life-experiences in Canada in order to develop a space of respect for Indigenous cultural sovereignty, resilience, and adaptation. Combining these views, in which one audience is encouraged, the other is reconfigured so as to revoke destructive colonial attitudes, builds toward a conciliatory future. Garneau emphasizes that "Conciliation is an ongoing process, a seeking rather than the restoration of an imagined agreement [of reconciliation]" (27). These works show how Indigenous-settler dynamics have always been fraught, but by honestly engaging with the cultural genocide attempted throughout colonial history, and reconfiguring the settler thinking that led to it, the stories establish dynamics that can facilitate the process of conciliation. As I show, the multimodal medium of comics is particularly salient for developing these layers of meaning through visual metaphors and counternarratives, all of which help the reader visualize and comprehend the path to a conciliatory future in Canada, which is grounded in Indigenous resilience and reclamation.

Colonial Traumas in *7 Generations: A Plains Cree Saga*

7 Generations: A Plains Cree Saga, written by David Alexander Robertson (Swampy Cree) and illustrated by Scott B. Henderson (English-Canadian), ranges across the expanse of Canadian colonial history by focusing on a single family through time, weaving together connections and contrasts between past and present experiences. It begins in the present with the attempted suicide of the protagonist Edwin, a teenager who is estranged from his father and feels lost and hopeless. While he is recovering, his mother, Lauren, recounts his paternal family's stories. These stories begin by initially establishing a series of parallels and contrasts between the ancient past and the present, before filling in the intervening processes of colonization and destruction surrounding the peoples' sense of identity and community. After several historically inflected chapters, the final chapter charts a path to healing for both the father and son, rebuilding their kinship relations with each other and their ancestors. Throughout, the comics medium plays a crucial role in establishing meaningful links between past and present stories to facilitate Lauren's teachings about history, identity, and cultural reclamation.

The historical narrative begins with the story of Stone prior to contact with European explorers and settlers. Rather than establishing a utopian time before European contact, as it is sometimes depicted, Robertson shows the tensions and raids between Plains Cree and Blackfoot nations, including the death of Stone's brother. The story also illustrates his connection to the land through his vision, in which he sees an Eagle and receives a stone amulet that "will remind you of your vision and what you need to do" (12). The amulet serves as a frequent narrative anchor that links the family through generations, as characters continue to inherit it. Stone's story develops a complex portrayal of a strong Plains Cree community through depictions of elders guiding the youth through ceremonies, Stone's marriage and fatherhood, and the avengement of his brother's death after he has become a warrior. The portrayal of this community, with a wide array of positive social roles and cultural values, is contrasted with Edwin and his mother's troubled present, with these characters first depicted as stooped and confined. The temporal contrast highlights a sense of present-day familial and cultural fragmentation and the loss of autonomy and connection to the land.

The contrasting content in this chapter is reinforced through page layouts that refract content off of facing pages, actively building resonances between the stories. For instance, figure 14.2 shows a portion of a two-page spread that builds mimetic elements between layouts, pictorial, and linguistic cues. On the left, Edwin lies in bed lamenting his emptiness and pain. The right-hand page parallels the emotional statements but regarding the death of Stone's brother. In the surrounding panels and pages, it is clear that the loss in the past is connected to a strong sense of purpose, responsibility, and connection to the community, such that the loss is indicative of dedication and communal well-being, setting up a culturally significant path for Stone of support, training, and finally retribution. In contrast, Edwin feels isolated from his community and surroundings, believing his ancestors to be what colonial ideology dictated "savages." His mother corrects this, "We were never savages. Back then family was important, community" (23) and affirms the kinship values that informed Stone's life. The storytelling parallels experiences but contrasts their communal and cultural engagement or isolation, building a clear contrast between confusion and purpose, between life and death.

After establishing a contrast between past and present identities, *7 Generations* traces changes within the Plains Cree family and communities through a devastating smallpox epidemic which fractured many communities and leaves Edwin's ancestor White Cloud scarred and without a family: "whether exposed to [smallpox] accidentally or given to us on purpose, we never stood a chance against it" (46). The resonances between Edwin and White Cloud's emotional states are visually enacted through a composite panel (fig. 14.3) that blends the temporal frames of the two characters running through a forest.

This scene follows the suicide of a sick Cree girl that White Cloud had initially left behind but then returned to try and help. He is understandably upset

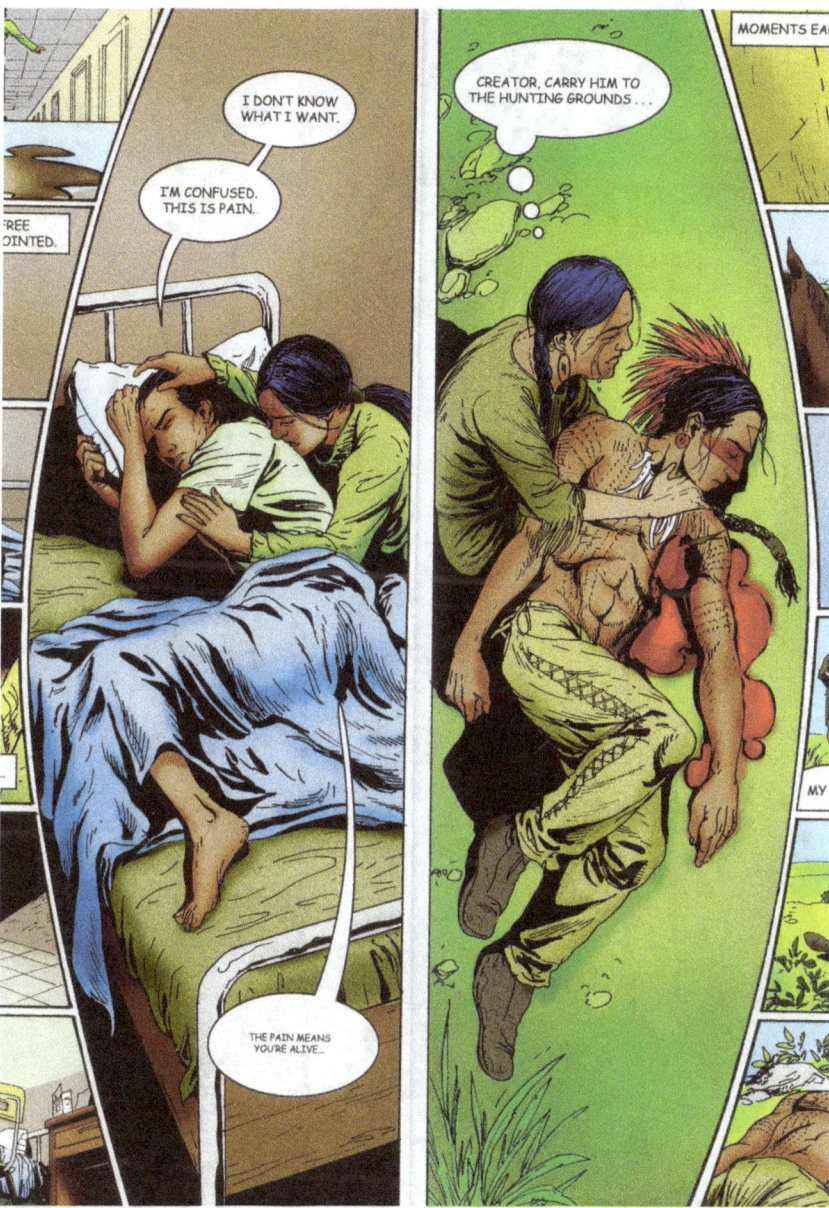

Figure 14.2. Parallel layouts and figurations that link Edwin and his fore-family across two pages (Robertson and Henderson 18–19).

and tries to run from the memory of losing his family and the vision of her death. This sense of loss and despair weaves with Edwin's reality through a dream, seen in this panel, of White Cloud and he running together. He wakes, and is reminded by his mother's presence, that he feels "still lost. / But maybe not alone" (56–57). The interweaving of historical losses and Edwin's sense of

Figure 14.3. Portion of a panel with interwoven temporalities between Edwin and White Cloud (Robertson and Henderson 56).

despair built in the initial panel is thus changed upon waking toward a crucial recognition: while his family is fragmented, it is still present in his mother. His kinship network is hurting, but not destroyed, which affirms the fact of Indigenous resilience and perseverance against colonial traumas. In subsequent panels, both White Cloud and Edwin are shown to embrace the vision-voice of their ancestor Stone to "Find your strength" and to "Face your fears with bravery" (59), with Edwin flushing the remaining pills that he originally attempted suicide with. His recognition of ongoing kinship is crucial to turning him away from despair, and shortly thereafter his mother gives him his father's stone amulet as a bearer of kinship connections and cultural resilience to "help you on your journey of healing" (60).

The story then turns to tell of how Edwin and his father, James, reunite. James tells his own story of his and his younger brother Thomas's experiences at residential school, beginning in 1963, which reflects the all-too-common traumatic experiences children sought to survive at these schools across Canada (see Fournier and Crey; Milloy). *7 Generations* shows how the school's staff beat children for speaking in Cree, and how the children were given subpar food and education, such that James observes that "I went to school, but what did I learn. Seems like I *unlearned* things" (80, emphasis in original). The story shows Thomas being physically, psychologically, and (it is strongly implied) sexually abused by the head priest. James only finds out later about the priest's actions and defends Thomas by intervening in a beating (fig. 14.4a), but Thomas flees and dies in the snow. James is haunted by the fact that he could not save Thomas from the assaults and his death. This haunting guilt leads to depression and alcoholism, depicted in images of him drinking while he narrates that "I couldn't bring myself to do anything. But those thoughts, they became too much. I tried to stop them [by drinking]" (109). The pressure to protect his kin while also surviving the ordeal undoes James's sense of self and purpose as a young man, despite his desire and actions to help, leading to years of mental health challenges and familial strife.

James's story also shows how the traumatic experiences of the schools informed intergenerational dynamics by removing positive role models and replacing them with colonial abusers. James later realizes his own potential to perpetuate the physical abuse he and his brother experienced on to his son Edwin when he pulls out his belt to beat him for playing unsafely at the road's edge (fig. 14.4b). James's anger is grounded in fear of losing his son, while the priest's anger is grounded in racist spite. Nonetheless, the link to the priest as a model for discipline and expression of anger is clearly established by the scenes' depictions. The scenes, separated by only several pages, present very similar actions, postures, perspectives, and power dynamics between the adult and child.

These visual resonances emphasize the intergeneration impact of residential school abuse, as it replaced the positive role models of elders and the cultural

Figure 14.4a. Intergenerational transmission of roles and traumas, beginning on the right priest and Thomas in the 1960s here (Robertson and Henderson 91).

connection to community and the land with the abuse of priests and broken senses of self and relationships. Such resonances, seen throughout the story, show how the school system disrupted healthy relationships grounded in cultural roles and values, and replaced them with negative colonial models of discipline and identity. *7 Generations* helps readers visualize the profound erosion of Indigenous identities and well-being through the ethnocidal practices of the residential school system and how it reverberates across generations.

Fig. 14.4b. Intergenerational transmission of roles and traumas continues to James and Edwin more recently (Robertson and Henderson 96).

7 Generations clearly depicts the challenges Indigenous communities face due to colonial legacies, charting key moments and processes across history in order to illustrate the concept of intergenerational trauma (see Bombay et al.). As Lauren says, "our past has shaped us all" (6). At the end of the story, this informing quality of history is acknowledged again, but not let to "define" the characters (126). Rather the story concludes with a strong focus on forgiveness and healing, a theme that builds across the story through the intergenerational stone amulet that represents cultural knowledge, strength, and connection. Edwin's mother, Lauren, at one point states, "I'm not your Saviour, James. I won't be" (116), but instead serves through her storytelling and care as a Knowledge Keeper,[5] who tells the history, and works to reconnect Edwin and James to each other and to their Plains Cree heritage. James ultimately confides in Edwin that he has only begun to heal from his mental health crisis through programs like Alcoholics Anonymous, traditional healing practices (119), and particularly by "coming to know our ways again" (125)—through cultural reclamation. In the final scenes of *7 Generations*, James takes Edwin back onto the land, to a river where, earlier in the story it is stated, "The Plains Cree believed their loved ones could be heard from the hunting grounds. The river's sounds and the valley's echoes were their voices" (20). There, Stone received a guiding vision from his brother which helps him overcome his grief and see his communal role more clearly. Upon return to the river, James describes the Plains Cree model of history and futurity:

> The elders say what was done to us will touch us for *7 generations*. So, too, the healing we do now will mend our people over that time. What happened to you doesn't define you. We are not our yesterday, we are our today, our tomorrow. This place [the river] is where that healing can begin for both of us. (126, emphasis in original)

With their own return to cultural practices upon the land, the father and son move toward healing themselves and their relationships to each other, their ancestors, and their future kin. Edwin goes on to give James back the stone amulet to help him heal by materially returning a symbol of cultural strength (upon which James receives a vision of Thomas), while Edwin heads off onto the land in search of his own vision. The visually dynamic final page of the comic shows Edwin's vision, which resonates visually with Stone's vision at the beginning of the story, conceptually returning the reader to the vibrancy of Stone's community. Through this visual mimicry, readers are shown how Edwin is beginning the process of healing his identity by reclaiming and actively participating in his Plains Cree culture and cosmology. By returning to his land and culture, including kinship with his ancestors and the creatures around him, Edwin enacts a sense of futurity that embraces Indigenous sovereignty and revokes colonial attempts at assimilation and erasure.

Through *7 Generations*, Robertson acts as a Knowledge Keeper who, with the help of Henderson's skilled illustrations and layouts, uses comics as a sovereign display territory to guide readers through the difficult story of Canadian colonial history and its impact on a Plains Cree community. He uses several characters as proxy Knowledge Keepers within the story to guide interpretations of culturally significant features and events, such as the stone amulet, the river, and various ceremonies. Originally, Lauren retells the history and guides interpretations, such that other characters (and the reader) can clearly understand their significance. For instance, it is clear the amulet is not a simple memento of an insightful vision, but is a sacred object with layers of meaning that we can only glimpse. Importantly, the fictional and constructed nature of the story helps build a sense of authenticity and accessibility without allowing a colonial assimilation of these experiences. As such, *7 Generations* teaches the traumas of colonial history to revoke colonial ideas of progress, Indigenous inferiority, and savagery, while teaching the necessary role of Indigenous cultural reclamation for the well-being of Indigenous communities. For the non-Indigenous reader, this graphic narrative offers the opportunity to recontextualize and decolonize one's sense of history. For Indigenous readers, it likely offers a model of healing grounded in a clear acknowledgment of the hard impacts of colonial history and the need to return to cultural kinship models and the land. Through this dual focus, the comic offers a model of conciliation grounded in historicized respect and cultural support.

Visualizing Complexity and Transformation in *The Outside Circle*

The award-winning graphic narrative, *The Outside Circle*, written by Patti LaBoucane-Benson (Métis) and illustrated by Kelly Mellings (Ukrainian / English-Canadian), offers a similar model of cultural reclamation for healing to *7 Generations*, but with a more detailed contemporary focus.[7] While *7 Generations* hints at Edwin's struggles, *The Outside Circle* explicitly explores contemporary Indigenous experiences of urban poverty, drug abuse, gangs, the child welfare system, and incarceration through the protagonist, Pete Carver, his younger brother Joey, and their mother, Bernice. These challenges are contextualized and complicated through integrated narration and diagrams of historical and institutional practices that continue to marginalize and stigmatize Indigenous peoples in Canada. Pete learns about these layers of challenge as he participates in a rehabilitation program while incarcerated. Through this woven storytelling, *The Outside Circle* helps readers visualize the complexity of current cultural forces and power dynamics that impact contemporary Indigenous youth, revealing their links to the intergenerational traumas of the residential school and child welfare systems. It also models a healing process for Pete through his embracing of his Cree culturally informed role as a provider and protector of his family and community: a warrior.

While charting important historical factors that inform Pete's familial story, the comic also establishes itself as a sovereign display territory for culturally specific healing practices and experiences. It offers a fictional depiction of the real *In Search of Your Warrior Program* (*Warrior Program*) for the rehabilitation of gang affiliated and incarcerated Indigenous men that LaBoucane-Benson works with at Native Counselling Services of Alberta (see Migdal). In the afterword to the graphic novel, she describes the program as "an intensive historical-trauma-healing process" (LaBoucane-Benson and Mellings n.p.). Through Pete's narrative, the novel expands on this process by contextualizing and sharing Indigenous needs for and strategies of cultural reclamation and revitalization. However, while accessibly presenting this process, the depictions of ceremonies are generally silent and only include framing narration to indicate their purpose and some basic practices. When Violet, the program facilitator, describes the ethnocidal and personal traumas of residential schools to introduce the need for healing at a sweat lodge ceremony, the story stops with her stating what she will sing and pray for, without showing her do either. At several other points, she states that they should pray and the images then silently show a prayer that is obviously being spoken. Thus, the storytelling grants partial access to the guest reader, while respecting the sanctity of that cultural space by keeping separate from the reader the language and some elements of the practices. Such controlled presentation implies that real access to such cultural practices can only happen in their embodied, participatory richness with the welcome and guidance of an Elder. The comic can only gesture to them and illustrate their impacts through the story of healing that follows.

The novel's creators guide readers in subtle ways by adjusting degrees of access, while also framing the story through more overt integrations of diagrammatic and infographic visual metaphors to educate readers about historical and contemporary policies and practices that can inform interpretations of character viewpoints and events. Through these visualizations, the graphic narrative seeks to expose personal, social, and institutional challenges for the characters, in order to establish the need for cultural reclamation and a conciliatory future.

The Outside Circle begins with Pete as an older man introducing the *Warrior Program* to two other men. He narrates the contemporary context of "a hard life in the inner city" for Indigenous people who feel "ashamed of their heritage," "hopeless and powerless," and who "still struggle with addictions, living in pain and confusion. There are no choices. Look what it does to our families" (n.p.). Pete then tells his story, which includes selling drugs, beating people, and abandoning his pregnant girlfriend. He is accepted into a gang that will be "just like family" (n.p.), during which he receives a tattoo. As a visual intervention into the story, a full-page panel zooms into Pete's arm, expanding the tattoo imagery, which is initially composed of a few letters and stylized blood just on his shoulder. In this image (fig. 14.5), however, the blood extends as pathways down his entire arm, and labels act as temporal markers to turn Pete's arm into a timeline.

The labels are in fact the titles of key colonial legislation since 1850 and of institutional spaces (residential schools) and practices (the 60s Scoop) that have directly controlled and attempted to assimilate Indigenous peoples and their territories in Canada. The use of this image at this very early moment is crucial, since it asks the reader to consider what role this history has in relation

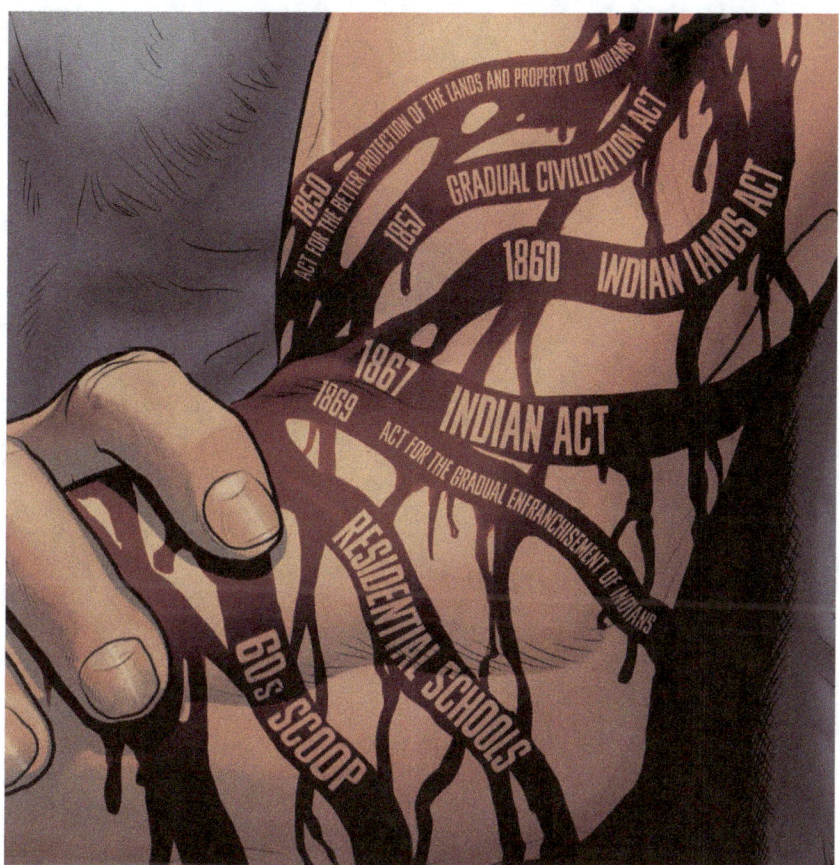

Figure 14.5. Close-up on the visual blend of tattoo and historical timeline of Canadian legislation and practices (LaBoucane-Benson and Mellings n.p.).

to the idea of family and the poverty, abuse, and gang violence that we have just witnessed. The timeline implies that historical knowledge should play an important role in explaining these challenging situations. Significantly, the visual blend of the timeline with Pete's blood shows how Indigenous peoples are deeply impacted by these colonial actions. As a visual metaphor for the intergenerational actions and impacts of colonization, the timeline-blood-tattoo blend grounds the conversation in a sense of living history, which sets up the story of intergenerational colonial trauma. Elsewhere in the story, another timeline blend—family trees—are drawn to highlight the recent histories of disruption. Readers will likely feel the resonances of this bloody tattoo as they read the narration of these family trees, and particularly as they witness Pete's anger at not being able to draw his own beyond his mother and brother. This clearly reflects the deep wounds of cultural and familial separation that this tattoo initially outlines, in particular with reference to residential schools and the 60s Scoop.

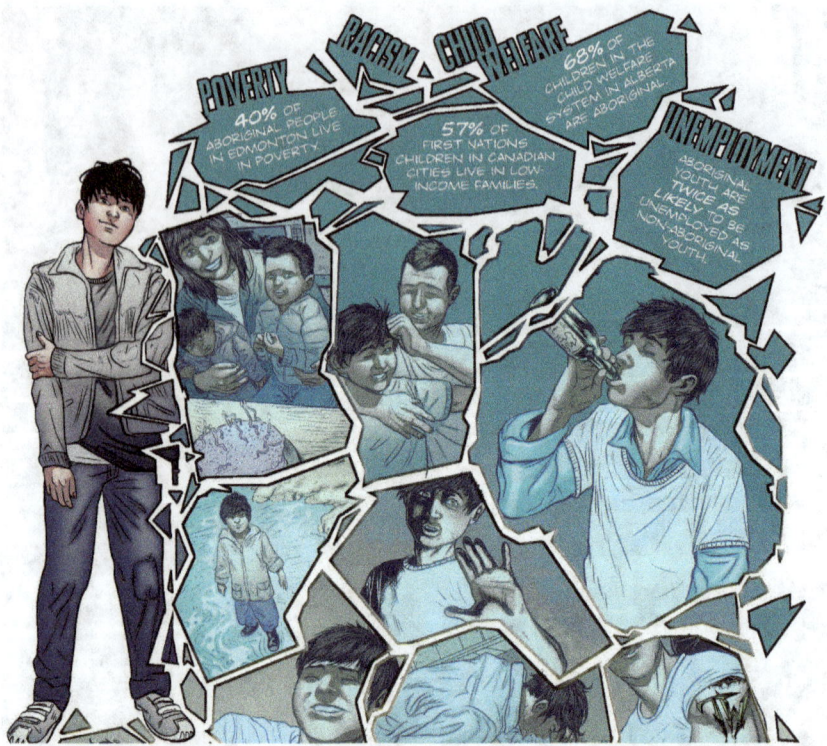

Figure 14.6. Portion of infographic summary of contemporary Indigenous statistics (LaBoucane-Benson and Mellings n.p.).

Another visual blend is seen when, following Pete's incarceration, his brother Joey is taken into child protective custody. His mother is obliged to sign a "Permanent Guardianship Order," which releases her parental rights to the state. The comic positions the reader to see the paperwork, with the page mimicking the form's title and opening lines, while replacing its contents with a concise history of forced removals of Indigenous children, noting especially that "Often children were apprehended due to poverty and negative preconceptions about Aboriginal culture" (n.p.). The final paragraph reads, "The Aboriginal child welfare case load continues to grow. In 2012, 68 percent of children involved in child welfare in Alberta were Aboriginal. My son is now a part of this history" (n.p.). The impacts of these removals are made particularly clear when Pete and Joey learn their familial history of disintegration through the residential schools and the 60s Scoop. *The Outside Circle* depicts these issues in order to acknowledge their impact on contemporary Indigenous people's lives, as well as to show a route to rebuilding Indigenous families and healthy communities.

The paperwork example also shows how *The Outside Circle* includes statistical information to ground the story in the Canadian present reality. Later in the story, as Joey tries to survive on the street after leaving an abusive group home, a full page (half shown in fig. 14.6) is taken over by a visual mosaic that blends brief images of Joey's life and surrounds them with key statistical information about Indigenous poverty, education, child welfare, and parenting.

Notably, the mosaic is composed of fractured paneling, a visual motif that reappears in particular when Pete and Joey learn from their uncle about his and their mother's 60s Scoop experiences of being separated from each other and their parents. Between this visual reminder of the socially fracturing challenges that Indigenous peoples face, and their clear link to colonial history, *The Outside Circle* guides readers to see these causal variables in order to understand the present situation and to support Indigenous cultural needs.

Finally, *The Outside Circle* not only charts histories, but shows a path to healing through Pete's experiences of ceremonies and reconnecting to his Cree background through his vision and acquiring a spirit name. These experiences are again illustrated in a visually conspicuous manner in order to signal how Pete changes, and why. Early in the story, whenever Pete became angry, his face would change into a white mask with red tears (which links to the blood of the previous tattoo example). However, he comes to learn that this mask of anger is a coping mechanism for deeper feelings of guilt, shame, and hopelessness. He comes to understand that he can control this anger, and draw strength from his true warrior spirit. The *Warrior Program* teaches him that he can take on his cultural role as a warrior who, as an Elder explains, protects and provides for his community and family as the outside circle around them. Through ceremony, he finds strength and control in his spirit animal and name, Waking Bear, which he sees in a vision. Through smudging (fig. 14.7), he learns to control and remove the negative reactive mask from before, with the strength of the bear being visually integrated into the smudging process through the paw prints in the smoke.

He later makes a literal mask with a bear on it to reflect his spiritual connection to this animal. Through this process of reconnecting to his cultural role and cosmology, Pete stands up against the violence of his old gang, finds peaceful work as a builder, and provides for his child. In the background of all of these later major events, a bear stands in support, emphasizing Pete's process of drawing strength from his cultural reclamation and new roles. Importantly, while the reactive mask of the early story appeared regularly as a clear visual intrusion that reflected his emotional state, the bear mask only appears once and then becomes hinted at through the background presence of the bear. This stylistic shift suggests that the earlier mask did not reflect Pete's inner nature, whereas the bear does. There is no need for the mask to indicate a change in identity, because Pete has embraced his true sense of self and is acting according to it. The shift from masked action to embodied presence indicates a path of healing and strength through the difficult process of cultural reclamation.

Figure 14.7. Pete's mask of anger being smudged away (LaBoucane-Benson and Mellings n.p.).

The Outside Circle employs a variety of visual and multimodal strategies to illustrate past traumas, present challenges, and future paths to Indigenous healing. There is much more within this excellent graphic novel to discuss regarding storytelling practices, but I have highlighted here some of the crucial ways that the creators have mobilized the comics medium to build complex depictions of Indigeneity in Canada. The comic acts as a sovereign display territory, since it makes accessible particular facets of ceremonies and identity, but also guides readers to see the need for cultural sovereignty and respect. For Indigenous readers, the story may offer insights into the past, present, and future of cultural reclamation, indicating a Cree perspective on this process, but in a way that likely entreats others to find strength in their own specific cultural traditions that have long been suppressed. The graphic novel guides non-Indigenous readers to a clearer understanding of historical factors that inform contemporary Indigenous experiences in Canada and makes a clear case for the embrace of cultural heterogeneity and respect. There are epistemic aspects of *The Outside Circle* that may cause a non-Cree reader to pause (for instance, an atheist may find the notions of spirit names and prayers problematic). But the powerful story of healing through the embrace of cultural practices that reaffirm kinship relations to family, community, and the creatures around us is necessary and instructive. In fact, being outside of these experiences does not negate their importance as they offer much to learn from and respect. As a display territory, the comic presents readers with opportunities to reflect on their assumptions about a wide array of familial, social, and cultural values. It shows the deeply destructive effects of governmental intervention that enacts a politics of assimilation and ethnocide rather than of respect and difference. Through the interweaving of history and the present, of insider and outsider perspectives and actions, and through a clear story of healing, *The Outside Circle* helps all readers envision healing and conciliation, modeling and guiding this through the strategic territorialization of the comics medium.

Graphical Conciliation

As the examples here have shown, Indigenous creators and their collaborative allies are using comics as a mediated form of Aboriginal sovereign display territories. The tensions between what is said and unsaid, shown and unseen, and how materials relate across the page and the story, allow the writers to act as Knowledge Keepers in guiding readers through complex colonial histories, intergenerational traumas, cultural practices, social needs, and healing processes. They articulate the need for cultural reclamation of kinship roles and values that have been actively eroded and fractured through attempted ethnocide, practices that produced what Cree scholar Neal McCleod calls the Cree "ideological diaspora" (28). These novels show the process of "coming home through story" by rebuilding kinship relations to family, ancestors, and the land, and finding "a place of speaking and narrating, wherein the experiences of the present can be understood as a function of the past" (33). Moreover, they attest to the decolonial healing this cultural reclamation can produce.

As I have shown, these Indigenous comics illustrate a complex interaction with readers through adaptations and manipulations of the medium, opening up opportunities to reflect on colonization and assimilation practices in Canada. As such, the multimodality of comics is mobilized and Indigenized to help readers visualize cultural reclamation, sovereignty, and healing, which fosters the empathetic and respectful imagination necessary for conciliation. Beyond the examples analyzed here range a wider variety of other fiction and nonfiction comics that further assert Indigenous representational autonomy through access and denial. The medium offers a complex space to strategically display Indigenous stories, which can only continue to add to the important work of Indigenous literatures that "build understanding, alliance, and respect, within, across, and beyond our differences" (Justice 112). As Daniel Heath Justice argues, Indigenous literatures unsettle a wide range of colonial stories about what it means to be human, to connect to the world as kin, to be a good ancestor, and to build a vibrant future. The Indigenous comics discussed here have shown how this heretofore Western medium's multimodality can be mobilized to contribute to these decolonial and alternative perspectives. Surely many more important interventions through Indigenous comics are to come.

Notes

A postdoctoral award from the Social Science and Humanities Research Council of Canada supported the research and writing of this chapter. My thanks to the David Garneau, HighWater Press, and House of Anansi Press for their kind permission to include the images found in this chapter. My gratitude to Sara Sultan and Bart Beaty for valuable feedback on this chapter. I am also thankful for the conversations I had years ago with Margery Fee, which have stayed with me and informed this work. I dedicate this chapter to Sara, Madeleine, and Zoë.

1. It is noteworthy that *The Globe and Mail* reprinted Lenore Keeshig [-Tobias]'s essay from January 26, 1990 again online on May 19, 2017. The problem of cultural appropriation in Canada has not been resolved.

2. See the excellent concise, introductory resource regarding the Canadian contexts of Indigenous rights, identities, cultures, legislation, and other related topics at *Indigenous Foundations* (Indigenousfoundations.arts.ubc.ca).

3. I am mindful of Tuck and Yang's critique of using decolonization as a metaphor to sidestep the place-based, material reality of decolonization efforts to reclaim territories and resources to support cultural and communal revitalization (for an important Canadian-specific argument in this vein, see Manuel and Derrickson's *Reconciliation Manifesto*). Such a critique is salient in the Canadian context, where treaty agreements have regularly gone unheeded and, in the case of most of the western province of British Columbia, territories remain unceded and in ongoing treaty negotiations. It is crucial to recognize that decolonizing space on paper and decolonizing space in place are distinct registers of experience. At the same time, the telling of these stories helps to inform the Canadian social awareness of territory and cultural rights and potentially facilitates the process of territory reclamation. Thus, the metaphorical usage may help support the material enactment of decolonization.

4. An earlier version of this chapter was published under the same main title in *West Coast Line* 74, no. 2 (2012): 27–38. I rely on the stronger revised version cited in this chapter. The source painting remains the same (2012. Oil on canvas, 5'x4').

5. Lauren is an interesting yet underdeveloped character unto herself. She is shown as a positive support for the men, by encouraging them to adapt to the challenges presented by colonial institutions while holding onto their stories. The men, it seems at the end of the story, are beginning their process of cultural reclamation through reconnection with the land and their

role as community providers, which Lauren sets them up for. At the same time, it is unclear how she has navigated the colonial institutions to maintain this perspective herself.

6. *The Outside Circle* does not announce its cultural tradition like *7 Generations* does of its Plains Cree tradition. The characters have grandparents from the Blackfish Lake Cree First Nation, and the Warrior Program seems to reflect similar Cree practices to those presented in *7 Generations*. I must leave it to a Cree or perhaps Métis reader or scholar to offer a more nuanced engagement with these depictions of cultural practices, objects, and attire.

Works Cited

Bombay, Amy, Kimberly Matheson, and Hymie Anisman. "The Intergenerational Effects of Indian Residential Schools: Implications for the Concept of Historical Trauma." *Transcultural Psychiatry* 51, no. 3 (2014): 320–38.

Borkent, Mike. "Mediated Characters: Multimodal Viewpoint Construction in Comics." *Cognitive Linguistics* 28, no. 3 (2017).

CBC Radio. "Curious about How Many of the TRC's Calls to Actions Have Been Completed? Check Ian Mosby's Twitter." *Unreserved*, 2017, http://www.cbc.ca/radio/unreserved/how-are-you-putting-reconciliation-into-action-1.4362219/curious-about-how-many-of-the-trc-s-calls-to-actions-have-been-completed-check-ian-mosby-s-twitter-1.4364330.

Chute, Hillary. "Comics as Literature? Reading Graphic Narrative." *PMLA* 123, no. 2 (2008): 452–65.

Coleman, Daniel. "Epistemic Justice, CanLit, and the Politics of Respect." *Canadian Literature* 204 (2010): 124–26.

Cutrara, Samantha. "Drawn out of History: The Representation of Women in Chester Brown's Louis Riel: A Comic-Strip Biography." In *Graphic History: Essays on Graphic Novels and/as History*, edited by Richard Iadonisi, 121–43. Cambridge Scholars Publishing, 2012.

Daschuk, James. *Clearing the Plains: Disease, Politics of Starvation, and the Loss of Aboriginal Life*. University of Regina Press, 2013.

El Refaie, Elisabeth. "Multiliteracies: How Readers Interpret Political Cartoons." *Visual Communication* 8, no. 2 (2009): 181–205.

Fee, Margery. *Literary Land Claims: The "Indian Land Question" from Pontiac's War to Attawapiskat*. Wilfrid Laurier University Press, 2015.

Forceville, Charles, Tony Veale, and Kurt Feyaerts. "Balloonics: The Visuals of Balloons in Comics." In *The Rise and Reason of Comics and Graphic Literature: Critical Essays on the Form*, edited by Joyce Goggin and Dan Hassler-Forest, 56–73. McFarland, 2010.

Fournier, Suzanne, and Ernie Crey. *Stolen from Our Embrace: The Abduction of First Nations Children and the Restoration of Aboriginal Communities*. Douglas & McIntyre, 1997.

Godard, Barbara. "The Politics of Representation: Some Native Canadian Women Writers." *Canadian Literature* 124–25 (1990): 183–225.

Gray, Brenna Clarke. "Border Studies in the Gutter: Canadian Comics and Structural Borders." *Canadian Literature* 228/229 (2016): 170–87.

Harper, Stephen. "Statement of Apology to Former Students of Indian Residential Schools." *Indigenous and Northern Affairs Canada*, 2008, http://www.aadnc-aandc.gc.ca/eng/1100100015644/1100100015649.

Harrison, Richard. "Seeing and Nothingness: Michael Nicoll Yahgulanaas, Haida Manga, and a Critique of the Gutter." *Canadian Review of Comparative Literature / Revue Canadienne de Littérature Comparée* 43, no. 1 (2016): 51–74.

Justice, Daniel Heath. *Why Indigenous Literatures Matter.* Wilfrid Laurier University Press, 2018.

King, C. Richard. "Alter/Native Heroes: Native Americans, Comic Books, and the Struggle for Self-Definition." *Cultural Studies—Critical Methodologies* 9, no. 2 (2009): 214–23.

Laboucane-Benson, Patti. *The Outside Circle: A Graphic Novel.* Illus. Kelly Mellings. House of Anansi Press, 2015.

Lesk, Andrew. "Redrawing Nationalism: Chester Brown's Louis Riel: A Comic-Strip Biography." *Journal of Graphic Novels & Comics* 1, no. 1 (2010): 63–81.

Manuel, Arthur, and Ronald Derrickson. *Reconciliation Manifesto: Recovering the Land, Rebuilding the Economy.* James Lorimer, 2017.

Migdal, Alex. "Graphic Novel 'The Outside Circle' Aims to Become a Tool for Aboriginal Healing." *Quillblog*, 2015, https://quillandquire.com/authors/2015/04/28/graphic-novel-the-outside-circle-aims-to-become-a-tool-for-aboriginal-healing/.

Miller, J. R. *Shingwauk's Vision: A History of Native Residential Schools.* University of Toronto Press, 1996.

Milloy, John S. *A National Crime: The Canadian Government and the Residential School System, 1879 to 1986.* University of Manitoba Press, 1999.

Palmater, Pamela. "Genocide, Indian Policy, and Legislated Elimination of Indians in Canada." *Aboriginal Policy Studies* 3, no. 3 (2014): 27–54.

———. "Stretched beyond Human Limits: Death by Poverty in First Nations." *Canadian Review of Social Policy* 65/66 (2011): 112–27.

Robertson, David Alexander. *7 Generations: A Plains Cree Saga.* Illus. Scott B. Henderson. HighWater Press, 2012.

Sheyahshe, Michael A. *Native Americans in Comic Books: A Critical Study.* McFarland, 2008.

Spiers, Miriam Brown. "Creating a Haida Manga: The Formline of Social Responsibility in Red." *Studies in American Indian Literatures* 26, no. 3 (2014).

Tuck, Eve, and K. Wayne Yang. "Decolonization Is Not a Metaphor." *Decolonization: Indigeneity, Education, & Society* 1, no. 1 (2012): 1–40.

Woolford, Andrew. "Ontological Destruction: Genocide and Canadian Aboriginal Peoples." *Genocide Studies and Prevention* 4, no. 1 (2009): 81–97.

Deep Time and Vast Place: Visualizing Land/ Water Relations across Time and Space in *Moonshot: The Indigenous Comics Collection*

Jeremy M. Carnes

In 1972, after the minor success of her album *She Used to Wanna Be a Ballerina*, Buffy Sainte-Marie (Plains Cree) released her eighth album, *Moonshot*. The title track focuses on both time and space, highlighting the ways in which settler conceptions fail to grasp how indigeneity complicates dominant ideologies of spatiality and temporality. In the refrain, which opens the song, Sainte-Marie sings: "Off into outer space you go my friends / We wish you bon voyage / And when you get there we will welcome you again / And still you'll wonder at it all." The narrator of the song addresses unknown individuals by wishing them good luck on their journey into space. Coming three years after the Apollo 11 moon landing, the song is likely a reference to the culmination of the infamous "Space Race" between the United States and the USSR. However, after immediately wishing these "friends" well, the same narrator notes that they will be "welcome[d] . . . again" in space. In this way, Sainte-Marie places Indigenous communities, a central concern in much of her music, in outer space prior to both global powers. In "Moonshot," reaching outer space is not necessarily a bodily experience, but one that relies on a spiritual connection with the creator.

Sainte-Marie further complicates settler ontology by denying a simple, causative association between the past and the present. Rather, Sainte-Marie simultaneously depicts how Indigenous voices are not solely marked as existing in the past, "enshrined in some great hourglass . . . entombed in some great English class," and establishes settlers as "primitive" themselves in the figure of the anthropologist who "spoke in a language oh so primitive, that he made sense to me." By, above, marking Indigenous communities as futuristic in their relationship to the cosmos and here marking settlers as "primitive," Sainte-Marie complicates notions of linear temporality or of progress. Rather, the relationships between past, present, and future are demarcated through Indigenous orientations to both spatiality and temporality, which champions Indigenous self-determination and ontologies over settler ones.

More than forty years after the release of Sainte-Marie's song challenging settler conceptions of time and space, the Toronto, Canada-based publisher Alternate History Comics produced the groundbreaking *Moonshot: The Indigenous Comics Collection*, Volume 1. The collection includes work by Indigenous artists and writers like Arigon Starr (Kickapoo), Elizabeth LaPensée (Anishinaabe/Métis/Irish), Richard Van Camp (Tłı̨chǫ), Jay & Joel Odjick (Kitigan Zibi Anishinabeg), and Michael Sheyahshe (Caddo), among so many others. The project was funded through Kickstarter and received $74,792 from 1,569 backers. Information on Kickstarter notes that the collection includes tales "From traditional stories to exciting new visions of the future." *Moonshot* provided one of the most concentrated efforts to centralize Indigenous voices and epistemologies as they extend outward from the stories being told. Editor Hope Nicholson notes that the collection considers similar concerns to Sainte-Marie's song, after which it is named. Nicholson writes in the foreword, "*Moonshot* is the title of this book as it is a song that I feel details the concepts of extraterrestrial and religious contact present in many Native communities across North America long before colonization" (7). *Moonshot*, like so much Indigenous art before it, is borne out of Indigenous ways of knowing and experiencing the world.

In their foreword to Thomas M. Norton-Smith's (Shawnee) *The Dance of Person and Place*, editors Agnes B. Curry and Anne Waters (Seminole/Choctaw/Chickasaw/Cherokee) write about their edited series "Living Indigenous Philosophies":

> [The series] is about a hope that documenting some thoughts and ideas about the ways worlds are, and how humans live in those worlds, might enable us to realize the vastness from which our ideas are born, and immeasurable openness to which we may turn for our creativity. It is about opening the life of our voices to the immense task that lies before us, as human, and as beings in the world, to reach for the horizon of our new worlds. (xiv)

Curry and Waters give voice to a wide envisioning of Indigenous being, which focuses on the interrelatedness of place, time, and Indigenous epistemologies. *Moonshot* is emblematic of this same envisioning, precisely because it highlights dynamic and fluid representations of Native communities that reach across time and space to make sense of "the ways worlds are, and how humans live in those worlds."

Scholars like Susan Bernardin have argued that comics specifically offer a form for Indigenous writers to "affirm dynamic relationships between Indigenous pasts and futures." Bernardin writes, "In refusing rigid boundaries between literary and visual arts, they [comics] also re-animate relationships with visual and sequential storytelling practices that stretch back millennia"

(480). The form of comics, a medium in which time is registered spatially through both the use of panels across the page and through the gutters, offers a particularly compelling medium through which to think about the importance of time and place in relationship to land/waters.[1]

Will Eisner has famously argued that the use of panels "indicates the duration of the event. Indeed, it effectively 'tells' time. The magnitude of time elapsed is not expressed by the panel per se ..." but "the fusing of symbols, images, and balloons makes the statement" (26). Thus, for Eisner, one of the ways time is told throughout a comic is with panels, across which artists can depict temporal movement. Yet, in a different vein, comics theorist Thierry Groensteen notes that panels, "situated relationally, are, necessarily, placed in relation to space and operate on a share of space" (21). For Groensteen, panels also help to demarcate the place of the narrative through the use of space on the page. Together Eisner and Groensteen indicate the ways in which the formal pieces of comics (panels, balloons, images) work in tandem to create a story in both space and time. In fact, spatiality and temporality are central concerns for all of comics storytelling, which is what makes exploring Indigenous conceptions of time and place so complex when reading a comics collection like *Moonshot*.

In the remainder of this chapter, I will follow Sainte-Marie's example and Bernardin's arguments about Indigenous comics form to explore how the art within *Moonshot* embodies a complex interweaving of time and place to think through the complex relations of living beings[2] and land/waters that pushes against settler orientations. By examining both specific stories in *Moonshot* as well as the specific organization of the text as a comics anthology, I argue that such artwork offers new and vital ways for re-envisioning relationships between art and land/water in local (tribally specific), global (trans-Indigenous), and even cosmic contexts. That is, while specific tribal communities view these interconnections in their given specific contexts, the overarching attitudes concerning these relations across time and space in local, global, and cosmic contexts require that we also think across tribal affiliations. As Chadwick Allen notes of trans-Indigenous methodology, "The point is not to displace the necessary, invigorating study of specific traditions and contexts but rather to complement these by augmenting and expanding broader, globally Indigenous fields of inquiry" (xiv). *Moonshot* is particularly useful in thinking through trans-Indigenous modes of meaning making because it is an anthology that already puts individuals from various tribal affiliations into conversation with one another.

Deep Time and Vast Place

Moonshot, as a collection of comics from multiple writers and artists from various tribal communities, foregrounds Indigenous understandings of the connections between living beings and land/waters in two ways. First, *Moonshot* depicts a wide temporal history of land/waters in association with both humans and nonhumans. In one theorization, Wai Chee Dimock has referred to a view across millennia as deep time. She argues that what deep time "highlights is a set of longitudinal frames, at once projective and recessional with input going both ways, and binding continents and millennia into many loops of relations, a densely interactive fabric" (3–4). Thinking in terms of deep time opens the possibility of thinking across the past, present, and future, simultaneously considering each. Yet, at the same time, considering cross-temporal frames reaches beyond national formations and people or groups of people. While individuals or communities do not cease mattering as critical relations, they become important in the larger web of the cosmos across deep time. As Dimock notes, "Scale enlargement along the temporal axis changes our very sense of connectedness among human beings" (5). Indigenous ontologies have, since time immemorial, been imbued with an eye toward deep time, which then shapes the interrelation between (non)humans and land/waters.

Indigenous orientations toward temporality are precisely what Mark Rifkin tries to address in his book *Beyond Settler Time*. Rifkin notes that attending to Native conceptions of temporality means purposefully thinking past settler temporalities and the "needs, claims, and norms" associated with colonial visions (4). In opposition to a shared time, where we all experience temporality collectively, Rifkin, following scientific theories of relativity and Indigenous anticolonial scholarship, suggests thinking through time in terms of "frames of reference." In Rifkin's view, "a notion of temporal frames of reference can provide ways that Native and non-native trajectories [. . .] might be distinguished without resorting to a notion of shared time (almost always skewed toward non-native framings), thereby opening up room conceptually for the expression of varied forms of temporal sovereignty" (30). In *Moonshot*, the attention toward deep time as a way of understanding the relations of all things, embeds the collection in an anticolonial conceit. Precisely because the collection decenters settler frames of temporality, it becomes a project in reclaiming Indigenous sovereignty and self-determination rather than simply a project with artwork by Native artists. It makes visible the ongoing emergence of Indigenous peoplehood, rather than becoming conscripted to the settler frame of reference that marks indigeneity as static, primitive, and Traditional.[3]

Second, *Moonshot* begins to constellate the relations between land/waters and living beings through what I am calling vast place. In this iteration, vast place is focused on stories that, in their vastness, lean into cosmic significance, that reach beyond the local, national, or even global. However, vast place is about more than showing stories that reach beyond specific locales, but also relies on those stories of cosmic significance providing meaning in and across local, national, and global contexts. In theorizing vast place, I follow geographer Tim Cresswell who writes that "the most straightforward and common definition of place [is] a meaningful location" and that "place is also a way of seeing, knowing, and understanding the world" (7, 11). *Moonshot* intermingles the cosmic with the local, the national, and the global to show the ways in which understandings of land/water matter for every place in the cosmos. All places rely on connections between land/water and living beings and are thus imbued with meaning and importance. Local understandings of these connections rely on cosmic ones, and vice versa; this is what *Moonshot* works to make visible in the comics medium.

The concept of vast place is deeply indebted to Glen Coulthard's notion of "gounded normativity," which he defines as "modalities of Indigenous and land-connected practices and longstanding experiential knowledge that inform and structure our ethical engagements with the world and our relationships with human and nonhuman others over time" (13). Indigenous practices of anticolonial resistance have always centered on questions of land, because land has been and continues to be the central element of settler colonial dominance. Vast place, like deep time, encompasses a wide view of place, seeing its importance as not relegated to a subset of specific lands, but embedded in all lands and places across and beyond this planet and into the cosmos. Vast place stretches Coulthard's account that, "Place is a way of knowing, of experiencing and relating to the world and with others; and sometimes these relational practices and forms of knowledge guide forms of resistance against other rationalizations of the world that threaten to erase or destroy our senses of place" (61). Vast place pushes toward a decolonial view of the local, national, global, and cosmic by contradicting settler conceptions of place as conquerable, ownable, or controllable.

In previous work, most notably Vine Deloria Jr.'s *God Is Red*, scholars have argued that a fundamental difference between Indigenous and settler views center on questions of land versus those of temporality. According to Deloria, Indigenous communities describe their lands (places) as having "the highest possible meaning," while settlers, because of movement from one place to another, mark history (time) "in the best possible light" (61). While in many ways this fundamental difference is of paramount importance, I follow Deloria in noting that, through a focus on place, temporality remains markedly important for Indigenous communities. In discussing the importance of sacred spaces to various religions, Deloria writes, "But it would seem likely that whereas religions that are spatially determined can create a sense of sacred time that originates in the specific location, it is exceedingly difficult for a religion, once bound to history, to incorporate sacred places into its doctrines. Space generates time, but time has little relationship to space" (70).[4] The relationship to specific lands for Indigenous communities is actually what allows for a more comprehensive view of time that refuses settler colonialism and western temporality.

The complex constellations of vast place and deep time can be encapsulated in a single term in some languages. For example, in the Indigenous

North American language, Anishinaabemowin (Ojibwe), the term might be rendered *giizhodibaa'iganeg*.[5] While this word literally means "heat time," it describes the notion of a core energy that exists beyond place and time, a kind of presence within nothingness—within the place before place and the time before time—an accounting of the core energy of the cosmos.[6] Such a presence, which is embodied in the animacy and connection of all things, lies at the center of *Moonshot*. Language comes together with visual representation in the comics medium to depict understandings of land/water, human, and nonhuman interconnections on all levels. To explore these depictions, I focus on two features of *Moonshot*: its organization as a comics anthology and the use of Indigenous science fiction in comics form to think beyond settler conceptions of time and space and the importance of relations between land/waters and living beings.

Moonshot, An Anthology

In his afterword to *Moonshot*, the president of Alternative History Comics, Andy Stanleigh, discusses the creation of the collection noting that "we ended up with 13 stories. Perhaps this was also serendipity" (158). He elaborates by quoting Elizabeth LaPensée: "Many Native Americans share the knowledge of the thirteen moons on a turtle's back. There are thirteen large segments which represent the thirteen moons which make up the lunar year. Every group of Native Americans has names for the thirteen moons and there are stories to go with each new moon." The number of stories in this collection carries with it a specific weight in many Indigenous traditions, but in all those traditions it is just as important to think about how the pieces make up the whole. The aesthetics of anthologies, in many ways, are based on the composition of the entire collection, similarly to the way the segments on a turtle's back make up the shell or the different moons make up the lunar year. The pieces and their relations to one another highlight some central concerns for the authors, artists, and a variety of Indigenous communities around the world.

The first few pages of *Moonshot* are not comics, per se. Instead art from Indigenous artists, some of which come directly from the comics themselves, introduces the collection. These pieces are mixed with the foreword by editor Hope Nicholson and the introduction by comics scholar and artist Michael Sheyahshe. The opening of the collection with these four images introduce what I am arguing are central concerns for the collection as a whole: the relations of land/waters, humans, and nonhumans across more comprehensive understandings of place and time. While each of these opening images might only depict some of these concerns, it is their juxtaposition that creates the larger narrative across time and space.

Moonshot: The Indigenous Comics Collection, vol. 1. Stephen Gladue (Métis), "Northern Crow."

The first image, Stephen Gladue's (Métis) "Northern Crow," focuses on Indigenous humanity and spirituality across space and time through what we might call a cosmic aesthetic. The entirety of the piece is made of small geometrical particles placed in relation to one another on a black background. The connections between these minute fractals creates the image of the Northern Crow individual. Yet, the aesthetic of the fractals alone seems to recall the stars spread across the night sky. In the same way that Gladue connected the fractals to create a picture with local meaning, cultures across the world have connected the stars to tell stories of local, national, and global significance. Such is a concern in some of the comics throughout the collection, which I discuss below.

"Northern Crow" also includes other small images that are contained within and alongside the fractals making up the central figure of the piece. The presence of the images, including the Native on horseback, the tepee, and the flying bird, mirrors artwork that has appeared throughout history across many Indigenous communities. They first resemble the pieces of art that appear as pictographs throughout the world. Yet associations to pictographs also exist as ledger art and hide records.[7] While mainstream views of Indigenous cultures might place these art forms distinctly in the past as ancient and "primitive," such a relegation ignores the engagements Indigenous artists have with these same forms across history. From before colonization to the contemporary moment, pictographs, ledger art, and hide records have been central to the way Indigenous storytellers mark an understanding of their past, present, and future in the world around them. These images tie into a narrative offered by "Northern Crow" that stretches across temporalities and locales, thus continually demonstrating that this art, then and now, is anything but simple. These forms alone embody the concept of deep time; the semiotics wrapped up in these simultaneously contemporary and ancient forms of composing and knowing are simultaneously active in the past, present, and future beyond any specific Indigenous nation.

Finally, throughout this piece, there are small splotches of red and blue that take on the aesthetic quality of liquid, which cause them to stand out from the more angular, sharp fractals that make up the bulk of the image. These splotches drip down the images giving them a feel of blood and water, respectively. These colors call to mind the histories of Indigenous communities, through both colonialism, that resulted in much spilled blood, and the continued return to the life-giving force of water. Thus, through the inclusion of the cosmic fractals, the smaller drawn images, and the liquid-like spots, this opening image, a smaller version of which is on the cover of the collection, alone foregrounds the connections of land/waters and living beings across deep time and vast place.

Gladue also offers two other pieces, which appear later in *Moonshot*. Both "Thunderbird" and "Untitled" lean even more explicitly into a cosmic aesthetic. While both images make use of the same type of fractal pieces that appear in "Northern Crow," they appear next to astral bodies like stars and nebulas. "Untitled," which appears nearly halfway through the collection, depicts a human body made up of fractals reaching out in front of it. "Thunderbird," which appears toward the end of the collection, shows a Thunderbird made up of these same images. These three images by Gladue, appearing throughout the collection, continue to accentuate the cosmic as readers encounter the specific stories of local significance. "Northern Crow" emphasizes the importance of local spirituality in the cosmos of all things through the representation of a Crow in regalia so important to Crow spiritual practice, while "Thunderbird" and "Untitled" draw attention to supernatural beings, the thunderbird and the creator, respectively. Gladue's images continue to urge the reader to remember the cosmic along with the local and the global.

The image which immediately follows "Northern Crow," Nicholas Burns's "Caribou," further extends questions of deep time by focusing beyond the human. The image shows a herd of caribou trekking across a snow-covered mountain, and it appears later in the collection as the title image to Richard Van Camp, Rosa Mantia, and Nicholas Burns's "Tlicho Nàowo." The lack of a represented human in the image decenters humans in favor of the natural world and processes of the caribou. Further, similarly to "Northern Crow," the lack of specific icons in the image marks it as existing outside of rigid understandings of time. Caribou have trekked across snow-covered mountains for millennia and will continue to do so. However, whereas "Northern Crow" highlights the cosmic through what I have called a cosmic aesthetic, "Caribou" focuses on the extremely local. Vast place and deep time conceptualize seeing beyond just the specifics so that relations across times and places can be relational rather than hierarchical. The juxtaposition of the two images requires that readers think in terms of both deep time and vast place, even from the opening of the collection.

A third image in the collection, which follows "Caribou," is "Water Spirit" by Hawei Hou. Next to the focus on land, humans, and nonhumans in the previous images, Hou's depiction of the spirit of the water forefronts the importance of the animacy of nonhuman beings in understanding both an Indigenous aesthetic and worldview. Hou's "Water Spirit" also pushes beyond the human to depict an animacy within the being of the land/water itself. Here we see a depiction of a small piece of the *giizhodibaa'iganeg*. Water is given an animacy, albeit still anthropomorphic, which enables readers to think about nonhuman actants and their effects in the fabric of life at large. Representing water imbued with life pictured next to a man-made creation of the water pump further illustrates the reliance of the human on water as a powerful and life-giving resource and hints toward a deep time wherein the spirit of the water exists beyond the human and yet in intimate relation to the human.

Where "Northern Crow" highlights the human and the cosmic, "Caribou" highlights the nonhuman and the local, and "Water Spirit" highlights the land/water animacy and the reliance of the human on said animacy, the final introductory image, "Preserver" by Jeffrey Veregge (Suquamish/Duwamish) brings these focuses together in a broad Indigenous context. In this image, we see an Indigenous woman sitting and weaving a basket above which is an almost ethereal lupine form. This is repeated along the top half of the two-page spread. According to the caption, the Indigenous woman weaving the basket is working to "preserve stories and culture . . . out of duty and honour to the ancestors, as well as [to leave] a marker for those in the future looking for their roots." The creation of the basket marks the importance of the nonhuman as evidenced by the wolf depictions being woven into the essence of the basket itself. Further, the cloudy shapes that come in to form the reeds of the basket and the small starlike spots also follow a cosmic aesthetic that pushes beyond the local in understanding the importance of relationality. Thus, the basket literally breathes in the cosmic and the nonhuman central to *giizhodibaa'iganeg*. Further, this image shows the ways these interrelations also include land/water through the placement of the woman herself. She sits on what seems to be at once land and water. The large circles that form the bottom of the image resemble concentric circles on the surface of a calm lake when it is touched. Yet, the alternating dark blue and dark maroon coloring convey both water and land. The deep red color calls to mind the soil of the land itself, and the ends of the woman's dress take on an almost liquid quality. Veregge's image encourages readers to keep relationality in mind, both across time and place as we enter the stories which, like the woman weaving the basket, the writers and artists are creating, both for their communities and for all who care to explore the complexities and importance of Indigenous stories.

Moonshot: The Indigenous Comics Collection, vol. 1. Jeffrey Veregge (S'Klallam/Suquamish/Duwamish), "Preserver."

Each of the stories throughout the collection, and oftentimes the juxtaposition of stories themselves, call attention to *giizhodibaa'iganeg*. One story, "Ochek," depicts an understanding of cosmic bodies, specifically constellations, and the ways that they constitute a Cree understanding of "what is above" being mirrored in "what is below." "Ochek" tells the story of the lynx who traveled to the highest point in creation and stole warmth from the sky people to end the seemingly endless winter. While trying to escape the sky people, Ochek is shot and killed. He is immortalized in the constellation of the Big Dipper.

Similarly, "Coyote and the Pebbles" accounts for an understanding of constellations through complex relationships between humans, nonhumans, and land/waters. In this story, all the animals are invited by the creator to create images in the sky using stones found in waters across the land. Coyote, who was running later than everyone else, realizes after gathering his rocks that there is only one place left in the sky for him to create his picture. As he moves toward the place he falls and his stones scatter across the sky, messing up everyone else's images. This short comic shows, again, the ways in which land/waters become foundational for an understanding of *giizhodibaa'iganeg*, the cosmic energy that constitutes interrelations in all things. What is particularly important in this story is the fact that Coyote gathers "sparkling pebbles" from both the land and the water and that these same pebbles constitute the relationships between the nonhumans featured in the story and the humans that exist beyond such. The story concludes:

> Tonight you might hear Coyote howling across the lake, in the field, or somewhere in the distance. You see, the night creatures are still upset with him, and will not let him join any of their celebrations. Know that Coyote is speaking to the great mystery, asking for another chance for the night creatures to draw their portraits again. And as you listen to Coyote, look up. Look above the tree tops, the mountains, the clouds, and moon . . . and you can see the pebbles Coyote scattered. We call these pebbles . . . stars. (46)

In both "Ochek" and "Coyote and the Pebbles," stories are used to demonstrate Indigenous understandings of the universe. Each story offers explanations for why things are the way they are—why we have stars, why Coyote howls, why the Big Dipper exists, why it is not always winter—and these explanations rely on *giizhodibaa'iganeg*, the relation of all things across time and space. From the hero of the lynx to the problematic Coyote, from the sky people to the great mystery, from the beds of the waters to the stars in the sky, Indigenous stories make sense of creation through relationality. These comics make those relations centrally visible.

Indigenous Science Fiction

In the introduction to her anthology *Walking the Clouds: An Anthology of Indigenous Science Fiction*, Grace Dillon notes that Indigenous science fiction (sf) "*change*[s] the parameters of [the genre of] sf" broadly (3). While sf is constantly changing, and has been for some time, the stories that have solidified the genre are entrenched in western conceptions of time, space, and being. Yet, the very nature of science fiction makes it a genre malleable to a variety of ontologies and understandings of the universe at large. Thus, Indigenous sf writers can play with character or setting and can "stretch boundaries" to represent Indigenous conceptions of time, space, and relationality in a way that "foundational" sf cannot. Rather than depicting yet another colonial expansion onto a distant planet inhabited by "simple" or "primitive" beings, Indigenous sf can represent the continuity of indigeneity itself. By representing indigeneity as existing beyond the colonial past and beyond the frontier, Indigenous sf stretches colonial understandings of time and space. As Dillon notes, Indigenous sf "returns us to ourselves by encouraging Native writers to write about Native conditions in Native-centered worlds liberated by the imagination" (11).

Many of the stories in *Moonshot* could be categorized as Indigenous sf. They each, following tribally specific traditions, use the genre of sf to represent Indigenous orientations to *giizhodibaa'iagneg*. Whether through retellings of traditional stories in a futuristic setting, through highlighting the continued importance of stories themselves across time and space, or through using aesthetic representation to call attention to the importance of our understanding of connections between living beings and land/waters, the stories in *Moonshot* are able to stretch the boundaries of the genre in order to make room for a wider understanding of orientations to time, space, and relationality. In many ways, these stories aid authors in "recover[ing] the Native space of the past, to bring it to the attention of contemporary readers, and to build better futures" (Dillon 4).

In Arigon Starr and David Cutler's (Qalipu Mi'kmaq) story "Ue-Pucase: Water Master," Starr makes use of sf to set a retelling of the Muskogee-Creek story "The Young Man Who Turned into a Snake" in the distant future where two Muskogee-Creek men travel to find the old Creek home world. After failing to follow off-protocol and eating a can of Spam, one of the young men becomes a snake, the water master. The other takes him to a lake and brings his grandmother to visit him. The water master then takes her with him underwater and they do not return.

While it would be possible in the realm of sf to explain why the transformation happened, perhaps through radiation soaked up in the food on the now uninhabited Earth, the point of the story is not to explain but to warn. The stories of the elders, Muskogee-Creek elders in this tradition, point out specific ways in which individuals are not to interact with other human or nonhuman beings. Failing to respect these warnings produces specific consequences. Issues of relationality are so central to the story of "Ue-Pucase" that they shape both the beginning and the ending. Warnings like "no off-world food" highlight specific ways Indigenous communities relate to the larger world, but those relations do not break down when the protocols are not followed. The consequence, the transformation of the young man into a snake, changes his relation to the world around him. He becomes a nonhuman being that remains important in the interaction between all things.

At the close of the story, the remaining young man tells readers, "He took her under the water. They never came back. I'm just an old junker. Who would believe me? I'm telling you now—those old stories are true. The Creek home world is real. So is Ue-Pucase, the water master. He's a friend of mine" (72). While this story focuses on the proper way to live out relations between all things, it also becomes a way to show the importance of traditional stories across times and spaces. As I stated above, this version of "Ue-Pucase" is based in a traditional Muskogee-Creek story. In that original story, the two young men are hunters that are not to eat eggs they find on the riverbank. What this version of the story shows is that the warnings do not stop being important when the Earth becomes uninhabitable. Beyond the Earth and beyond the contemporary moment, these stories are a part of time immemorial and write the relationship between all things in the cosmos.

Visualizing Land/Water Relations across Time and Space in *Moonshot* 311

Moonshot: The Indigenous Comics Collection, vol. 1. Todd Houseman (Cree) and Ben Shannon, "Ayanisach."

Similar to the story of "Ue-Pucase" are the stories "Ayanisach," by Todd Houseman (Cree) and Ben Shannon, and "Strike and Bolt" by Michael Sheyahshe and George Freeman. "Ayanisach," which is the Cree word for "He who tells stories of the past," shows a grandmother and her grandson as he tells her the story she once taught him about their people. In a veiled analogy for colonialism in North America, the young man tells of the coming of the dispectors, machines who "ate everything they could find" with the help of their machines called rippers (134). He closes the story by telling of the Chief Maskwa, who led the resistance against the dispectors and drove them from the planet. Upon completing the story, he realizes that his grandmother has died. He goes on to join a gathering of others and begins the story of their people for them. In the final panel of the story we see that they are at the base of a ruined, postapocalyptic Big Ben in London.

Within the collection, "Ayanisach" is one of the clearest examples of putting a settler orientation to the world next to an Indigenous one. The analogy of settlers to the dispectors, which are depicted as devouring machines interested only in the use of the land, is represented through an abstraction of settler colonialism itself. In Scott McCloud's terms, cartooning is about abstraction, which does not mean "eliminating details" as much as "focusing on specific details. By stripping down an image to its essential 'meaning,' an artist can amplify that meaning in a way that realistic art can't" (30). Using sf in comics form, Houseman and Shannon create icons of settler colonialism, which focus solely on the searching and utilization of land for materialistic and capital gain.

Yet, as the story plays out, the continued existence of a people is not marked by wealth or the capitalistic gain found in land, but by knowing and repeating

Moonshot: The Indigenous Comics Collection, vol. 1. Elizabeth La Pensée (Anishinaabe/Métis/Irish) and Gregory Chomichuk, "The Observing."

their place in the relationality of all things. As such, it is the dispectors, not Indigenous peoples, who are no longer on the Earth. As Houseman and Shannon note in their introduction to the story, "Storytelling in the oral tradition is an important part of Indigenous cultures" that "helps communities stay connected with their past, and preserve their culture for the future. This is a story that is set in a future that may be, or a present that might have been" (131). This story, along with many others in *Moonshot*, carries importance across times and spaces and even possible alternative histories. The use of sf and the comics medium encourages an Indigenous orientation to the relationality of all things to, as the original inhabitants of turtle island did, "[live] in harmony with mother earth" (133).

One of the most striking examples and embodiments of *giizhodibaa'iganeg*—this conflux of energies in the cosmic and the local, the human and the nonhuman, the land and the waters across time—arises in Elizabeth La Pensée (Anishinaabe) and Gregory Chomichuk's story "The Observing." This story is of Haida origin and is told across the Pacific Northwest. It recounts when the star people came to observe a hunt. The introduction to the story notes the use of Indigenous steampunk, an aesthetic specifically mobilized to introduce the Star People and their technology. The introduction states, "Indigenous steampunk is about recognizing water as in, around, and through all." Steampunk, which is used to re-envision past times with the inclusion of steam technology, has often been set in Victorian or Western times. However, as LaPensée has noted elsewhere, steampunk "overlooks Native . . . representations and forms of technology and aesthetics that did exist" (LaPensée n.p.). As "The Observing" shows, the basis of steampunk in indigeneity means that the steampunk will look quite different precisely because of the central concern of land/waters. Thus, water, rather than steam, becomes the notable aesthetic marker of Indigenous steampunk.

"The Observing" is also of specific interest because of the lack of dialogue or linguistic storytelling at all. The visuals are the story. As such, the visuals push readers to face the animate beings from the stars that are situated in relation to local communities as being constituted by a land/water complex. In the final panel, the star people soar away from the surprised hunter into the sky. While, as the introduction to the story notes, "how these beings come to observe us from their place of origin is protected knowledge," this comic version notes that a relationality exists between the human hunters and the star people. "The Observing" helps us to realize that language is not necessary to represent connection. Visualizing connections has been central to communities across times and places. While the other comics in *Moonshot* make use of language, the visualizations in comics are what highlight the ways these stories can think beyond any one specific community and point out how these complex relations of human, nonhuman, and land/water constitute each other in complex relations of deep time and vast place in the cosmos.

Notes

1. I am using land/waters with a slash between to note the difference of land and water, while also highlighting the inextricable relation between the two. Such a complex interrelation is clear given the ways in which land and water together make up the landscape on which

Indigenous communities live. If, as Patrick Wolfe argues, "Territoriality is settler colonialism's specific irreducible element" and, as Craig Womack (Creek-Cherokee) argues, "a landless Indian Literature is no Indian Literature at all," we must think about the complex relations between land and water that create territoriality and thus have central bearing on settler colonial relations and Indigenous literature more broadly writ.

2. In many Indigenous languages, like Anishinaabemowin (Ojibwe), words are marked as either animate or inanimate. What is seen as living in Indigenous epistemologies is much broader than Western ones. For instance, the word for "rock," *asin*, is animate. So rocks and stones are seen as animate. Similarly, when I discuss living beings in this chapter, I am following this wider view of the animacy of beings than what is offered in settler conceptions.

3. My use of "Traditional" here coincides with the settler understanding of the term that marks Indigenous peoplehood as simplistic and consistently relegated to the past. I differentiate it from "traditional," which refers to stories, beliefs, or communities embedded in a tradition that is not static but continually emerging and affecting the lives of Indigenous peoples in various tribal contexts. Thus, the latter term is used in an effort to separate tradition from settler concretizations of the term and understandings of what it means across time.

4. One marked issue with Deloria's discussion of time and place is that he often elides differences in the concepts of space and place. For my purposes, I consider all his uses of space as related to the definition of place by Tim Cresswell offered above.

5. My thanks to Margaret Noodin for helping to puzzle through the pieces of this term and develop an understanding of how one Indigenous language can represent the interconnections between time, space, (non)humans, and land/waters.

6. It is important to note that I am not using the Anishinaabe term *giizhodibaa'iganeg* as a broad overwriting of specific concepts arising from other Indigenous communities and languages. Rather, I am using a simple term to think through the complex relations of space and time as they constitute the nexus of human, nonhuman, and land/waters as centrally important for Indigenous worldviews especially as constituted in a comic collection like *Moonshot*. The complexities embodied in such terminology provide a simpler way to discuss a complex interrelation of multiple concepts that are, in many ways, inextricable.

7. More information on ledger art and hide records, especially as they relate to Plains Indians, can be found at plainsledgerart.org.

Works Cited

Allen, Chadwick. *Trans-Indigenous: Methodologies for Global Native Literary Studies*. Minneapolis: University of Minnesota Press, 2012. Print.

Alternate History Comics, Inc. "Moonshot: The Indigenous Comics Collection." *Kickstarter*. Accessed May 23, 2018. Web.

Bernardin, Susan. "Future Pasts: Comics, Graphic Novels, and Digital Media." In *The Routledge Companion to Native American Literature*, edited by Deborah L. Madsen. New York: Routledge, 2016.

Coulthard, Glen Sean. *Red Skin, White Masks: Rejecting the Colonial Politics of Recognition*. Minneapolis: University of Minnesota Press, 2014.

Cresswell, Tim. *Place: A Short Introduction*. Malden, MA: Blackwell Publishing, 2004.

Deloria, Jr., Vine. *God Is Red: A Native View of Religion*. Golden, CO: Fulcrum Publishing, 1992.

Dillon, Grace, ed. *Walking the Clouds: An Anthology of Indigenous Science Fiction*. Tucson: University of Arizona Press, 2012.

Dimock, Wai Chee. *Through Other Continents: American Literature across Deep Time*. Princeton, NJ: Princeton University Press, 2006.
Eisner, Will. *Comics and Sequential Art*. New York: W. W. Norton, 2008.
Groensteen, Thierry. *The System of Comics*. Trans. Bart Beaty and Nick Nguyen. Jackson: University Press of Mississippi, 2007.
LaPensée, Elizabeth. "Native Steampunk." *AbTec: Aboriginal Territories in Cyberspace*. September 18, 2009. Accessed on July 27, 2018. Web.
McCloud, Scott. *Understanding Comics: The Invisible Art*. New York: HarperCollins, 1993.
Nicholson, Hope, ed. *Moonshot: The Indigenous Comics Collection*. Toronto: Alternate History Comics, 2016.
Norton-Smith, Thomas M. *The Dance of Person and Place: One Interpretation of American Indian Philosophy*. Albany: SUNY Press, 2010.
Rifkin, Mark. *Beyond Settler Time: Temporal Sovereignty and Indigenous Self-Determination*. Durham, NC: Duke University Press, 2017.
Sainte-Marie, Buffy. "Moonshot." *Moonshot*. Vanguard Records, 1972. Web.
Wolfe, Patrick. "Settler Colonialism and the Elimination of the Native." *Journal of Genocide Research* 8, no. 4 (2006): 387–409.
Womack, Craig. *Art as Criticism, Story as Performance: Reflections on Native Literary Aesthetics*. Norman: University of Oklahoma Press, 2009.

Deer Woman Re-Generations: Re-Activating First Beings and Re-Arming Sisterhoods of Survivance in *Deer Woman: An Anthology*

Joshua T. Anderson

Deer Woman: An Anthology (2017) is at once a comics collection centering the stories and artwork of Indigenous women and a call to action in support of missing and murdered Indigenous women in the United States and Canada. Published by Native Realities Press and coedited by Elizabeth LaPensée, PhD (Anishinaabe, Métis, and settler-Irish) and Weshoyot Alvitre (Tongva/Scots-Gaelic), the anthology formed after the success of LaPensée's *Deer Woman: A Vignette* (2015), illustrated by Jonathan R. Thunder (Red Lake Anishinaabe). As CEO and founder of Native Realities Lee Francis IV (Laguna Pueblo) explains, "rather than reprint the original, Beth [LaPensée] and I concluded that an anthology featuring all Native stories by all Native women, as inspired by Deer Woman, was a necessary step in the evolution of this work" (iv). By re-activating the Indigenous first being, Deer Woman, the collection intervenes in what Francis calls the "eroticization and marginalization of Native women" in settler-colonial discourse and contributes to the mission of Native Realities, which he describes as an effort to promote a "community of Native people expressing themselves through the medium of sequential art" (iv). Moreover, Native Realities donates 10 percent of the profits from the anthology to Arming Sisters Reawakening Warriors (ASRW), a gender-neutral community healing organization that provides martial-arts self-defense training to Indigenous communities.[1] Combining Arming Sisters, the group founded in 2013 by Patty Stonefish (Lakota), with its "brother" course Reawakening Warriors, created by Stonefish's husband, Dereck Stonefish (Oneida) in 2015, ASRW strives to "reawaken and re-empower Indigenous communities through self-defense," and to redefine "what a warrior is" and how warriorhood applies to Indigenous communities in the contemporary world.[2]

In this chapter, I contend that the *Deer Woman* comics anthology, in coordination with ASRW, engages in the practices of visually "re-arming" Indigenous women and Two Spirit queer peoples, not simply through remembering the stories of Deer Woman, but through physically and metaphorically "re-membering" dismembered bodies and histories and re-activating "traditional" arts practices through resurgent, regenerative networks centering contemporary Indigenous women. Turning to the unique medium of comics or "sequential art," Native artists re-activate Deer Woman from her traditional places in Native oral stories and her encoded, visual representations in petroglyphs, winter counts, birchbark scrolls, and animal hides to envision contemporary Deer Women healing from ongoing legacies of sexual violence in contemporary settings. In several of the comics collected in the anthology, scars visibly mark the bodies of Indigenous women, and these "scar maps" chart an embodied cartography that re-members ongoing histories of violence and "survivance," or the term coined by Anishinaabe theorist Gerald Vizenor to connote not mere survival, but continuance, endurance, resistance, and resurgence.[3] Through the repeated imagery of scars, or the fibrous connective tissue around healing wounds, Native artists mark the bodies of Indigenous women as sites for Deer Woman re-generations, whereby a scar is at once an embodied symbol of violence and a regenerative site of power, healing, and transformation.

On the one hand, scars in the *Deer Woman* anthology re-map the interconnections among the gendered violence of heteropatriarchy, the geopolitical exploitation of Indigenous lands, and the generations of violence experienced by Indigenous women under settler colonialism. As Audra Simpson (Mohawk) argues at the outset of her keynote address "The Chief's Two Bodies" (2014): "Canada requires the death and so-called disappearance of Indigenous women in order to secure its sovereignty; and this is the sovereign death dance that requires us to think hard about the ways in which we imagine not only nations and states but what counts as governance itself."[4] Recently, the Native Women's Association of Canada (NWAC) has brought critical attention to the pervasive violence against First Nations women with its publication of *Voices of Our Sisters in Spirit* (2008) and its annual Sisters in Spirit Vigils, while in the United States, the enactment of the Tribal Law and Order Act (TLOA; 2010) and the reauthorization of the Violence Against Women Act (VAWA; 2013) represent significant legislative achievements resulting from growing grassroots and scholarly activism. However, while TLOA represents a concerted effort to streamline the jurisdictional quagmire in present-day Indian Country and the reauthorization of VAWA offers explicit protections for Native women in cases of domestic abuse, the fact remains that Indigenous women continue to experience a disproportionate share of violence. According to Amnesty International's report titled "Maze of Injustice" (2007), Native women in the United States are "more than 2.5 times more likely to be raped or sexually assaulted than other women," and "in at least 86 per cent of the reported cases . . . survivors report that the perpetrators are non-Native men" (n.p.).[5] With governance and jurisdictions still largely determined by the terms and conditions of settler colonialism, the "law of the land" remains inseparable from the gendered geopolitics of stolen sisters and stolen ground.

In *Deer Woman*, scars are not only embodied markers of this ongoing history of violence but empowering symbols of embodied "regeneration." As defined by Merriam-Webster, the term "regeneration" is at once biological and spiritual, emphasizing "renewal or restoration of a body, bodily part, or biological system (such as a forest) after injury or as a normal process," and the "renewal or revival" of the spirit. In addition to the biological and the spiritual components of regeneration, my work here emphasizes the potential for Deer Woman to track "re-generational" kinships through sisterhoods of survivance. Unlike Richard Slotkin's *Regeneration through Violence* (1973), in which he examines how settler storytelling transforms systemic land theft and systemic violence into the doctrine of discovery and manifest destiny, my work draws inspiration from the recent efforts in Indigenous feminisms that seek to "re-map" the intersections of gendered and geopolitical violence. As Mishuana Goeman (Seneca) asserts in *Mark My Words: Native Women Mapping Our Nations* (2013), "(re)mapping is not just about gaining that which was lost and returning to an original and pure point in history, but instead understanding the processes that have defined our current spatialities in order to sustain vibrant Native futures" (3). Remapping, in this sense, not only challenges the "settled" narratives of Indigenous dispossession and settler occupation, but also offers an alternative to the politics of "recognition" through what Audra Simpson calls the "cartography of refusal," which charts "a political and ethical stance that stands in stark contrast to the desire to have one's distinctiveness as a culture, as a people, recognized" on the terms set by settler governments (*Mohawk Interruptus* [2014]; 32, 11).

Crucially, the turn toward a politics of refusal disrupts and reworks the multilayered language of "consent" in settler colonialism, which derives its power through coercion and force, whereby the violence and violations against Indigenous women are central to the invasions and occupations of territory. As Audra Simpson asserts in *Mohawk Interruptus* (2014): "Nationalism expresses a particular form of collective identity that embeds desire for sovereignty and justice," however, "it does so only because of the deep impossibility of representation and consent within governance systems predicated upon dispossession and disavowal of [Indigenous] political histories" (18). The politics of refusal offers more than the rejection of settler maps of territorial jurisdiction or the disavowal of settler temporalities that set term limits on "authentic" Indigeneity and institute "statutes of limitations" that have long served to separate the contemporary missing and murdered from the ancestral dead and dispossessed. Instead, and more forcefully, the politics of refusal signals multiple forms of

Indigenous political reorganization coupled with resurgent art and activist practices grounded upon Indigenous forms of collectivity and relationality.

Drawing inspiration from Goeman's "(re)mapping" and Audra Simpson's "cartography of refusal," Nishnaabeg scholar Leanne Betasamosake Simpson calls for radical resurgent arts collectives comprised of Indigenous artists, activists, and storytellers who form what she terms "constellations of coresistance." As she asserts in her groundbreaking collection of essays, *As We Have Always Done: Indigenous Freedom through Radical Resistance* (2017), "constellations exist only in the context of relationships," and "constellations in relationship with other constellations form flight paths out of settler colonial realities into Indigeneity" (215; 217). Through "constellations of coresistance," in which individual artists and activists form collected networks, Simpson argues that Indigenous arts collectives engage in the "everyday renewal of Indigenous practices and in constellated relationships, meaning relationships that operate from within the grounded normativity of particular Indigenous nations" and the simultaneous formation of a larger, networked whole (217).[6] For Simpson, the emphasis on "constellated relationships" is rooted in the Nishnaabeg principle *kobade*, which she defines as "a link in a chain—a link in the chain between generations, between nations, between states of being, between individuals. I am a link in a chain. We are all links in a chain" (8). Through *kobade*, Simpson envisions a powerful, multigenerational embrace, or "the idea of my arms embracing my grandchildren, and their arms embracing their grandchildren . . . According to elder Edna Manitowa-bi, kobade is a word we use to refer to our great-grandparents and our great-grandchildren" (8). To ensure the future survivance of her kobade, Simpson asserts, "we need to . . . create constellations of coresistance, working together toward a radical alternative present based on deep reciprocity and the gorgeous generative refusal of colonial recognition" (9).

The *Deer Woman* anthology enacts a "constellation of coresistance" through what I call sisterhoods of survivance, in which Indigenous comics artists join forces with activist communities to tell stories that reconstruct lineages of survivance across generations of Native women and link the regenerative healing of Native bodies to the radical resurgence of Indigenous sovereignties and body politics. Like Leanne Simpson's powerful image of a multigenerational embrace, I argue that the *Deer Woman* anthology visually and metaphorically "re-arms" and, more broadly, re-members Indigenous body and sexuality sovereignties and, in so doing, counters the historical and ongoing efforts to disarm Native peoples and dismember Native lands and lifeways. Moreover, by engaging in the regenerative processes of re-arming sisterhoods of survivance, these contemporary comics artists offer a powerful "link in the chain" to previous generations of Indigenous arts collectives, such as the multi-tribal artists who produced ledger art at the prison camp in Fort Marion, Florida, after being forcibly removed from Fort Sill, Oklahoma, by Richard Henry Pratt in 1875. In the works of nineteenth-century ledger artists, Native peoples often appear literally "armless" or otherwise bound with arms hidden behind their backs. Consider, for instance, Walter Bone Shirt's (Brulé Lakota) famous image *On a Long March* from *The Walter Bone Shirt Ledger* (fig. 16.1). Produced at the Rosebud Indian Agency in the 1890s, the image depicts a Native woman leading a horse on a westward path with her arms bound (or disappearing) behind her back.[7] As Richard Pearce elaborates in *Women and Ledger Art: Four Contemporary Native American Artists* (2013), the "calculated attack on tribal culture" during the late nineteenth century "might explain Walter Bone Shirt's mid-1890s drawing of a proud and wealthy woman who seemed to be 'literally bound up'" (8). However, Pearce continues, "on the other hand, it might be explained stylistically, since there are nine other drawings of figures who seem armless in *The Walter Bone Shirt Ledger* (almost one third of the drawings)" (8).

This nineteenth-century image of a "disarmed" Indigenous woman on a "long march" offers a pictographic representation of the history of Indigenous dispossession and forced relocation, a history that Sarah Deer (Mvskoke) argues, "both necessitated and precipitated a highly gendered and sexualized dynamic in which Native women's bodies became commodities" (62). In *The Beginning and End of Rape: Confronting Sexual Violence in Native America* (2015), Deer traces the interconnections between Indigenous removals and rape, from the rampant sexual violence in boarding schools and along the many "trails of tears" during the nineteenth century to the modern-day "forced walks" of sex trafficking, which Deer contends, "is really a contemporary phrase for sexual slavery" (60). Linking the often legal (or de facto legal) history of sexual violence against Native women under settler colonialism to the contemporary "scourge of sex trafficking of Native women," Deer asserts, "the tactics used by sex traffickers today were used against Native peoples from the first moment of contact" (60; 62). The depiction of "armless" Native women in nineteenth-century ledger art offers a subtle but powerful recognition of the link between Indigenous women's body sovereignties and this history of dispossession. However, in *Deer Woman: An Anthology*, contemporary Native comics artists rework the visual grammar that links "armlessness" to dispossession, and instead, envision both literal and metaphorical methods for re-arming Native women and repossessing sexual and territorial sovereignties.

The first entry in the collection reprints "Deer Woman: A Vignette," a collaborative effort between mixed-media artist and writer Elizabeth LaPensée and artist Jonathan Thunder, "whose works," LaPensée argues, "expand tradition into survivance" (1). Set in the seedy, contemporary world of sex-trafficking along the Great Lakes, the vignette re-activates Deer Woman from her "traditional" role in oral stories, where she often seduces young men into abandoning their obligations to kinship and proper courtship practices.[8] As LaPensée writes in the introduction to the vignette, "the stories I've heard about Deer Woman tell

Figure 16.1. Walter Bone Shirt, *On a Long March*, Ledger Plate XX.

of a gorgeous, luscious, and downright deadly figure who lures men from fires and whose deer legs are hidden by the light and shadows of the flames until she leads a man off from a gathering far enough to stomp him to death" (1). "She's certainly empowered and made for killing," LaPensée continues, "but as I healed from personal experiences . . . I wondered how she came to be. Then Deer Woman came by for a visit" (1). By re-activating Deer Woman in a contemporary story of sexual violence and sex trafficking, LaPensée issues a call for justice for contemporary missing and murdered Indigenous women and a call "to take a stance to change the fact that Indigenous women are the most likely to experience sexual assault on Turtle Island" (1). Ending her introduction with an invitation and a disclaimer, LaPensée writes: "I welcome you to experience this comic with the warning that it is a brutal, beautiful, and unrelenting story that shows a glimpse of the serene chaos that Deer Woman is" (1).

The vignette begins with a haunting panel of a young Indigenous woman sitting in the passenger seat of a car, a man's hand draped over the steering wheel, his headlights shining like interrogation lamps at the reader. "He told me he'd introduce me to everyone at the party," a textbox reads, as the woman narrates from memory, recalling the night she was lured into the woods, only to discover when she arrives that "no one was there" (2). In the car, shadows cover both occupants' faces and stretch across the ground from leafless trees, while snow falls in the nearly depthless background. Juxtaposing shadows, which suggest depth and distance, with forced perspective, or the collapsing of depths of field, Thunder's artwork creates paradoxical spatialities. In the opening panel, for instance, the car and its occupants almost appear to be collaged over the snow falling in the background, while in the panels depicting the woman's rape, the formal technique of forced perspective visually reinforces the spatial and physical violations of the woman's body and the man's violent use of force. The effect of this thin, but textured layering of foreground and background extends to the collapsing of temporalities, which suggest that this memory of rape is not entirely past tense for the survivor who remembers. Moreover, the woman's act of remembrance breaks like light through shadows, as Thunder's black-and-white panels are divided by black gutters that cut at sharp, canted angles. In the page's final panel, the noir-like black-and-white color scheme is "cut" again, this time with bright red blood that drips from the woman's hand and pools underneath the picnic table, the silhouette of Deer Woman in the background making tracks through the snow. The vivid splash of blood in this panel is jarring in the otherwise black-and-white comic, an effect that recurs later, when the survivor lures a man away from a nightclub dance floor and stomps him to death in a bathroom stall, her deer hooves leaving blood-red tracks on the floor (6).

The vignette inverts or otherwise reworks elements of "traditional" Deer Woman stories, such as the Lakota story translated by anthropologist Ella Deloria in *Dakota Texts* (1932), in which Julien Rice observes, a Native man "is heading home, the completion of all circular excursions for hunting, war, or horse taking. But blocking his road to his relatives and his identity as provider and protector is a figure [Deer Woman] whose ability to plunge him into confusion is foreshadowed by the time of day, just before nightfall" (*Deer Woman and Elk Men* [1992]; 33). In the vignette, men lure Native women into the woods and Native girls into sex-trafficking boats; rapists corner women in dark alleys; cops brandish tasers and unholster sidearms, harassing homeless Native peoples who sleep on sidewalks. Moreover, in the vignette, Native women and girls are not merely "blocked" but stolen from the roads leading to their relatives and identities. For the woman in the first panel, the journey "home" begins not at "nightfall," but at the break of dawn, the morning after she survives rape. "In that moment, when it's already too late, what could I do?" she asks in a textbox, as she walks under crooked windows along trash-strewn streets and descends the stairs into her cracked-brick apartment, completing the first step in her version of the "circular excursion" home (3; see fig. 16.2).

Answering her own question with the empowered imperatives to "Survive" and "Transform," the following two panels graphically match the scenes of rape on the first page (3). In the "Survive" panel, the woman enters her home with the shadow of a deer hovering above her, its five-point antlers making a stunning graphic match with the five-point strands of the woman's hair on the opposite page, where she fights her rapist atop a picnic table. And, in the "Transform" panel, the woman stares at her own naked reflection in the bathroom mirror, where the imperative to "transform" graphically matches the scene of rape on the opening page, in which the woman's legs are bent at odd angles, her rapist

Figure 16.2. Elizabeth LaPensée (writer) and Jonathan R. Thunder (artist), "Deer Woman: A Vignette," in *Deer Woman: An Anthology*.

gyrating with motion lines above her, her feet transformed into deer hooves. The page's final panel depicts the woman's transformation from a survivor into a protector, enacting the multistep process of arming sisters promoted by ASRW, which calls on Native women to "heal the SELF first" in order to "be better equipped to help heal our families, communities, [and] nations."[9] Declaring that she has survived and transformed "so that it never happens again to anyone," the woman stands in an empowered posture in the center of a boxing gym, motion lines radiating from the speed bags behind her, a swoop of black hair covering her right eye, her dark left eye staring out at the reader (3). Overlaid with an insert—a close-up of the left eye of a deer—the panel reveals the empowered process of Deer Woman re-generation, in which the woman not only transforms herself physically through self-defense training, but also re-arms and reactivates herself spiritually and politically. In particular, her "deer eye" affords a powerful form of vision that refuses the settler-colonial gaze, which has long rendered Indigenous women invisible through narratives and policies that institute Indigenous "vanishing."

Visibility, in this sense, is not a passive act of recognition. Instead, Deer Woman's point of view enables an empowered mode of viewing and re-viewing, rooted in Indigenous feminisms, that radically "re-presents" the invisible as visible and transforms histories of settler violence into regenerations through survivance. Moreover, rather than merely bearing witness to the pervasive threats of sexual violence in settler-colonialism's long-standing rape culture, LaPensée and Thunder re-activate Deer Woman as a protector who violently kills sexual predators and enacts Indigenous forms of justice that extend beyond the juridical protections of TLOA, VAWA, and the Trafficking Victims Protection Act (2000). Casting the shadow of a deer, the re-empowered survivor walks through darkened streets, entering a dance club, where she lures a sexually aggressive man away from his date and stomps him to death in a bathroom stall (6). After making bloody deer tracks out of the bathroom, the re-embodied survivor travels backward through memory, recalling the night she sat alone on a park bench as a young girl. "There are days where the transformations are so deep I remember what it is to be innocent again," she tells us, as the young girl looks out on an empty playground with broken bottles surrounding a merry-go-round, a slide graffitied with an arrowed heart, the city skyline dotted with stars (7). Lured from the bench by a young white man, the girl is walked down the pier to a sex-trafficking boat, while the half-moon reflects on lake water and the shadow of a deer trails behind her (8–9). At the end of this "forced walk," the girl is thrown into the ship's cargo hold with other exploited Native women, girls, and boys. However, in this act of remembrance, the girl survives and transforms, sprouting small, spiked antlers and standing on deer legs, she brutally kills her captors and outruns the darkness that laps like flames at her feet (10). Returning to her adult form, she makes an empowered walk back into the present, where she cracks the skull of an abusive cop against a brick wall and stomps a rapist to death in a back alley with stiletto heels that transform into deer hooves (11–15).

In the vignette's final full-page panel, Deer Woman stands on a cracked sidewalk, her long arms stretched down at her side with palms facing out, her deer head sprouting ten-point antlers (16; fig. 16.3). Her black eyes shimmer with points of light, as she stares directly at the reader in this empowered stance, while the white folds of her striped shirt give the impression of hands embracing her around her waist. Behind her, Deer Woman's shadow splatters or "bleeds" onto the brick wall—the black inkblots entangling with the shadows of lush vegetation that seem to sprout from her, enacting a process of regeneration that completes the circular journey out of the leafless woods where the vignette begins. Over her left shoulder, a bright-red ladybug rests on one of the shadowed leaves, its symmetrical spot pattern—three spots on each side of its shell—suggests balance, while its color makes a near match with the splashes of blood in previous panels, suggesting multispecies regeneration from violence. "And in the end, whatever we have experienced, we always return to ourselves," the narrator declares (16). In this final declaration, Deer Woman powerfully reclaims body and sexuality sovereignties and rescripts the settler narratives that impose victimry and vanishing on Indigenous women and Two Spirit peoples. As Leanne Simpson contends, "A large part of the colonial project has been to control the political power of Indigenous women and queer people through the control of our sexual agency," asserting that "Indigenous body sovereignty and sexuality sovereignty threaten colonial power" (107). By ending the vignette with a "return to ourselves," LaPensée and Thunder envision Deer Woman as a protector of sexual agencies and body sovereignties and a healer who transforms physical and spiritual wounds into sites of radical regeneration and survivance. The endpapers of the original vignette extend this artistic practice of visually re-arming sisterhoods of survivance to its activist potential for Indigenous feminisms, in which "re-arming" is made literal through the hand-drawn page of "Self-Defense Moves" that includes techniques and instructions for punching, groin striking, eye gouging, and ear slapping. However, in the afterword that follows, ASRW founder Patty Stonefish asserts, "Women's self-defense isn't all about eye-gouging, throat punches, and striking. It's about reawakening empowerment, self-love, and ownership of body."[10]

Rather than reprinting the endpapers, the anthology builds upon the work of the vignette with short comics by other Native artists and storytellers who offer alternative methods for visually re-arming Native women through narratives of regeneration and survivance. In "Wives," written by Darcie Little Badger (Lipan Apache) and illustrated by Tara Ogaick, "Deer Woman" by Maria Wolf Lopez, and "Dog Woman" by Barbara Kenmille (Confederated Salish and Kootenai), the

Figure 16.3. Elizabeth LaPensée (writer) and Jonathan R. Thunder (artist), "Deer Woman: A Vignette," from *Deer Woman: An Anthology*.

imagery of scars and healing wounds make visible the often invisible or redacted histories of settler violence.[11] Inscribing the comics page with cartographies of scars, these comics artists offer methodologies for re-scripting and re-mapping this history of violence, whereby scars become constelled symbols of relationality and healing, transformation and regeneration. Much in the way that gutters on the comics page organize the spatial and temporal movements across panels, I contend that scars in these comics organize an embodied temporality *within* the visual grammar of individual panels and *across* the constellated network of panels in the construction of the larger whole. With their capacity to visibly and metaphorically re-member the interrelationships between the past and the present, the personal and the political, scars afford new readings of the multitemporal and multigenerational processes of healing from generations of violence and chart paths toward regenerations through survivance.

"Wives" tells the story of queer Lipan Apache newlyweds Cora, the IT professional, and Gabrielle, the librarian, as they endure gender and racial discrimination in Texas. "Outside the sanctuary of home," the title page explains, "people hunt them with arrows of violence, cruelty, and microagressions" (29). Sharing a morning cup of coffee, Cora and Gabrielle toast to a "happy Monday" before emerging from their apartment and embracing each other on the sidewalk (30–31). However, they are immediately confronted by a blond man who hurls insults at the couple and shoots them with arrows that remain lodged in their shoulders. Leaving the "sanctuary of home" for the routines of work, the couple encounters the daily violence of race and gender discrimination on public transit and public sidewalks before arriving at their respective workplaces. In the IT department, Cora huddles over her laptop that displays a multicolored "Trans Pride" sticker, while coworkers nock arrows, shooting her at her desk and across the boardroom table, where she sits with arms folded and eyes closed, arrows protruding like porcupine quills from her back (32). On Gabrielle's route to the library, a white man sporting a neck beard and a backward baseball cap follows her along the bright and busy sidewalk, stabbing her with an arrow in her back, just under her pink ponytail (33). And, later, while Gabrielle shelves books, a gray-haired librarian continues the assault, filling her body with arrows. When the couple reunites in front of their home, Cora asks, "Did my toast backfire?" to which Gabrielle exclaims, "No! Monday isn't over yet!" (34). Although arrows remain lodged in both of their bodies, the couple counters the presumed narrative of victimry, as they clap hands in a cheerful high-five.

In the poignant two-panel page that follows, Cora and Gabrielle sit on the floor of their bathroom, the vanity adorned with "Hers" and "Also Hers" towels, the floor littered with removed arrows, their bodies covered with gauze strips and band-aids from the first-aid kit (35; fig. 16.4). Below, the couple clasps hands, looking out through the bathroom door at a vase filled with cut flowers, their backs covered with brightly colored band-aids (35). To their left, Little Badger

Figure 16.4. Darcie Little Badger (writer) and Tara Ogaick (artist), "Wives," in *Deer Woman: An Anthology*.

and Ogaick include an image of Cora pulling a deeply embedded arrow from Gabrielle's back, as Cora exclaims, "this fucking arrow!! I'm so sorry," her apology punctuated with a heart. Crossing the gutter between the top and bottom panel, this image powerfully depicts the labor of mutual healing from acts of everyday discrimination that become embodied and embedded, leaving deep, internal scars that are not always visible on the surface. Like the vignette, "Wives" reworks tropes in traditional Deer Woman stories. Rather than male hunters "blocked" from their roads home, "Wives" tells the story of queer Indigenous women who are "hunted" and assaulted with everyday acts of violence. However, through their intimate and powerful acts of mutual healing, Cora and Gabrielle model the processes of everyday regeneration, through which victims become survivors, the "hunted" become "healers," who, in turn, become protectors. In the closing panels, the couple shares an evening meal of pizza and salad, reminiscing about their day, when they hear a young neighbor girl screaming for help (36). "Show us your weird drawings!" a blonde bully insists, threatening the girl with arrows, as she clutches her notebook to her chest (37). Armed with elaborate bows decorated with painted flowers and cats, Cora and Gabrielle emerge from their apartment, arrows nocked tight in their bowstrings (37). Together, Cora and Gabrielle embody the goals of ASRW, as their own healing wounds chart the intersections between ongoing violence and everyday survivance. Perhaps more importantly, as re-armed protectors, the couple defiantly resists everyday acts of violence through the multistep process of reclaiming their own body sovereignties and recovering the role of generational protectorship, in which they protect the young girl from her bullies. In so doing, the couple models the ways in which healing queer Indigenous bodies and reclaiming body and sexuality sovereignties can extend to broader acts of healing, protectorship, and justice for Indigenous families, communities, and nations.

Whereas "Wives" offers a brightly colored narrative of queer women healing from the violence of microaggressions, "Deer Woman" by Maria Wolf Lopez tells a darker, more graphic story of historical and ongoing physical violence. "I lived in a culture of both beauty and abuse," Lopez's narrator tells us, with "women as beautiful as wild flowers, and yet bruised and scarred on each side" (63). Inspired by tattoo designs, Lopez inks the comics page like a body in vivid black-and-white, her linework soaking down into the deep, subcutaneous layers, while, in the internal grammar of the panels, bulbous bruises swell up from the faces of battered Native women, tears and blood saturating the surface. In a powerful, full-page panel, Deer Woman's hand extends over blooming wildflowers, while below, Native women dressed in traditional regalia reach up with arms shackled and tears streaming down their cheeks (63; fig. 16.5). The iconography of shackled Indigenous women draws comparison to the "disarmed" woman in Walter Bone Shirt's *On a Long March*, while Lopez's artwork in this scene draws inspiration from the pottery and pictographic art of the Aztecs and

Figure 16.5. Maria Wolf Lopez, "Deer Woman," in *Deer Woman: An Anthology*.

other Indigenous peoples of modern-day Mexico and Central America. In a later scene, a man throws a punch from the left side of the panel, his clenched fist striking a young Native woman in the jaw, making a disturbing graphic match with Deer Woman's hand that offers protectorship to the shackled

Indigenous women from much earlier generations (65). With a bulbous eye and a split lip, the young woman holds her jaw, "trying to put [herself] together" (65). The woman's effort to "re-member" herself or "put [herself] together," extends to Lopez's broader political effort to "re-member" the interrelationships between ancestral and contemporary Native women through the figure of Deer Woman, who Lopez tells us, is "a mighty spirit who has crossed paths with many hurt women" (67). "She will see all your scars," Lopez continues, "each one tells a story of your pain" (67).

Although scars in the collection often help to re-map lineages of multigenerational violence, they do not always tell stories of "pain." In Kenmille's "Dog Woman," for instance, a Native grandmother "has many scars," one slashed from her right eyebrow down through her eyelid, another jagged scar cut across her throat, her right leg amputated below the knee (55; see fig. 16.6). Embodying a personal history of violence, Dog Woman's scars "follow into her clothing," cutting through Kenmille's beautiful watercolors to trace stitch lines that run across Dog Woman's blue shirt and through her red belt (55). However, Kenmille tells us, Dog Woman's scars "are stories that don't need vocalization," as "she shows them without shame and answers the questions she does get, but finds camaraderie in the ones that understand" (55). Refusing to tell scar stories that reinforce narratives of victimry and violence, Kenmille's Dog Woman wears her scars "without shame," and, in so doing, rescripts the personal and political histories contained in her scars toward narratives of ongoing survivance. Extending this politics of refusal, Kenmille tells us that Dog Woman's "tribal ID hasn't been reissued in years," leading some members of the community to "whisper that because of that she technically isn't even NDN" (53). However, much like the Iroquois National Lacrosse Team who refused to travel on US or Canadian passports in Audra Simpson's *Mohawk Interruptus*, Dog Woman quietly refuses to be authenticated as Indigenous by documents of colonial recognition, or the "only document that carries her English name" (53).[12] Instead, she feeds community members who come by for a visit, teaches Native youth "traditional activities" (56), and, "at the end of some visits," she offers guests one of her many dogs, who offer multispecies companionship and protectorship "from possible violence" (58). Similarly, in "Deer Woman," Lopez's protagonist recovers from personal histories of violence through the multispecies protectorship afforded by a pack of four wolves and a multigenerational community of four Native women. In the final panel, Lopez's protagonist transforms into "the powerful Deer Woman," standing "tall" and "strong" over a pack of four-eyed wolves, while ghostly antlers curl like smoke around her head, her powerful Deer Woman arms sprouting long hair and sharp nails (70). This image of a re-armed survivor graphically matches the arm of Deer Woman, which extends over shackled women in the opening pages of the comic (fig. 16.5). Reclaiming both multigenerational and multispecies protectorships,

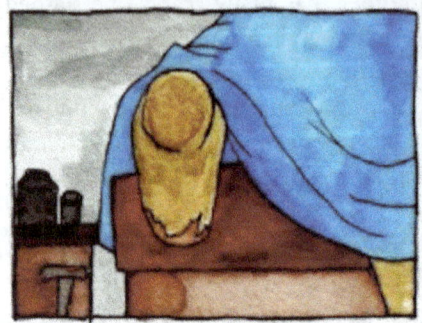
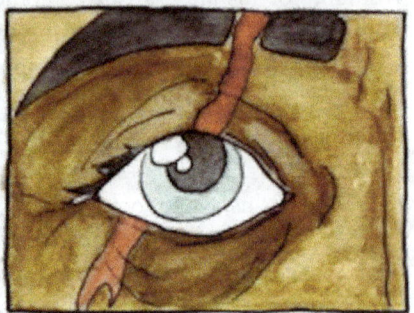
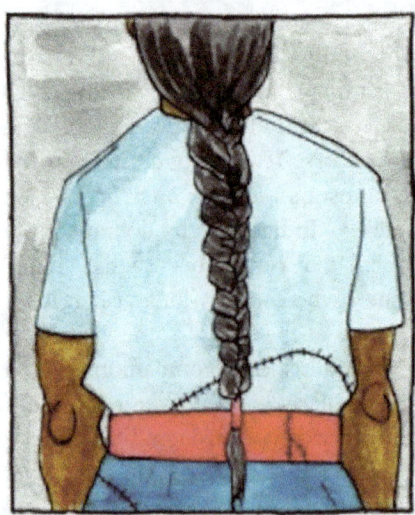

Figure 16.6. Barbara Kenmille, "Dog Woman," in *Deer Woman: An Anthology*.

Lopez's "Deer Woman" re-arms Native women across past and present generations through the blending of contemporary and ancestral arts practices, and concludes with a future-oriented call for survivors to "show those cowards that you *will* survive" (emphasis added; 70).

Through the repeated imagery of scarred and "re-armed" Indigenous women, and the blending of ancestral and contemporary arts practices, the *Deer Woman* anthology not only re-members the history of multigenerational violence, but participates in the regeneration of Indigenous futures through survivance (see Borkent, this volume). Re-arming, in this sense, offers a visual practice that reaches across temporalities and territories in the interrelated processes of reclaiming Indigenous body sovereignties and bodies of land and water. In "M.A.M.A.," for instance, Jackie Fawn (Yurok/Washoe/Filipino) traces a multi-generational narrative of survivance that shifts temporalities from the 1850s to the contemporary water protectors in Standing Rock, North Dakota. Inspired by the life of Julz Rich (Lakota), founder of the Mothers Against Meth Alliance or "M.A.M.A.," Fawn's comic recovers lineages of Lakota women as survivors and protectors, who embody multiple methods for re-arming Native women, from the title page depicting Rich armed with a shotgun, which she uses to protect a young Native woman from a meth dealer (87), to an ancestor from the 1850s cradling a newborn and "holding the future in her arms" (91), to the final page, in which a young water protector cradles a spotted fawn in arms tattooed with deer tracks (96; see fig. 16.7). Similarly, in "To Dress in Red," Weshoyote Alvitre depicts the hand of a murdered Native woman sticking up from red dirt, followed by hands painted on rocks alongside the petroglyphic images of Deer Woman, and, later, a pregnant mother with arms folded over her belly (72–73).

With armed Native women "holding the future" and offering protectorship to unborn, future generations, comics such as "M.A.M.A." and "To Dress in Red" disrupt and rework the long-standing rape culture of settler colonialism. As Sarah Deer argues, "rape" (and other forms of physical and sexual violence) is often directly linked "to conquest and genocide precisely because of its effects on reproduction" (112). From the title on down, "M.A.M.A." reclaims the role of Indigenous motherhood, joining several other comics in the collection that powerfully depict pregnant Indigenous women, such as "Dog Woman" (56) and "To Dress in Red" (73), or recover broader kinship relationships, from the queer marriage in "Wives" to Kimberly Robertson's (Mvskoke) collaged portraits commemorating her "auntie alliance" in "Las Aunties." In so doing, these works reveal how Indigenous women's body and sexuality sovereignties are directly linked to Indigenous futurities and the fight to reclaim and protect Indigenous territories. Through the use of the acronym M.A.M.A., Fawn's comic crosses the kinship term with the contemporary activist community Mothers Against Meth Alliance that Rich founded in response to the "man camps" and oil extraction in the Bakken Range. Linking the "oil boom" to the "meth boom," and the exploitation of Indigenous lands to the sexual exploitation of Native women and girls, both the comic and the activist organization call for an intersectional approach to violence across gendered, generational, and geopolitical lines.[13] Revealing the intersections of resource extraction, substance addiction, and sexual exploitation, Fawn's comic joins others in the collection that expose the politics of "consent" under settler colonialism as a thin cover for histories of coercion and force, whereby to "refuse" requires much more than Nancy Reagan's vapid antidrug plan to "just say no."

Instead, and more forcefully, the politics of refusal that emerges in the *Deer Woman* anthology involves the multistep processes of re-arming Indigenous women and recovering cycles of gendered and geopolitical regeneration. In Alvitre's "To Dress in Red," for instance, the first four sections cycle through an embodied cartography of loss and regeneration, from the "family weeping" over the grave of a murdered Native woman with a "hole dug deep in their hearts" to the belly of a pregnant woman juxtaposed with the image of "water collecting on new leaves," both of which are "life giving and essential" (73). Unfolding like a poem that begins with the imagery of burial and ends with gendered and geographic re-birth, this four-section sequence encodes the comic with Indigenous numerology—the number four suggesting the balance of the four directions and the calendric cycle of the four seasons. Moreover, the color-scheme and section headings define and redefine the word "red." Red, the comic suggests, can serve as a woman's name or nickname ("Red Is Missing"), as the color of blood and violence ("Red Is Murder"), as a coded reference to race and Native identity ("Red Is Indigenous"), and as the color of traditional jingle dresses and the flow of blood between mother and child in utero ("Red Is Woman"). Crossing imagery of pregnancy with imagery of water collecting on blades of grass, Alvitre powerfully depicts the constelled relationships between "re-generational" kinship through reproduction and the cyclical regeneration of Indigenous lands. In the fifth and final three-panel section, Alvitre writes, "Red is remembering her power, her song, her own language within more language" (74). Written over the hem of a jingle dress, these words emphasize multimodal remembrance and multigenerational protectorship, reinforced by the five Native women who stand together in the panel below, the elder's arms holding a young Native girl in a multigenerational embrace.

Re-arming in the *Deer Woman* anthology is at once a visual methodology linking the past to the present through multigenerational embrace, and a visual representation of activist solidarity, through which comics artists visually and metaphorically "join hands" with other contemporary arts and activist communities, such as ASRW, M.A.M.A., Idle No More, and the Mni Wiconi ("Water is Life") water protectors. In Fawn's "M.A.M.A." re-arming begins with a contemporary act of protectorship on the Pine Ridge Reservation that enables the recovery of ancestral memory, as the red color scheme shifts to blue, returning to "The Plains of South Dakota, Circa 1850," where a young Native woman escapes a scene of violence and cradles her newborn in her arms (91). On her desperate journey, the woman encounters a wolf named Unci (Grandmother), who tells her to "go defend the future" (91). "Holding the future in her arms," the narrator tells us, the woman "walked forth into the darkness," where future generations continue to "grow and stand against the suffering the people and Unci Maka [Grandmother Earth] would face in the coming years" (92). Tracing lineages of Lakota women as survivors and protectors, the comic returns to the present, where water protectors gather in Standing Rock to protest the Black Snake pipeline. In the final, full-page panel, a young water protector cradles a spotted fawn in her arms that are tattooed with deer tracks (96; see fig. 16.7). Much like her ancestor from the 1850s, this young survivor and protector "holds the future in her arms," while deer ears and three-point antlers mark her body with multiple forms of Deer Woman re-generations. Wearing a red bandana with the activist slogan, "No More Stolen Sisters," the young woman in Fawn's comic powerfully crosses Indigenous feminisms with the fight to protect Indigenous lands, or the intersections between stolen sisters and stolen ground.

More than exposing the links between gendered violence and geopolitical exploitation, *Deer Woman: An Anthology* envisions methodologies for re-activating Indigenous arts and activist practices and re-arming sisterhoods of survivance. Building from the work of Indigenous feminisms and activism, the collection represents a multilayered effort that combines regenerative arts practices with the politics of refusal, focused, in particular, on the refusal of settler-colonial rape culture. As Audra Simpson asks in the conclusion to *Mohawk Interruptus*: "how to stop a story that is always being told? Or, how to change a story that is always being told? The story that settler-colonial nation-states tend to tell about themselves is that they are new; they are beneficent; they have successfully 'settled' all issues prior to their beginning" (177). The comics collected in the *Deer Woman* anthology pose similar questions. How to stop the story that settler-colonialism tends to tell about sexual exploitation and murdered Indigenous women? How to refuse the versions of this story that suggest it is a "new" or recent phenomenon, a blameless "epidemic," a story that can be "settled" with changes to legislation or jurisdiction alone?

Crucially, like Simpson, the comics artists in the *Deer Woman* anthology take up the other side of these questions, moving from a politics of refusal toward the arts and activist practices of regeneration. In so doing, the comics collected in the anthology not only ask "how to stop a story that is always being told," but also, and more forcefully, how to regenerate the stories of Deer Women that refuse to remain untold? By re-activating the Indigenous first being, Deer Woman, the anthology transforms the "settled" stories of violence and victimry into unsettling and ongoing stories of Indigenous survivance. And, by combining the works of established comics and new-media artists, such as LaPensée and Alvitre, with emerging artists, such as Lopez and Kenmille, the *Deer Woman* anthology contributes to the broader efforts to "Indigitize" new media, telling Indigenous stories and re-activating Indigenous arts practices in video games, web and print comics, and other digital and new media platforms.[14] The endpapers extend this effort to the future of Indigenous communities, beginning

Figure 16.7. Jackie Fawn, "M.A.M.A.," in *Deer Woman: An Anthology*.

with the mother/daughter collaboration "Outfoxing Coyote" by Carolyn Dunn (writer) and her daughter Nashoba Dunn-Anderson (artist), and ending with a collection of one-page comics by Native middle-school students titled, "Youth Reflections on Native Women." As the editors write, the comics produced by Indigenous youth are "a combination of creative expression and a reorientation of negative associations of Native people, and women in particular" (101). This effort to protect and promote multigenerational arts practices challenges the "newness" of "new media." Far from "Columbusing," or claiming to discover that which was always there, *Deer Woman: An Anthology* reclaims multimodal and multigenerational storytelling as deeply rooted in Indigenous traditions and cycling onward into Indigenous futures. Through the politics and aesthetics of regeneration and "re-generational" kinships, the comics anthology joins Leanne Simpson, who asserts, "our revolutions will be our new dawn, our biidaaban, with the past and the present collapsing in on the present, *as we have always done*" (247).[15] The light that spreads from this "new dawn" is not the light mapping the "discovery" of the "New World" or the blue-glow of "newness" emanating from the latest new-media technology. Instead, it is a light that illuminates the processes of cyclical and radical regeneration of the self and of communities, grounded in deep and ongoing practices of Indigenous relationality across temporalities and territories. "Most of all," Patty Stonefish asserts, the stories collected in the *Deer Woman* anthology, "remind you of what you already possess—a light which refuses to die out" (v).

Notes

1. During the run of LaPensée's *Deer Woman: A Vignette*, Native Realities contributed one dollar per copy sold of LaPensée's comic.

2. In so doing, the founders of ASRW "envision a world where every individual will be on a healing path through discovery of self, love, empowerment, care, defense, and compassion." See the "Our Story" page on the Arming Sisters Reawakening Warriors website. http://www.asrw.co/our-story.html.

3. In his preface to *Manifest Manners: Narratives on Postindian Survivance* (1999), Vizenor defines survivance as "an active sense of presence, the continuation of Native stories, not a mere reaction, or a survivable name. Native survivance stories are renunciations of dominance, tragedy, and victimry. Survivance means the right of succession or reversion of an estate, and in that sense, the estate of Native survivancy" (vii).

4. View Audra Simpson's complete keynote address, delivered at the International R.A.c.e. Conference in Edmonton, Alberta, at https://vimeo.com/110948627.

5. These statistics are available in Amnesty International's summary of the "Maze of Injustice" report: http://www.amnestyusa.org/our-work/issues/women-s-rights/violence-against-women/maze-of-injustice.

6. Leanne Simpson's "constellations of coresistance" also draws inspiration from Jarrett Martineau's dissertation, "Creative Combat: Art, Resurgence, and Decolonization" (2015), in which he argues that contemporary Native artists "disrupt and interrogate" settler forms of recognition through what he calls "affirmative refusal," or the "refusing of forms of visibility within settler colonial realities that render the Indigenous vulnerable to commodification and control" (*As We Have Always Done* 199).

7. To view the full ledger, visit https://plainsledgerart.org.

8. For an example of a traditional Deer Woman story, see Dakota anthropologist Ella Deloria's famous translation in *Dakota Texts* (1932). See also Julien Rice's *Deer Women and Elk Men: The Lakota Narratives of Ella Deloria* (1992).

9. See the Arming Sisters mission statement in the endpapers of *Deer Woman: An Anthology*.

10. See Stonefish's "Words from Arming Sisters" in the endpapers of *Deer Woman: A Vignette* (2015).

11. In her artist bio, Tara Ogaick explains that she is an Iranian-Canadian artist, who has "only recently reconnected with her Anishinabeg relatives."

12. See Simpson's "Signpost 3: Refusing to Play the Game" (25–33), in *Mohawk Interruptus*.
13. See M.a.m.A.'s website: http://www.mothersagainstmeth.org/donate.html.
14. See, for example, LaPensée's side-scroller videogame *Thunderbird Strike* (2017), her web comics *Fala* (2008), which is "an urban Native remix of *Alice in Wonderland*," and *The West Was Lost* (2008), a steampunk web comic, as well as her award-winning print comics, such as *They Who Walk as Lightning* (2017), *The Observing* (2015), and *Copper Heart* (2015). Visit http://www.elizabethlapensee.com/. See also *Sixkiller* (2018), the new collaborative effort between Alvitre (artist) and Lee Francis IV (writer), a comic described as "*Alice in Wonderland* meets *Kill Bill* set in Cherokee Country," published by Native Realities Press. Visit https://www.nativerealities.com/collections/comic-books/products/sixkiller.
15. Biidaaban is an Anishinaabe (or Ojibwe) word meaning "dawn comes; it is daybreak." See *The Ojibwe People's Dictionary* entry: https://ojibwe.lib.umn.edu/main-entry/biidaaban-vii.

Works Cited

Alvitre, Weshoyot. "To Dress in Red." In *Deer Woman: An Anthology*, edited by Elizabeth LaPensée and Weshoyot Alvitre, 72–74. Albuquerque, NM: Native Realities Press, 2017.
Arming Sisters Reawakening Warriors. http://www.asrw.co/ Web.
Deer, Sarah. *The Beginning and End of Rape: Confronting Sexual Violence in Native America*. Minneapolis: University of Minnesota Press, 2015.
Dunn, Carolyn, and Nashoba Dunn-Anderson. "Outfoxing Coyote." In *Deer Woman: An Anthology*, edited by Elizabeth LaPensée and Weshoyot Alvitre, 102–11. Albuquerque, NM: Native Realities Press, 2017.
Fawn, Jackie. "M.A.M.A." In *Deer Woman: An Anthology*, edited by Elizabeth LaPensée and Weshoyot Alvitre, 87–96. Albuquerque, NM: Native Realities Press, 2017.
Francis, Lee. "Publisher Introduction." In *Deer Woman: An Anthology*, edited by Elizabeth LaPensée and Weshoyot Alvitre. Albuquerque, NM: Native Realities Press, 2017.
Kenmille, Barbara. "Dog Woman." In *Deer Woman: An Anthology*, edited by Elizabeth LaPensée and Weshoyot Alvitre, 53–60. Albuquerque, NM: Native Realities Press, 2017.
LaPensée, Elizabeth, and Weshoyot Alvitre, eds. *Deer Woman: An Anthology*. Albuquerque, NM: Native Realities Press, 2017.
LaPensée, Elizabeth, and Jonathan R. Thunder. "Deer Woman: A Vignette." 2015. In *Deer Woman: An Anthology*, edited by Elizabeth LaPensée and Weshoyot Alvitre, 1–16. Albuquerque, NM: Native Realities Press, 2017.
Little Badger, Darcie, and Tara Ogaick. "Wives." In *Deer Woman: An Anthology*, edited by Elizabeth LaPensée and Weshoyot Alvitre, 29–39. Albuquerque, NM: Native Realities Press, 2017.
Lopez, Maria Wolf. "Deer Woman." In *Deer Woman: An Anthology*, edited by Elizabeth LaPensée and Weshoyot Alvitre, 62–70. Albuquerque, NM: Native Realities Press, 2017.
Pearce, Richard. *Women and Ledger Art: Four Contemporary Native American Artists*. Tucson: University of Arizona Press, 2013.
Robertson, Kimberly. "Las Aunties." In *Deer Woman: An Anthology*, edited by Elizabeth LaPensée and Weshoyot Alvitre, 41–51. Albuquerque, NM: Native Realities Press, 2017.
Simpson, Audra. *Mohawk Interruptus: Political Life across the Borders of Settler States*. Durham, NC: Duke University Press, 2014.
Simpson, Leanne Betasamosake. *As We Have Always Done: Indigenous Freedom through Radical Resistance*. Minneapolis: University of Minnesota Press, 2017.
Stonefish, Patty. "Editor Introduction." In *Deer Woman: An Anthology*, edited by Elizabeth LaPensée and Weshoyot Alvitre. Albuquerque, NM: Native Realities Press, 2017.

Vizenor, Gerald. *Manifest Manners: Narratives on Postindian Survivance.* Lincoln: University of Nebraska Press, 1999.

"Youth Reflections on Native Women." In *Deer Woman: An Anthology*, edited by Elizabeth LaPensée and Weshoyot Alvitre, 112–15. Albuquerque, NM: Native Realities Press, 2017

Indigeneity, Intermediality, and the Haunted Present of *Will I See?*

Candida Rifkind and Jessica Fontaine

On August 19, 2014, over one thousand Indigenous and settler people marched through downtown Winnipeg, Canada, to the Forks, the sacred and traditional Indigenous meeting ground at the confluence of the Red and Assiniboine Rivers, to honor the lives and mourn the deaths of two Indigenous people, Tina Fontaine and Faron Hall (Sachgau). Fifteen-year-old Fontaine's body was found two days earlier while police searched for the body of a man who had been seen distressed in the water. Family later identified him as Hall, a homeless man who had won praise from the mayor of Winnipeg when he saved a teen from those waters in 2009. Yet, it was the death of Fontaine, originally from the Sagkeeng Nation north of Winnipeg, that seemed to shake the city and country. Vigils were held in cities across Canada in the week following the discovery of her body, and her death renewed calls by numerous national organizations, including the Assembly of First Nations, the Native Women's Association of Canada, and the Canadian Human Rights Commission, for a federal inquiry into the over 1,200 missing and murdered Indigenous women, girls, Trans, and Two Spirit persons (hereafter MMIWGT2S).[1] When Prime Minister Stephen Harper declared that Fontaine's death was a crime and not a "sociological phenomenon," Cree journalist Doug Cuthand wrote in the *Saskatoon StarPhoenix* that Canada has arrived at a "watershed event that cannot be ignored," echoing a more general public feeling that Harper's response was "the last straw" in a series of failed attempts to reconcile Indigenous-federal relations (Cuthand). Fontaine's story, often accompanied by her photograph, circulated widely in mainstream media and brought the MMIWGT2S epidemic to national prominence. Compelled by the outpouring of emotion, singer Iskwé (Cree/Dené) contacted graphic novelist David Alexander Robertson (Swampy Cree) to develop an animated music video for her song "Nobody Knows." According to Iskwé, this song is intended to "[force] the spotlight on the more than 1200 missing and murdered Indigenous women in Canada" (Bandcamp.com).[2] The collaboration grew to include settler illustrator GMB Chomichuk and Iskwé's cousin, digital artist Erin Leslie, all of whom worked on the graphic novel *Will I See?* published by Winnipeg's High-Water Press in 2016. While the official video for Iskwé's "Nobody Knows" (from her 2017 album *The Fight Within*) features footage of her in live performance, the animated music video for the same song adapted from the graphic novel was posted on YouTube by the publisher, HighWater Press. While they suggest it is a book trailer, we view the graphic novel *Will I See?*, the animated video "Nobody Knows," and the vocal recording of "Nobody Knows" as components of a collaborative multimodal project grounded in the politics and aesthetics of alternative comics.

In *Will I See?* the collaborators create an intimate narrative about the emotional and social effects of the MMIWGT2S epidemic in Canada. The gothic-styled, inky black-and-white graphic narrative follows May, an Indigenous teenager, as she learns about the tragic murders and disappearances of Indigenous women in her unnamed city and community by collecting personal items they lost during their violent disappearances. While her specific location is left vague, digitally distorted backgrounds in at least two of the panels use iconic New York cityscapes to evoke a large North American metropolis more generally as the setting and storyworld of *Will I See?*. This visual strategy to extend the experiences of MMIWGT2S beyond a specific locale, and indeed Canada, contrasts the Cree cultural specificity of May and her grandmother's identities, signaled by the Cree syllabics that appear as panel backgrounds, references to spirit animals based on the Seven Sacred Teachings, and the organization of the plot around the found objects that May places in her medicine bundle, all of which Robertson explains briefly in endnotes. In other ways, too, *Will I See?* achieves a delicate balance between specific Indigenous experiences and cultural practices and more general North American histories and legacies of settler colonialism and white supremacist violence.

We are two settler scholars learning about and from Indigenous writers and artists using comics to intervene in dominant discourses of Indigeneity in Canada and beyond. We come to this project with personal and scholarly interests in studying the multimedia *Will I See?* project. We have both lived and worked at the University of Winnipeg, located on Treaty One territory and in the heart of the Métis homeland, and the campus is a short walk from the hotel where Fontaine was last seen and the Alexander Docks where her body was found. We are both Canadianists exploring a variety of contemporary popular cultural forms, Indigenous creative expression, and affective relations between artists and audiences. We recognize that our locations, scholarly approaches, and standpoints shape our interpretations and investments in this project, and we offer what follows as a contribution to the conversation on Indigenous comics and graphic narratives from these positions. We believe that *Will I See?* is a significant development in Canadian and Indigenous comics because it crosses a series of conventional boundaries: print and video storytelling, documentary and gothic comics, political realism and Indigenous futurism, and individual experience and collective trauma. As such, it joins the growing field of Indigenous-created comics that Sarah Henzi argues "partake in the creation of a new space to voice, create and resist, as well as to restore and reaffirm experiences, histories and memory, and to rectify the falsity of colonial imagery" (36–37).

Will I See? as a Desire-Centered Narrative

Will I See? is a haunting, atmospheric representation of the emotional and social effects of systemic settler colonial violence on young Indigenous women, their families, and the larger Indigenous community in Canada. A sense of foreboding permeates much of the narrative, as the threat of violence lurks near May and is realized near the conclusion when a male predator attacks her. Yet, the collaborators refuse to circulate what Unangax̂ scholar Eve Tuck calls a "damage-based" discourse that only depicts the pain inflicted by colonial violence on Indigenous communities (409). Drawing from the Seven Sacred Teachings, May's grandmother teaches May and readers about the continued spiritual presence of Indigenous women who have been disappeared. Additionally, it is one of these spirits who saves May when she is attacked. As such, the *Will I See?* mixed media project facilitates a "desire-centered" educative narrative about MMIWGT2S and Indigenous culture, for both settler and Indigenous audiences. It fits with Tuck's proposal for works "concerned with understanding complexity, contradiction, and the self-determination of lived lives" that seek to engage us empathetically and responsibly (Tuck 416).[3] Throughout this analysis, we draw on Tuck's concept of centering desire as a productive framework for analyzing the ways in which the *Will I See?* project engages Indigenous traditions to imagine and long for an end of violence against Indigenous women, girls, Trans, and Two Spirit persons. Also underpinning our affective and anti-colonial approaches to these graphic texts are Amber Dean's concepts of "practices of inheritance" and "implicatedness," which she uses to think through public discourses around Indigenous women from Vancouver's Downtown East Side. Dean draws on Roger Simon's work on the ethics of remembering and memorializing past atrocities. Examining the role museum exhibitions play in the construction of the public history of the Holocaust, Simon locates museums as sites that bear traces of the past, giving testament as a "terrible gift" that is inherited by those of us in the present. Simon explains that "such a gift sets the demanding task of inheritance, a process with the potential to open a reconsideration of the terms of our lives now as well as in the future" (188). Recognizing such historic traces as testament shifts our responsibility from bearing witness to the past to acting as named heirs in the present.

Comics and graphic novels are well suited to this work of politicized spectatorship, and in different ways from museums as they draw readers into the tensions of the page layout and the dual presence and absence of panels and gutters. In *Ethics in the Gutter: Empathy and Historical Fiction in Comics*, Katie Polak argues, "Comics contain a metacognitive aspect of representation, emotion, and personal ethical positioning wherein the reading process itself causes us to reflect on the representation itself, our imaginative engagement with that representation, and our relationship to the content" (11). While Polak studies historical and meta-historical comics, we believe that such metacognition and ethical positioning is at work in *Will I See?* as well, and particularly in its personalization of the MMIWGT2S epidemic through the character of May. Dean argues that bearing witness to the violence inflicted on Indigenous women, girls, Trans, and Two Spirit persons often falls short of ethical engagement by removing Indigeneity from the disappeared and murdered through general narratives of violence against *any* woman (7). Dean argues that such empathic narratives are unethical and insufficient because they divorce violence against Indigenous women "from its colonial underpinnings" (5, 7).[4] She calls on us instead to "inherit what lives on from the disappearances of so many women" and explains that recognizing our "implicatedness ... evokes forms of empathic or felt engagement that necessarily tie feeling to responsibility leading us towards practices of inheritance" (17). Although the disappeared and murdered Indigenous women depicted in *Will I See?* are fictional, they are the imaginative inheritance and visual illustration of real disappeared women. *Will I See?* is thereby a graphic narrative that demands its readers engage with the "terrible gifts" of the MMIWGT2S epidemic, calling us into practices of inheritance and mobilizing us into politicized spectatorship.

The project's collaborators deploy a variety of visual and narrative strategies to facilitate these practices of inheritance between the text and us: setting and storyworld, irregular layout and gutters, images of May collecting the lost belongings of the disappeared women, and the depiction of May's relationship with her grandmother, her Kokum. Although Indigenous and settler audiences are implicated differently within the text, we are all implicated from the very beginning. On the first page of *Will I See?* the collaborators employ a setting textbox, inserted in a wide, narrow panel of an aerial view of a city, to situate the narrative and, therefore, the crisis of disappeared and murdered Indigenous women, girls, Trans, and Two Spirit persons in the present (fig. 17.1).[5]

Further, the aerial image of an unnamed city pairs with the following panel, a bird's-eye view of a city skyline. This multiplication of city images asserts that Indigenous girls, women, Trans, and Two Spirit persons are being disappeared from cities across these lands now known as North America. Their murders and disappearances are not isolated incidents. Rather, they are part of the ongoing toxic operations of settler colonialism. However, the collaborators create a more

Figure 17.1. The first page of *Will I See?* Reproduced with the permission of HighWater Press.

textured and complicated landscape through the use of Indigenous language and the figure of May. Cree syllabics lightly cover the page, descending to the left of an image of May through all of the panels, signifying the space and land of the city as Indigenous territory. These watermarks envision the comic's page as an Indigenous space, particularly one where Indigenous women are at the forefront. May's body crosses five panels, filling a large vertical portion of the page. She is on the far right of the page, facing right, but her head is turned to the left and her gaze looks behind her, as if she has walked from right to left and is now looking back. The non sequitur transitions between panels that provide vague setting information function as a background collage to the portrait of May that dominates the page. Her gaze appears extra-diegetic, directing readers to the three quotations on the left-hand page. On this page, floating objects that readers will later understand are items belonging to the disappeared women frame dedications by the three primary collaborators:

For each of the women we've lost, together we stand as One."—Iskwé

"For the over four thousand Indigenous women and girls we have lost and for my daughters, that they grow up strong, and in a safer space."—David Alexander Robertson

"For the seen and the unseen. For the forgotten and remembered."—GMB Chomichuk

Each of the collaborators in different ways dedicates this graphic novel to the disappeared and to the survivors, to the past and to the future. They position *Will I See?* as a textual memorial to commemorate the missing and honor their lives, and they attest to the healing work of their project for Indigenous communities. On the one hand, May's casual clothing, backpack, and arms full of books signify that she is a typical teenager; on the other hand, the Cree syllabics in the background and the dedications to which her gaze directs readers to situate her within the context of MMIWGT2S.

On these first pages, the collaborators thus initiate their desire-centered narrative that recognizes the context of settler colonial violence, but also asserts a dynamic, continued Indigenous presence. In "Suspending Damage: A Letter to Communities," Tuck explains, "Desire is involved with the not yet and, at times, the not anymore . . . There is a ghostly, remnant quality to desire, its existence not contained to the body but still derived of the body. Desire is about longing about a present that is enriched by both the past and the future" (417). The watermark quality of the Cree syllabics gives off a ghostly quality, and the black cat whose image appears three times on the dedication and first page introduces a gothic trope that resonates with the otherworldly, spectral visual tone. Against these visually haunting elements, the Cree lettering and May's powerful, large-scale embodiment that exceeds the panel borders center Indigeneity in the background and foreground of the generic North American metropolis. These visual techniques that open the narrative point to the past sovereignty of Indigenous languages and Indigenous bodies across the continent and express the desire for sovereignty in the future.

Gothic Gutters and Haunted Panels in *Will I See?*

One of the most common formal elements analyzed in comics criticism is the gutter, which Thierry Groensteen describes as a "forced virtual, an identifiable absence" that "is the site of a reciprocal determination" through which the reader participates actively and dialectically to create meaning with, in, and from the text (112–15). *Will I See?* uses irregular layouts and black gutters that can create a disorienting reading experience because of the text's heightened tensions between page and panel, presence and absence, foreground and background. The monochromatic palette splashed with occasional red, the digitally altered and layered hand drawings, and the relative lack of dialogue all demand a lot from readers who need to construct the narrative from what is implied as well as what is shown (fig. 17.2).

Along with these layered, distorted images and partial representations of the action, *Will I See?* uses a visual style that both participates in the long tradition of gothic comics and repurposes its central tropes to represent Indigenous experiences. In so doing, this project adapts gothic comics for Indigenous storytelling in ways that speak back to mainstream comics' celebration of horror in stories of terror and threat. *Will I See?* intervenes in popular forms of horror to ask what it means when the terror is neither imaginary nor a sign of female hysteria, but the real and brutal gendered violence of settler colonialism. The primary visual element that enacts this aesthetic and political intervention in *Will I See?* is the collaborators' use of gothic gutters. Indeed, Robertson has suggested that he wanted Chomichuk to illustrate this story because of his pulp and horror inflected visual style that is a clear departure from Robinson's previous collaborations with Scott B. Henderson, whose more realistic, clear line work illustrates such titles as *Betty: The Helen Betty Osborne Story* and *Sugar Falls: A Residential School Story* (also published by HighWater Press). Chomichuk is a Winnipeg-based settler illustrator whose speculative, noirish comics are influenced by Golden Age and pulp comics and shot through with dark and fantastical elements. This gothic style lends *Will I See?* a different visual tenor from Robertson's previous graphic novels and, while it remains no less educative than his other collaborations, the shift from visual realism to what might variously be described as horror, gothic, fantasy, and speculative comics styles plays with expectations of both Indigenous created comics and genre comics as it blurs the lines between political documentary and popular entertainment.

Chomichuk's style and *Will I See?*'s message that the dead disrupt the world of the living, and the past ruptures into the present, adapt and appropriate Euro-American gothic conventions to draw a story of the MMIWGT2S epidemic that also challenges the colonial and settler ideologies at the heart of much Canadian gothic literature. In her analysis of Euro-American gothic comics, Julia Round considers how the genre's spectrality can be conveyed in the very form of comics if we consider how gutters haunt panels. Round develops this further in her linguistic and conceptual play on the encryption of meaning/the gothic crypt to argue that the gaps between panels on the comics page depict, without showing, events present in the diegesis. The only way the reader can access the meaning of the gutter is by moving onto the next panel and then recursively reading content back into the gutter: "Through the process of recognizing its contents, they [readers] produce the content of the gutter ('crypting').

Figure 17.2. Gothic style and black gutters in *Will I See?* Reproduced with the permission of HighWater Press.

I thus define the crypt as the interior of this panel (whose shown content is its exterior)" (Round 101). Round describes this realization to be an inheritance or a legacy left to us by the artists (101). The gutter as a crypt that demands encryption by the reader and is the unspeakable of the panel content is evident throughout *Will I See?*, and the dual absence and presence it brings into play on the page reminds readers that our inheritance is simultaneously one of violence and loss, and one of Indigenous power and presence. At the beginning of the narrative, May, while walking home from school, meets a black cat, whom she later names Chípiy (Ghost). Chípiy leads May first to an egg that she places within a bundle around her neck, and then through the city to the lost belongings of women who have been violently disappeared. Parallel panels of the disappeared and/or murdered women over several pages depict the last moments they held their belongings. These belongings include an earring, a bracelet, and an arrowhead, among others (they are all displayed as though on a table in the bottom panel of the page where May returns home to show them to her Kokum). While some panels evoke simultaneiety through drawing washed-out background images of the violence inflicted on these unnamed women as haunting May's present, others use sequentiality to juxtapose panels of May and Chípiy in the present with panels of the women's violent disappearances in the past. In the latter, the past narrative of the women and the present narrative of May finding their belongings meet in the black gutters on the comics page.

For instance, on the page where May finds a feather and bead earring, the grayscale background images in the bottom panel depict a woman, wearing the earring, in the grip of a male attacker. This image overwhelms the metropolitan skyline, echoing B-film horror scenes of giant monsters stomping through the downtown. In the foreground, we see the everyday urban present of an outdoor basketball game on the left and a long shot of May and Chípiy in the bottom right (fig. 17.3).

As with the other objects she finds, in this sequence the disappeared woman slips out of the past and into the present through her belongings and through both simultaneity within the panel and sequentiality in the grid structure. Moreover, the violence inflicted on the women is also present with them in the gutters and in the panels. Round notes, "The gutter can also be the site of spatial exclusion . . . of events too graphic to be shown on the page" (104). Although their deaths are not graphically visualized, red splashes mark the violence inflicted upon the women and punctuate the monochromatic palette with gestures of violence that we must read into the action of the panels. At its core, the Euro-American gothic tradition is about the unspeakable, that which is individually repressed and/or culturally suppressed; gothic comics can make the unspeakable visible within the panel diegesis and they can also ask readers to interpellate meaning into the gutters, encrypting the blank/black spaces on the page with the spectral presence of that which is unspoken, even buried in cultural and discursive crypts. The *Will I See?* gutters are the absent presence on the page in which unspeakable violence is enacted. The choice of black gutters, instead of traditional white gutters, further asserts the darkness, the absolute unimaginability, of the terror that occurs within their seemingly blank spaces.

In addition, the red splashes that bleed over the panels emphasize the way the unspeakable past pours into the present. Via the work of reading into and through the gutters and red splashes, we inherit the past and present violence inflicted upon Indigenous women. Readers are implicated in its enactment and must consider how the silence often surrounding the disappearances and murders of Indigenous women, girls, Trans, and Two Spirit persons allows continued violence. As readers, we also follow Chípiy or Ghost and gather the lost items

Figure 17.3. May finds the earring. Reproduced with the permission of HighWater Press.

with May, implicating us in seeing the narrative of violence both within and outside of the text. May follows this gothic cat, and we follow them both, in ways that resonate with Dean's proposal that, "Following ghosts, as a practice of inheriting what lives on from the disappearances of so many women, might work to provide a more widespread grappling of the ways we are all differently implicated in those disappearances" (65). Although the ghosts we follow in *Will I See?* are fictional constructs based on real women, the present setting of the comic, structure of the narrative, and page layouts ask us to grapple with the disappearances of Indigenous women, girls, Trans, and Two Spirit persons beyond the page. In this way, as Dean notes, following ghosts refuses the trope of the "disappearing Indian" by asserting continued presence and by recognizing the ways Indigenous deaths have also come at the hand of intentional violence. They are forced to disappear by colonial systems and forceful actions. As Dean writes, "Settler colonialism and its ongoing effects are at the root of such ghostly-ness rather than some naturalized inherent predilection for disappearance" (62).

However, the project collaborators refuse to situate May within a context that only recognizes the ways in which violence and pain is inflicted upon her and her community and overlooks their survival, healing, and resistance. While May does experience direct violence and threat, and *Will I See?* implicates us in imagining the worst of it that lurks in the gutters and red splashes, this graphic novel refuses to let us leave May and the ghostly women as victims of violence. Instead, the collaborators use the gothic trope of the curious young woman who is subject to visions and drawn to otherworldly spirits to demonstrate inheritances of tradition and care among Indigenous women. Returning home, May reveals the items she found to her grandmother, who recognizes that the personal items must have belonged to disappeared women. Her grandmother helps May string together the belongings into a necklace as she tells her a story of how the disappeared women and girls blossom again from the earth: "They become animal spirits... and share their spirits with us" (n.p.). The visual image of the items tied together on a string points to the ways in which the community remains connected and held together, even when there are losses that fracture it. Similarly, as a piece worn on the body, the necklace may reflect a medicine bundle in sacredness and care. In a visual glossary at the back of the comic, Robertson explains that a medicine pouch or bundle contains sacred items and is worn around the neck to keep these items close to the heart. Like a bundle, the necklace may "bundle" or string together the disparate stories of the disappeared women, connecting the ways violence was similarly enacted against them while maintaining and caring for their individual autonomy, spirit, and legacy (Beeds 2014, 64).

The gothic style and story of *Will I See?* has counterparts in Indigenous literature in Canada, and most notably it shares with Haisla writer Eden Robinson's celebrated coming-of-age novel *Monkey Beach* a female protagonist who is subject to visions she must learn from her elders to understand. As well, both texts adapt and rewrite the Euro-North American gothic tradition to challenge white supremacist ideologies of gender and race particularly meaningful in the context of the MMIWGT2S epidemic. In her discussion of the gothic in *Monkey Beach*, Jodey Castricano suggests, "taking up the question of ghosts and spirits in a First Nations context challenges the Eurocentric version of Gothic as the signifier, par excellence, of psychological unease, perceptual disturbance, or atavistic, and, therefore, pathological tendencies to be explained—and, perhaps, normalized—in terms of hysteria, neuroses, or 'uncanny' primitivism" (806). Settler Canadian gothic literature has long relied on tropes of the Indigenous as monstrous other, and on the sexual availability of Indigenous women. So, while it may be risky for the collaborators of *Will I See?* to rewrite this literary and cultural tradition in an Indigenous gothic comic that could perpetuate the genre's worst stereotypes, this project joins *Monkey Beach* in disrupting the gendered and racialized ideologies of the Euro-American gothic. Castricano echoes Dean's language of inheritance and responsibility when she writes that "*Monkey Beach* demonstrates that learning to talk with one's own ghosts—instead of the imposed ghost of an/other that insists on telling you how, when, where, and why you are haunted—amounts to a transgenerational affirmation of an inheritance, thus involving a call to responsibility" (812). Similarly, the panels depicting May's relationship with her grandmother demonstrate a desire-based legacy and inheritance of and for Indigenous women. These images challenge negative stereotypes of Indigenous women, particularly those often applied to Indigenous women, girls, Trans, and Two Spirit persons who have been disappeared. Again, as comic readers, we must move back and forth across the gutters to construct the narrative in this scene (fig. 17.4).

Time moves both forward and backward, suggesting the endurance of Indigenous women and Indigenous traditions. For Indigenous readers, the decoding that occurs within this scene's gutters may be familial or memorial knowledge, possibly of mothers, sisters, or aunties who have been disappeared. The gutters may also contain embodied and embedded tradition. As settler readers, we cannot image and we cannot know the experiences of the missing and murdered in the same way. However, we are still implicated within these moments. Despite this opacity, we must still construct and decode, and we must still participate actively with the text to make meaning, a meaning that ultimately implicates settler readers in the events the text depicts. Here, the collaborators ask us to hold space for Indigenous tradition in the gutters and within our affective and political responses.

Transformation and Embodiment in "Nobody Knows"

Shifting focus from the graphic novel to the animated video for "Nobody Knows" reveals how differences in media render different artistic and formal

Figure 17.4. Kokum tells May a story in *Will I See?* Reproduced with the permission of HighWater Press.

operations, thereby providing new engagements with us, the audience. The video and the graphic novel both require not only witnessing and acknowledging violence against Indigenous women, but recognizing continued Indigenous presence, knowledge, and power. The video, which runs three minutes and thirty-four seconds, follows the same narrative as the graphic novel but adds animated movement and the song recording. Its motion-graphic style zooms on the comics's images, thereby giving the sense that we are being drawn into the narrative, and pans across visual frames, creating a continued momentum despite the animation's pauses on particular images. In doing so, the video directs viewers' eyes by animating certain panels and by pausing on or leaving still other images, and establishes a space for reflecting on our relationship to the narrative. Furthermore, Iskwé's voice and lyrics synthesize with the graphic novel images, generating a complex audiovisual experience.

The momentum of the video and the build-up of "Nobody Knows" seem to push toward the video's final sequence in which a ghoulish man kidnaps May. The quick animated transitions suggest an immediate danger threatening Indigenous women, girls, Trans, and Two Spirit persons. In the graphic novel, the man kidnapping May appears to be a different man to the one previously shown inflicting violence against one of the women (his hair is shorter than the first man's and his smirk appears more menacing). Through this visual difference, the collaborators assert that violence against Indigenous persons is not the work of one monstrous man, but rather the result of systemic violence embodied by many and manifested widely. However, in the video, the man appears consistent throughout the video, as his hair and silhouette is streamlined in his initial image, rendering a visual coherence to the attacking figure. As such, the threat against May feels persistent and acute. Yet, though attacked, May is not disappeared or murdered. Chípiy saves May and it becomes clear that, although cats are not traditional Cree spirit animals, Chípiy is a spirit animal born from one of the disappeared women. The spirit world holds more power than any individual violent man. As the man prepares to assault May, undoing his belt, Chípiy fills the bottom half of the screen. Her eyes glow white. Chípiy attacks the man and a red swatch streaks across the screen, much like the red splashes in the book. Chípiy's actions shift the power imbalance and stops the violence against May. Beginning when the man attacks May, the lyric "I won't let you look away anymore" repeats on the soundtrack. Unlike in the comic, where Iskwé's lyrics appear at the end of the graphic sequence as a paratext, Iskwé's disembodied voice accompanies the video as a ghostly presence speaking to us. With each repeat of "I won't let you look away anymore," Iskwé vocally exemplifies how the violence the video depicts has been repeated thousands of time against Indigenous women without consequence. Iskwé's voice uses the second-person address to demand that viewers become witnesses: its pairing with the eyes and actions of Chípiy suggest that Iskwé's voice may be understood as the voice of the disappeared woman. Her voice, in singing, refuses silence and inaction from us while asserting a continued presence for the disappeared women. As she does in the graphic novel dedication, Iskwé expresses solidarity with the disappeared women and Indigenous communities who have lost loved ones and seeks a community of inheritance.

Through the video's animation, the collaborators bring to life the tradition of spirit animals and the Seven Sacred Teachings as an intervention into violence inflicted on Indigenous women, girls, Trans, and Two Spirit persons. The transmission of intergenerational Indigenous knowledge represented by May's relationship with her grandmother is a vital part of a transformative Indigenous future this project at once imagines and enacts. Speaking from a Nishnaabeg perspective and addressing an Indigenous audience, Leanne Betasamosake Simpson explains that "*how* we live, *how* we organize, *how* we engage in the world—the process—not only frames the outcome, it is the transformation. *How* molds and then gives birth to the present" (19). She calls this "a *presencing of the present* that generates a particular kind of emergence that is resurgence" (Simpson 20). The video's "how," its moving images and narrative content, reveal traditional spirit animals and the Seven Sacred Teachings to be already at work in May's present. Thus, it generates a desire-centered narrative situated in and animated by the powerful presence of Indigenous community and tradition that is about "a present that is enriched by both the past and the future" (Tuck 417). Although the video contains violent images, the healing bundle, Chípiy, and later traditional spirit animals, take the visual foreground and through animation invite politicized spectatorship.

In the video, after the man falls off a cliff and May and Chípiy sit alone recovering, Chípiy paws at the medicine bundle around May's neck, placing Indigenous healing and knowledge traditions in the visual spotlight. She removes the egg and, in a burst of light, it hatches and a bird comes forth. At the same time, Cree syllabics move horizontally across the screen, filling the space. This sequence moves beyond envisioning May's survival and instead demonstrates the survivance and power of Indigenous traditions and people. As Tuck argues, "Survivance is a key component to a framework of desire" (422). Quoting Gerald Vizenor, who developed the term, she explains that survivance "is distinct from survival: it is 'moving beyond our basic survival in the face of overwhelming cultural genocide to create spaces of synthesis and renewal'" (Vizenor in Tuck 422). In the video, as the bird flies away, she takes the necklace from May. The items then fall to the earth, where they seed a flower, illustrating the transformation and even regeneration of the disappeared women's lives. From the flower then grows one of the disappeared women, who then transforms into a bear. In the endnotes to *Will I See?* Robertson explains that, in the Seven Sacred Teachings, the bear represents courage: "the mental, moral, and spiritual strength to overcome fears that keep us from living the way we are

Figure 17.5. The woman's transformation into a bear in *Will I See?* Reproduced with the permission of HighWater Press.

meant to live" (n.p.). The depiction of this transformation in the book varies from the video because of the different media: in the graphic novel, the collaborators draw the woman's transformation into a bear in a single horizontal panel that implies sequentiality without gutters (fig. 17.5).

The different creatures are linked by a spectral or otherworldly presence represented in the white light beam across the panel that is rooted in a Cree worldview. In both the video and the graphic novel, life, though not replaced, is renewed. However, the video form allows the collaborators to make this process more kinetic and, as the woman transforms, light beams through her to emphasize that she is a being in the process of becoming. This is accompanied by more Cree syllabics running over the screen, such that they trace her revitalization and perhaps also speak to the desire for Indigenous resurgence.

These images, and those that follow, embody Indigenous knowledge and tradition on the screen as the video comes to its conclusion. The video depicts May sitting before the spirit animals, some of whom draw connections to traditional Cree clans, including turtle, bear, and bird, and also represent the continuation of Indigenous kinship between humans and nonhuman beings. The animated animals sway or dance, illustrating their liveness and their movement within the world and the embodiment of Indigenous knowledge. As with the bear, each of the other spirit animals represent part of the Seven Sacred Teachings, which provide instructions for how to live the good life, Mino-Pimatisiwin (see the endnotes to *Will I See?*). For Indigenous audiences watching the music video, this image of May surrounded by the spirit animals may speak of how to both live in and disrupt settler colonialism. The layered meanings of the animals as spirits, teachings/teachers, and guides emphasize the importance of Indigenous community to individual survivance. Following ghosts to the end of the video may mean, for Indigenous audiences, following tradition and enacted traditional knowledge. For settler audiences, we may follow ghosts to learn about that to which we have been willfully ignorant. As the video finishes with a fadeout of the words "Nobody knows," the credits and project title *Will I See?* appears on the screen, asking us, particularly settler audiences, to internalize the question. The shift from Iskwé's pronouncement of "I won't let *you* look away anymore" in the lyrics to the words "Will *I* See?" posted on the screen reframe the demand to see and act as a moment of reflection that requires a response (emphasis added). When they appear after the images of the spirit animals, the words "Will I See?" suggest that our responsibility to see extends to seeing the power and value in Indigenous knowledge and communities, as well as recognizing the ways we are implicated, often in our silence or our looking away, in the violence inflicted upon Indigenous communities.

The final credits of the video roll over a washed-out grayscale image of a granite monument that will be familiar to viewers who have visited The Forks in downtown Winnipeg: it is the Missing and Murdered Women Monument, a collaborative project between the Ka Ni Kanichihk Indigenous cultural center and the Province of Manitoba, that was unveiled on August 12, 2014, five days before Tina Fontaine's body was discovered nearby. It continues to serve as a meeting place for individuals and group vigils to honor disappeared women and their families (fig. 17.6).

This image is not part of the graphic novel, whose locality remains ambiguous even though visual and linguistic signs point to May and her Kokum's Cree identity. That this actual monument appears in the final frames of the video sutures the speculative Indigenous storyworld of gothic transformations to the real territory on which the story was constructed. The image of the monument punctures this fictionalized narrative of the MMIWGT2S epidemic with an image of the ongoing and open wounds felt by those who gather at the real site to grieve and organize. Public memorials, to return to the ideas of Dean and Simon, materialize and mark the "terrible gifts" we inherit from past atrocities, and so the image of this monument at the end of the video at once locates the narrative in a real time and place and calls viewers to recognize that the representational world of the animation is in direct relation with the real world of racism and settler colonial violence.

Along with being a call for settlers to see, Iskwé's song may act as a healing bundle, a term Cree/Métis poet Gregory Scofield gives to Indigenous poetry for Indigenous people, and for Indigenous audiences. In the video, Iskwé's face is prominent on May's t-shirt as May drops the bird's egg (containing a spirit animal) into the medicine bundle, thus pairing Iskwé and her song with medicine and tradition. Scofield writes that poets "all carry, within ourselves, sacred bundles" (318). Sacred or healing bundles, for Scofield, are carried within the poet's body. It is the medicine of origin communities as well as communities yet to be. The medicine heals through the opening of the bundle that happens

Figure 17.6. Credit sequence of "Nobody Knows." Reproduced with the permission of HighWater Press.

in the sharing of stories, songs, histories, and ceremonies (318–19). Immediately following the image of the medicine pouch in the video, Iskwé sings, "I won't be afraid." The song she sings, and also the bundle she carries, speak to resurgence and survivance. Iskwé sonically and corporally mobilizes Indigenous medicine into the video. Scofield explains that "poetry is in your body. You have to use it like a rattle. You need to move silence around . . . When you think about the way medicine people work, they work with the body" (318). As Iskwé sings, she vocalizes the silences and embodies the disappearances surrounding the violence against Indigenous women, girls, Trans, and Two Spirit persons. Watching the video, it seems that as the egg hatches in the video and the bird flies across the city its medicine also moves from Iskwé and the *Will I See?* animation across the audience. It may be received as healing or as an image of Indigenous resurgence. Or, as settler audience members, we may receive the bird as implicating us in our responsibilities to this inheritance and its persistence in the present.

Endings and Beginnings

On February 22, 2018, a Winnipeg jury found Raymond Cormier not guilty of second-degree murder in the death of Tina Fontaine. The case rested on witnesses who said they had seen Cormier and Fontaine together, and other circumstantial evidence; the lack of forensic evidence was one of the factors that led to Cormier's acquittal. Just as the discovery of her body sparked national grief and outrage, so did this verdict. Rallies, vigils, and protests were held in cities across Canada, echoing the statement Manitoba Keewatinowi Okimakanak Grand Chief Sheila North made on the courthouse steps: "We've all failed her. We as a nation need to do better" (MacLean). Following the ghosts of *Will*

I See? to the narrative's ending that is also a beginning requires us to recognize the many ways we are implicated in the lives and deaths of Indigenous women through our reading, viewing, and listening activities. By implicating us in imagining the unspeakable violence within the comics gutters and through the demands of Iskwé's voice to see, the multimodal forms of the *Will I See?* project implicate us in the enactment of such violence and ask us how perception might be transformed into a more active and politicized practice of empathetic witness. The form of the gothic comic and the kinetic animation of the music video disrupt settler colonial Eurocentric divisions between human and nonhuman, living and dead, past and present, individual and community.

Judith Butler writes that grief is politicizing because it brings to the forefront relational ties on which we depend and for which we are responsible (12). However, any transformative political or public action for intervening in violence against Indigenous communities must be centered within Indigenous traditions and power, as illustrated in the ways May and her Kokum hold together the belongings of the disappeared and murdered women and the ways the spirit animals intervene to save May's life. This is not to say that the burden for change is placed solely on Indigenous peoples. Rather, we must see not only the damage inflicted by colonial violence on Indigenous communities, but look to their continued presence and survivance when seeking to develop inquiries or programs for change. *Will I See?* teaches us that ghosts may be more healing than terrifying, and that tracing their stories may lead to practices that include Indigenous-led appropriations, inversions, and reinventions of European forms, such as the settler colonial gothic. The setting, narrative, and layouts of the comic implicate readers as witnesses to colonial violence, and the animation of the music video highlights strength and power within Indigenous tradition as a means for intervening in violence. In both print and video, *Will I See?* repositions Indigenous women as having what Butler, in a different context, calls full and "grievable lives" within Canadian society. As a creative, collaborative intermedial project, *Will I See?* and "Nobody Knows" highlight the varieties of media, forms, genres, and styles available to Indigenous comics creators to mobilize, invert, and rewrite both settler ideologies and comics traditions.

Notes

We would like to thank Jenny Burman for her thoughtful critique and comments on an early draft of this work. We also thank David Alexander Robertson and GMB Chomichuk for informal conversations that provided insights into the creation of *Will I See?* and Laina Hughes at HighWater Press for assistance in preparing the images.

1. A 2004 Amnesty International report, *Stolen Sisters: A Human Rights Response to the Discrimination and Violence against Indigenous Women in Canada*, identifies multiple factors that contribute to the "heightened risk of violence against Indigenous women," including social and

economic marginalization; a history of government policies "that have torn apart Indigenous families and communities"; the failure of Canadian police to protect Indigenous women; the exploitation of the vulnerability of Indigenous women by Indigenous and non-Indigenous men; racism; and, the expectations of societal indifference that "will allow perpetrators to escape justice" (2).

2. Although Iskwé's Bandcamp page declares that "Nobody Knows" directs attention to missing and murdered Indigenous women specifically, it is important to acknowledge, as Iskwé and the collaborators do in interviews, that the high incidents of violence affect Indigenous girls, Trans, and Two Spirit persons as well. For that reason, we use the MMIWGT2S acronym to refer to these identity groups at multiple points.

3. A note on terminology: Following Amber Dean's lead in *Remembering Vancouver's Disappeared Women: Settler Colonialism and the Difficulty of Inheritance* (2015), we refer to the *Will I See?* audiences as "us" to illustrate how settler audiences, including both of us settler scholars, are implicated in the crisis and also in processes of recognition of Indigenous power and healing. At the same time, we note the ways the texts work to engage Indigenous culture particularly for Indigenous audiences. Like Dean, we refer to Indigenous women who are missing as "disappeared" or "have been disappeared" to further recognize that Indigenous women are often forcefully made to go missing (20–26).

4. Rauna Kuokkanen (2008) situates the epidemic of violence against Indigenous women in Canada as the result of Canada's colonial history, including the "dispossession of lands and livelihoods, abuse experienced in residential schools and assimilationist and racist policies seeking to erase identities and cultures" (219–20).

5. *Will I See?* is not paginated.

Works Cited

Amnesty International. *Stolen Sisters: A Human Rights Response to Discrimination and Violence against Indigenous Women in Canada*. Amnesty.ca. 2004. Web. March 5, 2016.

Beeds, Tasha. "Remembering the Poetics of Ancient Sound kistêsinâw/ wîsahkêcâhk's maskihkiy (Elder Brother's Medicine)." In *Indigenous Poetics in Canada*, edited by Neil McLeod, 61–71. Waterloo: Wilfred Laurier University Press, 2014. Print.

Butler, Judith. "Violence, Mourning, Politics." *Studies in Gender and Sexuality* 4, no. 1 (2003): 9–37. Print.

Castricano, Jody. "Learning to Talk with Ghosts: Canadian Gothic and the Poetics of Haunting in Eden Robinson's *Monkey Beach*." *University of Toronto Quarterly* 75, no. 2 (2006): 801–13. Print.

Cuthand, Doug. 2014. "Teen's Death Creates Pivotal Moment in History." *Star-Phoenix* [Saskatoon] August 29, 2014. ProQuest. Web. July 11, 2018.

Dean, Amber R. *Remembering Vancouver's Disappeared Women: Settler Colonialism and the Difficulty of Inheritance*. Toronto: University of Toronto Press, 2015. Print.

Groensteen, Thierry. *The System of Comics*. Trans. Bart Beaty and Nick Nguyen. Jackson: University Press of Mississippi, 2007. Print.

Henzi, Sarah. "A Necessary Antidote: Graphic Novels, Comics, and Indigenous Writing." *Canadian Revue of Comparative Literature* 43, no. 1 (2016): 23–38. Project Muse. Web. May 11, 2017.

Iskwé. "Nobody Knows." Bandcamp.com. August 18, 2017. Web. October 18, 2017.

Kuokkanen, Rauna. "Globalization as Racialized, Sexualized Violence: The Case of Indigenous Women." *International Feminist Journal of Politics* 10, no. 2 (2008): 216–33. Taylor and Francis. Web. October 18, 2017.

Maclean, Cameron. "Jury Finds Raymond Cormier Not Guilty in Death of Tina Fontaine." *CBC News*. February 22, 2018. Web. July 11, 2018.
Polak, Katie. *Ethics in the Gutter: Empathy and Historical Fiction in Comics*. Columbus: The Ohio State University Press, 2017.
Portage and Main Press. "Will I See?" *YouTube*. January 20, 2017. Web. October 18, 2017.
Robertson, David Alexander, et al. *Will I See?* Winnipeg: HighWater Press, 2016.
——, and Scott B. Henderson. *Betty: The Helen Betty Osborne Story*. Winnipeg: HighWater Press, 2015.
——, and Scott B. Henderson. *Sugar Falls: A Residential School Story*. Winnipeg: HighWater Press, 2011.
Robinson, Eden. *Monkey Beach*. Toronto: Vintage, 2000.
Round, Julia. *Gothic in Comics and Graphic Novels: A Critical Approach*. Jefferson, NC: McFarland, 2014.
Sachgau, Oliver. "Families Struck by Tragedy Consoled at Massive Vigil." *Winnipeg Free Press*, August 20, 2014, A3. Web. July 13, 2018.
Scofield, Gregory. "Poems as Healing Bundles." In *Indigenous Poetics in Canada*, edited by Neil McLeod, 314–19. Waterloo: Wilfrid Laurier University Press, 2014.
Simon, Roger I. "The Terrible Gift: Museums and the Possibility of Hope without Consolation." *Museum Management and Curatorship* 21 (2006): 187–204. Taylor and Francis. Web. October 18, 2017.
Simpson, Leanne Betasamosake. *As We Have Always Done: Indigenous Freedom through Radical Resistance*. Minneapolis: University of Minnesota Press, 2017.
Tuck, Eve. "Suspending Damage: A Letter to Communities." *Harvard Educational Review* 79, no. 3(2009): 409–28. *EBSCOHost*. Web. August 14, 2017.

Afterlives: A Coda

Susan Bernardin

In November 2016, the first Indigenous Comic Con took place in Albuquerque, New Mexico, through the visionary efforts of Lee Francis IV, publisher of Native Realities and author of the foreword to this volume, along with a cohort of Indigenous artists, cosplayers, and "Indiginerds." Indigenous and indigenized superheroes abounded that weekend: Jeffrey Veregge's Coastal Salish formline representations of Batman and Spiderman; Arigon Starr's "rez boy turned Super Indian"; Jonathan Nelson's "sheepish" hero Jonesy; Jay Odjick's Kagagi (Raven). That same weekend, one thousand miles north up I-25, the Standing Rock Reservation was a gathering place for thousands of Indigenous people and allies who came from all directions. The water and land protectors' months of superheroic resistance against the North Dakota Access Pipeline, or Black Snake, was met by a militarized police force that used water cannons, percussive grenades, rubber bullets, and tear gas against them.

Standing Rock—and the many preceding and ensuing sites of Indigenous resistance to assaults on homelands—viscerally demonstrates the old and very contemporary threats posed to Indigenous peoples across the Americas and Oceania. At the Indigenous Comic Con, solidarity and support for water protectors visibly abounded, from posters and t-shirts to a clay sculpture of a young Jemez Pueblo girl, fist raised up to a looming, coiled black snake. Created by Jemez artist Kathleen Wall, the sculpture was mirrored by the artist's daughter, whose cosplay made visible the power of Indigenous youth as change-makers in their communities and beyond. When children walked by Arigon Starr's booth at the third Con, held in November 2018, I would see them do a double-take upon seeing the life-size Super Indian poster ("Once a rez boy, now a Native American superhero!"). Some I heard repeating Super Indian's name, nudging their friends. Whether in cosplay or not, these children and youth underscore the generative power of Indigenous comics creation: to offer up new stories of representational possibility, and, given the specter of Black Snakes and all-too-real villains in our worlds, the encouragement that they themselves have power to create different futures.

As this volume shows, Indigenous comics work in part as a form of exuberant refusal: refusal of the formative representational legacies of mainstream comics. The interconnection between physical and representational violence endemic to colonization drives the urgency of this task to refuse stories that demean, erase, objectify. At the same time, Indigenous comics offer up alternative affinities to other stories, histories, and futures. Eight years before the first Indigenous Comic Con, the traveling exhibit, "Comic Art Indigène" opened in Santa Fe. The exhibit paired two images: Marvel superhero Captain America and a pictograph of a red, white, and blue, shield-bearing man located in what is now southwestern Utah. The exhibit's curator, Antonio Chavarria (Santa Clara Pueblo), shares that he was inspired to create the exhibit after seeing this pictograph, entitled "All American Man" in an archaeology journal: "As a devotee of comics from a young age, I immediately saw Captain America and I made a promise that some day I would share that insight with others" (*When Raven Became Spiderman* 36). "All American Man" asks us to consider affinities for super-figures and transformative stories across time and space. Perhaps more strikingly, like this volume, it upends conventional expectations by asserting the Indigenous origins of comics. For Arigon Starr, pictographs, what she calls "stories with pictures," make the case that "Native folks have always been doing "sequential art" (*Dreaming in Indian* 59).

The diverse Indigenous visual-verbal antecedents of contemporary comics in turn make possible new forms of visual storytelling. For example, Haida artist Michael Nicoll Yahgulanaas refuses kinship with North American comics, instead claiming manga in honor of trans-pacific intergenerational memories of Haida fishers being welcomed in Japanese communities. At the same time, he retools Haida visual language—popularly known as "formline" and familiar to anyone who has seen a totem pole—to create what he calls *Haida manga*. Like other Indigenous comics artists, Yahgulanaas sees the transformative potential of telling old stories anew. In *Red: A Haida Manga* and *War of the Blink*, he revisits family and community stories to offer cross-cultural lessons in healing, loss, and trauma, and reconciliation. He does so by purposely refusing conventional comics form, transmuting grids and gutters into black, fluidly curving lines that shape, stretch, and shrink. This fluid movement, much like the coastal setting for the story, directs its shifting meaning. Our efforts to make connections with the story's lessons are extended by the multiple forms the story takes. *Red* is composed of 108 individual watercolor panels that form both a sequential narrative and a narrative painting, what Yahgulanaas calls a "composite, one that will defy your ability to experience story as a simple progression of events" (109). Invited to turn the page at story's end, readers re-experience the story as one large interconnected formline that reveals a Haida crest. In *Haida manga*, the medium is also the message: a message of creative adaptation, collaboration, and engagement.

Such messages resonate across Indigenous comics as diverse as Roy Boney Jr.'s *We Speak in Secret*—about the undertold story of Cherokee codetalkers in World War I—and Beth LaPensée's story of upending gender violence in *Deer Woman*. Both herald the transformative power of recognizing one's own superhero powers, and those fueled by cultural stories and knowledge. At the heart of Indigenous comics is the question: what are the stories that nourish and sustain Indigenous peoples? What are the responsibilities of the different audiences that interact with these stories? What are the transformative possibilities of Indigenous-driven comics? How do they animate understanding about the past and imagine alternative futures?

In 2019, Indigenous Comic Con is in motion, with Cons in Denver, Melbourne, and Albuquerque. Similarly, Indigenous comics are in motion, offering new possibilities for imagining a Red Planet and inviting many welcome sequels.

Works Cited

"Arigon Starr: Comic Book Blues." In *Dreaming in Indian: Contemporary Native American Voices*, edited by Lisa Charleyboy and Mary Beth Leatherdale, 58–59. Toronto: Annick Press, 2014.

Chavarria, Antonio R. "Tales to Astonish: Heroes and Exhibitions." In *When Raven Became Spider*. Curated by Leena Minifie. Dunlop Art Gallery and Regina Public Library, 2017. 32–39.

Contributors

Frederick Luis Aldama is Distinguished University Professor, Arts & Humanities Distinguished Professor of English, Distinguished University Scholar, and Alumni Distinguished Teacher at The Ohio State University. He is the 2018 recipient of the Rodica C. Botoman Award for Distinguished Teaching and Mentoring and the Susan M. Hartmann Mentoring and Leadership Award. He is the award-winning author, coauthor, and editor of forty books. In 2018, *Latinx Superheroes in Mainstream Comics* won the International Latino Book Award and the Eisner Award for Best Scholarly Work. He is editor and coeditor of eight academic press book series as well as editor of Latinographix, a trade-press series that publishes Latinx graphic fiction and nonfiction. He is creator of the first documentary on the history of Latinx superheroes in comics (Amazon Prime) and cofounder and director of SŌL-CON: Brown & Black Comix Expo. He is founder and director of the Obama White House award-winning LASER: Latinx Space for Enrichment & Research as well as founder and codirector of the Humanities & Cognitive Sciences High School Summer Institute. He has a joint appointment in Spanish & Portuguese as well as faculty affiliation in Film Studies and the Center for Cognitive and Brain Sciences. His children's book, *The Adventures of Chupacabra Charlie*, will be published by OSU Press in January 2020.

Joshua T. Anderson is an assistant professor of American literature at the University of Saint Joseph. He is a non-Indigenous scholar and creative writer from rural North Dakota, and the former editorial assistant at *Western American Literature*, *Studies in American Indian Literatures*, and *Poetics Today*. His work is published or forthcoming in *Inks: The Journal of the Comics Studies Society*, *Studies in American Indian Literatures*, *Transmotion*, and *Weird Westerns: Race, Gender, Genre* critical collection. His short story "Playing Dead," appears in *Bourbon Penn*, and his creative nonfiction work appears in *Sonora Review*.

Chad A. Barbour is associate professor of English at Lake Superior State University. He is the author of *From Daniel Boone to Captain America: Playing Indian in American Popular Culture* (2016).

Susan Bernardin is director of the School of Language, Culture, & Society at Oregon State University, located on traditional homelands of the Mary's River or Ampinefu Band of Kalapuya. Recent publications in *Studies in American Indian Literatures* and *World Literature Today* address contemporary Indigenous comics and transmedia storytelling.

Mike Borkent is a lecturer in the Arts Studies in Research & Writing program at the University of British Columbia on unceded Musqueam territory. He completed a federally funded postdoctoral fellowship at the University of Calgary. He specializes in the study of visual poetry, comics, and cognitive poetics and has published several articles and reviews in such journals as *Visible Language, Cognitive Linguistics, Canadian Literature,* and *Literature & Translation*.

Jeremy M. Carnes is finishing his PhD in English Literature and Cultural Theory at the University of Wisconsin-Milwaukee. His dissertation explores how comics can help us theorize historicization and temporality differently to more radically dismantle Euro-American power structures surrounding history itself. He has written on indigeneity in Marvel's *The New Mutants* and Tim Truman's *Scout*.

Philip Cass, born in Papua, New Guinea, works as senior lecturer in the communication studies program at Unitec in Auckland, New Zealand, and as an associate editor of *Pacific Journalism Review*. He has published on a wide range of Pacific issues, including climate change-induced migration and Islam in the Pacific. His work with Jack Ford has focused on depictions of Australians and New Zealanders at war and representations of Asia and the Pacific in *Commando* comics.

Jordan Clapper is a doctoral candidate in the English program at Brandeis University. Jordan's research includes Indigenous narratives, video game studies, digital humanities, and narrative theory with ongoing projects in digital representation and immersion, Indigenous new media, and scholarly video games. Jordan is of Ponca of Oklahoma ancestry.

James J. Donahue is associate professor of English & Communication at SUNY Potsdam, where he also coordinates the minor in Native American studies. His most recent books include *Contemporary Native Fiction: Toward a Narrative Poetics of Survivance* (2019) and the coedited volume *Narrative, Race, and Ethnicity in the United States* (2017). His recent articles exploring the politics of race in narrative arts have been published in *African American Review* and *JNT: The Journal of Narrative Theory*.

Dennin Ellis is a long avid reader of comics and a musician. He earned his bachelor's in music and master's in English. He has been an English teacher in the United States and in South Korea. He is a PhD student at The Ohio State University.

Jessica Fontaine has an MA in cultural studies from the University of Winnipeg and is currently a PhD candidate in the Department of Art History and Communication Studies at McGill University. Her dissertation explores the relationships between feelings of belonging and care and affective labor in the professional wrestling media industry. She has presented conference papers on Tanya Tagaq's 2014 Polaris Music Prize Performance and on the visualization of Johnny Cash's songs in Reinhard Kleist's graphic biography *Johnny Cash: I See a Darkness*. She has published in *The Comics Grid*.

Jonathan (Jack) Ford is a member of Australia's Professional Historians Association, with a PhD in history (University of Queensland). Within Brisbane City Council's Heritage Unit (2001–2014), he gained heritage protection for 337 local sites. Jack is the author/contributor to ten books, fifteen commissioned reports, one heritage trail, thirteen journals, and eight conference papers. As a military historian, he, with Phil Cass, have examined how their shared ANZAC legend was appropriated for comics.

Lee Francis IV (Pueblo of Laguna) is the Head Indigenerd and CEO of Native Realities, the only Native and Indigenous pop culture company in the United States with the hope to change the perceptions of Native and Indigenous people through dynamic and imaginative pop culture representations. He is the author of poetry, short stories, and comics. His first solo comic book, *Sixkiller*, debuted June 2018. He is an advocate for Native youth, with a focus on community literacy and entrepreneurship. He lives in Albuquerque with his family (and dog).

Enrique García is associate professor of Hispanic Visual Culture at Middlebury College. He is author of *Cuban Cinema after the Cold War* (2015) and *The Hernandez Brothers: Love, Rockets, and Alternative Comics* (2017). His next book is about the role of Puerto Rican culture in the American superhero genre and future projects include a manuscript about orientalist trends in comic books from the Americas.

Javier García Liendo is assistant professor in the Department of Romance Languages and Literatures at Washington University in St. Louis. His work focuses on Peruvian and Latin American cultural production. He is the author of *El intelectual y la cultura de masas: Argumentos latinoamericanos en torno a Ángel*

Rama y José María Arguedas (2017). His work has appeared in *MLN*, *Latin American Research Review*, and *Discourse*, among other journals.

Brenna Clarke Gray holds a PhD in Canadian literature from the University of New Brunswick, where she was a Canada Graduate Scholar. She is a faculty member in the Department of English at Douglas College in New Westminster, British Columbia. Her research interests include Canadian superheroes and representations of Canada in mainstream American comics.

Brian Montes is assistant professor in Latin American and Latina/o studies at John Jay College, City University of New York. His research, teaching, and writing are grounded in US Latino/a studies, Latin American studies, and Maya studies, with particular interest placed on the lived experience of race and ethnicity within Latin American and Latina/o ethnic groups. Other areas of specialization include Latin American and Latina/o social movements, memory, critical race theory, Indigenous rights, Latinx popular culture, and Maya (Yucatán) identity.

Arij Ouweneel is associate professor at the Centre for Latin American Research and Documentation, Amsterdam, and Professor Emeritus at Utrecht University. His publications include several articles and books like *Freudian Fadeout* (2012) and *Resilient Memories: Amerindian Cognitive Schemas in Latin American Art* (2018). Currently he is working on a project on graphic narratives as public history.

Kevin Patrick, PhD, teaches media and communication studies at Fordham University, Bronx, NY. His scholarship on Australian comic books, pulp novels, and media fandom appears in numerous journals, including the *International Journal of Comic Art*, *Media International Australia*, and *Participations: Journal of Audience and Reception Studies*. He contributed entries to *A Companion to the Australian Media* (2014), and the *Planetary Republic of Comics* website. He curated a major exhibition on Australian comics at the State Library of Victoria (Melbourne, Australia) in 2006–2007 and is the author of *The Phantom Unmasked: America's First Superhero* (2017).

Candida Rifkind is professor in the Department of English at the University of Winnipeg, Canada, where she specializes in graphic narratives and Canadian literature and culture. In addition to numerous journal articles and book chapters in Canadian studies and comics studies, she is the author of *Comrades and Critics: Women, Literature, and the Left in 1930s Canada* (2009) and coeditor of *Canadian Graphic: Picturing Life Narratives* (2016). She serves on the Executive of the Comics Studies Society, the advisory board for the journal *INKS*, and is coeditor of the new Wilfrid Laurier University Press book series Crossing Lines: Transcultural/Transnational Comics Studies.

Jessica Rutherford is an assistant professor of Spanish in the Modern Languages department at Central Connecticut State University. She received her PhD from the Department of Spanish and Portuguese from The Ohio State University in 2017, specializing in Latin America from the colonial period to the present. Her current research works to decenter historiographical discourse via the study of Latin/x American popular culture to include marginalized perspectives and experiences in the historical archive.

Jorge Santos is Ecuadorian-Salvadorian Latinx and the first in his family to earn a PhD. He is assistant professor of Multi-Ethnic Literature of the United States at the College of the Holy Cross. His work has appeared in *MELUS*, *College Literature*, and *Image/Text*. He has contributed work to multiple collections on graphic narrative scholarship. His book, *Graphic Memories of the Civil Rights Movement*, was published in 2019.

Index

Aboriginal Curatorial Collective (Garneau), 278
Aborigines in comics, xii, xviii–xix, 21, 53–72, 75–97, 100–120
Acevedo, Ramón Luis, 212–13, 216
Action Comics, 101
Adams, Rachel, xiii
Adare, Sierra S., xv
Adolf, Hermann, and Musso, 55
Adventures of Devil Doone, The, 58
Adventures of Smoky Dawson, The, 59
Adventures of the Jolly Swagman, The, 61
Aguilar Peña, César, 134–36
AIDS crisis, 62, 117–19
Air Hawk and the Flying Doctors, 59
Alcatraz, 27
Aldama, Arturo, xiii, 129
Aldama, Frederick Luis, xi–xxiii, 129, 146
Alder, Alison, 117
Alec the Airman, 55
Alegría, Ricardo, 215, 225
Alexie, Sherman, xi
Allatson, Paul, 205
Allen, Chadwick, xiii–xiv, xvi, 301
Allen, Paula Gunn, 248
Alpha Flight, 5–24
Alter/native comics, 274
Álvarez Estrada, Edgar, 131
Álvarez-Rivón, Ricardo, 217–20, 222, 230–31
Alvitre, Weshoyot, 316, 333–34
A-Maze-In' Australia, 59
America: and colonialism, 19–23, 27–52, 147; and mainstream superheroes, 5–24
American Indian Movement (AIM), 27
American Weapon X program, 13
Amerindian, 127–43, 174, 176
Andean people in comics, 127–43

Anderson, Joshua T., xx, 316–39
Anzaldúa, Gloria, xiii, 127, 169, 177
Aotearoa Whispers, 69
Aotearoa people in comics, 53–72
Apache Kid, The, 44
Arabian Knight (Marvel), 77
Archive and the Repertoire, The, 169
Arguedas, José María, 34, 156, 225
Argus, 54
Arikirangi te Turuki, Te Kooti, 69
Arming Sisters Reawakening Warriors (ASRW), 316, 324–25, 329
Arohanui: Revenge of the Fey, 69
Asterix, 64, 220
As We Have Always Done, 319
Attawapiskat School Campaign, 16
Australia in comics, 53–72, 75–97, 100–120
Australian Chuckler's Weekly, 59
Australian Electoral Commission (AEC), 113, 115
Australian "Funnies," 53, 61
Australian Woman's Mirror, 102
Australian Women's Weekly, 102
Ausubel, David, 66
Authenticity, 280
Avengers, 15

Baker, Martin, 205
Ball, Murray, 61, 64
Bancroft, Brownyn, 62
Band Aid record (relief fund), 92
Banshee (X-Men), 76, 82
Barbachano, Miguel, 198
Barbour, Chad A., xii, xv, xviii, 27–49, 184
Barlock, Bart, 56
Batman, xv, 62, 220, 254–55, 257, 361

371

Bauldic, Michelle, xv
Beaty, Bart, 6–7
Beginning and End of Rape, The, 320
Bell, John, 8
Ben Bowyang (Dennis), 54
Bennett, Harry W., 63
Bernardin, Susan, xvii, xxi, 299–315, 361–63
Betances, Ramón Emeterio, 213
Betty: The Helen Betty Osborne Story, 346
Beyond Settler Time, 302
Beyond the Black Stump, 61
Bib and Bub (May Gibb), 54
Big Boss, 111
Big Chief Wahoo, 29–30
Big-2, 21–22. *See also* DC Comics; Marvel
Bin-Sallik, MaryAnn, 86
Bishop (superhero), 62, 88–89
Black Crow, 238
Black Panther, 256
Blake and Mortimer, 64
Blitzkrieg (Marvel), 78
Blood quantum laws, 265–66
Blue Hardy and the Diamond Eyed Pygmies, 55
Bluey and Curley, 55–56, 60
Bone Shirt, Walter, 320, 329–30
Borkent, Mike, xx, 273–98
Boy's Own Paper, The, 53
Brian Hibbs (Spider-Man), 77
Bredent, John, 61
Brodie, Ted, 64
Brown, Chester, 273
Burns, Nicholas, 306
Butler, Judith, 358
Byrne, John, 5, 7, 12–13, 17, 19

Callaghan's Kids, 59
Canada, 9, 13, 16, 18–22; and colonialism, 5–24; in comics, 5–24, 273–98; nationalist superheroes, 5–24
Canadian Whites, 6, 11, 13
Captain America, 6, 15, 76, 87, 362
Captain Atom, 58
Captain Britain, 9
Captain Canuck, 5–7
Captain Paiute, xx, 254–72
Captivity narrative, 42, 44–45
Carnes, Jeremy M., xx, 299–315
Carrasco, Davíd, 128

Carrasco Catalá, Jorge L., xii
Carter Brown Comics, 59
Cartography of refusal, 318
Cass, Philip, xviii, 53–72
Castanha, Tony, 224–25
Castellanos Casanova, Carlos, xix
Castricano, Jodey, 351
Caten, Dan and Dean, 9
Chato, Keith, 61
Chavarria, Tony, 184, 238
Cheyenne Kid, 44
Cheyenne people in comics, xvi, 33, 36–37, 40
Chi, Cecilio, 198, 202
Chicha, 161
Chickasaw, xvii
Chinnery, Tony, 112
Chola (term), 160–61
Cholas and Pishtacos, 160
Cholificación, 129
Cholo, 160–61
Chomichuk, Gregory, 313
Ch'ixi, 127, 129
Christchurch Star, 63
Chute, Hillary, 243–44, 277
Clapper, Jordan, xx, 237–53
Claremont, Chris, 76–77, 81–82
Classic Comics, 64, 68
Cleveland Indians mascot, 30
Clymer, John, 41
Colchado Lucio, Óscar, 156
Collective Man, The, 78
Colonialist binary, 182
Color Comics (Sunday Telegraph), 55
Colors of Australia, 62
Colossus, 76, 78, 80, 82
Colt, Jim, 55
Comanche Moon, 27–49
Comanche people in comics, 27–49
Comics Code, 27
Comics: Ideology, Power and the Critics, 205
Coming of Molo the Mighty, The, 55
Commando, 62, 64, 68, 70
Commonwealth Electoral Act, 115
Condoman (campaign), 62, 117–19
Condorito, 218
Contest of Champions, 77–80
Conversational remembering, 207
Coogan, Peter, 255–56
Cook, Noel, 64

Cooper, James Fenimore, 42
Corporate control, 5–24, 27
Cosmic aesthetic, 305–8
Coulthard, Glen, 303
Coupland, Douglas, 10
Cox, Eric, 54
Cox, James H., xiii–xiv
Crash Carson of the Future, 63
Crawford, Thomas, 42
Cree people in comics, 16–19, 273–98, 340–60
Cresswell, Tim, 302
Crimson Comet, The, 58
Critical impulse, 182, 184–85
Cross, Stan, 53, 56
Crosspollenization (Anzaldúa), 127
Crow of Whareatua, 69
Crypt-Keeper, 33–35
Cullen, Fred, 61
Cultural memory, 144, 162–63
Cultural nostalgia, 202
Cultural reclamation, xx
Curry, Agnes B., 300
Cutler, David, 310

Dad and Dave (Steele Rudd), 54
Daily Mail, 64
Dakota Access Pipe Line, 257
Dale, David, 110
Daley, Paul, 115
Dance of Person and Place, The, 300
Dances with Wolves, 265
Darkness Calls, xvii
Darkstar, 78
David and Dawn, 54
Davidson, Jim, xvi
Dazzler, 80, 89–91
DC Comics, 7, 16–18, 21–22, 58–61, 223, 226
Deadpool, 7, 13
Dean, Amber, 342–43, 350
Decolonial healing, xx
Deep time, 301–2, 306
Deep Waters: The Textual Continuum in American Indian Literature (Teuton), 182, 185
Deer Woman: An Anthology, xx, 243, 316–39
Defensor, 78
Degregori, Carlos Iván, 153
Dejo, Karen, 159
De las Casas, Bartholomé, 212

Dell (publisher), 59
Deloria, Vine, Jr., 303
Dembicki, Matt, xvi
Dennis, C. J., 54
Department H, 13
Derrida, Jacques, 182, 189
De Santiago Bouchez, Manuel, 131
Detective Comics, 59
Diamond Comics Distributors, 19
Diasporic intersectionality, 225
Didgeridoos, The, 60
Dillon, Grace, 309
Dimock, Wai Chee, 302
Dingle, Adrian, 12, 17
Disappearing Indian trope, 42, 350
Disney, 58, 60, 70
Dittmer, Jason, 5–7, 11–12
Dixon, Buzz, 238
Dixon, John, 59
Dixon, Les, 58
Dolan, Hugh, 62
Donahue, James J., xx, 254–72
Dot and the Kangaroo Meet Mr. Platypus, 61
Downing, Todd, xiv
Dreamguard, 87
Dreams of Looking Up, 197–206
Dreamtime: Aboriginal Stories, 62
D-Squaw (clothing line), 9
Duality (Andean), 154–56
Duany, Jorge, 225
Dumond, Don E., 197
Dunn, Carolyn, 336
Durack sisters (Mary and Elizabeth), 55–56
Dying Tecumseh, The, 42

Eagle, 64
EC Comics, 33–35
Echo, xvi
Editorial Manos, 218
Edmonds, Dayton, 237–53
Edwards, Jen Murvin, xvii
Edwardson, Ryan, 6
Eggenhofer, Nick, 41
Eisner, Will, 301
Ellis, Dennin, xviii, 62, 75–97
Ellison, Harlan, 92
El ultimo taíno, 214
El zorro de arriba y el zorro de abajo, 156
Equinox (*Justice League United*), 16–18

Espinoza Díaz, Martín, xix, 136, 144, 148, 159
Ethics in the Gutter, 343
Ethics of remembering, 342

Falcon Comics, 109
Falk, Lee, 101, 104–5
Family Court of Australia (FCA), 115
Fantomen, 108, 110
Fatty Finn, 54
Fawaz, Ramzi, 75
Fawn, Jackie, 333
Feature Productions, 63
Feliciano-Santos, Sherina, 224
Feral (Alpha Flight), 13
Fighting Indians of the West, 29
Firebrace, Francis, 62
Firehair, 44
Firehair (Fiction House), 44
Fitz, Earl E., xiii
500 Years of Resistance Comic Book, The, xvii
Flaherty, Louise, 274
Fleetway, 71
Fleetway picture libraries, 64
Flight of the Shepherd, 130
Fontaine, Jessica, xx, 11, 340–60
Fontaine, Tina, 340, 357–58
Footrot Flats, 61, 64, 67–68
Ford, Jack, xviii, 53–72
Forerunners, 61
Fragments, fragmentation, 127–43, 168–80, 206, 277
Franchise for Aborigines, 114
Francis, Lee, IV, ix–x, xi, 316, 361
Frank Oliver (Spider-Man), 77
Frederick Myers (Spider-Man), 77
Freud, Sigmund, 127, 163
Frew Publications, 58, 104
Frizzell, Dick, 66
From Earth's End, 64–65
From Sand Creek, 40
Furrow, Elena, 62

Gallipoli: The Landing, 62
Garage Graphix, 113–14
García, Enrique, xix, 210–33
García, Ivonne, 223, 225–26
García Liendo, Javier, xix, 144–67
Garneau, David, 274–75, 278, 280–81
Garroutte, Eva Marie, 265–66
Gateway (superhero), 61–62, 80–90
Geometrize, xii, xvi, xx
Giizhodibaa'iagneg, 307–13
Ginger Meggs, 54
Ginzburg, Carlo, 163
Girl Called Echo, A, 22
Gladue, Stephen, 305
God Is Red, 303
God Nose, 28
Goeman, Mishuana, 318–19
Gohier, Franck, 111
Golden Age (Canadian comics), 5
Golden Arrow, 44
Gold Key American comics, 60
Grace, Sherrill, 11
Grant, Andrea, xvii
Graphic violence in comics, 27–52, 66–67, 144–67
Gray, Brenna Clarke, xviii, 5–24
Great Depression, The, 53–54
Green Arrow, 257
Greenfield, Donald, 62
Green Lantern, 255
Green Lantern / Green Arrow, 27
Groensteen, Thierry, 185, 301, 345
Grozs, Chris, 68
Guevara, Rudy P., xiii
Gurney, Alex, 55
Gus of the Gulf, 55
Gutter in comics, 173, 248–49, 327, 345–55
Guzmán Reynoso, Abimael, 149, 153

Haka / Whiti Te Ra, 68
Hall, Faron, xx
HAN: Healthy Aboriginal Network, xvii
Hanna-Barbera cartoons, 61
Harper, Stephen, 10
Harrison, William Henry, 35
Hatfield, Charles, 185, 274, 277
Hautipua Rerarangi / Born to Fly, 68
Havok (Marvel), 80
Havok & Wolverine: Meltdown, 92
Hawke, Robert, 112
Hear N' Aid (relief fund), 92
Henderson, Scott B., xvii, 22, 281, 346
Henzi, Sarah, xii, xvii, 184, 238, 342
Heridas abiertas (open wounds), xiii
Heroes for Hope Starring the X-Men, 92
Hicks, Reg, 54

Hicksville, 64, 67–68
High Country News, 269
Highway (*We Stand on Guard*), 19
Hill, Gord, 277
Hine Poupou, 69
Historical trauma in comics, 273–98
Historietas, 197–207
Home space, ix
Hook Ups, 68
Horn, Maurice, 102
Horniman, Joanne, 112
Horrocks, 64–68
Horwitz (publisher), 58–59
Houseman, Todd, 311
Howe, LeAnne, ix
Huhndorf, Sheri, xii–xiv
Huna Smith, Ryan, xvii
Huria Matanga, 69
Hurricane María, 210–11, 223, 226, 228
Hybridity, 147, 162, 238

ICePé.cómic, 214, 225
Image Comics, 19
INC: The Indigenous Narratives Collective, xvii
Indian: Dying Chief of Contemplating the Progress of Civilization, The (Crawford), 42
Indian Act of 1876, 275
Indianness, xv
Indians (Jack Jackson), 29, 44
Indigeneity, ix, 5–24, 129, 184, 237–53, 340–60; in futurism, 342; in science fiction, 299–315; in thought, 144–67
Indigenous Comic Con, 361
Informe Final, The, 147–48, 153
In Search of Your Warrior Program, 289–93
Instituto de Cultura Puertorriqueña, 210–33
Intermediality, 340–60
Inuit people in comics, 10–14, 19, 21
Inuksuk, 10
Iron Man, 76
Iskwé, 340, 345, 353, 356–57
It's for Your Own Good, 111

Jack-in-the-Box, 88
Jackson, Andrew, 35
Jackson, Jack (Jaxon), xviii, 27–49
Janvier, Alex, 280

Jenkins, Henry, 112
Jiménez, Genero Pool, 198
Jindi the Picanniny Fairy, 60
Jindi's Australian ABC, 60
Johnny Canuck, 6
Johnston, Franz, 12
Jolliffe, Eric, 56–57, 59–60
Jolliffe's Outback, 62
Journey of the Healer, xvii
Justice, Daniel Heath, xiii–xiv, 276, 296
Justice League United, 16–18

Ka, Kaipel, 108
Kagagi: The Raven, 266
Kahe Te Rauoterangi, 69
Ka Mate (haka), 68
Kane, Katie, 33
Kenmille, Barbara, 325, 331, 335
Kimberley Aboriginal Medical Services, 117
Kimble Bent, 68
King, C. Richard, 237, 274–75
King, Stephen, 92
King, Thomas, 14
King Features, 102, 107
Kingston, Peter, 111
Kinnaird, 65, 68
Kinnane, Garry, 120
Kiss Me Deadly, xvii
Kiwi Black, 70
Klor de Alva, J., 230
K. G. Murray Comics, 58, 61
Kobade, 319
Kokoda: That Bloody Track, 62
Koliak (Inuit god), 11
Koostachin, Shannen, 16–17
Ko Wai hokitera Mauka, 69

La Boriqueña, xx, 210–33
LaBoucane-Benson, Patti, 22, 289
La Chola Power, xix, 127–43, 144–67
Lacourt, Luis, 218
La furia de Juracán, 214
Langston, Jessica, 238, 251, 277
La palma del Cacique, 213
LaPensée, Elizabeth, xii, xv, 243, 300, 304, 313, 316–39
Larsen, Soren, 5, 7, 11–12
Last of the Mohicans, The, 42
Last of the Wampanoags, The, 42

Leahy, Sean, 61
Leask, James, 21
Lederwasch, Dietmar, 111
Lemire, Jeff, 16–17
Lemos, Antonio, 115
Levitz, Paul, 205
Lewis, Pat, 238–39
Life of Helen Betty Osborne, The, xvii
Light in the Dark / Luz en lo oscuro, 169, 177
Lions Forge Comics, 211
Little Badger, Darcie, 325, 327–29
Little Hongi: Adventures in Māoriland, 65
Live Aid concert, 92
Llosa, Vargas, 153
Local ethnohistory in comics, 197–208
Logocentrism, 182
Logographic signs, 171
Long Shadows, 47
Longshot (Marvel), 80
Lone Avenger, The, 58
Look and Learn, 64
Lopez, Chris, 61
Lopez, Maya, xvi
López-Baralt, Mercedes, 212
Low, David, 64
Lubelicious (campaign), 62, 119
Lucioni, Mario, 147
Lyle, Tom, xvii
Lynn-Cook, Elizabeth, 87

MacLeod, Euan, 111
Macpherson, June and Bruce, 60
Mafalda, 218
Magic Boomerang, The, 60
Mandrake the Magician, 54
Mandrake the Magician, 102
Manifold, 87, 96
Mansfield, Jayne, 57
Mantia, Rosa, 306
Manuel Antonio Ay: El Primer Mártir de la Guerra de Castas, xix
Manzar the White Indian, 44
Manzour, José Luis, 131
Māori Challenge, The, 71
Māori people in comics, xii–xiv, xvi, xviii, 53–72
Marge's Lulu and Tubby in Australia, 59
Mark My Words: Native Women Mapping Our Nations, 318

Marks, Russell, 105
Marsh, Sid, 69
Marshall, James Vance, 62
Martínez-San Miguel, Yolanda, 224
Marvel, xviii, 5–8, 13, 16, 18, 21–22, 58–62, 65–66, 70, 75–97, 135, 223, 256
Marvel Comics Presents, 87, 91
Maus, 206
Mayans in comics, 197–208
McCleod, Neal, 295
McCloud, Scott, 172–73, 184–86, 190–91, 206, 241, 248, 251–52, 311
McGregor, Russell, 105
McKone, Mike, 16
McNickle, D'Arcy, xiv
Medak-Saltzman, Danika, xiv
Mega-narrator, 249–50
Meléndez, Magali, 218
Mellings, Kelly, 289
Memory, 197–208
Merino, Ana, 206
Mesoamerica in comics, 168–80, 181–96
Mestiza consciousness, 127
Mestizaje, xvi, 129, 203, 210, 214, 224–25
Metal Hurlant, 64
Metamora, 42
Michalak, Katja, 127
Middleton, David, 206
Mihalic, Francis, 106–7
Mikaere, Chaz, 69
Mikkonen, Kai, 240, 250
Mille Lacs Band of Ojivwe, 197–206
Miller, Mary E., 130–31
Miller, Syd, 55
Milton, Cynthia E., 148
Minnie's Story, 68
Minx: Dream War, xvii
Miranda-Rodríguez, Edgardo, 210, 224–26, 229–31
Misogyny, 38–40
Mitchell, Bill, 61
MMIWGT2S movement, 340–60
Mnemonic community, 129
Moa, xvi
Moana, 70
Modesty Blaise: The Stone Age Caper, 61
Mohawk Interruptus, 318, 331
Mohican syndrome, xv
Moir, Alan, 61

Monkey Beach, 350–51
Monroe, Marilyn, 57, 159
Montes, Brian, xix, 197–208
Montijo, Rhode, xix, 127
Moonshot, xvi, 22, 299–315
Moore, Ray, 101
Mopoke and the Necklace, The, 60
Morton, Tex, 58
Moses, Daniel David, 273
Moshman, David, 127
Mothers Against Meth Alliance (M.A.M.A.), 333–34
Mr. and Mrs. Potts, 53, 58
Mr. Pittialuk (*We Stand on Guard*), 19
Multicultural Comics: From Zap to Blue Beetle, 184
Multigenerational violence, 316–39, 340–60
Multimodality, 202–3, 206, 273–98
Mundo, El, 217
Muratti-Toro, José, 214
Museum of the Caste War, 198
Myth of Indigenous Caribbean Extinction, The, 224

Namja & The Dragon Goanna, 58
Napoleon Bonaparte, 59
Napoli, Donna Joan, 62
Nationalism, 5–24, 210–33, 318
Native, The. *See* Feral (Alpha Flight)
Native Americans in Comic Books, 70
Native art, 181–96
Native Realities, xvii, 316, 361
Nelvana of the North, 6, 11–12
NEOMAD, 72
Nepantla, 127, 129, 169, 182
New Mutants: Superheroes, The, 75
Newton (publisher), 60
New York Journal, 101
New Zealand comics, 53–72
New Zealand School Journal, 66
NFL Superpro, 238
Ngarara Huuarau, 69
Ngarimu Te Tohu Toa / Victory at Point 209, 68
Nicholson, Hope, 300, 304
Nightcrawler (X-Men), 76, 78, 82
No Hea Te Hau, 69
Nohelani, Stephanie, 239
Noori, Margaret, 184

North Dakota Access Pipeline, 361
Norton-Smith, Thomas M., 300
Novaro, Gonzalo, 69
Nuestros Muertos, 144–67
Nuevo Día, El, 217
Nungalla and Jungalla, 55
Nunukul, Oodgeroo, 62

Odjick, Jay, 266, 300
Odjick, Joel, 300
O'Donnell, Peter, 61
O'Neil, Dennis, 27
Ogaick, Tara, 325, 327–29
Old Timer, The, 60
Ookpik, xv, 10
Orality, 186, 190–93, 237–53, 312
Orange, Tommy, 40
Ortiz, Simon, 40
Outback, The, 62
Out of the Silence (comic strip), 54
Outsmarting Cognitive Schema, 128–30, 139
Outside Circle, The, xx, 273–98
Ouweneel, Arij, xix, 127–43
#OwnVoices, 21–22

Pablo's Inferno, xix, 127–43
Pachacuti (Andean), 154
Pacific Pictorial Comic, 57
Page Comics, 59
Pané, Ramón, 212
Pan-Indigeneity, 21
Panther, The, 59
Papua New Guinea, 100–120
Parada, Daniel, xix, 168–80, 181–96, 206
Paranjape, Makarand, 106
Parker, Cynthia Ann, 42–46
Pasarin, Fernando, xvi
Pasifika people in comics, 70
Pat, Jacinto, 198, 202
Patrick, Kevin, xviii–xix, 100–120
Patteson, Richard F., 104
Pearce, Richard, 320
Pearson, Noel, 112
Pereira, Claudia Matos, xii
Peruvian people in comics, 144–67
Pettrich, Ferdinand, 42
Petty, Bruce, 61
Peverill, Ralph, 60
Peyote in comics, 46

Phantom, The, 58, 62, 100–120
Phantom Commando, The, 59
Phantom Enrols & Votes, The, 113
Phantom Ranger, The, 58
Phelan, James, 237
Phillips, Nickie D., xii, xvi
Philosophygirl, 68
Phonetic signs, 171
Pickering, Larry, 61
Pictographs, 305
Pictorial clues, 172
Pictorial Social Studies, 109
Pogol, 58
Polak, Kate, 343
Political memory, public memory, 144, 148
Ponce Massacre, 226
Popol Vuh, 171–72, 175
Popol Wuj—The Book of the People, 131–35
Porter, Annaliese, 62
Post Courier, 108
Postmodern pastiche, 216–17, 224
Potts and Uncle Dick, The, 58, 60
Power of Comics: History, Form and Culture, The, 205
Practices of inheritance (concept), 342
Préfontaine, Darren, xvii
Prince and the Pauper, The, 220
Proudstar, Jon, xvii, 243, 267
Psylocke (Marvel), 80, 82, 84
Puerto Rican identity in comics, 210–33
Puerto Rico Strong, 210–33
Purgatory, 129–32
Pyro (X-Men), 77

Quechua in comics, 158–59
Queensland Association for Healthy Communities (QAHC), 119
Quesada, Joe, xvi
Quesada Cantuarias, Francisco Miro (Diodoros Kronos), xix, 136
Quetzal, 127, 130
Quintana Roo, 197–207

Rader, Dean, xii
Radical Imagination of American Comics, 75
Raeburn, Jack, 63
Raheja, Michelle H., 239
Rainbow Serpent, The, 62
Ramírez, Miriam, 214

Ranger (superhero), 59
"Rant, The" (advertisement), 20–21
Rauparaha, Te, 68
Ready to Dream, 62
Real Indians: Identity and the Survival of Native America, 265
Re-arming (concept), 317–35
Red (Yahgulanaa), xvii
Redback Graphix, 117–19
Reder, Deanna, xii, xv–xvi
Red Wolf, xvi
Reed, Nelson, 197
Regeneration, 318
Regeneration through Violence, 318
Reg Saunders: An Indigenous War Hero, 62–63
ReMatriate, 9
Remington, Frederic, 41
Resetar, Eric, 63
Residential schooling, 13, 275–76, 285–86, 289, 291
Resilient Memories, 129, 135
Resistance movements, xii, xviii, xxi, 200, 210–33
Rezum Studios, xviii
Ricanstruction, 226
Rice, Julien, 322
Rice, Norm, 58
Rifkin, Mark, 302
Rifkind, Candida, xii, xx, 340–60
Riggs, Lynn, xiv
Rivera Cusicanqui, Silvia, 127
Robertson, David Alexander, xvii, 22, 206, 277, 281, 340, 345
Rodríguez, Ricardo Walter, xix
Rogue (Marvel), 80
Rosa Cuchillo, 158
Rosado, Will, 227–28
Rosella and the Rain Cloud, The, 60
Rosnock, 60
Roughsey, Dick, 62
Round, Julie, 346
Rowlandson, Mary, 42
Royal Commission on Aboriginal Peoples, The, 276
Royal, Derek Parker, 208, 241
Rudd, Steve, 54
Rugeley, Terry, 197
Rupay: Historias de la violencia política en el Perú, 148
Russell, Charles, 41

Russell, Jim, 58
Rutherford, Jessica, xix, 168–80, 182, 206
Ryan, Marie-Laure, 244, 251

Sabra (Marvel), 77
Sabretooth, 13
Sacred Bullroarer, The, 55
Sacred Frog, The, 55
Sainte-Marie, Buffy, 299–315
Salisbury, Alan, 60
Saltbush Bill, 56, 60, 62
Sand Creek Massacre, 28, 40
Sanderson, Steven Keewatin, xvii
Sandy Blight, 56–57, 60
Santiváñez, César, 144, 148, 158
Santos, Jorge, xix, 127, 181–96, 206
Scalphunter (DC), 44
Secret of the Wreck, The, 55
Secret Valley, The, 66
Seduction of the Innocent, The, 64
Seminario de MedComics, 136
7 Generations: A Plains Cree Saga, xx, 281–89
Sexual violence, 316–39, 340–60
Shadow, The, 58–59
Shaman (Byrne), 13–16, 21
Shamrock (Marvel), 78
Shannon, Ben, 311
Shard, 88–89
Sheena, Queen of the Jungle, 54
Sherlock Holmes, 163
She Used to Wanna Be a Ballerina, 299
Sheyahshe, Michael, xii, xv, 70, 184, 238, 300
Shkolvsky, Viktor, 150
Silent Möbius, 62
Siles, Jorge, 137
Simon, Roger, 342
Simpson, Audra, 318–19, 331, 335
Simpson, Leanne Betasamosake, 319, 354
Simpsons, The, 211
Sinclair, Niigaanwewidam James, xii
60s Scoop, 276, 291–92
Skippy the Bush Kangaroo, 61
Skroce, Steve, 19
Slane, Chris, 69
Slotkin, Richard, 318
Slow Death, 27–49
Smith, Andrea, 239
Smith, Lindsay Claire, xii
Smith, Paul Chaat, xiii, 27

Smith, Will, 12
Smith's Weekly, 54, 56
Snake (comic strip), 60
Snowbird (Byrne), 12–16, 21
Solid, Coco, 68
Somerville, Alice Te Punga, xiv
Southern Cross Comics, 62
Souvenir of Canada project, 10
Sovereignty in comics, 273–98, 325, 345
Sparkles, 63
Spider-Man, 77, 255, 259
Spiegelman, Art, 206
Spiers, Miriam Brown, xii
Spirit animals, 15, 355
Spirituality in comics, 14, 18
Spivak, Gayatri, 224
Standing Rock, 333, 335, 361
Stanleigh, Andy, 304
Starr, Arigon, xvii–xviii, 262, 266, 300, 310, 361–62
Stereotypes, xii, xv, 14, 29, 31–33, 48, 55, 75–97, 147, 152–53, 184, 237, 273
Stockwhip Sam, 56
Stoked, Rosamond, 58
Stone, John Augustus, 42
Stonefish, Patty, 325, 336
Stories from the Billabong, 62
Storm (X-Men), 76, 80
Storm, Jennifer, 274
Strategic essentialism, 224
Streetwize comics, 61
Strobl, Staci, xii, xvi
Strömberg, Fredrik, 105
Stuller, Jennifer K., 159
Sugar Falls: A Residential School Story, xvii, 206, 347
Sunday Telegraph, 55
Sunfire (X-Men), 76–77
Sun-News Pictorial, 60
Supay, xix, 137–39
Supercholo, xix, 127–43, 147
Supergirl, 227–28
Superhero comics, xi, xv–xvi, xix, 5–24, 104, 109, 147, 210–33, 254–72
Super Indian, xvii, xx, 254–72, 361
Superman, 56, 119, 255–56, 265–66
Supreme Feature Comic, 63
Survivance, xiv
System of Comics, The, 185

Taínos in comics, 210–32
Talisman (Marvel), 13–16, 78–82, 86–88
Tametekapua, 70
Tapia, Alejandro, 213
Tapsell, Maia, 70
Tarzan, 54
Tate, Bernard, 60
Taube, Karl, 130–31
Taylor, Diana, 169, 177
Taylor, Drew Hayden, 274
Taylor, George F. H., 66
Tedlock, Dennis, 172
Tee Wees Adventures, 63
Temporality, 299–315
Te Orokotīmatanga o te Ao, 70
Testimonials, 206
Teuton, Christopher B., xv, 182–85, 189
Tex Moreton Western Comics, 58
There There, 40
This is not a Comic, 68
Thor: Ragnarok, 70
Three Words (anthology), 65
Threlfall, Adrian, 62
Thugine the Green Serpent, 55
Thunder, Jonathan R., 316–39
Thunderbird (X-Men), 76–77
Thunder Eagle (Proudstar), 267, 269
Tightrope Tim, 55
Tihosuco Community Heritage Preservation Projection, 198, 206
Tim Valour, 58–59
Tingle, Tim, 239
Tintin, 64
Tom Flynn Stockman, 56
Toronto Raptors, 9
Torres Strait Islanders in comics, xii, 53–72
Totem Pole History: The Work of Lummi Carver Joe Hillaire, A, 251
Trafficking Victims Protection Act, 324
Transnational concept, xiv–xv; and cultural networks, xiii
Treaty of Waitangi, 66
Trial by Battle, 71
Tribal Force, 243, 267, 269
Tribalography, ix
Trickster (anthology), xvi, xx
Trickster: Native American Tales, A Graphic Collection, 238–39
Trickster tales, 237–53

Trudeau, Justin, 11
Trudeau, Pierre, 13
Trump, Donald, 211, 231
Truth and Reconciliation Commission, 21, 276
Tuck, Eve, 342
Tukuna Aku Waikano, 69
Turbochaski, The Messenger of Peace, xix, 136–37
Turey El Taíno, xx, 210–33
Twain, Mark, 220
Two Indians, The, 213
Two-spirit peoples, 316–39, 340–60
2 Spirits Program, 119
2000AD, 64

Uchuyanay massacre, 149–53, 155
Última hora, 147
Uncanny X-Men, xviii, 62, 70, 92
Uncle Scrooge, 60
Underestimation (theme), 57
Underground comix, 27–28, 46–47
Understanding Comics, 241, 251
Understanding Comics: The Invisible Art, 172, 184, 190
Unredeemed captive, 42, 44

Valkyrie, 70
Van Camp, Richard, 277, 300, 306
Vanguard (Marvel), 77
Vasconcelos, Jose, 203
Vast place, 303
Vaughan, Brian K., 19
Vermette, Katherena, 22, 274
Violence Against Women Act, 317
Vizenor, Gerald, 316
Voices of Our Sisters in Spirit, 317
Von Schidt, Harold, 41
Vote 1 Phantom, 114
Vumps, 53

Waititi, Taika, 70
Walking the Clouds, 309
Wally and the Major, 55–56, 60
Walter Rodríguez, Ricardo, 136
Wanda the War Girl, 55
Wantok, 106–8
Warren Comics, 60
Warrior, Robert Allen, xiii, 27
Watchmen, 92

Waters, Anne, 300
Watson Smith, Joan, 60
Waugh, Coulton, 104
Waylon Williams (Bad Medicine), 260
Weapon X program, 13
Weismantel, Mary, 160
Welch, Raquel, 57
Wendigo (windigo), 18, 267
Wertham, Frederick, 63–64
We Stand on Guard, 19
Western discourse, ix
Westerns (genre), 29
"We the North," 22
Wheelahan, Paul, 59
Whitago, 18. *See also* Wendigo
White, Unk, 55, 64
White Boy, 44
White Chief of the Pawnee Indians, 44
White Indian, 44
White Indian (character type), 45
White supremacy, 12
Why I Love Australia, 62
Why Wanda said "No" in Broome, 117
Williams, Eunice, 42
Williams, Rhys, 55
Will I See?, 340–60
Wilson, Daniel H., xvi
Wisdom of the Phantom, The, 115
Witchetty's Tribe, 57, 60, 62
Witek, Joseph, 28, 38, 41, 47
Wogan (publisher), 58, 60
Wolf Lopez, Maria, 325, 329–32, 335
Wolverine, 7, 13, 77, 80
Woman's Weekly (Australia), 54
Women and Ledger Art, 320
Wonder Woman, 256
World War II, 5–6, 11, 13, 54, 68
Wounded Knee occupation, 27–28
Wright-McLeod, Brian, 274

Xibalbá, 131–33, 136, 171
Ximénez, Fray Francisco, 131
X-Men, 9, 12, 15, 75–97
X-Treme X-Men, 88

Yaffa (publisher), 59–60, 107
Yahgulanaa, Michael Nicoll, xvii, 22, 278, 362
You and Me (Stan Cross), 53
Yucatán's Caste War, 197–207

Zalles, Óscar, 137
Z Beach True Comics, 62
Zotz: Serpent and Shield, xix, 168–80, 181–96, 206

www.ingramcontent.com/pod-product-compliance
Lightning Source LLC
Chambersburg PA
CBHW070258240426
43661CB00057B/2580